C0-AAS-039

NATIONAL CONVENTIONS IN AN AGE OF PARTY REFORM

Recent titles in Contributions in Political Science
Series Editor: Bernard K. Johnpoll

WITHDRAWN
FAIRFIELD UNIVERSITY
LIBRARY

NATIONAL CONVENTIONS IN AN AGE OF PARTY REFORM

JAMES W. DAVIS

Foreword by
David S. Broder

Contributions in Political Science, Number 91

Greenwood Press
Westport, Connecticut • London, England

Library of Congress Cataloging in Publication Data

Davis, James W., 1920-
National conventions in an age of party reform.

(Contributions in political science, ISSN 0147-1066 ;
no. 91)
Bibliography: p.
Includes index.
1. Political conventions.   2. Political parties—
United States.   I. Title.   II. Series.
JK2255.D428   1983   324.5′6′0973   82-9382
ISBN 0-313-23048-X (lib. bdg.)   AACR2

Copyright © 1983 by James W. Davis

All rights reserved. No portion of this book may be
reproduced, by any process or technique, without the
express written consent of the publisher.

Library of Congress Catalog Card Number: 82-9382
ISBN: 0-313-23048-X
ISSN: 0147-1066

First published in 1983

Greenwood Press
A division of Congressional Information Service, Inc.
88 Post Road West
Westport, Connecticut 06881

Printed in the United States of America

10 9 8 7 6 5 4 3 2 1

Copyright Acknowledgments

Permission is gratefully acknowledged for the use of materials from the following sources:

"Conventions: Nominations by Rain Dance," by Paul O'Neil, *Life Magazine*, © 1968 Time Inc.
Reprinted by permission.

Search for Consensus by Ralph Goldman. By permission of Temple University Press.

Specified excerpt (p.119) from THE 103RD BALLOT: DEMOCRATS AND THE DISASTER IN
MADISON SQUARE GARDEN by Robert K. Murray. Copyright © 1976 by Robert K. Murray.
Reprinted by permission of Harper & Row, Publishers, Inc.

To Paul T. David—
Scholar, Gentleman, Friend
and Mentor

208045

10204°

Contents

Figures

Tables

Foreword _____

It is, I would suppose, a commonplace to observe that the test of any nominating system is the quality of the candidates it produces. The test of the American presidential nominating system is the quality of the presidents it produces. And by that test, the nominating system we have must be given a failing grade.

In the past twenty years, the United States has had six presidents, and each one of them has been judged to be seriously lacking in his performance. That may not be conclusive proof that something has gone wrong in the selection system, but it is surely suggestive that a study like this one is of more than academic interest and importance.

John F. Kennedy, in his brief tenure, started with a major miscalculation in foreign-military policy (the Bay of Pigs) and was frequently frustrated in his dealings with Congress. Lyndon B. Johnson pushed through a revolution in civil rights and social welfare legislation, saw the Congress revolt and then lost popular support over a war he knew no way to win or to end. Richard M. Nixon had more success in the policy field, particularly on the international scene, but was driven from office by the worst scandal in modern American history.

Gerald R. Ford (the only one of the six who was not picked for president or vice president by convention delegates) stumbled into difficulties in both the economy and the world scene, and was barely able to retain his party nomination. But he looked, in retrospect, like a model of competence compared to his successors, Democrat Jimmy Carter and Republican Ronald Reagan, whose absence of Washington experience made their presidencies nervous experiments in economic and international policymaking.

The gloomy history is darkened when one realizes that in many of the elections in which these men were chosen, the alternative candidates produced by the opposition party looked measurably worse to the voters. Three of the six elections in this span of time produced landslides, largely because the opposition candidate was deemed totally unacceptable by the voters. With Barry Goldwater in 1964, George McGovern in 1972 and Carter in 1980, the system produced "choices" that millions of voters found no choice at all.

That all this occurred in a period when our process of presidential selection was undergoing radical changes strikes me as more than coincidental. Up through the 1950s, the work of picking presidential nominees was left largely to insiders— to professional politicians, operating largely without instruction or inhibition, on the floor, in the corridors and, on occasion, in the smoke-filled rooms of the national convention.

That system has been changed dramatically by the impact of two forces, which are fully described in Professor Davis' book. One is the popularization and proliferation of presidential primaries as the favored device for choosing and instructing convention delegates. The second is the transformation of the convention hall from a shadowy shelter for political bargaining into a floodlit set for a scripted television drama.

Some would argue that the change began in 1952, when the Republicans chose Dwight D. Eisenhower over Robert A. Taft. That is certainly a defensible view, for the Eisenhower forces exploited his primary victories (starting in the now legendary New Hampshire leadoff battle) and the presence for the first time of national television in the convention hall, to overthrow Taft. But the powerbrokers were still operating in force, led by the ultimate insider, Thomas E. Dewey, at that convention. And both the Republican convention of 1956 (in its rejection of the dump-Nixon move) and the Democratic conventions that nominated Adlai E. Stevenson in 1952 and 1956 showed the persistence of the old ways of doing business. It was not until the 1960s that the new pattern was indelibly established— and the decline of the presidency became evident.

The source—and the heart—of the problem is defined in one sentence of Professor Davis' book. The changes in the process "have widened the gap between the ability to get elected and the ability to govern the country." As Anthony King, a distinguished British observer of American politics, put it, "A disjunction seems to have developed in the United States between the qualities required to win the presidential nomination of one's party and the qualities required to be a good president."

That gap is beginning to be recognized; it is impossible to ignore, given the succession of presidential failures we have experienced. And, gradually, people are coming to understand that the failure is rooted in the selection system. At the risk of oversimplification, the problem is that the delegates who now meet in convention hall do not know enough nor do they care enough to pick a president who can succeed.

They do not know enough, because they come from—and are answerable to—the ranks of voters who participate in the primaries in their states. Like the rest of the voters, most of the delegates know the candidates chiefly through meeting them in living-room or town-hall settings, or seeing them, fleetingly, on their television screens. They have not watched them function, at close range, as legislators or governors or cabinet members. Nor have they gauged their capacities over a long period of time, judging their growth potential, their range of skills. They know as much—or as little—as the average voter, which is to say, not very much at all. It is true that party rules these days tend to leave those delegates little discretion, binding them closely to the candidates they support. But even if they were free to exercise their judgments, they have little judgment to exercise.

They do not care enough, because, for the most part, theirs is a transient and passing involvement with the candidates and the process. Their loyalty is a fleeting thing, not a resource on which the candidate can count when it comes to the task of governing. When Mayor Daley (to choose a boss at random) committed to support a Kennedy candidacy, it was quite a commitment. Daley was around long after the campaign was finished, and he did not want to see the man he backed fail. When Kennedy needed help from the Chicago delegation in the House of Representatives, Daley could deliver help. When Jimmy Carter needed help from the Chicago delegation, the Carter delegates from Chicago were less than useless. They had virtually disappeared, their part of the game being over.

To some extent the Democrats, who went farther than the Republicans in pursuit of amateurism in the convention hall, have attempted to turn the clock back. The rules for the 1984 convention set aside one-sixth of the delegate seats for elected and party officials who may, if they wish, come into the convention uncommitted to any candidate. We will see if that is sufficient to change the character of the convention or whether the substantially larger proportion of uncommitted delegates of professional background that Professor Davis recommends is needed to bring about that change.

The point that is often forgotten—though not in this book—is that the national convention is the only time when our political parties assume reality. They are, for the most part, letterhead organizations, with small Washington staffs and occasional meetings of "national committees" of 150 to 300 members. It is only four days every four years that the national party meets in sufficient numbers to have any sense of its being a national organization. Those conventions ought to be times of renewal and network-building for delegates who expect to be long-term participants in the work of the party. That is their hidden agenda, no less important than the choice of the nominee (or the ratification of the primaries' choice) and the writing of the platform. The convention is the time when the Maricopa County, Arizona, chairman can learn how things look to the Bronx County chairman—and come to understand the terms on which they can work together, and govern, over the next four years. It is too valuable a learning experience to be squandered on people who will never be seen again at a Democratic Party meeting in Phoenix or the Bronx, as is so often the case now.

Professor Davis, following a distinguished tradition, argues that the deliberative as well as the networking functions of the convention would work better if its membership were smaller. That is undoubtedly the case. But my own view is that if the size of the quadrennial convention is reduced, then it becomes even more important to institutionalize and expand the mid-term convention: to bring in a wider range of "cadre party" workers and future leaders and allow them more time for the informal discussions that give them a sense of common purposes and shared commitments. The Republicans have not tried mid-terms at all; the Democrats are reducing the length and the size of theirs; and both those trends seem to me mistaken.

One final observation, before you begin this book. There is a tendency to say that the power that once was exercised by the convention has been transferred to the mass media. Professor Davis observes that

to win the nomination in the age of party reform a presidential candidate, above all else, must be able to attract the attention of the national television media and the working press and project a favorable "image" on the television screen. Indeed, the momentous shift toward media politics has seriously eroded the traditional function of parties to recruit presidential candidates capable of working with Congress, to develop party programs, and, if successful at election time, govern the country.

Let me say, as a member of the working press and (presumably) a beneficiary of the power shift, that it would be a mistake to think this is a power the press has wrested away or will fight to retain. Reporters will cover any kind of a presidential selection system the parties mandate—open, closed, or mixed. Reporters did not lobby for or advocate an explosion in the number of presidential primaries. Many of us can imagine better ways of spending our lives than walking behind some candidate down the aisles of the shoe factories in New Hampshire or the cigar factories in Tampa. We think of ourselves as professionals in our own business and we tend to respect—not denigrate—the judgment of professional politicians. It would not offend most of us if most of them reasserted their claim to a strong voice in the choice of their party's presidential candidate. Even those fearsome creatures—our brothers and sisters in television—would probably figure out how to cover an old-fashioned convention, which went beyond one ballot and where the name of the winner was not known in advance. I think they could adapt to that as well as they adapt to the risks of overtime in the Super Bowl or an extra-inning World Series game.

To put the point a bit more seriously, let us remind ourselves that it is the presidency—and therefore, the country—that suffers from the disabilities of our presidential selection system. It is in disarray, and it entails costs and risks which are unnecessary. The power to cure this malady rests in the hands of the political parties; the Supreme Court has made that amply clear. The politicians who manage those parties can serve the country well, and redeem more than a little of their own tattered reputation in the process, if they will reassert their rights and responsibilities in the presidential selection system. They can, in short, help restore the country by helping restore the conventions.

David S. Broder

Preface

National conventions survive, the late E.E. Schattschneider dryly observed more than 40 years ago, for two eminently sensible reasons: "(1) because they do a necessary task, and (2) because no feasible substitute for them has been discovered."[1]

Officially, the Republican and Democratic parties continue to select their presidential nominees at national nominating conventions by a simple majority vote of the delegates attending from all fifty states and the U.S. territories. But national conventions, as the title of this book indirectly suggests, are not what they were a generation ago. While the basic purpose of national conventions has remained the same—to find a presidential candidate who can win a majority of the Electoral College votes in the general election—a transformation in the function and operation of these party grand councils has occurred over the past quarter century. Most of these changes have reduced discretion in convention choice.

Efforts at making parties, especially the Democratic party, more popularly representative have, in effect, transformed the convention's main role from a deliberative assembly to a ratifying body. As a result, the importance of national conventions as decision-making bodies, it is generally agreed, has declined significantly. Since 1956, all nominations in both parties have been decided on the first ballot. Successful nominees in the party out of office have all traveled the route of the presidential primaries to win the nomination. As a matter of fact, no national convention has dared deny the nomination to a candidate of the challenging party who has won decisively in the primaries since the 1952 Democratic convention rejected Senator Estes Kefauver. Dark-horse or favorite-son candidates have almost completely disappeared from the convention scene. Nor has there been a genuine presidential draft in either party since the Democrats nominated Illinois Governor Adlai E. Stevenson in 1952.

Exhausting convention schedules of yesteryear, especially the interminable roll calls that frequently prolonged the party conclaves to five or six days, have been replaced by carefully orchestrated three or four-day scenarios built exclu-

sively around television prime time (7 to 11 p.m.). National conventions have
become theatrical events. Almost all commentators agree that the entire agenda
for national conventions in the current reform era has been constructed not for the
convenience of the delegates but to achieve maximum impact upon the 75 to 100
million nationwide television viewers watching the proceedings from their living
rooms. Nominating speeches have been cut drastically, and the time allotted to
seconding speeches has been pared to a few minutes each. Lengthy convention
floor snake-dance demonstrations on behalf of the various presidential contenders
(which often extended the convention proceedings into the wee hours of the
morning) have been banned.

The size of the national convention, especially within the Democratic party,
has continued to grow. Formerly, each convention numbered approximately
1,000 to 1,200 delegates, but the 1980 Democratic convention total reached
3,331 (the 1980 GOP conclave had 1,994 delegates). To most analysts, conventions are now simply too large to conduct party business.

Conventions of yesteryear were dominated by state and local party leaders
who, in the words of Frank J. Sorauf, "came as ambassadors to the convention
for the purpose of negotiating within a fragmented decentralized party."[2] But as a
result of the proliferation of presidential primaries and the recently established
open delegate procedures in the caucus-convention states, these leaders have
been displaced by the leading presidential candidates and their campaign organizations who have recruited huge blocs of pledged delegates in the primaries.
These delegates are, first and foremost, loyal to the presidential contender, not
their state delegation. This development partially explains why several recent
conventions have been marked by sharper cleavages among rival contenders and
why bargaining and compromise among the state delegations over the nomination have become more difficult. The idea that there are legitimate state party
interests to be represented and protected at national conventions has almost
disappeared as the candidate-centered delegate selection process has emerged as
the dominant factor at the party conclaves. The growth of various interest groups,
with their desire for recognition and insistence that their policy goals be integrated into the party platform, has affected not only the content of the platforms
but also the drafting process as well. Especially within the Democratic party, this
pressure group activity has produced more platform challenges.

In recent years most of the committing of delegates, the trading of support,
and the weeding out of weak candidates has taken place during the pre-convention
stages of the nominating process, not at the convention as was formerly the case.
Nor is it an exaggeration to assert that television commentators, the leading
polling organizations, reporters, national columnists of the leading daily newspapers, and the weekly newsmagazines *Time* and *Newsweek* have largely displaced delegates as certifying agents for ranking the various presidential contenders.
Long before the opening whistle of the primary race, the national press corps
have been keeping their own handicap sheets and rating charts of the various

contenders. Throughout the pre-convention period—indeed, even during the pre-primary stages—national pollsters check the pulse of American voters and report on the level of enthusiasm for each candidate, especially within the out-of-power party. Failure to run well in the polls, as well as the primaries, is now regarded as fatal to any candidate. Since most convention delegates are now pledged to a specific candidate there are consequently fewer secrets and fewer surprises at national conventions in this era of popular democracy. What do all of these changes hold for the future of national nominating conventions?

In his latest book, Theodore H. White, the veteran chronicler of presidential campaigns, describes the national convention's traditional function of choosing leaders as "a fading memory,"[3] since the winner has already been selected in the primary plebiscites. Gallup polls have consistently reported over the past fifteen years that two-thirds of the respondents nationwide favor abolishing national conventions and substituting a one-day national primary. Demands for convention reform or repeal occur as regularly as the conventions themselves. Indeed, no American political institution is more widely criticized or ridiculed—and less understood—than the national nominating conventions of the two major parties.

Have national conventions really outlived their usefulness? Have they become as outmoded as torchlight parades and front porch campaigns? In this author's view, national conventions are one of the nation's most undervalued resources. While the need for a national convention may not appear essential when one candidate clearly outdistances the field in the primaries, the convention will still continue to serve as an indispensable brokering agency—in a sense, a valuable party insurance policy—whenever a close race develops, such as the Ford-Reagan contest in 1976. Thus, if the parties were to abolish these 150-year-old national conclaves, they would be without a tried-and-tested political mechanism for sorting out rival contenders in a tight nominating race. Without national conventions the parties would lack the machinery to broker the interests of diverse and sometimes fragile components of their electoral coalitions. National conventions, it should not be forgotten, serve to unite the winner and the losers in a fifty-state party confederation which is not inherently united. In short, national conventions represent an all-out effort to find, to build, the widest possible party consensus on which to win power and then govern. Despite their outward carnival-like atmosphere, national conventions perform a valuable integrated function in the life of American national parties that is not always appreciated by its critics. Equally important, the conventions furnish a stamp of legitimacy on the nominee that tells all party members and the nation as a whole that the party stands behind the nominee as its standard-bearer in the general election. These quadrennial party grand councils also fill an indispensable role in helping build and maintain the independent stature of the President in the American system of government.

In this study a detailed review is undertaken of the various alternatives for selecting presidential nominees that have been used or offered since the early days of the Republic, but, in the view of this author, the national nominating convention is far and away superior to any substitute proposal advanced thus far. The pages that follow will explain why.

During the preparation of this study, I have been extremely fortunate to have benefited from the advice and counsel of several authorities on the presidential selection process. Especially, I would like to thank Professor Paul T. David, who, though formally retired from the University of Virginia, follows national conventions as avidly now as when he headed the team of scholars at the Brookings Institution who compiled the classic study, *The Politics of National Party Conventions* (1960). I am also deeply indebted to another shrewd convention observer, Professor John S. Jackson III, of Southern Illinois University, who suggested a number of conceptual changes in several chapters. Professor Steven S. Schier, Carleton College, was equally helpful with his recommendations for achieving greater clarity. Professor Stephen J. Wayne, George Washington University, though burdened with a heavy writing schedule, put aside his own work to read the manuscript and helped me to overcome a number of structural weaknesses. Chalmers M. Roberts, the widely respected diplomatic reporter of the *Washington Post*, now retired, has also read the manuscript and provided a number of valuable insights based upon his firsthand observation of more than a dozen national conventions. And I am especially grateful for the advice and encouragement of an old-time friend, Professor Charles H. Backstrom, of the University of Minnesota.

Both the Republican and Democratic national committee headquarters have been unfailing in their willingness to provide data whenever it has been requested by the author. The Gallup poll, as always, has also been most cooperative in making available its polling data.

Publication of this book, however, would not have been possible without the invaluable editorial support of Dr. James Sabin, Ms. Margaret Brezicki, and Ms. Susan Baker—all of Greenwood Press. Neither would this study have been completed without the permission of Barron's Educational Service, publisher of my earlier study, *National Conventions: Nominations Under the Big Top* (1971), to quote liberally from this paperback. Also, I wish to express my personal appreciation to Mrs. Patricia Houtchens and Mrs. Helen Peterson who have been unselfish with their time in preparing the manuscript.

As a convention observer and occasional participant since 1952, I have always been fascinated by the national conventions, often called—at least before the age of the Super Bowl—"the greatest show on earth." I am hopeful that the reader may come to share some of my enthusiasm and admiration for this uniquely American political institution—and perhaps come to appreciate more fully the vitally important role that these gatherings perform in picking nominees for the highest office in the land.

Notes

1. (E. E. Schattschneider, *Party Government* (New York: Rinehart and Company, 1942), p. 102.
2. Frank J. Sorauf, *Party Politics in America*, 4th ed. (Boston: Little, Brown and Company, 1980), p. 291.
3. Theodore H. White, *America in Search of Itself: The Making of the President, 1956-1980* (New York: Harper & Row, 1982), p. 312.

NATIONAL CONVENTIONS IN AN AGE OF PARTY REFORM

The National Convention System _____ 1

No American institutions so fascinate and so appall the citizenry of
the Republic (and so absolutely flabbergast foreigners) as do those
vulgar, those quarrelsome, those unspeakably chaotic rites by which
U.S. political parties choose candidates for the Presidency. The
quadrennial conventions assume the loftiest of partisan obligations;
but no other such convocations anywhere in the civilized world perform their functions amid such torrents of hoarse and lamentable oratory, such displays of hypocritical bedlam and such bare-faced re-
course to the mores of the poker table and flea market. They are
motivated by an arrant opportunism, will seize upon a Warren Harding as ecstatically as upon an Abraham Lincoln, and are such natu-
ral incubators of pathos and low comedy that their functionaries
sometimes seem to be engaged in some large-scale revival of 19th
century burlesque.[1]

National nominating conventions, as the quotation above explains, are "as American as cherry pie." Indeed, the national conventions are beyond doubt one of the
most unique and eminently practical political institutions ever devised by American party leaders. How else, barring a national primary system, could a huge
federal Republic of fifty states develop another political instrument that provides
relatively equal representation to rank-and-file party members in all 435 congressional districts, encompassing 3,000-plus counties, 10,000 cities and smaller
municipalities, and hundreds of townships and rural precincts? The answer to
this question almost defies a solution. It seems fair to conclude that party leaders,
if they had not developed the national nominating convention, would have had to
invent it. What other political organ could better serve the variegated interests in
each major party and provide the following benefits in an essentially decentralized party system: (1) provide for the diversity of representation; (2) possess the
flexibility to reconcile deep factional cleavages within a party; (3) produce a

binding nomination acceptable to virtually all elements within the party; and (4) select nominees who possess strong likelihood of winning voter support.

Clearly, the national nominating conventions have served the nation well. They have aided in the preservation of the two-party system; helped foster vigorous competition between the parties; and generally excluded extremists from winning the nomination, thereby facilitating the maintenance of a democratic consensus within the country. Though undreamed of when the United States Constitution was drafted, the national conventions have come to occupy a crucial role in the leadership selection process for the highest office in the land—the President of the United States. Certainly, the political machinery that selects candidates for the office that is commonly regarded as the most powerful in the Free World deserves close study.

Importance of the Nominating Phase in Presidential Selection

Nineteenth-century political boss William Marcy Tweed once observed, "I don't care who does the electing just so I can do the nominating." This sage observation underscores a basic political fact of life: nominations are the most decisive stage in the entire process of presidential selection.

Put simply, the presidential nominating process narrows the alternatives from a theoretical potential candidate pool of millions who meet the constitutional requirements for the office to only two candidates, one Republican and one Democrat, with a realistic chance of winning the White House. Donald R. Matthews has also noted, "The nominating decision is one of the major determinants of who wins in November."[2] Indeed, because electoral decisions usually take on greater importance in nominating decision-making than calculations on probable performance in the White House, the presidential nominating process has as much effect, if not more, as the presidential election itself in shaping the future direction of the country. The choice of Franklin Delano Roosevelt over Alfred E. Smith in the 1932 Democratic race, the Republicans' preference for Dwight D. Eisenhower over Senator Robert A. Taft in the 1952 GOP contest, the selection of John F. Kennedy over fellow Democrats Adlai E. Stevenson and Lyndon Johnson in 1960, and the Republicans' choice of Ronald Reagan over Howard Baker, George Bush, or John Connally in the 1980 GOP race are all cases in point.

It is sometimes forgotten that getting nominated may be a bigger hurdle toward winning the presidency than the general election itself. In 1952, for example, Dwight D. Eisenhower experienced far more difficulty in capturing the GOP nomination from his intraparty rival, Senator Taft, than in defeating his Democratic opponent, Governor Stevenson, in the general election. (Eisenhower led Taft by 595 to 500 votes on the first ballot at the GOP convention before several delegations quickly shifted to Ike, giving him a clear-cut majority before the first ballot roll call tally was officially announced.) For these reasons, the nominating system occupies a central role in the U.S. party system. Until the last decade, relatively little serious study has been devoted to the nominating phase of the presidential selection process.[3] But as the full impact of several Democratic reform commissions' recommendations have been felt, political scientists and party-watchers alike have developed a far keener appreciation of the vital importance that the nominating phase plays in the selection of our Presidents and the future leadership of the country.[4]

Since their founding almost 150 years ago, national nominating conventions— sometimes termed "the gatekeepers to the presidency" —have been vested by each major party with the final authority to select nominees for the highest office in the land. But the official duties of the national convention are not confined strictly to picking presidential candidates. Indeed, the quadrennial conclaves perform a number of other valuable functions, both manifest and latent, that should be explained briefly.

Functions Performed by National Conventions

Because the following functions are related to the basic purpose and intended consequences of national conventions, they are generally called *manifest* functions. For almost a century and a half national conventions have performed six manifest functions.

MANIFEST FUNCTIONS

1. National conventions have nominated presidential and vice presidential candidates acceptable to most factions within the party, except in 1860, 1912, 1924, 1964, 1968, and 1972. In a close race the convention has always served to break a deadlock between rival contenders. Indeed, we should not overlook the fact that, despite an unmarred record of first ballot nominations since 1956, a convention deadlock or stalemate continues to remain a distinct possibility. The proliferation of presidential primaries (even if a regional primary system were adopted) would seem, mathematically at least, to increase the possibility of future convention deadlocks. In the 1976 GOP nominating race, for example, the Republicans narrowly avoided a stalemate. Only 111 delegate votes separated President Ford and his challenger, Governor Ronald Reagan, on the first ballot at the Kansas City convention. If a third Republican candidate had been entered in the race and drained away, say, 200 delegate votes from Ford and Reagan, the 1976 GOP convention might well have become deadlocked. If that had occurred, the national convention would have had to revert to its original "brokering" function of coming up with a compromise candidate acceptable to most major factions of the party. The national convention is admirably suited to reconcile and reintegrate the various divergent forces operating within the party. Retention of the "brokerage" function alone—even if kept on the shelf except for emergencies— would seem by itself to justify continuance of the convention nominating system.

2. National conventions, it must be remembered, represent minorities as well as majorities. It is sometimes forgotten how long the bitter enmity between

supporters of rival contenders for the party nomination persists after balloting is over. Even among strong party loyalists, the losers' wounds are often slow to heal. The following remarks heard from a defeated Kennedy delegate at the badly split 1980 Democratic convention graphically reflect this attitude: "As a Kennedy delegate who has spent nine months in this fight, meeting the incredible, unethical and dishonest tactics of the Carter people, I don't think I can as a responsible citizen vote for Carter. I'm not ready to bolt the party," the delegate added, "but I'm looking."[5] Even the 1980 Republican convention director, Bob Carter, who had been attending GOP conventions for nearly thirty years, reported that he had once been so disappointed over Senator Taft's loss to General Eisenhower in 1952 that he decided to become a Democrat. But he was dissuaded by the Senator who told him "that losing a skirmish did not mean losing the war."[6]

Because the conventions endeavor to bring all party elements under the tent, they help foster party solidarity and national unity. Indeed, one of the strongest arguments in favor of the national convention is that it provides the impetus and encouragement to divergent elements of the party to close ranks behind the newly anointed nominee. This is no small accomplishment. Despite our federal system, most political forces in this country are centrifugal in nature. Sectional differences, state and local jealousies, special interest groups, and racial minority groups all tend to fragment power and pull the parts of our nation asunder. In the national conventions the parties long ago found a compensatory institution that fosters a modicum of unity.[7]

3. Another convention function that appears to be emerging, or reemerging in a new form, is the shaping of vice presidential choice. Although the national convention has always been vested with the authority to select the vice presidential nominee, this action in the past was often treated in a perfunctory manner. In a primary-dominated presidential nominating system, the top reward belongs almost exclusively to the winner. To finish second place in the primary races, especially the early primaries, is to finish out of the money, as Representative Morris "Second Place Mo" Udall, George Bush, and even Senator Edward Kennedy can attest. But, as David S. Broder and others have pointed out, there is an important consolation prize for backers of the also-rans. They can influence and shape the convention choice (sometimes their own choice) of the vice presidential nominee. In 1976, for example, President Ford, who belonged to the moderate wing of the Republican party, faced a convention more conservative than himself. When Ronald Reagan, his defeated rival, rejected overtures to be Ford's running-mate, the President selected another conservative, Senator Robert Dole of Kansas, to serve on the ticket with him. According to a number of political insiders, Ford had not settled on Dole as a running-mate during the first two days of the convention, but when the defeated conservative challenger Ronald Reagan refused all offers to join Ford on the GOP ticket, Ford picked Dole, a popular choice with many conservative delegates. Likewise, Governor Jimmy Carter, a moderate Southern Democrat, responded to the pressures of the

more liberally oriented national convention in 1976 by picking a favorite of the trade unions and more liberal wing of the party—Senator Walter F. Mondale of Minnesota. Postmortem reports indicated that Senator Mondale was not at the top of Carter's original list of possible running-mates, but, among other factors, important blocs of liberal delegates urged Carter to pick Mondale, the most liberal member on his candidate list. In both instances, President Ford and Jimmy Carter appeared to be responding to signals from the convention floor to pick a running-mate from another wing of the party.

Further evidence surfaced in 1980 confirming the use of the vice presidential spot on the ticket as a consolation prize. After Republican nominee Ronald Reagan dropped the idea of picking former President Ford as his running-mate, he selected his chief adversary in the primaries—George Bush—to be on the ticket with him. Bush's selection proved to be a popular choice with many middle-of-the-road Republican delegates, especially from the Northeastern states. Once again, the 1980 GOP convention provided the environment in which the successful presidential nominee picked his running-mate to placate a substantial bloc of delegates supporting another unsuccessful contender from another wing of the party. By this action Governor Reagan reassured these party adherents that he had their interest at heart, as well as his own, in the final quest for the White House.

In gun-slinging America the convention function of selecting a vice presidential candidate also takes on even greater importance when it is remembered that attempts have been made on the lives of nine Presidents; four have been assassinated in office. The odds on a vice president being elevated to the presidency have narrowed considerably in the twentieth century. Thus far in this century four vice presidents—Theodore Roosevelt, Coolidge, Truman, and Lyndon B. Johnson—have moved directly to the White House upon the death of the President. Theodore Roosevelt and Johnson assumed the Presidency following the assassinations of Presidents McKinley and Kennedy; Coolidge and Truman took over the presidential reins following the untimely deaths of Presidents Harding and Franklin D. Roosevelt. A fifth Vice President, Gerald Ford, was elevated to the presidency in 1974 upon the resignation of President Nixon, who chose to resign rather than face impeachment proceedings.

4. National conventions have hammered out party platforms each quadrennium for almost 140 years. This function evolved from the earlier occasional practice of presenting "an address to the people." Early platform-making was usually deferred until after the nominations had been completed. But in 1852 the parties sought to help reconcile party fissures arising over the slavery issue by adopting the platform before selecting presidential candidates. This order of the agenda has prevailed, with few exceptions, to the present. The valuable function that platform-building serves to reconcile divergent elements within the party, its utility as a campaign weapon and its role as a guide to future party and presidential action is delineated in much greater detail in chapter 4.

5. The national convention has served as the campaign rally mechanism for

the national party. This function of arousing party supporters to get behind the ticket has continued to take on greater importance, especially in recent decades. From the beginning, state conventions were held as public meetings. Thus, although the campaign function was not explicitly recognized, the publicity and rallying activities of conventions have always been an integral part of these huge party conclaves. Television has also, of course, helped the parties arouse the enthusiasm of the millions of home viewers for their nominee. This function is discussed more fully in chapter 5.

6. The national convention has operated as the supreme governing-body of the national party in a predominantly decentralized party system. This activity, which is exemplified by the election of a continuing national committee each four years, has been an integral part of national conventions since the 1850's. From the start, the federal nature of the American party system was always formally recognized by giving equal representation to each state (until the GOP voted in 1952 to give an additional seat to state chairmen, if their state had a Republican majority in Congress). In 1972, the Democratic National Convention accepted an O'Hara Commission recommendation to enlarge the Democratic National Committee and voted to give additional representation to the most populous states (for example, California was allocated a total of twelve seats on the national committee). Before every national convention the national commit- tee selects the convention city, prescribes the number of delegates allocated to each state, establishes the convention rules, appoints the chairmen of the various convention committees—credentials, rules, resolutions, and platform—issues the official convention "call," and handles all arrangements for the quadrennial conclave. These duties are spelled out in more detail in Chapters 3 and 4.

National conventions also have a number of latent (unintended) functions that are sometimes overlooked.

LATENT FUNCTIONS

First, the quadrennial gatherings over the years have performed a valuable legitimating function for a nonconsensus candidate. In 1912, for example, Dem- ocrat Woodrow Wilson, on the first ballot, only received 324 out of 1,094 votes, running second to Champ Clark who led with 440½; yet it took 46 ballots before Wilson finally won the two-thirds majority needed at the time to claim the Democratic nomination. As explained in chapter 4, Clark actually held an abso- lute majority of the convention delegates between the tenth and sixteenth ballots. Yet, once the convention made its decision on Wilson, he was viewed as the legitimate nominee by virtually all of the state delegations and rank-and-file party members. More recently, it is sometimes overlooked that in 1976 Democratic nominee Jimmy Carter was the choice of only 39 percent of the primary voters nationwide before the national convention, yet once nominated, he was accepted by almost all party groups as the legitimate nominee. Winning the acquiescence of other candidates and factions within the party, as demonstrated in convention hall, tells the party electorate and the nation as a whole that the nominee is legitimately the party standard-bearer.

Significantly, the convention's decision on its nominee has been accepted as legitimate (with only two or possibly three exceptions in each party) by most participants for nearly a century and a half. It is indeed surprising that in a large, decentralized confederation of fifty state parties, the conventions have had only four major party bolts (the Democrats in 1860 and 1948, and the Republicans in 1912 and 1964). That each party has been able to reach reasonable agreement on its nominee in 34 out of 36 cases within the Democratic party since 1836 and in 28 cases out of 30 within the Republican party speaks well indeed for the convention system.

Second, closely related to this latent function would be the consensus-building role performed by the national convention. The party conclaves that seem so offensive to the uninitiated are essential to develop party consensus. Our presidential form of government, combined with a two-party system, puts the major parties under severe pressure to bring together a coalition of state delegations large enough to nominate the one nationwide candidate who can pull all of the countervailing elements under the party banner and go on to victory in November. The national convention seems admirably suited to perform this consensus-building task, but the convention cannot operate, of course, without compromise among the divergent power groups within the party. Indeed, as Pendleton Herring observed more than four decades ago, the convention system, "provides an excellent instrument for compromise. . . .Here concessions of many types can be made and victories in various terms are possible. The range of satisfactions is great, and disappointment on one count may be compensated for on another."[8]

The national convention, which meets for a brief four days every four years, serves to unite fifty state parties into a single national party, if only for the duration of the general election campaign. The first few conventions functioned chiefly to ratify an established consensus on who should head the ticket, for example, Jackson, Van Buren, and Harrison; they were less successful in creating party unity in support of the vice presidential candidates. The nomination of James K. Polk at the 1844 Democratic convention marked the first instance in which a national convention generated a solid consensus on a candidate who had received no votes at all on the first ballot (Polk won on the ninth ballot) and united the party behind him.[9] But occasionally the convention fails to rally behind the nominee. In 1948, for example, the Democratic delegates from four Southern states, embittered by President Truman's forthright stand for a strong civil rights plank in the party platform, bolted the convention, formed their own States' Rights (or Dixiecrat) party and nominated their own presidential candidate— Democratic Governor J. Strom Thurmond (presently a U.S. Republican senator from South Carolina). Although President Truman was able to win reelection despite the formation of the Dixiecrats on his right and Henry Wallace's Progressive third party on his left, failure to win the acquiescence of intra-party rivals and their supporters at the convention usually spells disaster for the party nominee. Three nominees in recent years—Senator Goldwater in 1964, Vice President Humphrey in 1968, and Senator McGovern in 1972—all failed to win the general acquiescence of their defeated rivals' supporters and all went down to defeat in November. Presidential incumbent Jimmy Carter in 1980 also suffered from this same divided party syndrome—failure to win full acquiescence from the backers of his vanquished foe, Senator Edward Kennedy. That strong dissension of this nature is generally kept at a minimum at a national convention reaffirms the importance of this latent function.

Third, another latent function is the celebration of a ceremony or party ritual that reinforces the democratic nature of the huge conclave. Each of the 3,000-plus delegates at the Democratic convention and 2,000 delegates at the GOP convention possesses a full vote, and he or she can rise to challenge the convention vote on any issue reported by his or her state delegate chairperson.

Fourth, national conventions offer a forum for various interest groups to dialogue, debate their differences, and form voting coalitions on important issues facing the party and presidential nominee. If nothing else, leaders of these frequently competing groups learn once again at national conventions that it's impossible in a broad-based national party to win all the points on divisive issues. Compromise and accommodation are indeed integral features of a viable national convention system.

Finally, earlier national conventions performed a fifth latent function of rapidly nullifying the intent of the Founding Fathers, as prescribed in the Constitution, to have members of the Electoral College exercise independent judgment in voting for President and Vice President. Indeed, the national convention was the key device through which nineteenth-century political parties democratized the choice for President. The national convention succeeded far better than the congressional party caucus in transforming the Electoral College into a recording instrument for registering the popular choice for President. Once access to presidential power was freed from screening by a highly-centralized group of national party leaders in the congressional caucus, the presidency soon became more rooted in the support of the voting masses. Moreover, the evolution of the national convention as a nominating device is closely intertwined with the development of the president's independent base of power. In a broader sense, this latent function benefits the American political system as a whole rather than simply the parties and the candidates.

One can merely speculate how presidential nominations would have evolved if the national conventions had not emerged after the congressional caucus had collapsed. But it seems doubtful if any mechanism could have been as broadly representative and as responsive to the leadership recruitment process as the national conventions have been over the past century and a half.

National conventions, however, have come under increasing attack in recent years, especially since 1968, because the further spread of presidential primaries has enabled the winning candidate in the primaries to claim the nomination long before the convention opens. As a result, the critics argue that the deliberative function of the national conclaves has been so severely eroded that they have been transformed into mere vote-counting bodies whose political influence, like that of the Electoral College, has long been moribund. This recent erosion of the national convention's deliberative function raises some fundamental questions about representative assemblies and the role they should play in a democratic state.

Deliberative Body versus Ratification Assembly

More than a dozen years ago, the late Alexander M. Bickel reminded us that there are two main types of multi-member democratic institutions: (1) the representative, deliberative body and (2) a representative assembly meant to register a single prior-mandated decision of its constituency. Congress or state legislatures are, of course, typical representative institutions of the first type. The Electoral College is a good example of the second.[10]

Representative, deliberative assemblies, by their very nature, will reflect as many significant factions in the total constituency as possible. But the voting majority shall, after listening and debating the major issues, prevail in the decision-making. Institutions registering decisions already made by a majority of their constituency, for example, the Electoral College, should consist of members responsive to that majority and no one else. One example of this type of mandated electoral decision was made long ago by a Federalist voter who said of a member of the Electoral College in 1796 that he did not "choose Samuel Miles to determine for me whether John Adams or Thomas Jefferson is the fittest man for President of the United States. No, I choose him to act, not think."[11]

These two models of democratic decision-making are highly relevant as we assess the national convention in this age of political reform. Looking to the future, the crucial question remains: Is the national convention to be retained as a deliberative body consisting mostly of delegates acting as "trustees" to their constituencies in selecting presidential nominees? Or is the national convention to consist almost entirely of hundreds of delegates, acting as "instructed agents" or messengers of their constituencies, who convene every four years solely as a ratification assembly to give their imprimatur to the victor of the presidential primary sweepstakes?

Essentially these are the two basic options on delegate representation offered by the existing presidential nominating process. Prior to the late 1960's, the national convention served, of course, primarily as a deliberative body. Convention delegates, in theory at least, operated as "trustees" under the old Burkean theory of "virtual representation." Delegates, after careful deliberation, were expected to use their own best judgment in assessing the qualifications of the various candidates, their prospects of bringing victory to the party in November, and then to pick the nominee. The delegates also selected a vice presidential running-mate (usually the personal choice of the party nominee), hammered out a party platform, revised convention rules, and settled other unfinished party business. But the rise of the Progressive reform movement and the spread of presidential primaries, which provided for the popular election of convention delegates in a dozen or more states early in the twentieth century, transformed the presidential nominating process into a "mixed" or hybrid system. However, because most of these early primaries were advisory in nature, not mandatory, the bulk of the delegates still continued to function as "trustees," free to use their own best judgment in picking the party nominee. Until the late 1960's, the deliberative function of national conventions continued to dominate candidate decision-making. The party, in effect, retained its "gatekeeping" function of winnowing out the weak and unwanted aspirants in favor of a nominee who enjoyed the support of most elements within the party.

The near doubling of the number of primaries within eight years—from sixteen in 1968 to twenty-nine in 1976—and the further proliferation of this popular sovereignty system to nearly three dozen states in 1980, however, threatens to transform the national convention from a deliberative body into a predominantly plebiscitary assembly consisting mostly of popularly elected, instructed delegates chosen solely to anoint the winner of the primaries as the party nominee. With three-quarters of national delegates now popularly elected, the convention's deliberative function has been seriously undermined. Indeed, spreading participatory democracy in the presidential nominating process threatens to turn each party's national nominating convention into the functional equivalent of a party "Electoral College." But to halt the rapid growth of this popular sovereignty or plebiscitary system of candidate selection, to deny rank-and-file voters the final voice in the selection of the party nominee, is no small task.

As one commentator, James W. Ceaser, has wisely observed, "it is clear that the plebiscitary system is very difficult to challenge on the grounds of its formal legitimacy, as it is based on popular sovereignty, the strongest principal inherent in any democratic regime."[12] At the 1980 Democratic convention Senator Abraham Ribicoff (D.-Conn.), for example, effectively utilized the popular sovereignty argument to support President Carter's renomination. In defending the proposed new "faithful delegate" rule that would require delegates to vote, at least for one ballot, for the candidate they had originally supported, Senator Ribicoff implored the convention delegates to keep their commitment to the "nineteen million Democrats who went to the polls expecting their votes to mean something."[13] But this plebiscitarian democracy argument contains the seeds of dangerous doctrine, for if carried to an extreme, it would further undermine the already seriously weakened major political parties' role in selecting their presidential nominee. Equally important, this controversy raises a fundamental question about rival concepts of representation—the Progressive or instructed delegate versus the party regular or "trustee" delegate—within the national convention system. Separating the arguments of these two conflicting schools of representation is central to understanding the role of national conventions in this reform era.

Progressive versus Party Regular Concepts of Representation

For almost a century, two competing political schools of thought in American politics have been at odds over the best method to conduct nominations: the Progressives and, for want of a better name, Party Regulars or Burkean advocates. Each group interprets the role of the candidates, the party organization, and the rank-and-file voters quite differently. Each group advocates, as James W. Ceaser, Thomas R. Marshall, and others have pointed out, a different method for nominating candidates, especially for the Presidency. That both schools rest upon democratic assumptions is beyond question, since each relies directly or indirectly on the voters as a source of legitimacy. But the two groups strongly disagree on how best to represent the voters and on what role the rank-and-file voter should play in nominating candidates.

Since the turn of the twentieth century, the reform-minded Progressives have argued that a candidate should be popularly elected, instead of handpicked by party professionals. On the state level the Progressives would have direct primaries to allow the voters to nominate the party ticket directly. In national politics the Progressives would use presidential primaries to permit rank-and-file voters to choose national convention delegates who run pledged to specific candidates. Until recently, in some states (for example, Oregon) the voters also expressed their preference directly on the choice of presidential candidates. For a time the Progressives held high hopes that a national primary would be adopted, but the plan made little headway, despite endorsement in the Progressive Party platform in 1912 and by President Wilson in an address to the Congress in 1913. Frustrated at the national level, the Progressive forces shifted to the state level, even though the basic objective of the state presidential primary movement remained national in scope. But the major goal of the Progressives was to transform the delegate selection process into a type of national party plebiscite in which the citizenry would choose the nominee.

Under the Progressive doctrine, national convention delegates would become instructed agents of the voters' will at the national nominating convention, much as presidential electors in the early nineteenth century had been transformed into designated agents of the people's choice in the general election. Thus, if enough mandated convention delegates were chosen in the primaries, the convention would be converted from its earlier role as a deliberative assembly into the functional equivalent of the Electoral College. Some Progressives insisted that the national convention be abolished. But most of these reformers recognized that if none of the contenders won enough delegates in the presidential primaries to capture the nomination, the national convention would have to regain, temporarily at least, its former deliberative function. Even then, some early Progressives proposed that the convention choice be restricted to the top two or three vote-getters.

Progressive theorists also emphasized the importance of a direct popular mandate for the executive. They argued that the president, for example, should have a mandate separate from Congress and from state officeholders and professional politicians. If officeholders and party leaders controlled the nomination for president, the Progressives argued, then the nominee would be forced to trim or dilute his legislative program and court the favor of the party regulars in order to win support for his programs. An independent mandate, the Progressives insisted, would "energize" the executive. Even if Congress were preoccupied with defending local interests, a president chosen directly by the voters would possess a strong popular mandate to push his programs.[14] But shortly after the 1912 election the Progressive movement lost momentum as the gathering war clouds in Europe shifted national attention abroad. After the cessation of hostilities a conservative reaction submerged the Progressive movement.

More recently, the Progressive doctrine has been revived by its latter-day successors—the participatory Democrats and political amateurs. These recent critics of the party regulars, for example, the McGovern Democrats and the anti-war partisans of the late sixties and early seventies, castigated the existing convention system for its demographic underrepresentation of young people, women, and racial minorities. These modern reformers also pointed to the insufficient representation of members of the working class and underprivileged.

The party regulars or Burkeans, however, have disagreed over the years with virtually all of the Progressive doctrine insofar as nominations are concerned. First of all, the regulars argue that they can better represent the party's rank-and-file identifiers than can delegates chosen through presidential primaries. Second, the party regulars claim over-reliance on direct popular participation gives a special advantage to well-organized, but ideologically extreme, candidates. Third, the party regulars focus on reining in, not "energizing" the chief executive. The regulars disagree with the Progressives' contention that grass roots participation is the only adequate way to represent the party's electorate. Because many of those who participate in primaries are usually more ideological and extreme than the party's rank-and-file voters, say the party regulars, the primaries often overrepresent the extremist position and fail to reflect the average citizen.

By contrast, the party regulars emphasize compromise and coalition-building, which generally result in the selection of presidential nominees from the party center who will be more acceptable to the average citizen. Furthermore, the party regulars claim that their nominees will more likely attract the independent and crossover voters needed for victory. Indeed, the party regulars argue that the new reform system has a built-in bias toward nominating presidential candidates who are so extreme that they usually suffer electoral disasters. They cite the Barry Goldwater and George McGovern presidential candidacies as typical by-products of the popular participation nominating system.

Unlike the Progressives, the party regulars argue that a nominating system that ignores the party and elected officials is poor preparation for effective government during a president's term of office. Furthermore, the party regular school emphasizes the need to restrain the president. Defenders of the party regulars point out that the party's rank-and-file cannot effectively bargain and rein in a president, once elected. Only the elected officeholders in Congress and party leaders have the "clout" to restrain potential excesses and abuses by the president. Once this officeholder influence is removed, the regulars argue, the party organization is powerless to halt presidential abuses, such as those of President Nixon's reelection campaign committee (CREEP) and the White House "plumbers" involvement in the Watergate scandals.

In the Progressive school of politics party regulars have been viewed as unwelcome intruders attempting to block the political dialogue between the party's voters and its candidates. According to Progressive doctrine, the party regulars have not adequately represented the party's rank-and-file voters but instead have taken their marching orders from the party bosses and the vested interests. Furthermore, as Thomas R. Marshall has commented on Progressive doctrine, "Direct involvement by ordinary voters is seen as bringing benefits not only to the representative process, but also to the individual participants and to the political parties."[15] Direct personal involvement in the primaries, the party reformers argue, helps develop an awareness of the major issues that the presidential candidate, if elected, would have to face in office. Party regulars, the modern day Progressives insist, have been far more concerned with obtaining appointive positions and federal grants for their states from the victorious candidate than facing the crucial issues of the day.

To shift to a plebiscitary system with millions of voters electing most or all of the mandated delegates to a national convention, the regulars insist, would effectively destroy once and for all the power brokers within the party—the intermediaries who provide an effective check on the nominee and potential president-elect. If the party constraints upon the nominee are entirely removed, the regulars argue, the party standard-bearer can ignore party officials, conduct his general election campaign almost exclusively on the television networks, and hold himself accountable only to the voting masses in the primaries. This threatened transformation of the nominating process would, in this writer's view, too, have an extremely deleterious effect upon the presidential selection process, upon the Presidency, and eventually upon the system of democratic government itself.

Responsible Party Government Doctrine

In discussing the role of the party in the presidential selection process, brief mention should also be made of the responsible party government doctrine that influenced many political scientists in the 1950's and 1960's. Advocates of "responsible parties" believed that: (1) Modern mass democracy requires that the electorate be able to maintain control *over* government rather than participate *in* government on a regular basis. Emphasis should be on popular voter choice between the decision-makers of rival parties rather than having the people make governmental decisions themselves. (2) To achieve this kind of responsible popular control, it is essential to have competitive parties that offer alternative sets of leaders. These leaders must be identifiable, answerable for their actions, and strong enough to run the government. The parties must not only be unified and disciplined, but the majority party must also be responsible for the conduct of government.[16]

The American Political Science Association's Committee on Political Parties report, "Toward a More Responsible Two-Party System," which espoused the views of the "responsible parties" school, sought to strengthen the party's control over the national convention and yet make this large body more responsive to popular influence.[17] To make the national convention's deliberative process more effective, especially in reviewing the qualifications of the various presidential contenders and drafting the party platform, the Committee task force recommended reducing the size of the national convention to 500 to 600 members. This streamlined convention would consist of 300 to 350 delegates elected by party voters, and the other major portion would consist of national committee members, state party chairmen, congressional leaders, and other party leaders. Further discussion of the Committee's proposal will be reserved for the final chapter.

It is noteworthy that the three major party reform groups of the twentieth century—the Progressives, the party responsibility advocates, and the supporters of greater participatory democracy—have all focused on the presidential selection process as the most strategic control point for influencing public policy and the future direction of the country. No wonder, then, that party reformers and party regulars frequently clash over the virtues and shortcomings of the existing presidential nominating machinery.

In light of the frequent vitriolic criticism of the national convention from many quarters, what justification can be made in defense of an institution that has frequently been depicted as a combination carnival, Roman circus, and revival meeting? In this author's view, the critics seriously misunderstand the role performed by the national nominating conventions. James W. Ceaser, in his thoughtful study of the presidential selection process, has listed five normative functions of a sound presidential selection system: (1) It should minimize the harmful results of the pursuit of power by ambitious contenders. (2) It should help establish the proper kind of presidential leadership and proper scope of executive power. (3) It should help secure a competent executive. (4) It should help ensure legitimate accession. (5) It should provide for the proper degree of choice and change.[18]

In this study it will be argued that the present mixed system of primaries and caucus-convention delegate selection operating within the national convention framework (provided the number of delegates elected in mandatory, binding primaries does not exceed one-half of the total convention) satisfies these criteria more closely than any alternate institution—national primary, regional primaries, straight caucus-convention system, or congressional caucus—for selecting presidential nominees.

Still, it is the reader who will have to decide whether or not the virtues and operational flexibility of the national convention system delineated in this study justify continuance of this venerable institution that has selected every major nominee and future President of the United States—the outstanding chief executives, the undistinguished, and mediocrities—since the age of Andrew Jackson.

In the next chapter we will undertake a brief historical survey of presidential nominations from the early congressional caucus to the rise of the national nominating convention and then examine the recent collapse of the brokered convention system and its displacement by the new system of presidential primary popular appeal.

Notes

1. Paul O'Neil, "Conventions: Nominations by Rain Dance," *Life*, Vol. 65 (July 5, 1968), p. 19.

2. Donald R. Matthews, "Presidential Nominations: Process and Outcomes," in James David Barber, ed., *Choosing the President* (Englewood Cliffs, N.J.: Prentice-Hall, 1974), p. 36.

3. The major works in this earlier period were: Paul T. David, Malcolm Moos, and Ralph M. Goldman, *Presidential Nominating Politics in 1952*, 5 vols. (Baltimore: The Johns Hopkins University Press, 1954); Paul T. David, Ralph M. Goldman, and Richard C. Bain, *The Politics of National Party Conventions* (Washington, D.C.: The Brookings Institution, 1960); Gerald M. Pomper, *Nominating the President* (Evanston, Ill.: Northwestern University Press, 1963); and James W. Davis, *Presidential Primaries: Road to the White House* (New York: Thomas Y. Crowell, 1967).

4. A representative sample of recent books and monographs on the presidential nominating process would include: Thomas R. Marshall, *Presidential Nominations in a Reform Age* (New York: Praeger, 1981); Arthur T. Hadley, *The Invisible Primary* (Englewood Cliffs, N.J.: Prentice-Hall, 1976); William R. Keech and Donald R. Matthews, *The Party's Choice* (Washington, D.C.: The Brookings Institution, 1976); Donald R. Matthews, ed., *Perspectives on Presidential Selection* (Washington, D.C.: The Brookings Institution, 1973); Nelson W. Polsby and Aaron Wildavsky, *Presidential Elections*, 5th ed. (New York: Charles Scribner's Sons, 1980); and Austin Ranney, *The Federalization of Presidential Primaries* (Washington, D.C.: American Enterprise Institute, 1978). Chapters on presidential nominations will also be found in presidential chronicler Theodore H. White's series, *The Making of the President* (New York: Atheneum, 1961, 1965, 1969, and 1973); and his *America in Search of Itself: The Making of the President, 1956-1980* (New York: Harper and Row Publishers, 1981). See also Lewis Chester, Godfrey Hodgson, and Bruce Page, *An American Melodrama: The Presidential Campaign of 1968* (New York: Viking Press, 1969); and Jules Witcover, *Marathon: The Pursuit of the Presidency, 1972-1976* (New York: The Viking Press, 1977).

5. *Washington Post*, August 15, 1981.

6. Martin Tolchin, *New York Times*, July 14, 1980.

7. Donald Bruce Johnson, "Delegate Selection for National Conventions" in Cornelius P. Cotter, ed. *Practical Politics in the United States* (Boston: Allyn & Bacon, Inc., 1969), p.236.

8. Pendleton Herring, *The Politics of Democracy* (New York: W.W. Norton, Inc., 1940), p. 230.

9. V.O. Key, Jr., *Politics, Parties, and Pressure Groups*, 5th ed. (New York: Thomas Y. Crowell, 1964), p. 327.

10. Alexander M. Bickel, *The New Age of Political Reform: The Electoral College, the Convention and the Party* (New York: Harper & Row, 1968), pp. 26-27.

11. Ibid.

12. James W. Ceaser, *Presidential Selection: Theory and Development* (Princeton, N.J.: Princeton University Press, 1979), p. 300.

13. *New York Times*, August 12, 1980.

14. See James W. Ceaser, *Presidential Selection: Theory and Development*, chapter 5; Thomas R. Marshall, *Presidential Nominations in a Reform Age*, chapter 6.

15. Thomas R. Marshall, *Presidential Nominations in a Reform Age*, pp. 160-161.

16. This brief summary has been adopted from Austin Ranney and Willmoore Kendall, *Democracy and the American Party System* (New York: Harcourt, Brace and World, Inc., 1956), pp. 151-52, 525-27).

17. *American Political Science Review*, Vol. 44 (September 1950), Supplement, pp. 1-99.

18. James W. Ceaser, *Presidential Selection: Theory and Development*, p. 307.

History of the
National Convention System _____ 2

> Nominations are made from necessity. In an extended territory,
> comprising a numerous population, men having the same object
> in view, and governed by the same political principles, to give ef-
> fect and success to their objects and principles, must act in con-
> cert. Meetings of some kind must be held—an interchange of senti-
> ment take place, and the candidate agreed upon.
>
> Albany *Argus*, June 2, 1826

If the first three presidential elections before 1800 are excluded, a history of
American presidential elections shows three distinct systems by which parties
have chosen their nominees. For convenience sake, we have borrowed Thomas
R. Marshall's classification of these three systems—the Congressional Caucus
System, 1800-1824; the Brokered Convention System, 1832-1968; the System
of Popular Appeal, 1972-present.[1] Each of these systems, Marshall reminds us,
differs from the others in several respects: the type of candidate favored, the
focus of the nomination, the role of party leaders and rank-and-file members, and
the role of the media. Each system has had both formal and informal rules; each
system has also had different stages and focal points in the decision-making
process. In the course of our discussion we will delineate the salient features of
each system and seek an explanation of why each of the first two systems
ultimately collapsed.

Nominations by Congressional Caucus

Although the Founding Fathers recognized that the need for a strong chief
executive in the fledgling Republic—they considered at least a half dozen proposals at the Constitutional Convention before settling upon the independently
elected chief executive outlined in Article II of the U.S. Constitution—they did
not bother to construct machinery for nominating presidential candidates. No

method of nominating presidents was written into the Constitution because the Founding Fathers assumed the choice would be limited to a very small number of obviously well-qualified men, and the best man would be selected. Nor should it be forgotten that parties were still non-existent at the time the Framers met in Philadelphia in 1787. The first presidential nomination presented no problem, since George Washington was the unanimous choice of his countrymen. In 1796, however, President Washington's announcement that he would not seek a third term signaled the opening of the first presidential nominating contest. But his belated announcement in his Farewell Address left no time for potential con- tenders to organize their campaigns. Rival factions in Congress—the Federalists and Democratic-Republicans—convened into the newly formed congressional caucuses to select their choice for president. The Federalists chose Vice Presi- dent John Adams as their nominee and Thomas Pinckney as his running-mate. The Democratic-Republicans (soon to be called Democrats) selected Thomas Jefferson to head the ticket and Aaron Burr as his running-mate. In neither case did the parties make formal nominations; they merely decided among themselves and depended upon their political influence to keep the presidential electors in line. These informal nominations, however, did not assure complete elector loyalty, and as a result, the president and vice president were elected from different parties! Federalist electors gave 71 votes to Adams but only 59 to vice presidential nominee Pinckney. Democratic-Republican electors cast 68 votes for Jefferson but only 30 for Burr.[2] Thus, the Federalist Adams was elected president and Jefferson, the Democratic-Republican, vice president. (This anom- aly was not corrected until passage of the Twelfth Amendment in 1804, as will be explained below.)

Four years later, however, party lines had hardened. President Adams and Vice President Jefferson were generally acknowledged to be leaders of their respective parties. The party caucuses nominated these candidates as well as their vice presidential running-mates, Federalist Charles C. Pinckney and Democratic- Republican Aaron Burr. Under the newly established party discipline, the win- ning ticket of Jefferson and Burr was tied for first place with 73 votes each. It was widely understood that Jefferson was to be president and Burr, vice presi- dent. But the opportunistic Burr refused to step aside, thus sending the decision to the House of Representatives, as provided for in the Constitution. Many lame-duck Federalist congressmen saw this electoral deadlock as a prime oppor- tunity to humiliate the despised Jefferson, but Alexander Hamilton, formerly his leading adversary in Washington's Cabinet, viewed Burr as far more unscrupu- lous. Hamilton successfully prevailed upon several Federalists in the House of Representatives to cast ballots for Jefferson and thus put him in the Presidency.[3] To prevent a repetition of this deadlock, Congress passed and the states soon ratified (in 1804) the Twelfth Amendment, which stipulated that members of the Electoral College must designate both the presidential and vice presidential candidates on their ballots.

From 1800 to 1820, the Democratic-Republicans relied exclusively upon their congressional caucus to nominate their presidential candidates—Jefferson, Madison, and Monroe. But it would be an exaggeration to contend that Jefferson, Madison, or Monroe reached the White House exclusively as a result of a caucus nomination. Each of these men was widely recognized at the time of his nomination as the party leader or heir apparent. Actually, the congressional caucus seemed to devote far more time to selecting vice presidential running-mates.[4] But the congressional caucus (known as "King Caucus") was a centralized or national mechanism that contained some representatives from all or nearly all of the states. It was also a convenient system in the young Republic. Members of Congress, having already made the long painful journey to the nation's capital over indescribably muddy roads at the beginning of the session, were readily available to handle the quadrennial selection duties. Congressmen were also quite knowledgeable about potential presidential candidates from all sections of the new country. For almost a quarter of a century the congressional caucus gave its official seal of approval to each Democratic-Republican nominee and thereby suppressed any serious challenge to his candidacy. The rival Federalists, their numbers in Congress dwindling in face of widespread Democratic-Republican popularity, resorted to other means to pick nominees. In 1808 and 1812, the Federalists used an informal nominating convention to select nominees. Unlike the national conventions subsequently developed in the Jacksonian era, the Federalist conventions consisted of small groups, designated in a variety of ways, meeting in secret! These parleys furnished a measure of legitimacy to the presidential candidates they nominated, even though many states were not even represented. But in the presidential elections, the Federalist candidates were easily overwhelmed by their far more popular Jeffersonian opponents. By 1820, the Federalists had faded into history. (Since President Monroe had no opponent in 1820, the Democratic-Republicans did not even bother to convene a congressional caucus to renominate him for a second term.)

Did the congressional caucus provide the same kind of legitimating authority before 1824 that the national convention has supplied since 1832? To all outward appearances it did. From 1800 to 1820, the caucus nominees for president and vice president were acceptable to the vast majority of Democratic-Republicans, and the nominees won easy victories in the Electoral College. But the superficial solidarity of the congressional caucus disintegrated in 1824 because there was no opposition party to force the reigning Democratic-Republicans, faced with a multi-candidate field, to unite and make a binding nomination. Clearly, one-party politics do not necessarily translate into political harmony, as the late V.O. Key, Jr., and other twentieth century students of American parties have repeatedly explained.[5]

By 1824, the dominant Democratic party had fragmented into warring factions. William Crawford, former Secretary of the Treasury in Madison's Cabinet, was the caucus choice, but he won the support of only 64 votes out of the 240 eligible members of Congress (see Table 1). Almost three-quarters of the congressmen boycotted the caucus. Indeed, ten states were unrepresented at the

TABLE 1

DEMOCRATIC-REPUBLICAN CONGRESSIONAL CAUCUS NOMINATING
AND ELECTORAL COLLEGE VOTES, 1804-1824

| Date of Caucus | Democratic-Republicans in Congress | | Democratic-Republicans | | Presidential | Vice-Presidential | Democratic-Republican Electoral College Majorities |
	House (Total)	Senate (Total)	Attending Caucus	Abstentions			
Feb. 25, 1804	102 (142)	25 (34)	110	15-20 Burr men	Jefferson, acclamation	Clinton, 67; Breckenridge, 20, others, 21	162-14
Jan. 23, 1808	118 (142)	28 (34)	94	50-55 "anti-caucus" congressmen	Madison, 83; Clinton, 3; Monroe, 3	Clinton, 79; Langdon, 5; others, 4	122-47
May 12, May 18, June 8, 1812	108 (186)	30 (36)	About 83	50-55 Clinton men	Madison, 82	Langdon, 64; Gerry, 16, others 2; Langdon declined. Gerry, 74; others, 3	128-89

22

Date					President	Vice-President	Electoral vote
March 16-17, 1816	117 (186)	25 (38)	About 119	About 23	Monroe, 65; Crawford, 54	Tompkins, 85; Snyder, 30	183-34
1820	156 (186)	35 (46)	No caucus held, no formal action	—	Monroe	Tompkins	231-1
Feb. 14, 1824	187 (213)	44 (48)	68	Over 160	Crawford, 64; others, 4	Gallatin, 57; others, 9; Gallatin declined	Jackson, 99; Adams, 84; Crawford, 41; Clay, 37; (vice president: Calhoun, 182, others, 79)

Sources: Compiled by Ralph M. Goldman from Louis C. Hatch, *History of the Vice-Presidency* (Westport, Conn., reprint of 1934 ed.: Greenwood Press, 1970), pp. 13-43, 149, 162-66; and Edward Stanwood, *A History of the Presidency* (Boston: Houghton, Mifflin, 1928), vol. 1. pp. 90-91, 99 109-10: *National Intelligencer* (February 16, 1824). In Ralph M. Goldman, *Search for Consensus: The Story of the Democratic Party* (Philadelphia: Temple University Press, 1979), p. 29. Reprinted by permission of Temple University Press.

meeting, and five others had only one member representing the state.[6] The caucus boycott was led by the anti-Crawford forces who wished to scuttle "King Caucus" once and for all. But they had no distinctive alternate system available to select a nominee. Three candidates—Henry Clay of Kentucky, Andrew Jackson of Tennessee, and John C. Calhoun of South Carolina—were nominated by their home state legislatures. John Quincy Adams was endorsed by several New England legislatures. All of these candidates were subsequently endorsed by the legislatures of other states.

Since none of the presidential candidates in 1824 received a majority of the Electoral College votes, the decision was again, in accordance with the Constitution, thrown into the House of Representatives. Although Jackson had led the field in popular and electoral votes, the House (with each of the 24 states casting one vote apiece) chose John Quincy Adams to be the next President, thanks to special support from Henry Clay's partisans in the House. The thirteen states that cast ballots for Adams included five states that the Jacksonians said Clay had "thrown" to Adams. Understandably, Jackson and his followers complained vociferously that they had been the victims of an Adams-Clay deal, and when it was announced that Clay would become Secretary of State in Adams' Cabinet, there appeared to be additional grounds, whether true or not, for claiming that they had been cheated. In any event, this unfortunate set of circumstances totally discredited the congressional caucus.

The Transitional Period

The election of 1824 marked the end of an era—the demise of the congressional caucus and the short-lived one-party system. The congressional caucus system was abandoned because it smacked of aristocratic privilege; it violated the great touchstone of Jacksonian democracy—popular sovereignty. Another charge against the caucus, an argument that came to a head in 1824, was that the caucus violated the separation of powers, a basic principle of the United States Constitution. "King Caucus" grew increasingly unpopular because it threatened to make Presidents the creatures of Congress. Contemporary critics pointed out that the congressional caucus amounted, in effect, to the selection of the chief executive by the legislative branch. This could lead, the critics said, either to domination of the President by Congress or the corruption of Congress by presidents or would-be presidents. The astute Daniel Webster, for example, expressed fear that without strong parties the president would become a captive of Congress.[7]

The most serious objection to the congressional caucus, however, was its unrepresentativeness. Democratic-Republicans who lived in districts represented in Congress by Federalists, or Federalists who lived in congressional districts represented by Democratic-Republicans could argue persuasively that they were not represented in presidential nominations at all. Furthermore, wide fluctuations of party membership in Congress led to a serious imbalance of representation in the congressional caucus. If a party did poorly in one section of the country for a few years, its representation in Congress from this area would be small, and it would, in effect, be deprived of a major voice in the presidential nominating process. Thus, if Northern Democrats suffered a series of reverses in one or two elections, the Southern wing of the party would dominate the candidate choice. Under the congressional caucus system Southern candidates did in fact monopolize the nominations. In areas where the party was weak the attempts of leaders to nominate their favorite candidate would be frustrated by the sectional leaders from the party's dominant area. Spokesmen for the expanding sectional interests complained that the Virginia Dynasty (Jefferson, Madison, and Monroe) and their congressional caucus system of presidential nominations had transformed the selection process into an oligarchical scheme to perpetuate control of the national government. Moreover, interested and informed citizens who participated in politics at the grass roots level, especially during campaigns, were totally excluded from the presidential nominating process. As William G. Carleton explained some years ago, "The caucus consisted of only a handful of leaders not fresh from the people and alert to the latest trends in public opinion, but far removed in Washington from their home communities, remote (in that day of poor communications) from the latest developments in their constituencies, at the end of their terms, many of them to become lame ducks."[8]

Other factors in the Republic were also undermining the caucus system. Expansion of the suffrage and changes in voting procedures for presidential electors (by popular election in most states) were opening up the political system. Between 1800 and 1824, the popular vote rose from 400,000 to 1.1 million. The number of states in which presidential electors were chosen by the popular vote rather than by state legislatures rose from four out of sixteen states in 1800 to eighteen out of twenty-four states in 1824. Along the Atlantic seaboard states, the propertied classes found themselves outvoted by the rising groups of artisans and farmers. Demands for presidential nominations by state legislatures, state conventions, and mass meetings reflected this popular challenge to the eastern-southern oligarch system. Sharp alterations in the distribution of power were occurring across the land, and these shifts paralleled a transformation in the method of selecting presidential candidates.

The demise of the congressional caucus, Theodore Lowi and Austin Ranney have both pointed out, not only altered the character of the young political parties but changed the constitutional system as well. From 1800 to the 1820's, "the main impact of caucus nominations was to convert the formal separation of powers between the President and Congress into a de facto 'fusion of powers' not unlike such modern parliamentary systems as the British."[9] But the collapse of the caucus, the rise of the popular favorite Andrew Jackson, and the emergence of presidential nominations by national conventions consisting of delegations from state parties gave "him and succeeding Presidents a base of power independent of Congress . . . totally split Congress off from the presidential succession and established for the first time an institutionalized, *real* separation of powers."[10]

State and local parties, though their leaders may not have recognized it at the time, had won a great victory in ending presidential nominations by the congressional caucus.[11]

It is worth taking a moment to speculate about the possible effect that a congressional caucus system for presidential nominations would have in the present era. If this system were ever adopted (which is highly unlikely), might not a modern congressional caucus nominating mechanism lead to better coordination of the executive and legislative branches within our separation of powers system? Instead of a one-party system that prevailed in the last days of the congressional caucus, today such a caucus nominating system involving strong two-party representation in most of the 50 states would probably be far more responsive to the popular will than the early nineteenth century version. But the threat of congressional domination of the President under this system would, of course, still hover over the country, as it did in the early days of the Republic.

The national convention, however, did not immediately displace the hodge-podge decentralized nominating structure that had filled the institutional vacuum following the demise of the congressional caucus. If the congressional caucus was too centralized to represent the state and local units of the party, contemporary leaders noted that the selection of presidential nominees by individual states was too decentralized in the young federal Republic. How, they asked, could a presidential aspirant win the exclusive nomination of a united party? Some mechanism was needed that would represent party elements throughout the country and at the same time facilitate the nomination of a broadly supported candidate, since a "no-nomination" system promised to throw every presidential election into the House of Representatives—a prospect abhorrent to informed opinion of every persuasion.[12]

During the transitional period from the congressional caucus system to the national nominating convention, four decentralized methods for nominating the president were used in the various states. The most popular method of presidential nomination was by state legislative caucus, typically a joint meeting of both houses. The second method used was by the "mixed" convention, composed of the party members of the legislature and independently elected delegates from those counties and towns which were not represented in the legislature by the party holding the convention. Indeed, this method of nominating a presidential candidate carried over to the early period of the national convention. According to Frederick W. Dallinger, a nineteenth century authority on nominations:

...in February 1843, a convention composed of the Whig members of the Virginia Legislature, and of two hundred delegates from different parts of the state, was held at Richmond at which resolutions were adopted nominating Henry Clay as the Whig candidate for the Presidency, and referring the nomination of a candidate for the Vice Presidency to the national convention.[13]

Third, state conventions, as indicated earlier, were also used to nominate presidential candidates during the interim period. In some states the party continued to "nominate" presidential candidates—the action serving merely to reflect party sentiment within the state. Fourth, in other states it was a common practice to obtain the presidential preferences of rank-and-file voters at various types of public meetings. Throughout the country mass meetings were held, at which formal resolutions nominating a candidate for president were adopted. These various meetings were, in effect, gatherings to ratify the nomination of candidates who had been previously nominated by state conventions or legislative caucuses.[14] Today we would term these meetings party rallies, though these early meetings formally adopted nominating resolutions. Briefly, then, the switchover from legislative caucuses, state conventions, and mass meetings to the national convention took place gradually over a period of two decades.

None of the four nominating methods sketched above adequately met the needs of the emerging party system in the young, sprawling Republic. Indeed, it is entirely possible that if the state convention or legislative caucus system had persisted, a multi-party system might have evolved, since each state conclave was completely free to put forward any candidate that captured its fancy. That this patchwork system lacked the cohesiveness to make binding nominations, however, facilitated the emergence of the national nominating convention, in which delegates from all states of the Union would meet under one roof to select a presidential and vice presidential candidate. Also, the fact that party conventions had been used extensively on the county and state level in most states for more than two decades before the first national convention undoubtedly made easier the transition from earlier nominating procedures to the national convention system. In the words of one commentator, "The practiced ease with which American politicians organized national nominating conventions during the age of Jackson was made possible by long experience with low-level conventions during the Jeffersonian era."[15]

Clearly, the idea of a national nominating convention was not exactly new when Senator Martin Van Buren, leader of the Jacksonian forces on Capitol Hill and a former supporter of William Crawford, proposed it in 1827.[16] No immediate action, however, was taken on Van Buren's proposal. For the moment it was unnecessary because the Tennessee legislature had already renominated Jackson, who in the meantime had resigned from the U.S. Senate to commence presidential campaigning. Jackson became an announced candidate three years before the 1828 election—a record that twentieth-century "early bird" presidential candidates still have not matched. President Adams' renomination in 1828 was accepted as a matter of course by his followers, though no formal endorsement was made.

The Brokered Convention System: 1832-1968

With the demise of the congressional caucus, party leaders began casting about for a new mechanism to nominate a presidential candidate. While nomination by state legislatures was still available, this decentralized form of nomination lacked a binding national mandate needed in the expanding Republic. Three years later, a small splinter group, the Anti-Masonic party, experimented with a unique nominating mechanism—a national nominating convention.

EARLY PERIOD

Almost by accident, the Anti-Masons discovered that a party convention would serve as a forum to assess and discuss prospective candidates before choosing the party standard-bearer. The Anti-Masonic leaders also concluded this same forum could help facilitate development of a national organization and foster a favorable national party image. Thirteen states sent a total of 116 delegates to the Anti-Masonic convention, held in Baltimore, Maryland, September 1831—fourteen months before the general election. William Wirt, United States Attorney General in James Monroe's Cabinet, was selected as nominee of the Anti-Masonic party. Though the Anti-Masons did not survive to hold another convention, this minor party established several precedents that have influenced major party convention and national party organizations ever since:

1. Delegations were chosen in a manner determined by each state.
2. Each state was entitled to as many votes as the state's representation in Congress.
3. A special majority—the Anti-Masons had decreed three-fourths of the delegates—was required for nomination.
4. An Anti-Masonic national committee was appointed to carry on national party business between elections.
5. The first national party platform (called "an address to the people") was approved by the delegates.[17]

Three months after the Anti-Masonic party met in Baltimore, the newly established National Republican Party convened in the same city for the party's first and only convention. Elements of this newly formed party had supported President John Quincy Adams' reelection bid in 1828, but they had so few members in Congress that caucus selection seemed futile. The party needed a new mechanism to give it a semblance of nationwide representation. Although Henry Clay had already been nominated by several state legislatures, party leaders soon agreed that the national convention idea, recently developed by the Anti-Masonic party, was an eminently practical instrument for selecting a presidential nominee.

Weather conditions in Baltimore were so bad that only 130 delegates were on hand when the National Republican convention was called to order. Late arrivals kept straggling into the convention throughout the proceedings, even after the balloting had been completed. Eventually all states, except Tennessee, were represented, although in disproportionate numbers. The National Republicans nominated Henry Clay for President and John Sergeant, his running-mate, by a unanimous vote and then composed an address to the people castigating President Jackson's policies. Within the Democratic party President Jackson's renomination was assured in 1832; instead, his major concern was the selection of his vice presidential running-mate. Jackson, after a falling-out with his first term Vice President, John C. Calhoun, wanted Martin Van Buren of New York on the ticket with him. But Jackson felt that he could not depend on endorsement for Van Buren from state legislatures, who might decide to nominate several different candidates, or possibly members of the congressional caucus might seek to get back into the nominating business. Since General Jackson was keenly aware that no party can successfully vie for power unless it can prevent the fragmentation of its own supporters, he was looking for a mechanism by which state party leaders throughout the country could agree on a single vice presidential candidate. Borrowing a page from the Anti-Masons and National Republicans, Jackson instructed his managers to convene a nominating convention to select his running-mate. Jackson leaders agreed, too, that a national convention would serve to emphasize his great popular strength. Ironically, the "calls" for the first two Democratic conventions were issued by the legislature of New Hampshire.[18] Like their rivals, the Democrats convened in Baltimore in May 1832. Surprisingly, most of the basic organizational structure of the first Democratic convention— committees on credentials, permanent organization, and rules—was an early version of the modern-day convention. The national nominating convention has been a part of the American party scene since 1832.

In 1836, however, leaders of the newly emergent Whig Party (formed mainly from elements of the defunct National Republican party and anti-Jackson Democrats) could not agree on a united strategy to oppose the Democratic nominee, Martin Van Buren, Jackson's handpicked successor. Instead of convening a national convention, the Whigs decided to run several strong state and regional leaders for President in regions where each was strong. The "divide and rule" strategy was to nominate several candidates in hopes of preventing Van Buren from winning enough electoral votes to capture the White House, thus forcing the presidential selection once again into the House of Representatives. According to the plan, Senator Daniel Webster was to capture New England; the Northwest was to unite behind General William Henry Harrison; and Tennessee's Hugh White was expected to hold down the Southwest. The Whig plan almost succeeded. Van Buren's majority was only 25,688 out of a popular vote of 1,505,290 in a highly competitive race. But Van Buren carried the Electoral College vote, 170 against a combined total of 124 votes for his three rivals.[19]

Compared with the modern national convention, early conventions showed certain irregularities or imperfections. State delegates were chosen under a variety of ways—congressional district conventions, state conventions, local meetings, informal caucuses—depending upon the organization and leaders of the party in each state. The early conventions might even recognize as delegates visitors in attendance from a state which sent no delegates. At the 1835 Democratic convention, for example, a Mr. Edward Rucker cast the entire vote of unrepresented Tennessee because he happened to be in Baltimore and was a Van

Buren man. Distance, poor transportation, or lack of interest sometimes kept states from sending delegates to early conventions. Still, at the 1835 Democratic convention 181 delegates showed up to represent their states. From the outset, however, the major parties restricted the voting strength of a state in the national convention to its electoral vote, regardless of oversize delegations or other irregularities.[20]

NATIONAL CONVENTIONS COME OF AGE

With the newly emerging party system in a state of flux, the authority of the national party conventions to determine presidential nominations was not accorded full recognition until the 1840 campaign. After the Democrats held a second national convention in 1835 and a third in 1839, and the newly formed Whig party adopted a national convention to select its candidate—William Henry Harrison—for its 1840 campaign, the national nominating convention became established as a permanent element of the American party system. Indeed, the national conventions have become one of the most durable political institutions in the Western world. National conventions have been held by the major parties quadrennially—in peace time or war—ever since 1840. Fortunately, the growth of canal and railroad systems improved transportation during this period so that national conventions could depend upon delegates from all the states reaching a central site.

By 1848, the national nominating convention had become completely divorced from the congressional caucus. The year 1848 marked the last time the Democratic congressional caucus issued the "call" for the Democratic convention; four years later, the Whig congressional caucus also performed this function for the last time.[21] Henceforth, the presidential branch of each national party asserted its complete independence of congressional influence. No specific provision for party continuity between national conventions existed, however, until 1848. In that year the Democrats formed a Democratic National Committee with one member from each state to serve until the next convention. Thereafter, the call for each subsequent national convention was issued by the national committee, which determined the time and place and handled other arrangements. The Republican party, which held its first convention in 1856, soon copied this same party structure and plan for convening its national conclaves.

Beyond question, the national nominating convention was well suited for the young nation because:

1. It was representative in character.

2. It divorced presidential nominations from congressional control.

3. It provided for a broad-based formulation of a party program.

4. It concentrated the party's strength behind a single presidential ticket.

5. It reconciled personal rivalries and group or sectional interests.[22]

Before the convention system emerged, no caucus of the party leaders in Congress could adequately represent all party elements or areas of the country. The problem of how to achieve congressional caucus representation in a congressional district held by the opposition party had never been resolved. In contrast, the party convention provided delegate representation, no matter which party controlled office, for all party constituencies—the congressional districts, the cities, the small towns, the rural areas. The national convention also provided voting rights for elected officeholders—senators, governors, congressmen, and state legislators— as well as party officials and rank-and-file delegates. In short, the national convention, as its name implies, served as an instrument to give representation nationwide to all constituencies within both major parties. Because the American system abounds in centrifugal forces arising from decentralized parties and the division of powers between the federal and state governments, the national convention helps cement the divergent interests that exist on all levels within each party. From the start, national conventions have made it possible for the peculiarly decentralized American parties to have their own national existence. Most importantly, the national convention system has concentrated the electorate behind the two major party nominees, thus keeping the final selection away from Congress and giving the President a base of support independent of the legislative branch. Clearly, the national convention has strengthened the nominee's ability not only to lead his party but—if successful at the polls—to lead the nation as well. Thus it can be said that the national convention, though it has escaped constitutional regulation, has profoundly shaped the nature of the Presidency as much as the party system itself has.

CANDIDATES VERSUS PARTY LEADERS

Although the national conventions remained essentially unchanged in their format from the 1840's to the age of television more than a century later, the role of the convention underwent several changes. For the first decade or so, national conventions served merely as legitimizing forums for the front-running candidates. But within a short time, the national conventions and the party system underwent a major transformation. State party leaders took over control of the conventions and forced the various aspirants to bargain with them over matters of cabinet posts, patronage, or major issues facing various regions of the country before putting their stamp of approval on the favorite. This change was facilitated by the decentralized party system in which each state party was treated almost as an independent member of a nationwide confederation. Upon arrival at the conventions state party leaders could reaffirm their pre-convention deals or, if no candidate appeared the sure winner, strike the necessary bargains. The rapid shift of power over nominations from the candidates to the state party leaders must have surprised some leading presidential contenders. Three-time nominee Henry Clay suddenly discovered this political fact of life in 1840 when the Whig party managers passed over him in favor of the veteran Indian fighter, General William Henry Harrison—"Tippecanoe and Tyler, too"—because the aging general and his running-mate, John Tyler of Virginia, appeared more electable. Four years later, the Democratic party leaders dumped former President Martin Van Buren, Jackson's protege and the early front-runner, in favor of a "dark-horse" candidate, former Governor of Tennessee James K. Polk.[23]

Until the advent of the presidential primaries, most of the political bargaining took place at the convention itself rather than during the pre-convention period. Leading contenders, however, usually sent their "drummers," that is, veteran professional politicians with numerous contacts in the state party organizations, to circulate around the country building up support for their candidate and seeking delegate commitments long before the opening convention gavel. In yesteryear national conventions were often protracted multi-ballot conclaves because the party choice usually did not bubble to the surface until after state party leaders had reached consensus or at least discarded most of the unacceptable candidates. Within the Democratic party, conventions were often prolonged by the long-standing "two-thirds rule" (repealed in 1936), which required that the eventual nominee receive a two-thirds, not a simple, majority to claim the nomination. (This extraordinary rule is discussed further in chapter 4.) Usually several ballots were necessary just to shake out the various favorite-son candidates and to get a better reading on the sizeable blocs of uncommitted delegates. Political bargaining occurred amidst a good deal of uncertainty, confusion, rumors, and attempted efforts to stampede the uncommitted delegates. Generally, convention decision-making during the brokered convention era took place privately in the "smoke-filled rooms" between the candidates themselves and the state party leaders who controlled sizeable blocs of delegates. Rank-and-file party voters had nothing to do with the convention choice, though the party kingmakers seldom passed over a popular candidate who looked as if he would lead the party to victory in November. Similarly, convention delegates were usually left cooling their heels on the convention floor between ballots while their leaders were cutting deals in the back room.

EMERGENCE OF PRESIDENTIAL PRIMARY MOVEMENT

Until the turn of the twentieth century, presidential nominating politics remained chiefly under the control of state party leaders. Rank-and-file voters had virtually no voice in the selection of presidential nominees. But as the evils of boss-controlled conventions became more widely known toward the end of the nineteenth century, the demand for reform echoed across the land. The Populists and, more importantly, their successors, the Progressives, demanded that the state party "kingmakers" and political machines be replaced by popularly elected national convention delegates chosen in state presidential primaries. By 1912, a dozen states, spurred on by Wisconsin's Progressive Republican Senator (and former governor) Robert LaFollette, had adopted presidential primaries to pick delegates and, in some instances, to register their personal choice for president. Structurally, the Progressives' institutional plan called for shifting the locus of decisionmaking in the nominating process from the national convention itself to the preconvention stage—the primary season. Moreover, the Progressives hoped to transform the nominating process in the words of one party expert, "from its existing status as a 'privately' controlled associational activity to a state-run public function, ideally through a national primary, but failing that, through a system of delegate selection primaries enacted by individual states."[24] By 1916, more than two dozen states had experimented with some form of popular selection of delegates. But at no time were a majority of delegates chosen in the primaries. Nevertheless, the primaries introduced an important element of popular participation in the presidential nominating process heretofore lacking. That the Progressives' dream of a popularly selected nominee never came to pass, however, could be attributed to several factors. The conservative reaction after World War I took the momentum out of the Progressive movement. Party regulars in a number of states, capitalizing on complaints of low voter participation and the high cost of primaries, succeeded in repealing the presidential primaries or diluting their effectiveness by making them "advisory" rather than mandatory. By 1935, only 15 states retained their presidential primaries, and the party regulars had long ago moved back into the driver's seat at the national conventions.

During the interwar period (1920-1940) both the traditional caucus-convention and presidential primary system, it might be noted, operated side by side. In 1920, for example, three popular leaders who had campaigned in the primaries—General Leonard Wood (the Douglas MacArthur of this era), California Senator Hiram Johnson, and Illinois Governor Frank O. Lowden—were so hopelessly deadlocked at the GOP convention that the party leaders moved to the "smoke-filled room" to come up with a compromise candidate—Senator Warren G. Harding of Ohio. Other subsequent nominees—Herbert Hoover (1928), Alfred E. Smith (1928), and Franklin D. Roosevelt (1932)—all used the presidential primaries effectively to publicize their candidacies, but in the final analysis they still all relied heavily on state party leaders to deliver the needed delegate votes to clinch the nomination.

NEW PRE-CONVENTION CAMPAIGN STYLE

After World War II, several "outsider" candidates—most notably former Minnesota Republican Governor Harold Stassen and Senator Estes Kefauver (D.-Tenn.)—recognized the value of the presidential primaries to develop popular appeal, attract a solid base of delegates, and also expose their rivals as weak vote-getters. Though Stassen and Kefauver were unsuccessful in their nomination ventures, their out-front campaign style marked the beginning of a new era in presidential nominating politics. Shortly thereafter, an impressive record in the primaries enabled a popular vote-getter, John F. Kennedy, in 1960 to convince the state party and big city leaders—and a majority of the delegates (still elected in the party caucuses and state conventions)—that he was the winning type of nominee the party needed.

The advent of television's instant nationwide communication and the rise of nationally syndicated opinion polls helped usher in the gradual transformation of the presidential nominating process in which presidential candidates began again to dominate convention choice, even though a majority of delegates were still selected by party caucuses and conventions. Clearly, popular vote-getters, such as General Dwight D. Eisenhower and John F. Kennedy, used presidential primary campaigning to demonstrate their popular appeal as a major step toward the nomination. Still, the impact of the primaries during the latter part of the brokered convention era served mostly as a psychological weapon for the front-running candidate to impress state party leaders and to win over uncommitted delegates. To win the nomination outright required extensive coalition building and political bargaining. Successful nominees still concentrated on building up a base of regional support and focused their sights on state party leaders in many of the thirty-plus caucus-convention states in hopes of generating bandwagon support on their behalf. Favorite-son candidates often had to be persuaded to give up their candidacies in favor of the front-runner.

But with the birth of network television, the growth of syndicated opinion polls, and the reemergence of presidential primary campaigning, candidates began using their popular appeal to go directly to the electorate, over the heads of the state party organizations in the primary and caucus-convention states, to win delegate support. However, the big breakthrough on presidential candidate influence with rank-and-file voters did not take place until the rapid spread of the presidential primary movement in the early 1970's. This recent period Thomas R. Marshall calls "the system of popular appeal," a term that may overstate the case, but we will use it nonetheless throughout this study.[25]

The System of Popular Appeal: 1972 to Present

Since the tumultuous 1968 Democratic national convention, the modern-day reformers and participatory Democrats have succeeded in overturning the party regulars' domination of the presidential nominating process. Actually, the cracks in the brokered convention system had begun appearing shortly after World War II, as previously explained. In 1952, for example, General Dwight D. Eisenhower grabbed the GOP nomination away from the conservative Republican organization favorite, Senator Robert A. Taft, by demonstrating his popularity in the primaries. Eisenhower's success with the primaries as well as John F. Kennedy's showed that the transformation of the nominating process has not been exactly an overnight event.

By the early 1970's, however, the spread of the presidential primary legislation (mostly with mandatory delegate commitments) to almost thirty states, broad popular participation in presidential primaries—32 million citizens voted in the 1980 primaries and caucuses—and direct mass media candidate appeals to the voters had completely displaced the party regulars' kingmaker role in the presidential nominating process. As Thomas R. Marshall has recently noted, "The media, not the party regulars, now stand between the candidate and the voter."[26]

Similar to the demise of the congressional caucus in the 1800's, the brokered convention system collapsed because it was viewed by party reformers as undemocratic. Several factors, in particular, contributed to its sudden disintegration. The McGovern-Fraser Democratic party reform rules—an outgrowth of the divisive 1968 Democratic convention which saw Vice President Humphrey deprive his anti-Vietnam War opponent and former fellow Minnesota Senator Eugene J. McCarthy of the nomination—severely undermined the role of party regulars at future national conventions. The eighteen McGovern-Fraser "guidelines," which became a major part of the 1972 delegate selection ground rules, assured rank-and-file party identifiers a far greater voice in future conventions.[27] In the process the new reform movement virtually removed the party regulars' control over delegate selection.

Though unintended by the McGovern-Fraser Commission, the Democratic guidelines suddenly encouraged more than a half dozen states to adopt presidential primaries and give to party members, especially within the Democratic party, the exclusive right to select the state's national convention delegates. Between 1972 and 1976, another seven states joined the presidential primary club. Thus, within a period of eight years popular election of national convention delegates had spread to nearly thirty states, including nine out of the ten of the most populous states. As a result of these state actions, approximately 75 percent of the national convention delegates attending the 1976 Democratic convention (the figure was slightly lower at the Republican convention) were chosen by rank-and-file voters, and most of these delegates were pledged to specific presidential candidates. In a number of states the Republicans were swept along by the Democratic tide of reform, since the state primary laws usually covered both parties.

Suddenly, through a combination of party rule changes, state delegate selection laws, and the 1974 federal campaign finance legislation (which provided matching money subsidies to presidential contenders and imposed a $1,000 ceiling on individual contributions), the national convention was transformed from an essentially deliberative body into a ratifying assembly which merely anointed the popular favorite in the primaries. No longer did state party leaders, big city mayors, or leading members of the U.S. Senate and House of Representatives have a major voice in determining who would be the party standard-bearer. Plebiscitarian choice replaced the system of party brokers. However, one would be hard-pressed to defend the position that the nominees of the post-1968 period—for example, George McGovern and Jimmy Carter—have been more representative of the party electorate than, say, earlier nominees Franklin D. Roosevelt or John F. Kennedy. The term "popular appeal" for the present era is intended only to reflect the participatory democracy ethos that overlays the nominating system, not the superiority of the present method over earlier models.

Unique Aspects of Presidential Leadership Selection

The American presidential nominating process is unique among Western political systems. Indeed, the presidential nominating procedure permits a degree of popular participation and accountability not found elsewhere in the Free World. That rank-and-file voters should have a voice in the selection of a national party leader seems bizarre to a foreigner. In the European democracies, there is a clear distinction between the nominating and electing processes. Instead of national conventions, parliamentary leaders are selected entirely through internal party machinery. Generally, the list of potential leaders is trimmed down by a small group of party executives and former officeholders. Members of parliament or the national party conference are then given the privilege of voting on the choice of the party's inner circle. The leader of the British Conservative party, for example, is chosen by the party's members in the House of Commons. But the choice of the potential leader has already been narrowed down by demonstrated ability in the Commons and in the Cabinet. On the Continent, leadership has followed much the same pattern. In West Germany, for example, leadership has long been concentrated in the party executive committee, especially within the Social Democratic Party (SPD).[28]

CANADIAN LEADERSHIP CONVENTIONS

Until recent changes in the British Labour Party's leadership selection process, the only Western parliamentary democracy that has permitted rank-and-file participation in leadership selection is Canada. Since 1919, the two major parties— the Liberals and Progressive-Conservatives—have both used national party conventions. Like their American counterparts, the Canadian conventions are huge gatherings numbering over two thousand delegates from all ten provinces. Unlike national party conventions in the United States, however, the Canadian party conclaves are not held quadrennially, but meet only when the leader is rejected or a vacancy occurs in the national party leadership by death or resignation.[29] There are no direct primaries in Canada; national convention delegates are chosen via party machinery.

The Canadian national leadership conventions are only slightly less flamboyant and boisterous than their U.S. counterparts. Much of the same terminology and format has been adopted. Like the U.S. convention, there is a keynote speaker. The platform-making task is also undertaken before the delegates (chosen mostly in the 260-odd parliamentary constituencies) settle down to the serious business of choosing their leader.

Unlike the U.S. conventions, the rival contenders in Canada each address the convention briefly before the balloting; usually a twenty-minute time limit is imposed. These prenominating speeches can "make or break" a candidate's chances; and a poor performance will most surely eliminate a contender from serious consideration. The delegates then vote by secret ballot individually (not orally on a roll call by state delegations as in the United States); a simple majority is sufficient for election.[30] Both the Liberals and the Conservative party—technically, the Progressive-Conservative Party—have a rule that if three or more candidates run and no one receives a majority, the low man is automatically eliminated after each ballot.

Canadian national conventions have not displayed as much flexibility and, until recently, have lacked the degree of popular influence possessed by their American counterparts, since the primary system is nonexistent north of the border. Canadian convention choice is generally restricted to Cabinet members, leading members of the Opposition, or provincial premiers. American conventions, however, can search afar for their nominees—Vice Presidents, governors, U.S. senators, Cabinet members, corporate lawyers, generals, and even movie stars! Since the American national convention is the supreme governing body of the party, the only limitation on its choice is the nominee's degree of "electability." This wide latitude of choice is in some ways both a blessing and a curse, for the convention decision on the type of nominee, as explained earlier, can sometimes be more critical for the future of the country than the voter's choice in the general election.

How does the national convention go about its business of picking a presidential nominee? This will be our main topic of discussion in the next three chapters.

Notes

1. Thomas R. Marshall, *Presidential Nominations in a Reform Age* (New York: Praeger, 1981), pp. 17-64.

2. Paul T. David, Ralph M. Goldman, and Richard C. Bain, *The Politics of National Party Conventions* (Washington, D.C.: The Brookings Institution, 1960), p. 12.

3. Ibid., p. 13.

4. James S. Chase, *Emergence of the Presidential Nominating Convention, 1789-1832* (Urbana, Ill.: University of Illinois Press, 1973), p. 60.

5. See V.O. Key, Jr., *Southern Politics* (New York: Alfred A. Knopf, 1949).

6. Four states accounted for more than two-thirds of the members attending the congressional caucus: New York (16), Virginia (15), North Carolina (9), and Georgia (8). See James S. Chase, *Emergence of the Presidential Nominating Convention, 1789-1832*, p. 60.

7. Ibid., p. 294.

8. William G. Carleton, "The Collapse of the Caucus," *Current History*, Vol. 25 (September 1953), p. 147.

9. Theodore J. Lowi, "Party, Policy and Constitution in America," in William Nisbet Chambers and Walter Dean Burnham, eds., *The American Party Systems* (New York: Oxford University Press, 1967), p. 248, as quoted by Austin Ranney, *Curing the Mischiefs of Faction* (Berkeley, Calif.: The University of California Press, 1975), p. 173.

10. Ibid.

11. Ibid., p. 174.

12. Karl O'Lessker, "The National Nominating Conventions," in Cornelius P. Cotter,

ed., *Practical Politics in the United States* (Boston: Allyn & Bacon, Inc., 1969), p. 240.

13. Frederick W. Dallinger, *Nominations for Elective Office in the United States* (Cambridge, Mass.: Harvard University Press, 1897), p. 43.

14. Ibid., pp. 31-35.

15. David H. Fischer, *The Revolution of American Conservatism* (New York: Harper and Row, 1965), p. 81.

16. Paul T. David, Ralph M. Goldman, and Richard C. Bain, *The Politics of National Party Conventions*, p. 17.

17. Ibid., p. 18.

18. Ibid., p. 19; James S. Chase, "Jacksonian Democracy and the Rise of the Nominating Conventions," *Mid-America*, Vol. 45 (October 1963), p. 249.

19. Paul T. David, Ralph M. Goldman, and Richard C. Bain, *The Politics of National Party Conventions*, p. 20.

20. In the Whig convention of 1848, for example, the Louisiana delegates cast both their votes and those of Texas, because the Lone Star Whigs had given them their proxies. Eugene H. Roseboom, *A History of Presidential Elections* (New York: The Macmillan Company, 1957), p. 106.

21. The Whigs held national nominating conventions in 1840, 1844, 1848, and 1852, but the party then rapidly disintegrated as the warring pro- and anti-slavery factions pulled the party asunder. Most elements of the anti-slavery faction found a home in the newly emerging Republican party; the "Cotton Whigs" ultimately moved into the Democratic party.

22. Eugene H. Roseboom, *A History of Presidential Elections*, p. 106.

23. Van Buren actually received 151 votes out of 266 convention votes—a clear majority—on the first ballot. But the recently adopted two-thirds rule required the party nominee to collect two-thirds of the convention's vote to be selected. On each subsequent vote Van Buren lost support. By the seventh ballot he was down to 99 votes. On the eighth ballot the only avowed vice presidential candidate, James K. Polk of Tennessee, whose name was not even before the delegates during the first seven ballots, received 44 votes. Amidst great confusion, Polk went over the top on the ninth ballot. The convention then voted to make the first "dark-horse" nominee a unanimous choice. See Richard C. Bain and Judith H. Parris, *Convention Decisions and Voting Records*, 2nd ed. (Washington, D.C.: The Brookings Institution, 1973), pp. 33-34.

24. James W. Ceaser, *Reforming the Reforms* (Cambridge, Mass.: Ballinger Publishing Company, 1982), p. 23.

25. Thomas R. Marshall, *Presidential Nominations in a Reform Age*, pp. 22-32.

26. Ibid., p. 159.

27. *Mandate for Reform*, Report of the Commission on Party Structure and Delegate Selection to the Democratic National Committee (Washington, D.C.: Democratic National Committee, 1970), pp. 39-48.

28. See Lewis J. Edinger, *Politics in Germany* (Boston: Little, Brown and Company, 1968), pp. 254-255.

29. For an excellent discussion of the Canadian leadership selection process, see John C. Courtney, *The Selection of National Party Leaders in Canada* (Hamden, Conn.: Shoe String Press, 1973).

30. Unlike most delegates to United States national conventions, delegates to Canadian leadership conventions receive little direction or guidance from their constituency

units on candidate preference. As explained by a leading Canadian parties expert, "Instructions to delegates or pledges from delegates to their constituency associations to support a particular leadership candidate (at least on the first ballot) are virtually unknown in Canadian convention politics, and in any event are of questionable value to the delegating body, given the secrecy of the balloting" (Ibid., pp. 107-08).

Convention Machinery and
Organization _____ 3

> There is something about a national convention that makes it as fas-
> cinating as a revival or a hanging. It is vulgar, it is ugly, it is
> stupid, it is tedious, it's hard upon both the cerebral centers and the
> *gluteus maximus*, and yet it is somehow charming. One sits
> through long sessions wishing heartily that all the delegates were
> dead and in hell—and then suddenly there comes a show so gaudy
> and hilarious, so melodramatic and obscene, so unimaginably
> exhilarating and preposterous that one lives a gorgeous year in
> an hour.
>
> H.L. Mencken, 1924

National nominating conventions are one of the more enduring features of the
American political system. Although in continuous use for almost 150 years, the
convention system was never envisioned by the Founding Fathers. Nor was it the
subject of Congressional legislation until the Federal Election Campaign Act of
1974 authorized a $2 million subsidy (with a built-in inflation factor) to each
national committee to help fund its national convention.

While the political setting and the proceedings have changed significantly over
the years, the basic functions of the national convention have remained essentially unchanged. Indeed, if a foreign observer had monitored the Republican
National Convention of 1860 which nominated Abraham Lincoln and then mi-
raculously returned to earth to watch the proceedings of the 1980 GOP convention which nominated Ronald Reagan, he would know without a moment's
hesitation that one of America's major parties was in the process of picking
another presidential nominee.[1] To be sure, the television cameras and lights, the
loudspeakers, the huge press gallery, the modern attire of the delegates, and the
presence of a large number of women delegates would be completely unfamiliar
to this imaginary observer, but the convention format would not differ basically
120 years later. Conventions, however, simply do not automatically happen.

Extensive planning and preparation are required to mount these quadrennial extravaganzas. Let's take a moment to look into the detailed planning that must be done before the temporary chairman of the convention pounds the gavel and announces: "The delegates will please come to order...."

Role of the National Committee

National committees, which are responsible for handling all arrangements for their party's national conventions, are extra-constitutional agencies that date back to the mid-nineteenth century. The Democratic National Committee, first organized in 1848 was an outgrowth of a "central committee" appointed in 1844 to "promote the election of Polk and Dallas."[2] In 1852, the short-lived Whigs created a national committee, but the party expired before the next national election. The soon-to-be-organized Republican party, capitalizing on the practical experience of these parties, began its national organization in more advanced form. In February 1856, an informal meeting of Republican leaders established a National Executive Committee; one month later this committee issued a "call" for a national convention in June. At its first national nominating convention, the GOP delegates passed a resolution recommending formation of a Republican National Committee. Among the first duties assigned to this newly established committee was the planning of the 1860 Republican convention. Like its Democratic counterpart, the Republican National Committee has performed its quadrennial duties without interruption since before the Civil War.

Originally, both national committees consisted of one member from each state and territory and the District of Columbia. With the adoption of women's suffrage in 1920, however, each party stipulated that its national committee should be composed henceforth of one man and one woman from each state and territory. In 1952, the Republican National Convention approved a new rule to permit any state chairman to serve on the national committee if at the preceding presidential election his state had cast its vote for Republican electors, or if the state had elected a Republican governor or sent a Republican majority of the state's delegation to Congress. (The 1968 GOP national convention voted to make all state chairmen members of the Republican National Committee.) In 1972, the Democratic National Convention approved a compromise proposal to expand the size of its national committee, almost tripling its size from 110 members to 303 (with a voting strength of 234 votes). Additional seats were allocated on a combined basis of population and presidential vote. Populous states, such as California and New York, saw their representation jump from two to twelve votes.

Making arrangements for national conventions has always been the foremost duty assigned to the party's national committee. Indeed, for more than 140 years the party's national committee has been the key link between one convention and the next. As Cotter and Hennessey observed some years ago, "The national committees were created not to institutionalize a theory or from any impulse of good or evil, but simply to do a job. At first mere *ad hoc* arrangements, they are still to a large degree creations of unclear dimensions and uncertain traditions."[3] The national committee, as will be explained later in this chapter, performs a variety of duties: it selects the convention city, issues the official call for the convention, apportions the delegates on the basis of rules approved by previous national conventions, prepares a temporary roll of delegates, approves the selection of a national convention director, recommends a slate of temporary and permanent officers for the convention, and conducts the national party's business between conventions.

With the establishment of permanent year-round national headquarters for each party in the 1930's and the hiring of a permanent office staff, coupled with the expanded duties of a full-time national party chairman, the day-to-day planning of the national conventions has gradually shifted from the national committee to the national party headquarters. This professionalization should occasion no surprise; for a regular, paid, full-time national chairman and staff based in Washington, D.C., are in a much better position to handle the extensive preconvention planning than 100 to 300 unpaid national committee members scattered over the fifty states. As the size and cost of national conventions has steadily ballooned, especially since the advent of nationwide television, convention planning has become a big business. No longer do the national committees have the expertise in handling media arrangements, printing contracts, processing thousands of hotel reservations, and handling the endless number of other details for these massive gatherings. The growing complexities of organizing a huge national convention have led to a shift from amateur to professional management. But if the committee members have given up the convention "housekeeping" duties, they have not abdicated decision-making on site-selection, approval of delegate apportionment rules, and selection of temporary convention officials.[4]

Growth in Size of Conventions

Starting with the new Democratic "bonus" rule in 1944, the size of Democratic conventions began to increase steadily. Patterned after the GOP bonus rule system, the new Democratic apportionment rules soon opened the door to expanded delegations. Even more important, the Democratic National Committee in 1956 authorized all states to send delegates on a half-vote basis. Most states jumped at this opportunity. As a result, the size of Democratic conventions increased by 50 percent between 1952 and 1956—from 1,642 delegates with 1,230 votes to 2,477 delegates with 1,372 votes.[5] By 1960, the bonus rule produced another 149 delegate votes. As will be explained later, the Democratic National Committee refused to penalize any state delegation when it failed to carry the national ticket; therefore, under this "no loser" rule, Democratic conventions could only get larger—and they did. Between 1956 and 1968, the number of delegate votes to Democratic conventions nearly doubled—from 1,372 in 1956 to 2,622 in 1968. "Elephantiasis" is the term one critic has attached to this rapid swelling of convention size.[6] By 1972, it reached 3,016 and in 1980 the total number of Democratic delegate votes hit an all-time high of 3,331. Compare this figure with the 303 delegates who participated in the 1860 Democratic convention or the 466 delegates who attended the second Republican convention, held in Chicago's famed nineteenth century hall, the "Wigwam," that saw Lincoln capture the GOP nomination on the third ballot with 340 votes.

Democratic conventions in the mid-twentieth century have come to resemble a mass rally rather than a deliberative body. Republican conventions, too, have been gradually expanding in size, but at a somewhat slower pace, as Figure 1 shows.

FIGURE 1
SIZE OF NATIONAL PARTY CONVENTIONS, 1932-1980

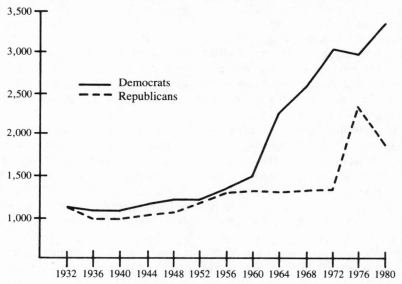

Size by Year	Democrats	Republicans	Size by Year	Democrats	Republicans
1932	1,154	1,154	1956	1,372	1,323
1936	1,100	1,003	1960	1,521	1,331
1940	1,100	1,000	1964	2,295	1,308
1944	1,176	1,059	1968	2,522	1,333
1948	1,234	1,094	1972	3,016	1,333
1952	1,230	1,206	1976	3,008	2,259
			1980	3,331	1,994

Sources: Richard C. Bain and Judith H. Parris, *Convention Decisions and Voting Records*, 2nd ed. (Washington, D.C.: Brookings Institution, 1973), appendix C; for the period 1932-1972. The 1976 and 1980 delegate totals have been provided by the Democratic and Republican national committees.

But the likelihood that future Democratic or Republican conventions will be "downsized," to borrow a term from the automotive world, exists only in the minds of a few persistent reformers. Conventions continue to grow in size because zealous party leaders wish to include all of the diverse elements in the party, particularly the previously underrepresented, while not excluding any groups or persons who have previously attended the national conclaves. Increasingly, more party activists want to attend the conventions. Attendance is viewed by the delegates and alternates as the ultimate political prize, an opportunity to have a direct voice in the choice of the party nominee. Others consider it a status symbol, and, for some, an exciting vacation.

The expanded size of conventions reflects the democratization of conventions, the disappearance of political bosses as more and more states switch to presidential primaries to permit the popular selection of delegates, and the dramatically expanded membership of youth, women, and minorities among the state delegations. Increased representation for these groups was one of the major reasons given by the GOP for the 60 percent increase in delegate strength authorized by the 1972 Republican convention, effective for the 1976 conclave. Between 1972 and 1976, the number of Republican delegates jumped from 1,333 to 2,259. The Democratic National Committee adopted a new rule in June 1978 expanding the number of delegates further by ten percent to give extra representation to elected and party officials.

The growing size of national nominating conventions is not confined exclusively to the United States. Canada, the only other Western democracy that uses the national convention system, has also seen a marked growth in recent years in the size of its national leadership conclaves. Had the Liberal party convention been held in early 1980 to choose a successor to Pierre Elliot Trudeau (who decided not to resign), no fewer than 3,200 voting delegates would have been in attendance, a record for any Canadian convention. The 1976 Progressive-Conservative leadership convention that picked Mr. Joe Clark, a young Alberta MP, as its new party leader had 2,360 voting delegates—a slight increase of 120 delegates over the last convention held in 1967, which picked Robert Stanfield, but 947 more delegates than attended the previous leadership convention that selected John G. Diefenbaker in 1956.[7]

Advanced Convention Planning

Planning for the next quadrennial convention commences more than a year and one-half in advance of the opening gavel. The task begins with the appointment of a site-selection committee by the party's national chairman. Consisting of approximately one dozen leading members of the national committee, the site-selection committee first reviews the invitations and financial offers from the various cities. One unwritten rule observed by the committees is that the convention city must not be located in a state which has a contender for the party's nomination. Another unwritten rule is not to hold a national convention while the

Olympic games are running, as they do every fourth year in the summer of presidential election years. Another practice of the past several decades, although not formalized, is to let the out-of-power party hold its convention first, since it needs more time for its campaign. Before making a final choice, committee members tour the various convention centers and explore the facilities in the prospective cities. Committee members are often treated lavishly on these inspection tours by civic and business groups trying to book the convention. For example, a two-day excursion of New York City by the 1976 Democratic site-selection committee cost the Association for a Better New York and the Convention and Visitors Bureau approximately $10,000. But the civic group's success in convincing the Democrats to meet in "the Big Apple" meant far more than a thousand-fold return on this small goodwill investment. Delegates, it was estimated, would spend approximately $10 million per day while at the convention.

Once the convention site has been selected, the parties shift their planning into high gear. In 1976, the Democratic site committee supervised the extensive construction to convert Madison Square Garden from a sports arena to a convention hall. More than two months' work was required to build special seating platforms and special overhead booths for the television networks, a false floor, and a bulletproof podium. The total construction bill cost New York City $1.4 million. In addition, the site committee and convention director spent $210,000 for insurance coverage, $30,000 to rent a parking lot for VIP's, and $90,000 for buses to transport delegates to and from their hotels. The committee was also instrumental in helping to obtain a $2.6 million grant from the Law Enforcement Assistance Administration (LEAA) to the New York police for overtime and other security costs incurred during the four-day convention. Likewise, the Republicans also helped secure a $2.4 million LEAA grant for the Kansas City police force for improved security at the 1976 GOP convention. All told, the Democratic and Republican committees obtained a grand total of $9.5 million from sources other than the $2.2 million in federal subsidies for each of the 1976 national conventions.[8]

In recent years both major parties have hired a full-time convention director to handle the party's quadrennial conclave. Before the Civil War, however, conventions were conducted in relative obscurity. Held in small buildings or public halls, the conventions attracted a few hundred delegates and a handful of spectators and reporters. Management of the conventions was left to members of the national committee. Because the national committees closed up shop for more than three years after each national convention and did not reopen their offices until a few months before the next national gathering, convention management was handled with a minimum of planning. More than anything else, the age of television in the mid-twentieth century has prompted party leaders to give national convention management top billing. Blessed with a captive prime-time nationwide viewing audience that sometimes exceeds 90 million persons, party leaders soon decided to make the national conventions into grand productions. Party leaders also concluded that the conclaves could serve as the kickoff for the general election campaign. No longer would hour-long "spontaneous" marching demonstrations on behalf of a presidential hopeful be permitted to bore the millions of viewers comfortably watching the televised proceedings in their living rooms. Bitter floor fights over credentials challenges would have to be kept to the minimum or, if unavoidable, scheduled in the early afternoon or the wee morning hours when the television networks have their smallest audiences.

To minimize pre-convention "flaps" and to put the party's best foot forward, the national party chairmen have, with the concurrence of the national committees, hired a full-time convention director for at least a year's contract before the next convention. Democratic party rules stipulate "A Convention Manager shall be elected by the Democratic National Committee. . . . Subject to the authority of the Arrangements Committee, the Convention Manager shall be responsible for all business and financial affairs of the Democratic National Convention."[9]

The convention director must, first of all, book and reserve a large block of hotel rooms in the convention city and surrounding suburbs. Coordinating all three television networks' coverage of the convention will also occupy a major share of the director's time. Since each of the networks invests several million dollars to provide priceless cost-free convention coverage to the parties, the director can ill afford to ignore network executive requests for camera placement, adequate work space for technical and production staffs, telephone service, and so forth. Bus transportation to and from the convention hall to the various hotels (each state or group of states is assigned to a specific hotel) must be obtained for the delegates. Extensive security arrangements must be coordinated with the local police and the Secret Service. (All presidential candidates are assigned, if they wish, Secret Service protection; and, of course, the party nominee must be given special protection as soon as the convention approves his nomination.) Credentials and special passes must be printed and distributed— generally, separate delegate and alternate passes are printed for each day of the convention to cut down on counterfeiting and to help provide tighter convention hall security. Since visitor seats are prized almost as highly as tickets to the Super Bowl, the printing of limited visitor credentials must be handled under tight security. Obviously, the convention director cannot perform all of these tasks by himself. Generally, members of the national committee staff—and sometimes special consultants— are drafted to help with the convention planning. Over the past two decades the Democrats have hired such convention directors as Mr. Leonard Reinsch, a veteran television producer-executive, and Mr. Andrew Shea, a Washington lawyer and close associate of Mr. Robert Strauss, Democratic National Chairman (1972-1976). Shea, hired one year in advance of the 1976 convention, was paid $90,000 for his year's labor—plus expenses, including a $1,150 a month apartment on Central Park South.[10] The Republicans, more reliant on permanent staff, have had much less staff turnover in critical jobs than the Democrats. For more than 20 years (1960-1980), Miss Josephine Good was in charge of convention arrangements at the Republican National Committee, until her retirement after the 1980 GOP convention in Detroit.

Site Selection

In the pre-Civil War period national conventions were usually held in late spring in a city centrally located on the Atlantic seaboard. Baltimore, Maryland, was the favorite meeting spot during this pre-railroad era, hosting the first six Democratic conventions (1832-1852), two Whig conventions, one National Republican convention, and the 1831 Anti-Masonic conclave.

With the spread of railroads and the nation's westward expansion, Chicago became the favorite convention city for both parties. Located in America's heartland, Chicago has been the site of 24 major party conventions (14 Republican and 10 Democratic). But with the arrival of the jet age, other factors have weighed more heavily than central location in site selection. Pledges of financial contributions—at least until passage of the 1974 Campaign Election Reform Act, which authorized federal subsidies to fund each national convention—have played an important role in site choice. Municipal contributions in the form of goods and services (for example, rent-free convention hall, extra police protection, free bus transportation) may be even more valuable than cash. These contributions, plus heavy corporate advertising in the party's official convention program (prohibited by the 1974 federal legislation), generally have enabled each party to avoid a big national convention deficit before entering the fall campaign.

Adequate hotel accommodations—upwards of 20,000 rooms—are also a prime requirement, since modern-day conventions attract thousands of delegates, party officials, spectators, and media personnel. Parties may sometimes decide upon a particular city for reasons of campaign strategy. For example, the Republican 1980 site-selection committee chose Detroit ahead of Dallas or Kansas City again to convey a special message to the American public: The Republican party is not just the party of corporate boardrooms, country clubs, the "Sun Belt," and the White Anglo-Saxon Protestant minority; it seeks the support from all classes and ethnic groups in the population. Detroit was also chosen for other related symbolic reasons. The Motor City is, as one observer put it, "a back-from-trouble renaissance city, much as the GOP sees itself as a party restored to health. Detroit also is a Northeastern industrial city with a black majority and high unemployment, a union town, and a blue-collar, ethnic, Catholic town but simultaneously with a high inflation rate and suffering from a deep recession."[11] Convention security, especially during the period of anti-Vietnam War demonstrations, became an increasingly important factor in choosing convention sites. Miami Beach, Florida—a unique island location connected to the mainland only by causeways—was considered an ideal location. In 1972, both the Republicans and Democrats met in Miami Beach. Thus, Miami Beach joined Chicago (1888 and 1952) and Philadelphia (1948) as the only cities to host two conventions in the same year.

For the party controlling the White House the personal preference of the incumbent president is usually the overriding factor in the final choice of the convention city. In 1968, President Lyndon Johnson sided with Chicago Mayor Richard J. Daley's request to hold the Democratic convention in the Windy City, in spite of the TV networks executives' pleas, for economic reasons, to hold it in Miami Beach, site of the 1968 GOP conclave. The massive anti-war demonstrations and brutal Chicago police counteraction that produced a brawling, divided party were not, of course, anticipated when President Johnson and the Democratic National Committee turned down the networks' request to avoid a costly second move to Chicago by also meeting in Miami Beach. In 1972, President Nixon's first choice was San Diego, only 55 miles from his summer White House in San Clemente. However, when word leaked out that a San Diego subsidiary of a multinational corporation, which had recently received a favorable anti-trust ruling from the Nixon Administration, had made a generous contribution to the Republican convention fund, White House staffers "persuaded" the Republican National Committee to make a last-minute shift to Miami Beach. Eight years later, the Carter White House originally favored a southern city as a convention site. But when Atlanta and other major southern cities were ruled out because their states had not ratified the Equal Rights Amendment, the White House did not push for any specific city, leaving the choice up to the site-selection committee. President Carter had no difficulty, however, in accepting New York City since he considered it a lucky city after his first nomination there in Madison Square Garden in July 1976 and his subsequent election victory. Nor did he ignore the possibility of enhancing his chances of carrying New York state's 41 electoral votes in November—possibly the margin of victory in a close race.

More than two years before the 1984 GOP convention, the Republican National Committee selected Dallas as the site of its next convention. This decision was made after President Reagan indicated that Dallas, a runner-up in the 1980 convention city sweepstakes, was his first preference. Presumably heavy Texas conservative support for Reagan at both the 1976 and 1980 GOP conclaves and the anticipated friendly galleries in Dallas were factors in the President's choice of that city.

From time to time it has been suggested that a permanent national convention center be established, for example, in Washington, D.C., to be used by both parties every four years. While all three television networks would welcome one location for all the national conventions for reasons of economy, none of the three major networks has been willing to push the proposal for fear of being charged with exerting undue influence in the political process.[12] Neither of the major parties has evinced much enthusiasm for a single site. They prefer to maintain the traditional flexibility of choice for opportunistic political reasons.

Official Convention Call

The "call" to the convention sets the dates and site of the convention. Although formerly announced early in the presidential year, it is now issued in the preceding year. The Democratic "call" for the 1980 convention, for example, was issued on May 29, 1979. Moving the call back to the previous year reflects, in part, the lengthening pre-nominating phase of the presidential selection process that has evolved as a result of extensive presidential primary campaigning. Issued by the national committees to the 50 state and territorial parties, the "call" of both parties includes the allocation of delegates to each state and rules governing credentials contests. In recent years, the Democratic "call" has also included: detailed rules regulating the activities of the arrangements committee; size of each state's membership on the platform and credentials committees; affirmative action rules; duties of the temporary chairpersons of the standing committees; and procedural rules governing the order of business, the time allocated to each presidential candidate's nominating and seconding speeches (a total of 15 minutes), and even the method to fill a presidential or vice presidential nominee vacancy created by death, resignation, or disability (the Democratic National Committee performs this function, if needed).[13]

Major Convention Committees

For more than a century the basic work of each national convention has been done by four major committees: Permanent Organization, Credentials, Rules, and Platform (resolutions). In recent years, however, the Democrats have shifted the work calendar so that in some instances committee sessions, for example, platform hearings, are held several weeks ahead of the convention. The O'Hara Commission recommended that all committee work be completed well ahead of the convention, and this has since been done. Also, the O'Hara Commission recommended that a final draft copy of the Democratic platform be in the hands of all delegates ten days before the opening convention gavel, and this rule has been observed since 1972. This extra time gives the delegates more time to deliberate on platform planks. The Republican committees still do substantially all of their committee work, including the platform, in the week before the convention, as they did in 1980, though the GOP national committee staff does extensive preparation work for the convention committees in the months before the party conclave. Generally, the more tightly organized GOP platform-drafting schedule allows the incumbent or dominant faction to dictate its contents. In 1980, for example, the GOP delegates did not get a final copy of the platform until after they had voted for it.[14]

PERMANENT ORGANIZATION COMMITTEE

Traditionally, this committee selects the permanent officers of the convention— permanent chairman, secretary, and sergeant-at-arms. In the past these designees were picked by the national chairman and ratified by the committee. In the aftermath of the Democratic defeat in 1968, the O'Hara Commission recommended elimination of the Committee on Permanent Organization, with the transfer of its functions to the Committee on Rules. Thus, the Democrats have had no Committee on Permanent Organization since 1968. In the past these permanent officers have sometimes played an important role in shaping the convention outcome—especially if the delegates were evenly divided between two leading contenders—because they controlled speaker recognition and the agenda of the convention.

CREDENTIALS COMMITTEE

In terms of influencing the outcome of a hot nominating battle, the Credentials Committee has in the past been the most important committee of the convention. Indeed, in a close contest the Credentials Committee's recommendations on delegate challenges can often be decisive in determining who can vote and, thus, ultimately who will be the nominee. Probably the most famous credentials fight took place at the tension-filled 1912 Republican convention, in which the pro-Taft majority on the Credentials Committee recommended seating 235 contested pro-Taft delegates, mostly from Southern "rotten borough" districts, instead of Teddy Roosevelt's rival delegates from these congressional districts.[15] This recommendation, which was upheld on the convention floor by a 557 to 501 vote, in effect, assured Taft renomination and doomed Roosevelt's candidacy.[16] Following this convention action, Roosevelt and his Progressive Republican supporters bolted the convention, formed their own third-party (the Bull Moose or Progressive party), and nominated Roosevelt to be their standard-bearer.

Forty years later, another memorable credentials fight occurred at the 1952 Republican convention when the Credentials Committee, dominated by the backers of Senator Robert A. Taft (son of the former president), recommended the seating of pro-Taft delegations from Texas, Georgia, and Louisiana, only to have the decision overturned on the convention floor after an impassioned "Thou Shalt Not Steal" speech by an Eisenhower spokesperson. The seating of the pro-Eisenhower Texas delegation and a majority of challenged Eisenhower delegates from Georgia and Louisiana put the smiling former Supreme Allied Commander in strategic position to capture the GOP nomination on the first ballot.

In recent years, mainly since 1972, the credentials contest process in both parties has been "judicialized" to a point where it would be hard to argue that the decisions are typically unfair. Especially within the Democratic party, the Compliance Review Commission (CRC), established by the O'Hara Commission, closely monitors each state's selection process to see to it that the participants observe all of the procedural "ground rules" to the letter. Indeed, a strong case can be made that establishment of the Compliance Review Commission has probably erased future credentials fights at the Democratic party conclaves. More will be said about the role of the Credentials Committee in the next chapter.

RULES COMMITTEE

Since the beginning of convention history before the Civil War, major parties have included a Rules Committee as an integral part of each national convention.

As the name implies, the Rules Committee establishes the rules under which each convention will operate. Generally, most rules of previous conventions are readopted. Until 1936, for example, Democratic conventions used the century-old "two-thirds" rule which required the party nominee to receive two-thirds—not a simple majority—of the convention vote. First used in 1836 and readopted at each convention for a century, the two-thirds rule often resulted in marathon balloting—the most famous case being the 103-ballot, 16-day Democratic convention of 1924. Long endorsed and defended by southern delegations, the two-thirds rule gave the South, in effect, a veto over any unwanted nominee. It was not until President Franklin D. Roosevelt ran for a second term in 1936 that the southerners were persuaded to drop their opposition to repeal of this long-standing rule. President Roosevelt had his own special reason for pushing for abolition of the two-thirds rule. In 1932, the Roosevelt forces, although they controlled a majority of votes through each of the first three ballots, were stalled by their inability to win over the needed extra votes to give them the required two-thirds majority. Fearful that they might begin to suffer delegate erosion on subsequent ballots (usually viewed as a sign of weakness by party insiders) Governor Roosevelt's managers offered the vice presidential nomination to Speaker John N. Garner of Texas, in return for his 90 delegates won in the Texas convention and California primary.[17] Garner's managers accepted the deal. These additional delegates were enough to put Roosevelt over the top on the fourth ballot; he then chose Garner as his running-mate.

In 1968, the outnumbered supporters of Senator Eugene J. McCarthy, who knew beforehand that they did not have the votes to win the nomination, nevertheless convinced the Humphrey majority on the Rules Committee to recommend repeal of another anti-majoritarian instrument, the "unit rule." This long-standing rule, used most frequently in the Southern states, required all members of a state delegation instructed under this rule to vote according to the wishes of the delegation majority. After a short, heated debate the unit rule was abolished on a voice vote, much to the disappointment of several Southern delegations. In view of recent delegate selection rule changes, especially in the Democratic party, it is probably not an exaggeration to state that the Rules Committee, not the Credentials Committee, is where the action will be when two or three candidates are locked in a close pre-convention race. The role of the Rules Committee will be discussed in greater detail in Chapter 4.

PLATFORM COMMITTEE

Voters who comprise the two major American parties are, of course, never completely united on every issue. Consequently, platform writing has become the most widely used means for reconciling basic intra-party differences over issues. In the process the American voters become better informed about the party's position on basic issues. In the early nineteenth century conventions, the platform-drafting function had evolved out of the periodic efforts to prepare "an address to the people."[18] By 1850, it had become accepted as a normal part of convention activity. Early platform-drafting had been deferred until after the presidential nominating had been completed. In 1852, however, both the Democrats and Whigs adopted their platforms *before* undertaking nominations. Though the action stirred up deep fissures in each party over the Compromise of 1850 on the slavery question, it set a precedent for the standard convention agenda that has been followed to the present day. More will be said about platform writing in the next chapter.

Delegate Apportionment

The outcome of all national conventions is, in the final analysis, determined by a majority of delegates. The rules that determine how many delegates each state is allocated to the national convention are, in many respects, the most important rules in the entire nominating process because they determine how the units of power are to be divided. Consequently, this allocation influences every important decision taken by the states. When the national convention system was first established, apportionment of delegates was erratic and unequal. Some states had larger delegations than others solely because they were geographically closer to the convention city. This unstructured system, however, was changed before the Civil War.[19]

Because elections in the United States are held on a territorial basis, both major parties early on conveniently adopted the same system for apportioning delegates to the national party conclaves, with the state serving as the basic electoral unit and the Electoral College votes used for basing the total delegate votes allocated to each state. Other systems of delegate representation could, of course, have been used, for example, party officeholders exclusively, functional representation of farmer, labor, and business organizations, and so forth. But party managers from the first conventions in the 1830's chose instead to adopt the "Connecticut Compromise" solution that the Founding Fathers had used to resolve the small state-large state controversy over legislative representation (each state was allocated two U.S. Senators, and the House seats were based on population) in the presidential nominating process. This eminently sensible approach also directly tied the nominating procedures to the general election campaign, since the size of each state's congressional delegation also determined the total number of votes they cast in the Electoral College. Thus, the basic allocation of delegate voting power to each state was equal to the sum total of senators and representatives within the state (which could be multiplied by some constant figure if and when they wanted to allow for a larger number of delegates at the convention). As the Founding Fathers had recognized in the Constitution when they established Congress, this plan gave a special advantage to small states (because all of them, large or small, had two senators). This apportionment method, however, failed to reflect whether a state made a significant contribution to the party's victory in the general election. But the combination of equal Senate representation plus population (for the congressional districts) was not seriously questioned until the emergence of one-party areas after the Civil War, especially in the one-party Democratic South. Within the one-party area the minority party's abnormally small voter constituency meant that the minority party (in this case, the Republicans) would be overrepresented at its national conventions. This vexing problem, which haunted the Republicans for decades, will be discussed in more detail later in the chapter.

DEMOCRATIC APPORTIONMENT

Most Democratic conventions during their first century of operation encountered more problems with fractional voting than with questions of representation. In 1852, the Democratic convention voted to allow each state twice as many delegates as it had votes in the Electoral College, giving each delegate a half vote. In 1872, however, the number of votes was doubled so that each delegate might have a whole vote.[20] Nevertheless, throughout the next half-century, fractional votes occasionally appeared on the convention roll calls. In 1924, for example, after passage of women's suffrage, the Democrats split up the four at-large delegate seats from each state (representing the state's two senatorial votes in the Electoral College) into eight delegates with one-half vote each "to give adequate representation to women as delegates at-large, without disturbing prevailing party customs."[21]

Bonus votes, as will be explained elsewhere in the chapter, were adopted later by the Democratic party than their Republican counterparts. As a concession to the South, following abolition of the century-old two-thirds rule at the 1936 Democratic convention, the Democratic National Committee was directed to modify delegate selection rules by taking into account "the Democratic strength within each state."[22]

In 1940, the Democratic national convention that nominated President Franklin Delano Roosevelt to a third term approved a rule, effective in 1944, by which two bonus votes would be allotted to each state going Democratic in the last preceding presidential election. Four years later, the Democratic National Committee increased the bonus to four votes for states going Democratic in the previous presidential election.

Congressional reapportionment after the 1950 census, which had resulted in significant population shifts, created a special headache for both parties because nine states lost seats. The Republicans, faced with an unpleasant task of reducing delegate representation in these states, did nothing about it and left the states to adjust to their delegate loss. The Democratic National Committee, however, yielded to pressure from party leaders in the nine states, led by New York, and adopted a special rule for the 1952 convention that no state should lose convention votes by reason of congressional reapportionment. Earlier, the Democrats had taken similar actions in 1912 and 1932, when conventions followed close after reapportionment, but each time they returned to normal apportionment rules in 1916 and 1936.

Reducing the size of state delegations, as party leaders know, is an unpleasant assignment. In 1956, the Democratic National Committee once again yielded to the complaining states by passing another generous bonus rule. The new rule stipulated that every state would receive *all* of the votes previously allotted to it in the 1952 convention and four *additional* votes if it had either cast its electoral votes for the Democratic nominees in 1952 or had elected a Democratic governor or senator on or after November 4, 1952.[23] Thus, the new rule had the effect of carrying over into 1956 the compensatory votes authorized four years earlier to alleviate the painful effects of the 1950 congressional reapportionment in states that had lost congressional seats. This action established the precedent under which the delegate votes corresponding to lost congressional districts might be continued indefinitely from census to census by states losing population.

Before the "call" was issued for the 1960 Democratic convention, Democratic National Party Chairman Paul M. Butler led an effort to put an end to the bonus rule and to compensate states for their loss of bonus delegates by increasing the number of regular votes allotted to every state. Under Butler's plan, 15 states would have lost delegates. To avoid this cutback, a compromise delegate plan was adopted that retained major elements of Butler's plan, but the new plan also provided that no state should suffer any reduction in the number of votes that it had received in 1956. More importantly, the Democratic National Committee authorized each state either one or two delegates per vote; consequently, most states split their delegate votes in half, with the result that approximately 3,000 delegates (with a voting strength of 1,521 votes) attended the 1960 convention in Los Angeles. More and more, the Democratic conventions were coming to resemble mass rallies. The 1964 Democratic convention vote was increased to 2,316, but a grand total of 5,260 delegates and alternates attended the Atlantic City convention. The newly approved vote allocation formula reflected both a state's electoral vote and voting support for the Kennedy-Johnson ticket in 1960.

The Democrats continued to experiment with their apportionment formula, with every opportunity taken to reward states for carrying the national ticket. Eight years later the Democrats modified their delegate vote formula, basing it almost equally between Electoral College strength (53 percent) and the Democratic vote in the three most recent presidential elections (47 percent). As a result, the size of the 1972 Democratic convention jumped to 3,016 delegates— an increase of 394 delegates over 1968.

Prior to the 1980 convention, the Democratic National Committee approved a Winograd party reform commission recommendation that the number of delegate seats in each state be increased by 10 percent to provide delegate slots for party leaders and elected officials.[24] In the aftermath of their 1980 electoral defeat and the belief that President Carter, a political outsider, had failed while in office to work closely enough with party members in Congress, the Democratic National Committee adopted rules for the 1984 convention requiring that 14 percent of the delegates to the nominating convention be chosen on the basis of their office or party status and without commitment to a candidate. If past experience can be relied upon as an indicator, the Democratic party rule change can be expected in

1984 to expand further the size of its national convention to avoid depriving or penalizing rank-and-file prospective delegates from attending.[25]

Until the 1970's, the delegate apportionment formulae (from which the state convention vote totals are derived) did not stir much controversy in either major party. But in recent years the apportionment formulae of both parties have triggered court challenges, as will be discussed in a moment.

REPUBLICAN APPORTIONMENT

Within the GOP the adoption of a new formula in 1972 provoked extensive debate that soon took on ideological and geographical overtones—right-wing conservatives versus moderate or liberal Republicans. The issue has focused on the victory bonus rule, by which states regardless of size are awarded a set number of extra delegate votes if the party's presidential, senatorial, gubernatorial, and a majority of House candidates have carried the state in the previous election. Republicans have been using some type of victory bonus since 1916, but in 1971 the rule was challenged in federal courts by the Ripon Society, a group of liberal and moderate young Republicans. The Ripon suit maintained that a uniform bonus rule ran afoul of the Fourteenth Amendment, violative of the one-person, one-vote standard set forth in the U.S. Supreme Court's ruling on apportionment in congressional and state legislative districts. In their court fight against the Republican National Committee the Ripons claimed the victory bonus denied larger states their fair share of convention votes. Instead, the Ripons urged the courts to overturn the bonus rule and institute a new apportionment formula which would allocate votes to the states on the basis of two criteria: population and popular vote for the Republican presidential candidate in the previous election. Although the U.S. District Court for the District of Columbia upheld the Ripon contention, Associate Supreme Justice William Rehnquist issued a stay order prior to the 1972 GOP convention and thereby negated the lower court's ruling. Subsequently, the U.S. Court of Appeals dismissed the suit as moot.

In December 1972, the Ripon Society returned to court, challenging the 1976 delegate allocation formula approved by the GOP convention. The initial court ruling satisfied neither side. The uniform bonus system was held unconstitutional, but the court deemed legitimate the proportional-bonus aspect of the GOP formula. Both sides appealed the case. In March 1974, a three-judge appeals-court panel sustained the Ripons on both counts. The decision, however, was vacated until the full Appeals Court for the District of Columbia could review the case. On reargument, the appeals court reversed the lower court's rulings, and in so doing upheld the paramount authority of the Republican National Convention to determine delegate apportionment. This court ruling in favor of the Republican national organization was in accordance with the High Court's ruling in the 1972 Illinois primary case that involved the unseating of Chicago Mayor Richard J. Daley's Cook County delegation at the 1972 Democratic convention.[26]

By a nine to one vote, the full appeals court reversed a previous decision of a three-member panel of the same court which had ruled in favor of the Ripon Society's challenge against the GOP bonus rule. In overturning the three-member panel, Judge Carl McGowan opined that courts should be "slow to interfere with the internal processes of political parties. . . . It is the essence of the First Amendment rights which the parties exercise that they make their own contrary judgments without interference from the courts."[27] Undeterred, the Ripon Society appealed to the Supreme Court, but in February 1976, the High Court refused to grant a hearing.

The Ripon Society had also unsuccessfully fought its battle on another front— at the 1972 GOP National Convention. After a debate in the Rules Committee and on the convention floor, the 1972 convention rejected the Ripon challenge and adopted a formula for use four years later that included a victory bonus. Within the Democratic party the victory bonus rule had also come under fire in 1971. At the urging of the party's reform commission on Rules, the Democratic National Committee adopted a new formula based almost equally on two criteria: a state's population and its popular vote for the Democratic presidential candidate in the past three elections. Before issuance of the "call" to the 1972 Democratic convention, a group of party liberals challenged this formula in court, arguing that it should reflect a one-Democrat, one-vote standard and be based entirely on a state's Democratic presidential vote. While the reformers were successful with their challenge in the U.S. District Court, a U.S. Court of Appeals in the District of Columbia overturned the decision. In January 1972, the U.S. Supreme Court refused without comment to hear the case, in effect upholding the national committee's new formula. The Democratic National Committee adopted the same delegate apportionment formula for its 1976 convention.

Almost from its birth, the Republican party has been plagued with controversy over delegate apportionment rules. At the first GOP convention in 1856 each state was allocated six delegates at-large and three for each congressional district. Four years later, this was changed to four at-large and two for each district— an apportionment plan that remained in effect, despite growing dissatisfaction, until after the strife-torn 1912 Republican convention. The newly founded Republican party, essentially a Northern party, had no delegations south of the Potomac at its first convention. In 1860, however, delegations from Virginia and Texas appeared at the Chicago convention. The Texas delegation faced a challenge, since the party had no significant voter membership in the Lone Star State. The GOP Credentials Committee, as a compromise, suggested seating the Texans with a reduction in voting strength from eight to six delegates. The convention agreed to this compromise—the first instance of recognition that lack of party strength would not require total exclusion but might involve a reduction in delegate voting strength.[28]

In 1864, however, the Republican National Union convention delegates from three Southern states—Tennessee, Arkansas, and Louisiana (where the Union armies were in sufficient control to enable Unionist governments to be established) —were seated with full voting rights. During the Reconstruction Era all southern states were given their full apportionment of delegates. With the end of Reconstruction, however, the white supremacists in control of the dominant Democratic party disfranchised most black voters. Since blacks had supported the Republicans—the party of Abraham Lincoln—the GOP electorate shrank drastically. Indeed, with the emergence in 1880 of the Democratic "Solid South," Republican delegates below the Mason-Dixon Line represented little more than thinly populated "rotten borough" districts.

Comprised mostly of appointed federal officeholders (postmasters, collector of the customs, and internal revenue officers were all patronage jobs in this pre-civil service era) when the GOP controlled the White House, the Southern delegations were a constant embarrassment to the Republican party. Efforts of the GOP conventions in 1884 and 1892 to reduce the representation of the South were unsuccessful. In the 1896 nominating race, with the GOP out of power, widespread bribery of Southern delegates by Northern presidential candidate staff members reportedly occurred in several states.[29] In 1908, a minority report of the GOP convention Rules Committee proposed that for the 1912 convention each state should be allocated four delegates at-large and one additional delegate for each 10,000 Republican votes or major fraction thereof in the last preceding presidential election. Since only a handful of Southern congressional districts had 10,000 Republican voters, this proposal would have reduced by half the number of delegates going to the 1912 GOP convention. This proposal was narrowly defeated on the floor of the convention by a vote of 506 to 471, with the bulk of the opposition coming from the heavily overrepresented Dixie Republicans.

If this apportionment proposal had been adopted, former President Theodore Roosevelt would probably have been nominated instead of President Taft. Why? The reason was simple: the eleven former Confederate states had 252 votes (mostly pro-Taft) in the 1912 convention, or 23 percent of the total, even though they had contributed less than seven percent of the Republican popular vote in 1908. These Southern delegates, almost all federal officeholders appointed by the Taft administration, virtually guaranteed Taft the nomination. Taft won the first test of strength on the vote for convention temporary chairman in 1912 by 558 to 501, with 256 contested delegates voting. Of the 256 challenged votes, 176 were from the eleven states of the Confederacy, and the delegates from these Southern "rotten boroughs" gave Taft far more than the 57 vote margin needed to control the 1912 GOP convention. To illustrate the GOP overrepresentation in the South early in the twentieth century, Republican delegations from Florida, Louisiana, Mississippi, and South Carolina together cast more delegate votes (70) on the basis of 34,000 popular votes for the Republican President in 1908 than Kansas, Connecticut, New Hampshire, Oregon, and West Virginia (68 delegates in all) did with their 550,000 Republican votes in 1908.[30] Outmaneuvered and outvoted by the Taft forces, Roosevelt's Progressive faction bolted the GOP convention and formed the "Bull Moose" third party. As a result of this Republican schism and a three-way presidential race, Democrat Woodrow Wilson swept into the White House with 435 electoral votes but only 44 percent of the popular vote.

Reacting to the 1912 electoral disaster, the GOP National Committee (with no official authority to act) soon moved into the breach. Less than a year later, the Republican National Committee proposed a reform plan for the 1916 convention that would become effective if approved before the end of 1914 by state conventions in states having a majority of the electoral votes. Under the new plan, each state would retain its four delegates at-large, along with one delegate for each congressional delegate. One additional delegate in 1916 would be allowed to each district in which 7,500 Republican votes had been cast for President in 1908 or for congressmen in 1914—because the 1912 Republican general election vote was not considered a fair reflection of Republican nationwide strength.[31]

By October 1914, the reform plan had been approved by party conventions in 22 states, including five Southern states. Under the new rules the 11 states of the Confederacy lost 78 delegates in 1916 and seven more in 1920. Only two Northern states were affected unfavorably—New York lost three delegates in 1916 and two in 1920, and Massachusetts lost one in 1920.[32]

For the 1924 convention the Republican requirement to qualify for a second district delegate was raised from 7,500 votes to 10,000. The new higher figure was calculated to take into account population growth and the advent of women's suffrage in 1920. Also, the GOP adopted a new system of bonus delegates. Under the new plan three bonus delegates at-large were allotted to each state carried by the party in the last preceding presidential election—a provision favoring Northern states. This new rule also favored small states at the expense of the large, because the number of bonus delegates was in no way related to state size. No other major changes in delegate apportionment rules were made until the 1940 Republican National Convention. To reflect more accurately Republican voters in each congressional district, the GOP national convention meeting in Philadelphia voted to approve a new plan, effective in 1944, which required a congressional district to produce at least 1,000 GOP votes in the last preceding presidential or congressional election in order to qualify for even *one* district delegate.[33] In 1952, effective 1956, the requirement was raised to 2,000 votes. The 10,000 vote requirement, established in 1924, for the second district delegate remained unchanged.[34]

Bonus votes have been, as might be expected, extremely popular over the years. In 1940, effective 1944, the GOP rules stipulated that a state that failed to carry in the presidential election for the GOP could still have its three bonus votes if it should elect a Republican U.S. Senator in the following off-year election.

In 1948, effective 1952, the number of GOP bonus delegates for a party victory in a state was increased from three to six and the bonus was made available for electoral success in the last preceding presidential, senatorial, or gubernatorial election. With the rise of the Republican party south of the Mason-Dixon Line in the 1960's, the problem of overrepresentation in the South has almost disappeared. In 1968, for example, the Southern states held approximately 26.7 percent of the national convention delegate vote (356 of 1,333 delegates).

In 1972, after a federal court challenge from the Ripon Society, an organization of Republican moderate and liberal intellectuals, the GOP continued searching for an equitable apportionment plan that would satisfy both the populous and small states. Finally, the 1972 convention rules committee came up with a compromise solution, which after limited debate was accepted by the full convention: six delegates at-large for each state; three delegates for each House district; 14 votes at-large for the District of Columbia; eight for Puerto Rico and four each for Guam and the Virgin Islands; for each state carrying the Republican ticket in the previous election, four and a half delegates plus 60 percent of the state's electoral vote total, rounded upward if necessary; one delegate for each GOP senator elected; a maximum of one delegate for states going Republican for governor; and one delegate for states electing a House delegation at least half Republican for President. Each delegate would have a full vote; thus the size of the 1976 convention jumped from 1,348 in 1972 to 2,259 delegates in 1976. The GOP also copied the frequently used Democratic "no loser" rule, which guaranteed that every state is assured of at least as many delegate votes as it had in the previous convention.[35]

In 1980, the Ripon Society once again sought to reform the GOP convention rules but without success. The Society argued that the party's system of awarding bonus delegates for Republican victories was an anachronism. The Ripons contended that the bonus system consistently underrepresented Roman Catholics, blacks, Jews, Hispanics, and Southern Baptists in the South and the larger states. The Society proposed that delegate selection be tied more closely to a state's population.[36]

The different apportionment criteria used by the two parties tends to favor some states over others at the national conventions. The Republican party's allocation of delegates based upon the Electoral College vote and mere electoral victory, not on the number of votes cast for party candidates, translates into a special advantage to small states, especially those one-party states that the GOP has carried in the last presidential election. In contrast, the Democratic party now places equal emphasis on the total number of votes cast in presidential elections and Electoral College apportionment. As a result, the populous states, most of which tend to be competitive, generally benefit from the Democratic apportionment system.

Recent Democratic and Republican rules governing delegate selection, it might be pointed out, also differ on a number of key points.

Major Differences between Democratic and GOP Delegate Selection Rules

Primary and Caucus Time Frames. In 1980, for example, the Democrats required states to hold their primaries or first stage of their caucus processes between specific dates (March 11-June 10, 1980). Only states that started earlier in 1976, for example, Iowa, New Hampshire, and Massachusetts, were permitted to apply for exemptions. But for 1984, the Democratic National Committee has ruled that Iowa cannot hold its precinct caucuses until the last week in February, only eight days before the New Hampshire primary. All states must hold their 1984 primaries or first-stage caucuses within a three-month period, known as the "window," running from the second Tuesday in March through the second Tuesday in June. Republicans have no restrictions on dates, other than that delegates must be chosen after the call of the convention is published (usually at least eight months before the convention). Democrats require primary states to set their filing deadlines 75 days before the election. Republicans have no restrictions.

Proportionality.   Democratic party rules no longer require proportional representation on the basis of presidential preference. For 1984 the Democrats will permit states to keep proportional representation, but states also have two options: they may adopt a winner bonus plan that would award the top vote-getter in each district one extra delegate; or the state may return to the "loophole" primary— winner-take-all by congressional district. In 1980 the Republicans had no such requirement and permitted winner-take-all primaries, for example, California. If a state primary law requires proportional allocation of delegates, the Republicans of course adhere to this requirement.

Crossovers.   Democratic party rules ban crossover voting, allowing only Democrats to participate in its primaries and caucuses. But the Democratic National Committee has tried to enforce this ban in only the most flagrant cases of violation, with the leading controversy centering on Wisconsin. The 1981 Supreme Court decision on the Wisconsin open primary, discussed in the next chapter, is expected to strengthen the hand of the Democratic National Committee in dealing with crossover voting violations. The Republicans prohibit crossovers unless permitted by state law.

Voter Preference.   The Democratic party requires delegates in the primaries and caucuses to declare their presidential preference or uncommitted status. Also, Democratic presidential contenders possess the authority in each state to certify their list of delegates to prevent any "trojan horse" delegates from winning seats on the candidate's convention delegation. The GOP does not require delegates to declare their preference or authorize the candidate to veto delegates who might be untrustworthy.

Ballot Commitment.   In 1980 Democratic delegates were bound to vote their presidential preference for one ballot. But the 1984 rules have weakened this "faithful delegate" commitment. The new language allows delegates to respond to changing political conditions by requiring only that they "reflect in good conscience the sentiments of those who selected them." Republicans require delegates bound to a candidate by state law in primary states to vote for that candidate.

Sex Apportionment.   The Democratic party requires states to elect an equal number of men and women delegates. The GOP requests states to elect an equal number.

With the 1980 census dictating a subsequent shift of 17 congressional seats from the Northeastern and Midwestern states to the "Sun Belt" states of the South and Southwest—the largest shift of congressional seats in the twentieth century—the 1984 and subsequent national conventions can be expected, more and more, to reflect the regional interests of these burgeoning areas. Florida's four additional congressional seats, for example, can be translated into at least twelve additional delegates and will transform the Sunshine State into the seventh largest delegation at both Democratic and Republican conventions. Texas, which gains three additional congressional seats, will move into third place, ahead of Pennsylvania. It has been predicted that both the Republican and Democratic conventions will take on an increasingly conservative tone as more Southern and Western delegates displace those from the liberal-oriented areas of the Northeast (New York, for example, will lose five congressional seats) and Midwest, but it is too early to make a conclusive judgment on this point.

Methods of Selecting Delegates

Throughout the twentieth century both major parties have used a "mixed" nominating system to send delegates to national nominating conventions. The term "mixed" refers to the optional, dual-tracked method involving both presidential primaries and the caucus-convention system used in the 50 states to select national convention delegates.[37] As explained earlier, the United States is the only Western country to utilize a type of popular election in a majority of states to select delegates to attend an equally unique nominating body—the national convention.

CAUCUS-CONVENTION SYSTEM

Prior to 1900, presidential candidates were nominated by national convention delegates chosen exclusively through a "closed" caucus-convention system. To many citizens, the multi-tiered caucus-convention system still remains a mystery. But the system which dates back to the time of President Andrew Jackson, and, even earlier, is not that complicated, though it may vary somewhat from state to state. In the 15 states using the caucus-convention system, the opening round of the delegate selection system begins in January, February, or the early spring with precinct caucuses or some other type of local mass meeting open to all party voters. No national convention delegates, it should be noted, are directly elected at the precinct meetings, but the precinct outcome ultimately dictates the composition of the congressional district delegation.

As a first step, the caucuses elect delegates to county conventions. At the county level a smaller group of delegates is then elected to congressional district conventions (or caucuses); these same delegates usually also go to state conventions. The time frame for the caucus-convention system is similar though slightly longer than the presidential primary season—the final state conventions are sometimes not held until late July. As political insiders have long known, the key phase of the caucus-convention delegate selection process takes place at the precinct level, because it is the persons elected from this level who eventually decide who will attend the congressional district conventions, which pick 75 percent of the state's delegates to the national convention.

Congressional district conventions (or caucuses) elect a minimum of two delegates to the national conventions. (The Democratic party allocates between two and seven delegates, based upon a combined formula of Electoral College representation and the size of the party's presidential vote in the past three elections.) The Democratic party sets aside 25 percent of its delegates to be chosen at-large by the state conventions; within the Republican party the number of at-large delegates may run as high as 50 percent, and even higher in small states carried by the GOP presidential candidate in the last election. The at-large arrangement was originally adopted to enable state parties to select governors, U.S. senators, congressmen, state party chairpersons, and other high party officials to serve as national convention delegates without competing against party members at the district conventions.

Three states—Hawaii, Arizona, and Delaware—are listed officially as caucus-convention states, but they also hold what are known as "firehouse primaries." In these states party members attend local mass meetings (often at a fire hall, school, or other type of public building), vote on their presidential choice, and send delegates to congressional district conventions, which pick national convention delegates committed to specific presidential candidates.

Between 1968 and 1976, the number of caucus-convention states declined from 34 to 21. Four years later, the number dwindled to 15 states. By 1980, less than 30 percent of the national convention delegates were selected under the caucus-convention system (see Table 2). Of the twelve largest states in the Union, only Texas uses the caucus-convention system (in the Democratic party only).

The year 1980, however, may represent the high-water mark of the presidential primary movement. The 1981 Supreme Court decision on the Wisconsin open primary upholding the Democratic National Committee's constitutional right—regardless of any state law—to insist that only Democrats participate in the process of choosing national convention delegates may inhibit additional states from adopting presidential primaries.[38] Moreover, if Democratic state party organizations—especially those in the 15 primary states now using crossover

TABLE 2
CAUCUS-CONVENTION VERSUS PRESIDENTIAL
PRIMARY DELEGATE APPORTIONMENT IN 1980

Delegates by Region

Democrats

	Total Selected	Carter	Kennedy	Others	Uncommitted
East	948	415	531	1	1
South	793	645	125	0	23
Midwest	932	592	277	1	62
West	581	288.6	266.8	0	25.6
Territories	57	30.5	22	0	4.5

Republicans

	Total Selected	Reagan	Bush	Anderson	Others	Uncommitted
East	498	310	109	19	4	56
South	475	415	48	0	5	7
Midwest	553	436	68	31	0	18
West	446	415	14	1	0	16
Territories	22	4	14	0	0	4

Delegates by Selection System

	Democrats					Republicans					
	TOTAL SELECTED	CARTER	KENNEDY	OTHERS	UNCOMMITTED	TOTAL SELECTED	REAGAN	BUSH	ANDERSON	OTHERS	UNCOMMITTED
Caucus states	933	596.1	231.8	0	105.1	478	397	36	1	5	39
Primary states (by primary type)											
Proportional	2,164	1,191	961	1	11	463	307	131	19	4	2
Loophole	214	184	29	1	0	516	406	27	25	0	58
Winner-take-all						426	380	40	6	0	0
Mixed						111	90	19	0	0	2
TOTAL (primary states)	2,378	1,375	990	2	11	1,516	1,183	217	50	4	62
GRAND TOTAL	3,311	1,971.1	1,221.8	2	116.1	1,994	1,580	253	51	9	101

Source: *Congressional Quarterly Weekly Report*, Vol. 38, No. 27 (July 5, 1980), p. 1873. Quoted by permission, Congressional Quarterly, Inc., Washington, D.C.

voting—operate with the knowledge that their national convention delegates will not be seated if Republicans have voted in the Democratic presidential primary, they may well be disinclined to continue with the presidential primary system of choosing national convention delegates in their state.

PRESIDENTIAL PRIMARY SYSTEM

With the rapid spread of state presidential primary laws in recent years, 35 states now use some form of popular election to select delegates to the national conventions. Despite their wide variation in form, state presidential primary laws can be divided into two general types: (1) presidential preference votes, for example, between Taft and Eisenhower, McGovern and Humphrey, Ford and Reagan, or Carter and Kennedy—the so-called "beauty contest" or popularity poll; and (2) direct election of delegates to the national conventions.

The Republican party uses two variations or combination forms of the preference primary—binding or advisory; the Democrats in 1980 required that all binding primary preferences be based on proportionality. Further, if a state wished to hold an advisory primary, Democratic rules in 1980 required that the delegates be selected by a caucus-convention system, in which delegates are allocated proportionately on the basis of the candidate vote in the primary, but this rule has been modified for 1984, permitting states to readopt winner-take-all "loophole" primaries. In a loophole primary state, voters ballot directly for delegates, with each delegate candidate identified by presidential preference. Under this plan a presidential candidate can sweep all of the delegates within a congressional district, if his or her delegates win their races by a plurality. (Formerly, five big states, among others, in the industrial "Frost Belt"—Illinois, New Jersey, New York, Ohio, and Pennsylvania—used the loophole primary before it was banned by the 1976 Democratic convention.)

In the 1984 Democratic nominating race, states, as an option, may elect to keep proportional representation but adopt a winner bonus plan that will award the top vote-getter in each congressional district one extra delegate; otherwise the votes will be divided proportionately. In a binding Republican preference primary, the results of the primary election bind the delegates to the plurality or majority winner of the preference primary in each congressional district and at-large delegates to the statewide winner. California's Republican primary, however, is a "winner-take-all" binding preference vote, which requires the entire state delegation to vote for the primary winner. Thus, in 1976 and 1980 former California governor Ronald Reagan captured the entire California delegation by winning the California primary (167 votes in 1976 and 168 in 1980).

Under the proportionality rules used in 1980 in the Democratic party primaries (or caucuses and conventions), delegates were apportioned to each of the candidates, for example, President Jimmy Carter, Senator Edward Kennedy, or Governor Edmund G. "Jerry" Brown, on the basis of the percentage of votes received in each congressional district or statewide. Before the 1976 nominating season opened, the Democratic National Committee voted to put a "floor," or minimum level of support (15 percent) that all candidates had to meet before they could acquire a proportion of the national convention delegate votes in a state primary, caucus, or convention. The newly established 15 percent rule was widely but not universally followed in 1976. Under the 1980 Democratic rules recommended by the Winograd Commission, a minimum vote of 15 percent was established in the early primaries, caucuses, or conventions to acquire a proportion of the delegates, 20 percent was required in the midseason contests, and 25 percent in the final third of the season (in 1976 almost 60 percent of the delegates were chosen during this period).[39]

This action by the Democratic National Committee, which reflected the wishes of the Carter White House, was intended to make it extremely difficult for potential challengers of President Carter to mount a major campaign against his renomination. The sliding scale of proportionality, however, did not deter Senator Edward M. Kennedy or California Governor Edmund G. "Jerry" Brown from entering the 1980 presidential nominating sweepstakes against Carter. But it was sound electoral strategy for a presidential incumbent to erect these nomination barriers, since it is widely recognized that victories in early primaries and caucuses enable any candidate to build momentum, and drain away money, volunteers, and network TV coverage from all competitors, thereby making it more difficult for rivals to win additional delegates.

Presidential Primaries versus Caucus-Convention System

Defenders of the existing presidential primary system endorse the mixed or dual system of primaries and conventions because it permits rank-and-file voters in 30-plus states to participate directly in the selection of presidential candidates by electing delegates or expressing candidate preferences (or both) without destroying the nominating function of the national convention. Indeed, the existing primary-convention system avoids the revolutionary changes that a national primary would have upon the nominating system.

The mixed primary-convention system, as it exists today, still serves as a national forum and testing ground for the presidential candidates. There is no better "school for presidents" than the presidential primaries. They give the national convention delegates and the voting public the opportunity to assess first hand, over a period of several months, a presidential candidate's behavior, reaction under pressure, and statesman qualities—a comprehensive "on the job" type of training. The 30-plus primaries put a premium on a candidate's organizing ability—his deployment of campaign funds, management of campaign staff and his own time, and his decisiveness. Also, the primaries test the candidate's capacity to recover from campaign gaffes, his reaction to the unexpected, and, above all, his physical stamina. Despite its cost, length, and physical demands, the present system furnishes an invaluable measuring stick for comparing candidates' qualifications. The primaries subject the candidates to a variety of election conditions, shifting sets of competitors, and close scrutiny by the national media.

Under the present system the candidates are tested in a sequential series of primaries over a four-month period to an intensive degree never contemplated by our Founding Fathers—and all the time under the relentless lenses of the television camera. The present system also provides an excellent round-robin elimination contest, a broad cross sampling of voter opinion in various geographical sections—almost a form of regional primary—without the necessity of holding presidential primary elections in each of the 50 states. In 15 weeks the primaries weed out with relentless efficiency the weak vote-getters. Among the major victims of the primary competition the names of Senator Estes Kefauver in 1956, Governor George Romney in 1968, Senator Henry Jackson in 1972 and 1976, and former Secretary of the Treasury John B. Connally in 1980, immediately come to mind.

One of the chief virtues of the existing string of primaries spaced over a period of several months is that the sequential nature of the mixed system permits the outsider or insurgent candidate to build success upon good showings in one state at a time. Campaign "start up" costs are relatively modest. A presidential candidate with a limited budget and a corps of volunteer workers (such as Jimmy Carter, George McGovern, or Eugene McCarthy) can concentrate all of his resources and firepower on a single primary in the early stages of the campaign. If he is successful, say, in New Hampshire, he can move all of his troops and wagon trains to Florida or Wisconsin and repeat the process, thus building up presidential support gradually among the delegates and among the national opinion polls. The serialized testing of candidates enables them to assess their chances after one or two forays in the primaries. Some presidential aspirants may find that they do not have the necessary vote-drawing or finances after the early round competition and withdraw from the race—without serious financial loss or loss of face.

When the primary returns are all in and the results have been fully assessed, the majority of the convention delegates are still technically free to make their choice of the candidate they feel best merits the nomination.[40] The national convention can still operate, if there is no popular choice, as a broker to reconcile factional differences with a compromise candidate and draft a platform acceptable to the various constituencies within the party. The national convention still remains far and away the best forum for putting together a winning ticket combination and platform that are most likely to appeal across party lines and to the millions of independent voters (now more than one-third of the electorate). Finally, the existing mixed system of primaries retains the national convention to legitimize the winner of primaries. In some nominating campaigns the primaries alone are not enough to anoint the nominee. In the 1976 primaries, for example, Jimmy Carter was the choice of only 39 percent of the approximately 16 million participating Democratic voters. By utilizing the national convention for the legitimization of the presidential choice, parties are able to foster consensus-building after the tension-filled rivalry of the primary campaign.

The chief shortcoming of the existing "mixed" system, in the minds of some critics, is that the national media devote an inordinate amount of attention and attach such extreme importance to the early round small state primaries and caucuses in such states as New Hampshire and Iowa that it distorts the entire nominating process. Thus, these states, unrepresentative of the country as a whole, play a predominantly heavy role in picking the front-runner and, in effect, "wash out" a number of well-qualified contenders who fail to run well in the early primaries and caucuses. More will be said about the deleterious effects of media distortion in chapters 8 and 9. The other major objection, at least within the Democratic party, has been the requirement that delegate commitments are binding—in both the primary and caucus-convention states—for the first convention ballot.[41]

Proponents of the caucus system—party professionals and advocates of strong party responsibility—argue, as explained in the opening chapter, that the *quality* of participation in caucuses is superior to the quality of participation in primaries. Party members who attend caucus meetings and participate in debate are generally viewed as more knowledgeable about presidential candidates and their qualifications—and their weaknesses—than the rank-and-file voters. Caucus participants make a greater commitment of time and energy than do primary voters who simply cast a ballot and return home. Caucuses can be a valuable tool for involving more people in the party organization. In states where the caucuses have functions other than delegate selection, such as the drafting of a state party platform and nominating party and public officials, the caucus system helps promote party unity and recruits campaign workers.

Critics of the straight caucus system claim that it is unrepresentative and would mean the return of the same old "courthouse gang" and party oligarchs of an earlier era controlling delegate selection. Until the early 1970's, these charges were often true. But recent changes in delegate selection rules, especially within the Democratic party, have removed most of the "smoke-filled" (or air conditioned) room influence from the delegate decision-making process. Generally, state laws require that dates and times of all caucuses be posted and publicly announced in the media. Democratic party rules also require all caucus participants to declare their presidential preferences or uncommitted status at the initial caucus-level meeting. As the competition for the presidential nomination has intensified with the spread of presidential primaries, party officials in the nonprimary states have also found it harder to keep their delegations uncommitted. In recent years the wire services have publicized delegate commitments and kept a running box score on the number of delegates supporting each presidential aspirant. Clearly, the new "open" caucus system has removed much of the backroom, behind-the-scenes manipulation that formerly characterized the delegate selection process in some caucus-convention states. As Leon Epstein recently observed, "The more open method character of the [caucus-convention] method, particularly under post-1968 Democratic rules, means that its import is not so radically different from that of the primaries as it was when there were stronger state party leaders."[42] Clearly, in recent years there has been a convergence of the two delegate selection processes that begin with the opening caucuses in snow-swept Iowa, followed by the New Hampshire primary and then through a four-month-long campaign in the other 30-plus primary and 14 caucus-convention states. Since 1976, the national media have also begun to give almost as much television and press coverage to the first-round Iowa caucuses as the first-in-the-nation New Hampshire primary. All of this delegate selection publicity is, of course, a part of a general shift to a more open participatory politics.

Comparisons of the two delegate selection processes now reveal almost as many similarities as differences. While the voter turnout in the primary states (approximately 30 percent) is four or five times as large as in the caucus-convention states (turnout rarely exceeds eight or nine percent), participants in both systems are drawn heavily from strong partisans. Survey Research Center data for 1976 indicate that persons who identified strongly as either strong Democrats or Republicans voted at a 38 percent rate in the presidential primaries while only 22 percent of other adults voted in these springtime elections. Moreover, with the opening of selection processes in the nonprimary states, participants in these states now have virtually the same range of voter options among the presidential aspirants as found in the primary states. Popular support of presidential contenders is, according to one respected source, probably as fairly represented as it is in the primary states.[43] Thus, it would appear to the neutral observer that there is now relatively little to choose between the primary and nonprimary delegate selection systems, insofar as the caliber and representativeness of the delegates are concerned.

Members of the party responsibility school, however, would not be satisfied with the process used under either of the existing delegate selection systems. To achieve maximum party input in the presidential nominating process, many party responsibility advocates, for example, would like to see the delegate selection process confined to "card-carrying" members, or at least those with a strong commitment to party membership and support of party leaders and their programs. The original Democratic Party Charter proposal, drafted for consideration at the 1972 convention but shelved before it ever reached the floor, aimed toward this goal.[44] But the strong responsible party concept did not reappear in the redrafted Democratic Charter, finally approved by the Democratic mid-term convention in Kansas City in December 1974. Nor is it likely to appear among the convention "ground rules" in either major party in the foreseeable future.

Who Are the Delegates?

To most party activists their selection as national convention delegates represents the culmination of one's party career. How many times do they attend national conventions? The common belief that national conventions are populated by the same group of loyal party "insiders" year-in and year-out is inaccurate. Delegate turnover is, on the contrary, high. Most delegates get the opportunity to attend a national convention only once in their lives.

Between 1944 and 1968, for example, approximately 63 percent of Democratic and 65 percent of the Republican delegates during this period had not previously attended a national convention.[45] Thus, roughly only one-third of the delegates attending national conventions during this period could be described as experienced. Delegate participation in all GOP and Democratic conventions during this period showed comparable patterns. According to Johnson and Hahn, the proportion of new delegates at each convention did not differ by more than nine percentage points in the GOP or by more than 16 percentage points in the Democratic party. Nor did the percentage of returning delegates increase progressively with each succeeding convention. Ironically, the greatest increase in the proportion of new delegates attending their first convention during this period occurred at the 1968 Democratic convention, when the party was severely criticized for failing to open up the delegate selection process to new elements within the party! Four years later, the Democratic National Committee reported that 80 percent of the 1972 Democratic convention delegates were newcomers; the GOP National Committee reported that 67.7 percent of the Republican delegates to the 1972 GOP convention were first-timers.[46] According to a 1976 GOP delegate sample, approximately 75 percent had never previously attended a convention. Only 10 percent had attended the 1972 Republican convention; moreover only nine percent had ever attended more than two national conventions.[47] In some presidential years, however, certain types of party activists will be attracted to the convention by particular candidates or issues. In 1976, for example, slightly more than eight percent of the GOP delegates had attended the 1964 convention, which had nominated conservative Republican Barry Goldwater—an unusually high repeater rate considering an interval of 12 years. Most of these delegates, the sample indicated, were a large number of conservative Goldwater supporters who were attempting to nominate another GOP conservative, Ronald Reagan.[48] Within the Democratic party John S. Jackson III and his associates surveyed delegates attending the 1980 Democratic convention in New York City and found that 19 percent of the respondents had attended the 1976 convention; 10 percent had attended the 1972 convention; seven percent, the 1968 convention; five percent, the 1964 convention; and four percent had been in attendance at the 1960 or earlier Democratic conventions. Jackson's data do not, however, reveal how many conventions each of these respondents attended within this time span.[49]

According to extensive survey data, delegates in both parties are drawn mostly from the upper-middle and higher-income brackets. Clearly, they are not a representative cross-section of rank-and-file voters. In view of the fact that delegates in virtually all states are expected to pay all of their own expenses— $800 to $1,500, depending mostly upon distance from the convention—this preponderance of affluent delegates should come as no surprise, though it means that many able, potential delegates must forego attendance because it is too expensive.

Education, Occupation, and Group Affiliation.   According to a CBS News survey of virtually every delegate to the 1980 Democratic national convention, two out of every three Democrats were college graduates, or had done post-graduate work (see Table 3). Four years earlier, the percentage of delegates with college degrees or post-graduate work was at the same level.[50] The average income of Democratic delegates was $37,000—$10,000 less than their Republican counterparts. Jeane J. Kirkpatrick's study of the 1972 delegates revealed that the proportion of professionals—lawyers, teachers, journalists—had increased while the proportion of businessmen, workers, and farmers decreased.[51]

Age. In 1968, approximately 80 percent of the delegates to both the Democratic and Republican conventions were middle-aged, white males. But conditions have changed. The number of young people at the 1972 Democratic convention jumped sevenfold (3 percent to 22 percent) and the number of under-30 delegates at the 1972 GOP convention doubled (4 percent to 8 percent). But since then, the number of young delegates has trailed off (see Table 3). Adoption of the Twenty-sixth Amendment (the 18-year old vote) in 1971 was expected to bring more young people into the political process as both parties courted the young voters; indeed, competition for their votes was expected to open the doors to more young people. But the record shows that both parties, especially the Republicans, have a long way to go before the under-30 voters are fairly represented at the conventions.

Sex. In 1968, only 13 percent of the delegates attending the Democratic convention were women; approximately 16 percent of the delegates to the 1968 GOP convention were women. The growing role of women at the Democratic national convention in 1972 was one of the most significant political developments of the year. Indeed, the number of women delegates increased threefold— from 13 percent at the 1968 convention to almost 40 percent (1,163 of 3,103 delegates) in 1972. This increase in feminine representation was largely the by-product of the new party rules and affirmative action guidelines, initiated by the McGovern-Fraser reform commission. Some party insiders predicted that the percentage of women delegates would climb to 50 percent at the 1976 Democratic convention. The number of women delegates, in fact, decreased significantly at the 1976 parley; therefore, the Democratic National Committee voted two years later to require that 50 percent of the state delegations to the 1980 convention be women. This goal was nearly reached—49 percent of the delegates at the 1980 New York City convention were women. Within the Republican party, the proportion of women delegates increased to 29 percent of the delegates at the 1972 GOP convention, and it hovered around that figure at the 1976 and 1980 Republican conclaves (see Table 3).

Race. Until 1972, black representation at Democratic conventions increased at a glacial pace. Not a single black delegate or alternate had attended the 1924 Democratic convention in New York City. In 1964, only two percent of the Democratic delegates were black. Of the 3,331 delegates attending the 1980 Democratic convention in New York City, however, blacks constituted 15 percent—

TABLE 3
PROFILE OF
NATIONAL CONVENTION DELEGATES, 1968-1980

| | National Convention Delegates | | | | | | | | Public | |
| | 1968 | | 1972 | | 1976 | | 1980 | | 1980 | |
	DEM.	REP.	DEM.	REP.	DEM.	REP.	DEM.	REP.	DEM.	REP.
Women	13%	16%	40%	29%	33%	31%	49%	29%	56%	53%
Blacks	5	2	15	4	11	3	15	3	19	4
Under thirty	3	4	22	8	15	7	11	5	27	27
Median age (years)	(49)	(49)	(42)		(43)	(48)	(44)	(49)	(43)	(45)
Lawyers	28	22	12		16	15	13	15		
Teachers	8	2	11		12	4	15	4		
Union official	4	0	5		6	0	5	0		
Union member			16		21	3	27	4	29*	18*
Attended first convention	67	66	83	78	80	78	87	84		
College graduate	19		21		21	27	20	26 }		
Post—graduate	44	34	36		43	38	45	39 }	11	18
Protestant			42		47	73	47	72	63	74
Catholic			26		34	18	37	22	29	21
Jewish			9		9	3	8	3	4	1
Ireland			13		19	14	15	9		
Britain			17		15	28	15	31		
Germany			9		9	14	6	12		
Italy			4		6	5	5	6		
Liberal					40	3	46	2	21	13
Moderate					47	45	42	36	44	40
Conservative					8	48	6	58	26	41
Governors (number)	(23)	(24)	(17)	(16)	(16)	(9)	(23)	(13)		
Senators (number)	(39)	(21)	(15)	(22)	(11)	(22)	(8)	(26)		
U.S. Representatives (number)	(78)	(58)	(31)	(33)	(41)	(52)	(37)	(64)		

Source: CBS News Delegate Surveys, 1968–1980. Characteristics of the public are average values from seven CBS News/*New York Times* polls, 1980. Poll figures used by permission of CBS Polls. For additional details, see Warren J. Mitofsky and Martin Plissner, "The Making of the Delegates, 1968–1980," *Public Opinion*, Vol. 3 (October-November 1980), pp. 36-43.

*Households with a union member.

approximately the same number as 1972. Close to six percent of the delegates were drawn from other minority groups.[52] Since the massive switchover of blacks from the Republican party to the Democrats during the New Deal era of the 1930's, the GOP appears, at least to the outside observer, to be less concerned than the Democratic party about having blacks serve as delegates. Though blacks now constitute over 11 percent of the population, they have always been underrepresented in ratio to population at Republican national conventions. Blacks constituted two percent of the delegates to the 1968 GOP convention and four percent of the delegates at the 1972 GOP convention—a two percent (or 100 percent) increase over 1968.[53] Only three percent of the delegates to the 1976 and 1980 GOP conventions were black (see Table 3). Approximately one percent had Hispanic surnames and approximately one percent were Asian or American Indian.

Public and Party Office.   European commentator Moisei Ostrogorski's turn-of-the-century observation about the large number of public and party officials attending national conventions is less valid today.[54] As recently as 1968, however, over 42 percent of the GOP delegates had held public office. But the number of officeholders has dropped steadily since then. Within the Democratic party the drop-off has been even more pronounced (see Table 3). In the pre-reform era, it was standard operating procedure in most states to reserve a sizeable batch of delegate slots for the parties' major elective officials, especially governors, U.S. senators, and U.S. representatives. (In 1956, for example, two-thirds of the governors and U.S. senators were members of their state delegations.) Frequently, they were major decision-makers. Between 1968 and 1980, however, the number of U.S. senators and representatives attending Democratic conventions has dropped significantly—only eight U.S. Senators and 36 House members attended in 1980. The McGovern-Fraser reform rules for the 1972 Democratic convention were a major factor in upsetting this special office-holder privilege. Rule 13, for example, stipulated that "no person shall serve as an automatic or *ex officio* voting delegate at any level of the delegate selection process by virtue of holding a public or party office." Thus, any public or party official who wanted to be a delegate to the 1972 or 1976 national conventions had to compete in the congressional caucuses, state conventions, or presidential primaries just like everyone else. Apparently, many were reluctant to commit themselves to a specific candidate or preferred not to deprive some hard-working party volunteer of a seat at the convention. In other cases, especially in the 1972 Democratic nominating race, they risked defeat in the delegate contests. For example, George McGovern's young anti-war delegate candidates frequently won delegate seats from U.S. senators and U.S. representatives backing Senator Hubert H. Humphrey or Edmund S. Muskie.

In 1978, as explained earlier in the chapter, the Democrats sought to reverse this anti-party trend and expand public and party influence in the nominating process by requiring that ten percent of the state's delegate slots at the 1980 convention be reserved for elected officeholders and party officials. Within the Republican party the number of U.S. senators and representatives has not, however, fluctuated as widely (see Table 3). Two CBS News pollsters have pointed out that "Contrary to a common belief, prominent public and party officials are not quite a vanishing race at the convention of either party. As a matter of fact, the Republicans actually had more members from both houses of Congress present at the 1980 Detroit convention than at their 1968 Miami Beach convention."[55] Governors also continue to be well represented at the gatherings of both parties. In 1980, one delegate out of four held some public office at both conventions. Also, three out of five Republicans and half the Democrats held some party office.[56]

Government Employees. Before passage of the two Hatch Acts (1937 and 1938) during the New Deal era which banned political activity by government employees, government patronage-holders constituted an important segment of the incumbent party's national convention. But these federal appointees could no longer serve as delegates after the Hatch Acts went into effect. In 1980, however, another type of government employee delegate (mostly members of teachers' unions or government employees' unions) increased remarkably, especially within the Democratic party. CBS News estimated that about a third of the Democratic convention delegates worked full-time on some government payroll. This high figure represented the exceptional number of teachers activated by the Carter campaign (and to a lesser extent the American Federation of Teachers delegate drive for Senator Kennedy). Using the same criteria in defining a government employee, approximately 21 percent of the Republican delegates in 1980 could be counted as government employees.[57]

Policy Preferences. Herbert McClosky's classic study, completed more than 25 years ago, comparing the policy preferences of the convention delegates and rank-and-file party identifiers in 1956, found that Democratic delegates were considerably more liberal than rank-and-file Democratic identifiers, and Republican delegates were comparably more conservative than ordinary Republicans.[58] Four conventions and 16 years later, Jeane J. Kirkpatrick's study of delegates to the two 1972 conventions found the same kind of leader/follower differences that McClosky had uncovered, but she discovered much greater differences among Democrats than among Republicans.[59] Surprisingly, she found that the differences between the Democratic delegates and rank-and-file party identifiers were so great that the policy preferences of rank-and-file Democrats were much better represented by GOP delegates than Democratic delegates! Indeed, on five of seven leading policy issues in 1972, for example, social welfare, school busing, crime prevention, government action toward inflation, and so forth, Kirkpatrick found that the preferences of ordinary Democratic identifiers were much closer to those of Republican delegates than to those of Democratic delegates.

In a combined study of 1980 Democratic and Republican delegates, plus a national sample of state and county chairmen and members of the Republican and Democratic National Committees, John S. Jackson III and associates found the GOP elites to be much more conservative than the national public and the Democratic elites to be much more liberal than the mass public. Jackson's research team noted tentatively that, "If anything, these differences have probably increased considerably since McClosky's 1956 study although the lack of directly comparable indicators make such conclusions tentative at best."[60] This study, a general replication of McClosky's study a quarter of a century ago, included not only the mass base of the two parties and the American electorate in general but also a number of items drawn from the Center for Political Studies 1980 study and the Gallup and Harris polls. Jackson's data showed, it might be noted, that the Democratic party identifiers still contain a rather large number of self-proclaimed conservatives (42 percent). The Jackson team also found that the Republican identifiers are significantly less conservative than the Republican elites. But Jackson and his colleagues did not find Republican leaders to be further removed from their mass base than the Democrats from theirs. One of the more revealing facets of Jackson's data was the finding that "There are almost no liberals left among the Republicans and very few conservatives left among the Democratic party elites (one percent and nine percent respectively)."[61]

Decline of Party Professionals

New party rules and the recent proliferation of mandatory presidential primaries, as explained above, have been chiefly responsible for the decline in the number of political professionals and public officeholders at the national conventions. Now delegates to national conventions are elected on the basis of their candidate preference, not as rewards for service to the state party. Thus, in the primaries professional politicians must compete one-on-one with the political enthusiasts supporting a specific candidate and representatives from special interest groups, for example, members of the National Education Association (NEA), the National Organization of Women (NOW), the Right-to-Life, the Moral Majority, and so on. While name recognition may help some political professionals win delegate seats, they frequently discover that they are outnumbered by large voting blocs of teachers, women, trade unionists, or right-wing conservatives.

The anti-Vietnam War protest movement was partially responsible for the rapid increase in the percentage of first-time participants, especially within the Democratic party. In 1972, for example, 83 percent of the Democrats were attending their first convention. The newly recruited supporters of Senator George McGovern helped swell the ranks of new participants at the Democratic convention. The Republican presidential primaries also attracted a large number of first-time participants—76 percent of the 1972 GOP delegates were attending their first convention. Four years later, Jimmy Carter's newly recruited backers in the primary states displaced many old-line politicians at the 1976 Democratic convention. Presidential candidates who appeal to the extreme wings of their party, for example, George McGovern or George Wallace in the Democratic party, and Barry Goldwater and Ronald Reagan in the GOP, have generally been able to attract and help elect more activists as delegates than the more moderate candidates, who frequently discover that their less-dedicated, rank-and-file supporters stay home on primary day.

Within the Democratic party, new delegate selection rules designed to transfer power over presidential nominations from party regulars to persons committed to a particular presidential candidate or policy have led to a drastic cut in party professionals at the conventions. Most delegates now owe their seats not to the special favor of any state or local party leader, but rather to their commitment to a specific national presidential contender who has done well in their state primary or within the caucus-convention delegate selection process—or to the special interest groups who have turned out in record numbers in the caucuses or primaries to elect their supporters to the national convention.

New affirmative action rules, especially within the Democratic party, increased the number of women, blacks, and youth at recent conventions. Clearly, affirmative action policies in both parties have attracted more newcomers who soon become competitors with party professionals for delegate seats.

Growth of Organized Interest Group Delegates

In recent years the increasing institutionalization of organized groups—labor unions, teachers, black organizations, women's groups, and so forth—has generated demands for more recognition and greater participation in setting policy goals at national conventions. The growing voice of these groups has affected not only the content of party platforms but also the process of drafting them as well. With the declining influence of state parties, the rise of candidate organizations and the popular election of most convention delegates in primaries has resulted in the election of more special interest delegates. Issue-oriented delegates elected by the National Education Association, the Right-to-Life groups, the National Organization of Women, and spokespersons for the Moral Majority are all less inclined to compromise on party platform planks. Less dependent on and loyal to party leadership, these issue-oriented delegates have become better organized and more adept at bargaining to achieve their policy objectives. Especially within the Democratic party, the development of caucus groups, for example, the women's caucus and Hispanic caucus, has generated additional demands on the platform and opened up the delegate selection process further.

To counteract the declining role of party professionals in convention decision-making, the Democratic National Committee approved the 1978 Winograd Commission recommendation that ten percent of each state's delegates to the 1980 national convention be reserved for party and elected officials. Even so, the 1980 Democratic national convention had the largest single-interest group delegation in the history of national conventions—302 members of the National Education Association served as delegates. Ninety percent of the NEA delegates backed Carter. Without this large bloc of "teacher power" delegates, President Carter might well have lost the nomination to Senator Edward Kennedy. (Carter's margin over Kennedy on the crucial binding delegate rule change was 1,936.42 for the Carter forces and 1,390.58 for Kennedy's supporters—a margin considerably less than a swing of, say, 300 delegates, which immediately translates into a 600-vote difference.) One Carter delegate in seven was an NEA member. Every state delegation had at least one NEA delegate or alternate NEA delegate give their heavy backing to Carter, chiefly because he supported increased federal aid to education and persuaded Congress to establish a separate Department of Education—a favorite long-term goal of NEA. The smaller teachers' union—the 500,000 member American Federation of Teachers (AFT)—which heavily backed Carter's challenger, Senator Edward M. Kennedy, had 66 delegates at the 1980 Democratic convention. Of the Democratic delegates, 49 backed Kennedy, 10 supported Carter, and seven were uncommitted before the New York convention opened.[62] Nor does Big Labor seem inclined to stay on the sidelines in future nominating contests. In August 1982 the executive council of the 15 million-member AFL-CIO labor federation, for the first time in history, voted to endorse a presidential aspirant in December 1983, even before the primaries begin, if two-thirds of the executive council agree on a single candidate then.[63]

Members of the Democratic Hunt Commission task force on delegate selection reform, however, have indirectly halted the expansion of special interest delegates at future Democratic conventions. By stipulating that at least 14 percent of the 1984 Democratic delegate seats be reserved for elected officeholders and professional politicians listed as officially uncommitted, the Hunt Commission's recommendation (already approved as an official rule for the 1984 convention by the Democratic National Committee) should reduce, to some extent, the number of delegate seats that the special interest groups have previously occupied. The rapid growth of special interest delegates over the past 15 years, it would appear, has now generated a countervailing force within the Democratic party to reduce their influence at national conventions. Indeed, the new "ground rules" in the Democratic party now make it possible to select a bloc of party professionals more attuned to compromise and more concerned than the special interest zealots about selecting an electable nominee.

If an increasing number of single interest group delegates pledged to specific candidates should continue to be elected to national conventions, voting behavior of the delegates and the functions of national conventions can be expected to undergo further changes. As Christopher Arterton has noted recently:

To the extent that conventions have become arenas for competing candidate organizations, the question of the correspondence of delegate attitudes on public policy issues to the attitudes of party voters becomes a tangential matter. Rather, as delegates come to resemble mere instruments of their campaign, the germane issues involve mechanisms for insuring delegate loyalty and the correspondence in candidate preferences between voters and convention delegates. Second, in a candidate-centered convention, platform-writing and party governance issues will naturally and inextricably become linked to the nomination question. Although the platform and rule issues do provide real and symbolic prizes, useful for unifying the party around the nomination outcome, we need to consider the consequences of having all party business determined by the nomination struggle. Such a system is tantamount to parties being no more than arenas for party competition.[64]

This topic will be discussed further in the final chapter.

Public Funding of National Conventions

Until 1974, both major parties always picked up the tab for the entire cost of conducting their national nominating conventions. But this was not all out-of-pocket for the parties. In one manner or another, parties managed to recapture most convention costs by obtaining heavy financial pledges or services-in-kind offers from the convention city. In 1967, for example, Miami Beach officials offered the Republican National Committee $850,000 (a new high) to hold their 1968 convention on the sun-drenched shores of Biscayne Bay. To keep the Democrats from also holding their 1968 convention in Miami Beach, Chicago Mayor Richard J. Daley and his businessmen associates topped the Floridian bid by offering the Democrats just under $1 million to hold their national convention in the Windy City. In addition, both parties invariably collected substantial sums from solicitation of corporate advertising ($10,000 to $15,000 per page) for the official convention program book. But in 1974, the traditional way of funding conventions was altered in the aftermath of the Watergate scandals. Congress decided that it was bad public policy to expect political parties to pay the full cost of national conventions by, in effect, forcing the parties to solicit large sums (several millions) from major corporations and special interest groups via corporate advertising in the party's official convention program.

During 1975, the Republican National Committee (RNC) opposed in principle the public funding of their 1976 convention. The RNC adopted a resolution against accepting the money while seeking alternate private sources. But when they failed to locate the needed convention funds, and not wanting to yield any special advantage to their Democratic counterparts, the GOP reluctantly agreed to accept Uncle Sam's money to help underwrite their 1976 convention.

Amendments to the Federal Election Campaign Act of 1974 established for the first time an option for public financing of party conventions.[65] Yet, the new law and the Federal Election Commission (FEC), charged with administering the new law, left partially intact the parties' privilege of soliciting private and municipal funds to help defray the cost of running the national conventions because the $2.2 million federal subsidy did not cover the full cost of running the quadrennial conclaves. Indeed, it fell far short of the total bill. Direct and indirect costs (which included the heavy security protection costs) for each of the 1976 conventions were in the neighborhood of $8 million. Direct subsidies from New York City to the 1976 Democratic National Convention, for example, totaled $3,630,000![66]

In shifting toward partial public funding of national conventions, Congress eliminated income tax deductions (listed as a business expense) for advertising in convention program books—a major source of funding for past party conventions. Previously, corporations simply charged these advertisements—more accurately, campaign contributions—as a standard business expense. In response to complaints from the Democratic and Republican national committees that the

$2.2 million federal subsidy was far too low to run a national convention, the FEC ruled that state and local governments could provide free-of-charge certain services and facilities such as convention halls, transportation, and security assistance—costs that would not count against the parties' expenditure limits in the general election campaign.

The Federal Election Commission also made two exceptions to the general prohibition on corporate contributions and free services. The first exception allowed the parties to accept such items as free hotel rooms and conference facilities in return for booking a certain number of room reservations, so long as other conventions of similar size and length received comparable benefits.[67] The FEC also made another exception concerning corporate contributions to host city committees and civic associations working to attract or assist the political conventions. National corporations with local branches were permitted to contribute to host committees as long as the contributions were made "in the reasonable expectation of a commensurate commercial return during the life of the convention."[68] Thus, by sanctioning the solicitation of certain corporate donations and municipal contributions, in addition to the federal subsidies, the FEC permitted a partial return to traditional private financing of national conventions. The chief advantage of the federal convention subsidy is that the $2.2 million federal nest egg permits both parties to conduct early convention planning and incur heavy bills, since they know that they can count on using Uncle Sam's dollars to help meet many of these heavy pre-convention costs.

By way of summary, national conventions in the twentieth century have more than doubled in size (tripled in the Democratic party) over their nineteenth century counterparts. Convention cities are still selected with a dual goal in mind: (a) to select a city in a state that can strengthen the party's chances of victory in the presidential election and (b) to choose a large city with adequate convention facilities and hotel rooms for delegates and the mass media. Representatives of the mass media now outnumber the convention delegates by ratios of four or five to one, and this ratio continues to grow each four years. Delegate apportionment rules continue to be scrutinized closely in both parties—and by the federal courts, in a few cases— because state party leaders know that apportionment rules determine how big a voice each state will have when it comes time to ballot for the presidential nominee. As a result of party reforms and the rapid spread of presidential primaries, the number of elected officeholders and professional politicians serving as delegates has declined seriously in recent years, chiefly because they do not wish to risk defeat supporting the wrong contender in the delegate race, nor do they want to alienate the large corps of party activists and political amateurs seeking delegate seats. Delegates to recent conventions in both parties consist mostly of the well-educated, upper middle-class partisans who become involved in politics for ideological or policy reasons, not patronage jobs. Delegates of Republican conventions tend to be more conservative than rank-and-file GOP voters, and delegates of Democratic conventions are, by and large, more liberal in their political orientation than rank-and-file Democratic voters. Recent conventions have also seen a steady growth of organized interest group representation, for example, trade union delegates, teachers, minority groups, "pro-Life" advocates, members of the "Moral Majority," and a variety of other groups wishing to advance their special causes. Since 1974, national conventions have received federal subsidies ($4 million in 1980) to help underwrite the cost, but Uncle Sam's allocation has been insufficient to meet the expenses of putting on these quadrennial extravaganzas. Consequently, the Federal Election Commission has agreed to permit host city committees to contribute several million dollars to underwrite transportation, convention site security (also subsidized by federal law enforcement agencies), and convention hall remodeling costs. This joint public-private financing of national conventions appears to be a sensible compromise for all parties concerned.

Unlike the raucous, unpredictable conventions of yesteryear, national conventions in the reform era have become tightly programmed mass rallies with relatively few surprises. To many party veterans, the convention schedule has been carefully tailored for the television networks and their multi-million member viewing audience, not the parties or the individual delegates. More than anything else, this absence of spontaneity and emphasis on conflict avoidance differentiates the streamlined modern convention from the wide open national conclaves of the pre-television era.

So much for the planning and mechanics of a national convention. The next chapter will discuss the actual gavel-to-gavel operation of a typical national convention.

Notes

1. Lincoln's biographer, Carl Sandburg, tells us that the second national convention of the Republican party at the Wigwam in Chicago in 1860 had many of the elements associated with modern national conventions. Some 40,000 visitors, 500 delegates, and 900 reporters jammed the Windy City whose population, according to the recently compiled census, exceeded 106,000 inhabitants. Straw votes of the delegates conducted on the dozens of trains converging on the city from all directions showed Senator William Seward of New York to be the front-runner. According to Sandburg, an enthusiastic staff of "Lincoln hustlers, evangelists, salesmen, pleaders, exhorters, schemers" and, it might be added, veteran politicians spread out from the headquarters hotel to strike bargains with the vitally important Indiana and Pennsylvania delegations, offering Cabinet posts (without Lincoln's knowledge) in return for delegate votes and collecting political debts from various political and business associates throughout the Midwest. Inside the newly constructed convention hall, Lincoln's Chicago managers carefully arranged the state delegation seating to isolate key supporters of the favored Seward from effectively communicating with each other. Moreover, Lincoln's people quietly printed hundreds of counterfeit visitor passes to pack the galleries with the Rail Splitter's vociferous supporters on the crucial third day of the convention. Carl Sandburg, *Abraham Lincoln: The Prairie Years*, Vol. 2 (New York: Harcourt, Brace and Company, 1926), pp. 339-47.

2. Hugh A. Bone, *Party Committees and National Politics* (Seattle, Wash.: University of Washington Press, 1958), p. 4.

3. Cornelius P. Cotter and Bernard C. Hennessey, *Politics without Power: The National Party Committee* (New York: Atherton Press, 1964), p. 16.

4. To reinforce the role of the national committee in convention planning, however, the Democratic National Committee, in 1971, established a fourth standing committee— the Committee on Arrangements. Proposed by the O'Hara Commission on convention reform, the newly established committee, consisting of fifteen members elected by the Democratic National Committee, was given full authority over the convention's operations, except as otherwise provided for in the Rules. The Committee's responsibilities included: housing, communications, delegate seating, security, transportation, and finance. Each presidential candidate was also authorized to appoint a non-voting representative to the Arrangements Committee to see that the candidate's supporters received fair treatment in all aspects of the convention planning. *Call to Order*, Report of the Commission on Rules of the Democratic National Committee, Rep. James G. O'Hara, Chairman (Washington, D.C.: Democratic National Committee, 1972), pp. 35-36.

5. Paul T. David, Ralph M. Goldman, and Richard C. Bain, *The Politics of National Party Conventions* (Washington, D.C.: The Brookings Institution, 1960), p. 213.

6. Alexander M. Bickel, *The New Age of Political Reform: The Electoral College, the Convention and the Party* (New York: Harper & Row, 1968), p. 40.

7. The last Liberal party convention, held in 1968, that selected Mr. Trudeau had a total of 2,366 voting delegates. Ten years earlier, the Liberal convention that picked Lester B. Pearson as its leader in 1958 had 1,380 voting delegates in attendance. John C. Courtney, *The Selection of National Party Leaders in Canada* (Hamden, Conn.: The Shoe String Press, Inc., 1973), pp. 146-47.

8. Herbert E. Alexander, *Financing the 1976 Election* (Washington, D.C.: Congressional Quarterly Press, 1979), pp. 342-43.

9. *Call to Order*, p. 80.

10. Richard Reeves, *Convention* (New York: Harcourt Brace Jovanovich, 1977), p. 62; Herbert E. Alexander, *Financing the 1976 Election*, p. 346.

11. Morton Kondracke, "The GOP Gets Its Act Together," *New York Times Magazine* (July 13, 1980), p. 18.

12. Judith H. Parris, *The Convention Problem* (Washington, D.C.: The Brookings Institution, 1972), pp. 164-65.

13. *Final Call, The Democratic National Convention, 1980* (Washington, D.C.: Democratic National Committee, May 29, 1979).

14. I am indebted to John S. Jackson, III, for this observation.

15. The term "rotten borough," borrowed from British politics, refers to an election district that has many fewer inhabitants than other election districts with the same voting power. In the nineteenth century, one rotten borough in Great Britain along the North Sea was reported to be completely under water at high tide.

16. Paul T. David, Ralph M. Goldman, and Richard C. Bain, *The Politics of National Party Conventions*, pp. 166-67.

17. To win over the reluctant Southern delegations, FDR's managers promised to obtain additional representation for the South in the form of "bonus" votes at future conventions. Roosevelt and his high command did not want to risk the fate of two earlier Democratic front-runners—Martin Van Buren and Champ Clark—who had received convention majorities but then failed to reach the required two-thirds mark.

18. Paul T. David, Ralph M. Goldman, and Richard C. Bain, *The Politics of National Party Conventions*, p. 29.

19. Richard C. Bain and Judith H. Parris, *Convention Decisions and Voting Records*, 2nd ed. (Washington, D.C.: The Brookings Institution, 1973), p. 21.

20. Paul T. David, Ralph M. Goldman, and Richard C. Bain, *The Politics of National Party Conventions*, p. 165.

21. Democratic National Committee (DNC) *Proceedings*, 1924, p. 5, as quoted by David, Goldman, and Bain, p. 165.

22. Ibid., p. 168.

23. Ibid.

24. *Openness, Participation and Party Building: Reforms for a Stronger Democratic Party*, Report of the Commission on Presidential Nomination and Party Structure (Winograd Commission) (Washington, D.C.: Democratic National Committee, 1978), pp. 100-101.

25. In 1984, the Democratic delegate total will be 3,921—an increase of 590 delegates (or almost 15 percent) over 1980. *New York Times*, January 7, 1983.

26. This litigation is discussed more fully by Charles Longley, "Party Nationalization in America," in William J. Crotty, ed., *Paths to Political Reform* (Lexington, Mass.: D.C. Heath and Company, 1980), pp. 184-85.

27. F. Rhodes Cook, "National Conventions and Delegate Selection: An Overview," in Jeff Fishel, ed., *Parties and Elections in an Anti-Party Age* (Bloomington, Ind.: University of Indiana Press, 1978), p. 201.

28. Paul T. David, Ralph M. Goldman, and Richard C. Bain, *The Politics of National Party Conventions*, pp. 165-66.

29. Ibid., p. 166.

30. George E. Mowry, *Theodore Roosevelt and the Progressive Movement* (Madison, Wis.: University of Wisconsin Press, 1947), p. 241.

31. Paul T. David, Ralph M. Goldman, and Richard C. Bain, *The Politics of National Party Conventions*, p. 167, footnote 11. Source of this information is *New York Times*, December 18, 1913.

32. Howard R. Penniman, *Sait's American Parties and Elections*, 5th ed. (New York: Appleton-Century-Crofts, 1952), p. 400.

33. Paul T. David, Ralph M. Goldman, and Richard C. Bain, *The Politics of National Party Conventions*, p. 167.

34. In 1956, the rules were amended to make clear that votes for the Republican candidate for President would be recognized even when the candidate had received the votes as an "independent" (as in Mississippi and South Carolina in 1952). RNC *Proceedings*, 1956, p. 162, as quoted by David, Goldman, and Bain, p. 167, footnote 15.

35. *New York Times*, August 22, 1972.

36. "GOP Convention Rules Adopted without Dispute," *Congressional Quarterly Weekly Report*, Vol. 38 (July 19, 1980), p. 2012.

37. For additional information on the presidential primary and caucus-convention systems, see James W. Davis, *Presidential Primaries: Road to the White House*, 2nd ed. (Westport, Conn.: Greenwood Press, 1980), chapter 3.

38. For further discussion of the Supreme Court's ruling on the Wisconsin open primary, see below, chapter 3, pp. 97-99.

39. *Openness, Participation, and Party Building: Reforms for a Stronger Democratic Party*, Report of the Commission on Presidential Nomination and Party Structure (Washington, D.C.: Democratic National Committee, 1978), p. 54.

40. In 1976, however, the Ford-controlled Republican convention adopted a rule (Rule 18) binding delegates elected in primaries to vote according to their delegate pledge, if

required by state law. Four years later, President Carter's forces pushed through a "faithful delegate" rule, requiring Democratic delegates to vote in accordance with their delegate commitment made at the time they announced their candidacy.

41. The Hunt Commission, the Democratic reform task force drafting the 1984 delegate selection rules, has already agreed without dissent to repeal this rule for the 1984 Democratic convention.

42. Leon D. Epstein, "Political Science and Presidential Nomination," *Political Science Quarterly*, Vol. 93 (Summer 1978), p. 187.

43. Thomas R. Marshall, "Caucuses and Primaries: Measuring Reform in the Presidential Nomination Process," *American Politics Quarterly*, Vol.7 (April 1979), pp. 155-74.

44. According to the Charter draft, "Membership in the Democratic Party of the United States shall be by periodic registration in a manner specified by the Democratic National Committee. Members. . .shall be eligible to vote for congressional district delegates to regional and national conferences only if they have been members continuously for at least 30 days prior to such vote. . . ." The entire draft Charter of the Democratic Party of the United States will be found in *Call to Order*, appendix D.

45. Loch K. Johnson and Harlan Hahn, "Delegate Turnover at National Party Conventions," in Donald R. Matthews, ed., *Perspectives on Presidential Selection* (Washington, D.C.: The Brookings Institution, 1973), pp. 147-48. The Johnson-Hahn study, based upon the official rosters of the Republican and Democratic national conventions between 1944 and 1968, included more than 50,000 delegates and alternates.

46. Ibid., p. 149, footnote 15.

47. Thomas H. Roback, "Recruitment and Motives for National Convention Activism: Republican Delegates in 1972 and 1976," in William J. Crotty, ed., *The Party Symbol* (San Francisco: W.H. Freeman, 1980), pp. 193-94.

48. Ibid.

49. *1980 Results of Survey of Political Party Leaders*, data supplied by John S. Jackson, III, to author.

50. Warren J. Mitofsky and Martin Plissner, "The Making of the Delegates, 1968-1980," *Public Opinion*, Vol. 3 (October-November 1980), p. 43.

51. Jeane J. Kirkpatrick, *The New Presidential Elite: Men and Women in National Politics* (New York: Russell Sage Foundation and the Twentieth Century Fund, 1976), chapter 3.

52. *Washington Post*, August 11, 1980.

53. Thomas Roback, "Recruitment and Motives for National Convention Activism: Republican Delegates in 1972 and 1976," p. 194.

54. M.I. Ostrogorski, *Democracy and the Organization of Political Parties*, Vol. 2, translated by Frederick Clarke (New York: The Macmillan Company, 1902), pp. 278-79.

55. Warren J. Mitofsky and Martin Plissner, "The Making of the Delegates, 1968-1980," p. 42.

56. Ibid.

57. Ibid.

58. Herbert McClosky, Paul J. Hoffman, and Rosemary O'Hara, "Issue Conflict and Consensus among Party Leaders and Followers," *American Political Science Review*, Vol. 54 (1960), pp. 406-27.

59. Jeane J. Kirkpatrick, *The New Presidential Elite*, chapter 2.

60. John S. Jackson III, Barbara Leavitt Brown, and David Bostis, "Herbert McClosky

and Friends Revisited, 1980 Democratic and Republican Elites Compared to the Mass Public," *American Politics Quarterly*, Vol. 10 (April 1982), pp. 158-80.

61. Ibid.

62. For further details on NEA influence in the 1980 Democratic nominating sweepstakes, see "Teacher Organization Unites Behind Carter—For a Price," *Congressional Quarterly Weekly Report*, Vol. 38 (August 9, 1980), pp. 2277-79.

63. Under federation rules, however, members of the 99 affiliated unions would still be free to continue backing a candidate not chosen by the union's policy-making body, according to AFL-CIO President Lane Kirkland. *New York Times* August 6, 1982; see also "Labor's Love," *Time*, Vol. 120 (August 16, 1982), p. 31.

64. F. Christopher Arterton, "Strategies and Tactics of Candidate Organizations," *Political Science Quarterly*, Vol. 92 (Winter 1977-1978), pp. 663-71.

65. Herbert E. Alexander, *Financing the 1976 Election*, p. 339.

66. Ibid.

67. Ibid., p. 340.

68. Ibid., p. 341.

Convention Preliminaries ⎯⎯⎯⎯⎯⎯ 4

> It's the Fourth of July celebration of national politics. It's a clambake
> of big politicians. . . . But as bad as we are, and as funny as we
> do things, we are better off than the other countries, so bring on
> more conventions.
>
> Will Rogers

The mounting tempo of excitement that accompanies the national convention can
be detected several days before the curtain rises at the quadrennial extravaganza.
Already the headquarters of the various contenders, especially the front-runner,
are operating at a frantic pace. To add to the excitement and confusion, hundreds
of television network staff personnel and newsmen descend upon the convention
city to report on "the greatest show on earth." According to the *New York Times*,
the news media in 1980 outnumbered the Republican delegates at the Detroit
convention by more than a five to one ratio. Over 10,000 reporters, editors,
cameramen, and technicians—some estimates placed the number closer to
12,000—swamped the Joe Louis Arena and its environs in the Motor City, while
the 1,994 delegates prepared to nominate the GOP front-runner, Ronald Reagan,
as its standard-bearer. At the 1980 Democratic National Convention in New
York City, the media outnumbered the delegates by a ratio of more than three to
one—11,500 media representatives versus 3,381 delegates.[1]

By the time the 50-state delegations and territorial representatives begin flock-
ing into the convention city the weekend before the opening session, the platform
committee has already been hard at work putting the final touches on the careful
phraseology of the various planks.[2] The credentials committee will also be in
session, striving to arrive at an amicable compromise on contested delegation
controversies or merely checking out the delegates' documentation, if there are
no challenges. Until 1972, all of these major convention committees in both
parties provided equal representation to all 50 states in the Union—another
recognition of the confederate nature of American parties. Thus, the platform

committee in each party had two members, one man and one woman, from each state; the same arrangement was also followed on the other regular committees. But at the 1972 Democratic convention it was decided that large states with a heavy Democratic vote would be given weighted representation and the small states only one vote.

The final pre-convention hours are usually marked by various party festivities—receptions, cocktail parties, dinners, and caucus meetings of the various state delegations—as the tension builds up and the curtain rises on the great political drama.

Order of Business

Despite the carnival-like atmosphere of the convention, the usual order of business does not vary much from one convention to the next. On the first day (usually a Monday) the delegates listen to the various welcoming addresses, approve the installation of temporary officers and the formal appointment of committees (which have been tentatively selected several months earlier by the national committee), and listen to the keynote address. (See Figure 2 for a copy of the 1980 Republican convention agenda.)

The chief item of business on the second day is devoted to the committee reports. It is at this juncture that heated floor fights over the seating of contested delegations may take place. Once these disputes have been settled, the convention is ready to consider the party platform.

The climax of the convention comes on the third day with the nomination of the various presidential contenders and the selection of the nominee. Nominating speeches and balloting for the party's presidential candidate may extend into the late evening hours—and into the next day, if necessary. Since 1956, however, presidential nominees in both parties have all been selected on the first ballot.

The fourth day of the convention is somewhat anticlimactic as the delegates select the vice presidential candidate—usually the handpicked choice of the presidential nominee. After the two nominees for the national ticket make their formal acceptance speeches, the defeated contenders are invited to the podium to share briefly the limelight, arm-in arm with the nominee, and to pledge their full support against the opposition in the fall campaign. The curtain then rings down for another four years. The delegates then turn homeward, emotionally exhausted from nearly a week of sleepless nights and endless speeches, but usually confident that their party is destined for victory in November. Not for another four years will the supreme governing-body of the national party convene again in convention hall for another ritualistic series of tribal rites that presage the nomination of another presidential candidate or the renomination of an incumbent. Let's take a few moments to review the step-by-step operation of a typical national convention.

Before the delegates sit back to hear the keynote speaker deliver an old-fashioned speech praising his own party to the rafters while thoroughly blistering

FIGURE 2
THE ANNOUNCED SCHEDULE OF MAJOR EVENTS AT THE 1980
REPUBLICAN NATIONAL CONVENTION
(ALL TIMES ARE EASTERN DAYLIGHT.)

Joe Louis Arena, Detroit
Monday, July 14, 1980
First Session (11 A.M.)

Call to order: Bill Brock, party chairman
Pledge of allegiance: Pat Boone
National anthem: Glen Campbell and Tanya Tucker
Address: Mayor Coleman A. Young of Detroit
Roll-call for the convention
Election of temporary chairman
Adoption of rules
Address: Senator Richard G. Lugar of Indiana

Second Session (8 P.M.)
National anthem: Representative Robert H. Michel of Illinois
Invocation: The Rev. Billy Graham
Address: Governor William G. Milliken of Michigan
Film on Alf Landon, introduced by his daughter, Senator Nancy Landon
    Kassebaum of Kansas
Addresses: Senator Kassebaum, temporary chairman
    William E. Simon, former Treasury Secretary
    Donald H. Rumsfeld, former Defense Secretary
    Former President Gerald R. Ford
    Benjamin Fernandez, former Presidential candidate
    Vincent Cianci Jr., Mayor of Providence, R.I.
Entertainment program, "Together...A New Beginning," with a cast including
    Susan Anton, Vikki Carr, Buddy Ebsen, Chad Everett, Dorothy Hamill,
    Gordie Howe, Michael Landon, Vicki Lawrence, Wayne Newton, Donny
    and Marie Osmond, Richard Petty, Ginger Rogers, James Stewart, Lyle
    Waggoner, Efrem Zimbalist, Jr.

Tuesday, July 15, 1980 (5 P.M.)
Pledge of allegiance: Don DeFore
Reports: Committee on Credentials
         Committee on Rules
         Committee on Permanent Organization
Address: Representative John J. Rhodes of Arizona,
    permanent chairman
Report: Committee on Resolutions (platform)
Addresses: Senator John W. Warner of Virginia
    Senator Barry Goldwater of Arizona
    Former Governor John B. Connally of Texas
    Anne Armstrong, former Ambassador to Britain
    Representative Jack F. Kemp of Buffalo
    Henry A. Kissinger, former Secretary of State
Keynote speech: Representative Guy Vander Jagt of Michigan

Wednesday, July 16, 1980 (7 P.M.)
Addresses: Governor David C. Treen of Louisiana
   Bill Brock
   George Bush, former Presidential candidate
Roll-call of states for nomination of Presidential candidate
Roll-call of states for selection of Presidential nominee

Thursday, July 17, 1980 (8 P.M.)
Address: Senator Howard H. Baker, Jr., of Tennessee
Roll-call of states for nomination of a Vice Presidential candidate
Roll-call of states for selection of Vice Presidential nominee
Acceptance speech of the Vice Presidential nominee
Acceptance speech of the Presidential nominee
Benediction

Source: Republican National Committee.

the opposition party, the temporary chairman is usually installed in routine fashion. If there is a floor fight over the temporary chairmanship (which is rare), one can usually detect signs of a badly divided party. The deep cleavages within the Republican party in 1912, for example, surfaced immediately during this opening session, as the Taft and Roosevelt factions squared off to battle over the temporary chairman (won by the Taft forces). To some veteran party professionals, the selection of the temporary chairman is more important than the permanent chairman.[3] Under normal convention procedure the permanent chairman isn't chosen until the delegate contests have been decided. Twice in this century (both times at GOP conventions), the rules under which delegates could be temporarily seated, and could vote while under challenge, have ultimately determined the nominee—Taft in 1912 and Eisenhower in 1952. In 1972, Democratic temporary Chairman Lawrence F. O'Brien's favorable ruling on the seating of part of the challenged California delegation paved the way for Senator George McGovern's nomination. Especially in the out-of-power party, the temporary chairman's rulings can convey or withhold tactical advantage to rival candidates. Generally, though, the selection of the temporary chairman and keynote speaker has already been ironed out at earlier planning sessions of the national committee.

Selection of Permanent Officers and Action on Committee Reports

On the second day of the convention the party officers and committee chairmen begin to roll up their sleeves for the serious business ahead. First of all, the permanent chairman and the chairmen of the various committees must be approved. Ordinarily, the delegates endorse these selections *pro forma*. Indeed, the name of the scheduled permanent chairman has already been publicized for several months, since his name has been proposed at an earlier meeting of the party's national committee. The last big fight over the permanent chairmanship occurred in 1932 between the forces of Governor Franklin D. Roosevelt and the 1928 Democratic presidential nominee, Alfred E. Smith. The selection of Roosevelt's choice—Senator Thomas Walsh of Montana—was the tip-off that FDR held the inside track for the nomination, which he won on the fourth ballot.

The strategic importance of the permanent chairman's power of recognition and his rulings on motions for a recess or adjournment on the day's proceedings can sometimes be decisive. In 1940, for example, Senator John Bricker of Ohio, a key backer of his fellow Ohioan—the late Senator Robert A. Taft—moved for a recess before the crucial sixth ballot. This recess might have enabled the Taft and Dewey forces to make a deal and thereby halt the surging Willkie drive. Convention Chairman Joseph Martin, who was sympathetic to the Willkie cause, refused the request; Willkie won the nomination on the sixth ballot.[4] The advent of televised convention proceedings has probably lessened the possibility of cavalier, unfair rulings from the chair (for fear of alienating many independent voters watching), but the role of the permanent chairman should not be underestimated.

As soon as the permanent chairman has been installed, the other three major committees—Rules, Credentials, and Platform—offer their reports. If there are to be any firefights, this is the time they will break out.

Rules Committee Report

Veteran politicians, aware that control over the rules more often than not translates into control over events, always keep a watchful eye on the Rules Committee of the national conventions. Perhaps the most important battle over convention rules in recent times occurred at the 1952 Republican National Convention in Chicago. Focal point of the bitter fight between the forces of General Dwight D. Eisenhower and Senator Robert A. Taft was the so-called "fair play" resolution, on contested delegations in Texas, Georgia, and Louisiana, offered by the underdog Eisenhower forces. Prior to the convention, the Taft-dominated national committee had recommended by majorities of 60 percent to 40 percent to seat the Taft delegates from Georgia, most of the delegates from Louisiana, and to split the Texas delegates with a majority portion going to Taft. But the astute Eisenhower convention managers cleverly moved adoption of the "fair play" amendment to the rules, suggested earlier by the Republican governors' "manifesto" drafted at a recent governors' conference in Houston, to restrict the voting rights of delegates on the temporary roll call if they had been seated by less than a two-thirds vote in the national committee. On this crucial vote, which had been preceded by some of the most emotional speeches in memory, especially by the Eisenhowerites, the Taft forces lost by a 658 to 548 vote, despite inclusion of 47 challenged votes in the Taft count.[5] Senator Taft may not have realized it, but the final vote on the "fair play" resolution spelled defeat of his candidacy. Indeed, after the floor debate on the contested delegations, Taft lost the vote on the Georgia delegation and conceded the Texas delegation after another flurry of dramatic arguments—"Thou Shalt Not Steal"—by the Eisenhower spokesmen. (Earlier the Taft members on the credentials committee had conceded the Louisiana delegates to Eisenhower.) Seldom, if ever, has the tide of a convention shifted so rapidly—and all under the relentless eye of the newly present television cameras. (The 1952 conventions were the first to be televised nationwide by the three networks.)

At the 1968 Democratic National Convention a heated controversy erupted over the so-called "unit rule," requiring all members of a state delegation instructed under this rule to vote according to the wishes of the delegation majority. Earlier, the supporters of Senator Eugene McCarthy had pushed Vice President Humphrey and his convention majority to join forces to put an end to the undemocratic unit rule. This strategy was aimed primarily at several Southern delegations still adhering to the unit rule. Unhappily for Humphrey, most of these Southerners were Humphrey backers. After a short, heated debate the unit rule was abolished on a voice vote. Not only was the unit rule declared illegal at the 1968 and all future conventions, but the committee report also stated that the unit rule would not be used in any state or local party proceedings either. A last-minute attempt by the Humphreyites to mollify the huge 104-member Texas delegation (which had long used the unit rule) by delaying application of the unit rule ban until the 1972 national convention was voted down with a resounding "no."[6]

In 1976, the Republican National Convention treated millions of television viewers to one brief but decisive rules debate between the rival forces of President Ford and Ronald Reagan. Supporters of the former California governor, faced with a 110-delegate vote deficit in the closing days of the pre-convention race and desperate to shake loose some "soft" Ford delegates in the final hours before the balloting began, proposed a rule change that would have required President Ford to indicate his choice for vice president before the vote for president, just as Reagan had done in announcing that Senator Richard Schweiker (R.-Pa.) would be his choice for running-mate if he were nominated. But the Ford forces, sensing a nomination victory within their grasp, voted down this Reagan stratagem, 1,180 to 1,069.[7] The vote on this rule change also foretold the GOP choice for nominee would be President Ford. On the first ballot he won the nomination by the almost identical vote 1,187 to 1,070. No wonder convention experts monitor key rule votes for the tip-off on who most likely will be the nominee in a tight convention race.

The outcome of the 1980 Democratic nominating battle between President Jimmy Carter and Senator Ted Kennedy hinged, in the minds of most veteran observers, on the single roll of the dice—the convention vote on the "faithful delegate" rule change that would require delegates elected in the primaries or caucuses to vote according to their pledged commitment (made at the time of his or her election) for at least one ballot. Known officially as Rule 11(h) and more popularly, by its proponents, as the "faithful delegate" rule and by its opponents as the "bind and yank" rule, this proposed change in the 1980 Democratic convention rules became a key test between Carter and Kennedy. The proposed rule defined, in essence, the role of delegates at a national convention. Should they be able to cast their votes only for the candidate they were instructed, often months earlier, to represent, or should they be free as "trustees" to change their minds and vote their consciences? Clearly, this dispute symbolized the classic conflict between the Progressive instructed delegate versus the Burkean-party regular concept of representation delineated in Chapter 1.

President Carter's supporters, of course, favored adoption of the new "faithful delegate" rule since they had nearly a 600-vote lead over Kennedy in pledged delegates. Indeed, they viewed the proposed rule as a logical extension of the Democratic reform movement that, since 1968, had aimed to take the nominating process away from the party leaders and professional politicians and put it into the hands of rank-and-file voters in the primaries and caucuses. Senator Abraham Ribicoff (D.-Conn.) speaking for the pro-Carter forces supporting the loyalty rule, said that both the candidates had competed throughout the primaries with the understanding that delegate commitments were binding and that it wasn't fair to change the rules now. "It isn't fair to 19 million Democrats who voted," Ribicoff argued, "and it isn't fair to the candidates who won the most delegates."[8] If Rule 11(h) had been rejected by the convention majority, pledged Carter delegates would have been released of any binding commitment to vote for any candidate nominated. Kennedy and his supporters placed all their bets that enough "soft" Carter delegates would jump ship and vote for Kennedy who, though an underdog, had won five of eight final-round primaries, including victories in the big electoral vote states of California and New Jersey.

For the Kennedy team the proposed rule change was viewed as an unprecedented break with long-standing rules of Democratic conventions, dating back to President Andrew Jackson's era, that would take away each elected delegate's freedom of action to vote as he or she pleases. "No similar rule has ever been proposed, let alone adopted, in the 148 years of Democratic National Conventions," Senator Kennedy wrote in a two-page memorandum to all 1980 convention delegates. The Kennedyites argued that the proposed rule change would turn delegates into robots, forced to support a candidate they were chosen to represent many months earlier, no matter how events may have changed in the interim. With the formal nominating process stretched out from January to July, the rule opponents pointed out, a candidate may look very different at the time of the mid-January Iowa caucuses than in the final stretch before the July or August convention. If the new rule were in place, the Kennedyites said, the party might nominate a candidate who stands no chance of winning in November. Indeed, opponents of Rule 11(h), pushing their arguments to the limit, said that the binding rule could force delegates to vote for a candidate who had just been unmasked as "triple-ax murderer!" To counter this argument, Carter campaign aides noted that any convention rule could be suspended by a two-thirds vote of the delegates. But New York Governor Hugh L. Carey, who may have harbored presidential ambitions of his own, urged rejection of the instructed delegate rule, declaring that the issue was not between Kennedy or Carter but the future of the party and whether the Madison Square Garden convention would resemble "a central party conference" in a totalitarian country or would be "a typical Democratic convention in which unity is achieved through debate." His voice rising, "You're not cattle, you're delegates, and you have rights," Carey told the packed audience. "Don't give away the powers of yourselves as delegates," he concluded.[9]

Carter loyalist Dan Fowler, former South Carolina chairman, responded that the "plain, simple fact [was] that nobody raised the principle about a closed convention and robot delegates until it was clear who was winning the primaries and caucuses. Don't start the race and change the rules the last 20 yards."[10] The decisive roll call vote came after an hour of intense debate on prime-time television. Carter won handily 1,936.4 to 1,390.6 votes, with one abstention. "The vote pretty much rings down the curtain on the Democratic convention for this year," declared Senator John Durkin (D.-N.H.)—and he was right. Kennedy's defeat was sealed. Ninety minutes later, Senator Kennedy withdrew from the race, saying, "Carter's forces have won an impressive victory this evening and I'm a realist and I know what this result means. . . . The effort on the nomination is over."[11] All that remained for the Kennedy team was to challenge Carter's party platform, particularly the economic sections, and to propose some future rules changes dealing with the party charter and future party affairs. Unlike the bitter quarrel over the "faithful delegate" rule on the opening night of the 1980 Democratic convention, the second part of the Rules Report was approved without dissent two nights later. Originally scheduled for the final night of the convention, two other Kennedy-backed minority reports were heard a day earlier when a block of free time opened up. Both were approved by a voice vote. One of the minority reports that was approved prohibited members of the Democratic National Committee (DNC) from also serving on the party's Judicial Council, a party tribunal that acts as a type of supreme court in interpreting party rules. The second minority report approved called for a sweeping review of the Democratic presidential nominating process by the DNC. The report stipulated that the national committee should complete this assignment by the end of 1982. The Carter-backed majority report had proposed a more limited review by the DNC Executive Committee.[12] Adoption of this minority report paved the way for the establishment of the Democrats' fourth party reform task force in twelve years— the Commission on Presidential Nominations chaired by North Carolina Governor James B. Hunt, Jr. The Hunt Commission subsequently approved a number of recommendations on the presidential nominating process designed to increase the power of party regulars and give the 1984 convention more freedom to act on its own.

Looking ahead, it is safe to predict that the 1984 Democratic Convention will not see a replay of the 1980 fight over the faithful delegate rule. In March 1982, the Democratic National Committee, acting on recommendations from its Hunt Commission on presidential nominating rules, repealed this rule for the 1984

Convention and thus ended the threat of replacement of delegates who bolt their original choice. Instead, the new rule requires only that the delegates "reflect in good conscience the sentiments of those who elected them." However, the new rules preserve the right of the presidential candidate to approve all delegates running in his name.[13]

Credentials Committee Report

Generally speaking, the processing of delegate credentials is a routine matter at national conventions. But whenever one of the major parties is faced with a close nominating race, challenged credentials of rival state delegations have usually surfaced. Major convention battles have often revolved around the credentials of contesting rival delegations from one-party states, especially in the South. Until the late 1950's, southern Republican organizations usually consisted of self-appointed party officials who presided over thinly populated GOP constituencies and then arranged to select themselves as delegates to the national conventions. Whenever the chances of a Republican presidential victory were bright, the impending possibility of federal patronage in the area often attracted a second, competing GOP group—also self-appointed—into the delegate contests. Since each of the rival factions usually identified with a major presidential contender or the conservative and liberal factions within the national party, the odds were high that the two factional groups would collide head-on before the GOP Credentials Committee. It was almost a rule-of-thumb that the convention's decision on the seating of these competing delegations portended which major candidate would win the nomination. President William Howard Taft's victory over Teddy Roosevelt in the 1912 GOP credentials fight and Eisenhower's triumph over Robert A. Taft in the 1952 credentials controversy have already been cited as the best-known cases.

In recent years, the Democratic conventions have also been the scene of bitter controversy over the same general question—the credentials of competing Southern delegations. Unlike the GOP, however, most Democratic credentials fights have been offshoots of the civil rights movement, not the case of two rotten borough delegations quarreling over patronage plums.

At the 1964 Atlantic City convention, for example, a credentials fight emerged over the question of whether the "regular" Mississippi Democratic party could systematically discriminate against blacks in the selection of delegates. When the dust had settled at the convention, the integrated Free Democratic party of Mississippi had won only token representation—two at-large delegates in the state delegation. But it was not entirely a hollow victory, for the 1964 Democratic National Convention adopted a rule prohibiting such discriminatory practices against blacks in the future.[14] Four years later at the 1968 Chicago convention, this issue added fuel to an already volatile confrontation between the forces of Vice President Humphrey and Senator Eugene McCarthy. Challenges by integrated delegations against the segregationist old-guard Democratic delegations in

Mississippi, Georgia, Texas, and Alabama were reviewed, first by the Credentials Committee and then by the full convention. To the chagrin of many veteran Southern Democrats, the convention refused to seat the regular, all-white Mississippi Democratic delegation, replacing it with an integrated, moderate group. In a close decision on the Georgia contest the convention voted to seat both the conservative, "regular" Georgia delegation and the integrated McCarthy-oriented delegation led by Julian Bond, a young black Georgia legislator—each group receiving half of the allotted votes (one-half vote for each delegate) for Georgia.[15] The predominantly segregationist Texas and Alabama delegations, after the fight of their lives, won their seats by narrow margins.

In 1972, the final-round pre-convention skirmishing on delegate challenges at the Democratic national convention in Miami Beach was some of the most acrimonious in memory. Surprisingly, the two major pre-convention credentials challenges were fought in the courts, not in the political arena.

The showdown contest between George McGovern and the rival ABM (Anybody but McGovern) forces for control of the key convention delegates began on June 29, ten days before the convention. The firefight erupted when the anti-McGovern majority on the Democratic Credentials Committee (which had to handle more than 80 challenges involving over 1,300 delegates) voted to strip Senator McGovern of 151 of his 271-member California delegation. This move immediately reduced McGovern's delegate count to approximately 1,300 (1,509 were needed for nomination). With the ten pro-McGovern members of the Credentials Committee from California ineligible to vote on their own challenge, the committee majority asserted that the California "winner-take-all" primary law violated the party's reform commission rules. In the committee majority's view, the California law denied all other entrants—in this case, chiefly Hubert Humphrey, who won 39 percent of the California primary vote (1,352,379 voters) —of any representation on the California delegation. McGovern and his supporters cried "foul," claiming that Humphrey and other ABM backers were changing the rules after the game had been played. Humphrey, they pointed out, had not objected to the California winner-take-all law before the West Coast primary.

In retaliation, the Democratic Credentials Committee (with the ten pro-McGovern California delegates now eligible to vote) then unseated 59 uncommitted Illinois delegates of Chicago Major Richard J. Daley's organization, including the mayor himself, who had been duly elected in the Illinois presidential primary. According to the majority report, there were two reasons for unseating the Chicagoans: (a) these delegates had been "slated" in private meetings by Mayor Daley's organization, in violation of party reform rules, and (b) they did not reflect adequate numbers of women, young voters, or minority groups—also required by the reform guidelines.[16] Instead, the Credentials Committee replaced the Daley contingent with an insurgent group headed by dissident city alderman William Singer, composed of mostly pro-McGovern delegates who had not been popularly elected.

Supreme Court's Role in Settling Delegate Seating Disputes

The 1972 Democratic National Convention Credentials Committee's transactions triggered a flurry of court cases that ultimately reached the United States Supreme Court. Even before the convention opened, the McGovern and Daley forces appealed the Credentials Committee's ruling to the U.S. District Court in Washington, D.C. Federal District Judge George L. Hart, Jr., held that in the California case the Credentials Committee had not committed any unconstitutional acts that warranted court intervention. He stressed the reluctance of the courts to enter "the political thicket" of convention politics.

Two days later, however, the United States Court of Appeals in the District of Columbia restored to McGovern his 151 California delegates and upheld the Committee's unseating of the Daley slate. The Court of Appeals declared that the Democratic Credentials Committee had been "arbitrary and unconstitutional" in depriving Senator McGovern of 151 delegates. It awarded McGovern the full 271-vote California delegation. In the companion Illinois case the federal court denied seats to the Daley delegates and prohibited the Daley forces from pursuing an action in Illinois state courts to regain their seats.

Immediately, two appeals were carried to the United States Supreme Court, which had already adjourned for the summer. In an unprecedented move concerning political parties, Chief Justice Warren Burger summoned seven of his colleagues (only Justice William J. Brennan did not return to Washington) for a series of conferences and reconvocation of the tribunal, which had been done only three times in history.

Three days before the opening of the Democratic convention, the Supreme Court, in a six to three verdict, voted to stay (or block) the Court of Appeals ruling. In effect, the High Court stated that the federal judiciary had no business interfering with a political party's right to quarrel about its delegate representation. "For a century and a half the national parties themselves have determined controversies regarding the seating of delegates to their conventions," declared Chief Justice Burger.[17] The net result of the High Court's decision was to deprive Senator McGovern temporarily of his 151 California delegates and to throw the credentials controversy back to the nominating convention. It was small comfort to the McGovern camp that the Supreme Court simultaneously let stand a Credentials Committee vote to unseat Chicago Mayor Richard J. Daley and his 58 uncommitted delegates.

Technically, the Supreme Court did not pass judgment on the merits of the California and Illinois challengers. The court majority merely stayed the decision of the Court of Appeals until the fall session of the High Court. In a stinging dissent, Associate Justice Thurgood Marshall pointed out that by staying the lower court's ruling the Supreme Court could still take up the issue *after* the convention and perhaps "have no choice but to declare the convention null and void and to require that it be repealed."[18] But the Supreme Court having spoken, the Democrats resumed their feuding for the contested delegates. The outcome of this credentials battle, later events confirmed, was the indicator on who would be the 1972 Democratic nominee.

The McGovern forces, temporarily denied the 151 contested California delegates, intensified their lobbying for additional delegate support, and more importantly, sought a favorable parliamentary ruling on two points: (a) who could vote on the seating of the contested California and Illinois delegates and (b) how many votes were needed to win the challenges.

According to Rule 6E of the Democratic Convention, all questions before the convention "shall be determined by a majority vote of the delegates to the convention." But it was unclear to the convention managers as to what was meant by the word "majority." The anti-McGovern coalition forces argued that the word "majority" meant a majority of all the convention delegates—meaning that McGovern needed 1,509 votes to win the California challenge. The McGovern spokesman argued that it meant a majority of the convention delegates minus the 151 Californians—an interpretation that would permit them to win the credentials fight with fewer (1,433) votes.

FAVORABLE PARLIAMENTARY RULINGS

Some veteran convention-watchers felt that McGovern, in effect, won the nomination—even before the convention opened—on the basis of two favorable procedural rulings by Democratic National Chairman Lawrence O'Brien. In one ruling, O'Brien decreed that the 120 pro-McGovern California delegates not challenged by the anti-McGovern coalition were eligible to vote on the seating of the 151 challenged California delegates, awarded temporarily to the anti-McGovern forces. However, O'Brien ruled that the 151 anti-McGovern delegates under challenge could not vote on their own case. The chairman's other favorable procedural ruling permitted the California credentials issue to be settled by a majority of delegates eligible to vote (1,433), rather than by a majority of the entire convention (1,509 votes). If Democratic Chairman O'Brien (who also served as permanent Chairman of the Convention) had ruled that the 120 unchallenged pro-McGovern California delegates could not vote on the 151 challenged delegates, and if he had ruled that all credentials challenges must be decided by a majority of the entire convention (1,509 votes), Senator McGovern would have lost the California credentials challenge by eleven votes—and with it, possibly the nomination.[19]

Bolstered by these favorable parliamentary rulings, the McGovern forces were ready to meet the anti-McGovern coalition head-on at the opening session credentials fight. As the clerk read the roll, managers of the various contenders knew that the side which won the California roll call vote would control all major convention decisions, including the choice of the party nominee. The suspense lasted less than an hour. When the roll had been completed, McGovern had a clear majority with 1,616.28 votes—and the nomination. To be sure, the formal nomination would not take place for another two days, but the anti-McGovern forces knew they had lost the war.

One more credentials fight on the challenged Chicago delegates had to be resolved before the convention could settle down to platform-making. With the entire California delegation safely in McGovern's hands, the Chicago challenge was more likely to have an impact on the general election campaign in Illinois than on the outcome of the convention's choice for President. In an attempt to retain Mayor Daley's support—or at least to avoid a total break with the Chicago mayor whose political organization would be needed in the general election campaign—the McGovern high command tried unsuccessfully to push through a compromise plan giving half of the contested seats to Mayor Richard J.Daley's contingent and half to the liberal insurgents. But Daley rejected this compromise outright. Then, the convention rejected the minority report that would have seated Daley and 58 of his Chicago delegates, 1,371.55 to 1,486.45. Some old party hands declared that the McGovernites had won a battle that would cost them the general election—at least in Illinois. In retrospect, it more accurately helped cost them the national election, for the credentials challenges showed the 50-million-person national viewing audience that the Democrats were a party in complete disarray.

All convention activity after the California and Illinois challenges seemed almost anticlimactic. The Daley versus anti-Daley delegation fight, however, did not end with the Supreme Court's ruling that because there was insufficient time to conduct hearings and render an authoritative opinion on the constitutional questions involved, the issue would have to be decided by the Democratic party machinery.

SECOND ROUND OF LITIGATION

Soon after the Credentials Committee denied the Daley contingent their seats, one of the Daley delegates—acting on behalf of Mayor Daley—obtained an injunction from the Cook County (Chicago) Circuit Court prohibiting any anti-Daley delegates from taking their seats or acting as the legally recognized delegates from Illinois. Led by dissident alderman William Singer, the anti-Daley group ignored the Illinois injunction and participated fully in all of the convention proceedings. Shortly thereafter, criminal charges were initiated against the Singer group for disobeying the court injunction. The Illinois Appellate Court upheld the injunction, declaring that the election laws of Illinois were legally of higher standing than the rules of the national Democratic party. In the words of the Illinois court:

In this case, the law of the State is supreme and party rules to the contrary are of no effect.... We think the convention, a voluntary association, was without power or authority to deny the elected delegates their seats in the convention and most certainly could not force them upon the people of Illinois as their representatives contrary to their elective mandate. Such action is an absolute destruction of the democratic process of this nation and cannot be tolerated.[20]

Rebuffed in Illinois, the anti-Daley group appealed the Illinois decision to the United States Supreme Court. While the Illinois court's view was considered to be the prevailing interpretation of state versus national party authority, the Supreme Court overturned this traditional view.

In a landmark case, *Cousins v. Wigoda* (1975),[21] the High Court ruled that the national party rules are in most circumstances superior to state laws. Speaking for the majority, Justice William Brennan ruled that the right to organize and associate with others in a political party is part of the freedom of association protected by the First and Fourteenth Amendments of the U.S. Constitution. These rights can therefore be abridged or limited by state law only when "a compelling state interest" makes it absolutely necessary. In Justice Brennan's view, Illinois' interest in protecting the integrity and authority of its presidential primary was not sufficiently compelling to warrant any infringement of freedom of association—the right of the party to organize and conduct its presidential nominating convention. According to Justice Brennan, states have no constitutionally mandated role in the nomination of candidates for President and Vice President. Since this role is performed by the national party conventions, the party agencies have the final word about whether or not a delegation should be seated. The High Court concluded:

If the qualifications and eligibility of delegates to National Political Party Conventions were left to state law "each of the 50 states could establish the qualifications of its delegates to the various party conventions without regard to party policy, an obviously intolerable result." Such a regime could seriously undercut or indeed destroy the effectiveness of the National Party Convention as a concerted enterprise engaged in the vital process of choosing Presidential and Vice Presidential candidates—a process which usually involves coalitions cutting across state lines. The convention serves the pervasive national interest in the selection of candidates for national office, and this national interest is greater than the interest of any state.[22]

The concurring opinion of Justices Rehnquist, Burger, and Stewart indicated that while all national party rules may not be superior to all conflicting state laws under all circumstances, the justices did not specify the conditions under which state laws would prevail. On the basis of this definitive ruling by the U.S. Supreme Court on the supremacy of the national convention to resolve credentials disputes between rival state delegations, it seems unlikely that the national conventions would again see a replay of the same vitriolic confrontations that characterized the 1972 Democratic National Convention.

In 1976 and 1980, neither the Republican nor Democratic conventions had to review any serious credentials challenges, but a credentials dispute over the Wisconsin delegates, elected in an open, crossover primary, would undoubtedly have arisen at the 1980 Democratic conclave if the case were not still pending in the U.S. Supreme Court. The High Court did not hand down its decision until nearly a year after the 1980 Wisconsin presidential primary. But its ruling will, it seems fair to say, have a far-reaching effect on national-state party relations—in favor of the national party—in the presidential nominating process.

THE WISCONSIN "OPEN" PRIMARY CASE

By a 6 to 3 vote, the Supreme Court in the *Democratic Party of the United States et al. v. LaFollette et al.*[23] overturned a ruling of the Wisconsin Supreme Court, which ordered the Democratic National Convention to seat the Dairyland State's delegation in 1980, even though it had been chosen in violation of the national party's "Democrats-only" rule. The issue before the High Court was not the long-established open primary itself. At least 15 states conduct open or "crossover" presidential primaries that, like Wisconsin's, are not limited to enrolled members of any party; neither the Republican nor Democratic parties forbid this practice. But Democratic party rules insist that only Democrats may participate in that phase of the nominating process that selects delegates for the national convention. Under Wisconsin law, national convention delegates are chosen separately, by party caucuses, after the primary. Because these delegates are legally bound to vote at the national convention in accordance with the results of the open primary, the Democratic National Committee argued that the state delegation was not entitled to be seated at the convention. Before the 1980 convention the Democratic National Committee, in view of the impending court case, relented and agreed to seat the Dairyland State delegation—but without waiving its right to refuse to seat future delegations selected under the challenged open primary. Justice Potter Stewart, speaking for the majority, said that the open primary case was controlled by a 1975 case, *Cousins v. Wigoda*,[24] in which the Supreme Court ruled that the 1972 Democratic National Convention had the right to refuse to seat a popularly elected Illinois delegation that was chosen in violation of the national party's affirmative action rules on participation of women, young people, and minorities.

In the Illinois case, Justice William J. Brennan, Jr., upheld the national convention decision against state law because, he said, "the convention serves the pervasive national interest in the selection of candidates for national office, and this national interest is greater than interest of an individual state." Moreover, because "delegates perform a task of supreme importance to every citizen of the nation," Brennan ruled no single state may be permitted to dictate terms for its delegates that "could seriously undercut or indeed destroy the effectiveness of the National Party Convention as a concerted enterprise engaged in the vital process of choosing presidential and vice presidential candidates."[25] In the 1975 decision, the justices held that political parties are private organizations with rights of "free association" under the First Amendment.

This "freedom to associate for the common advancement of political beliefs," Justice Stewart added in the Wisconsin case, "necessarily presupposes the freedom to identify the people who comprise the association, and to limit the association to those people only."[26]

The High Court reviewed the history of the "Democrats-only" rule, adopted in

1976 to halt the crossover voting in open primaries. Crossover votes had the effect of diluting the votes of Democrats and distorting the outcome. The opinion noted in the 1972 Wisconsin open primary that 34 percent of the voters were non-Democrats and approximately 29 percent of the crossovers voted for Alabama Governor George Wallace. Wisconsin, the justices said, is free to make its own rules for holding primary elections, but the national Democratic party is free to ignore them, unless there is a "compelling" constitutional reason to the contrary.

Against this background, the High Court said that Wisconsin had failed to prove the "compelling interest" necessary to justify its "substantial intrusion into the associational freedom of members of the national party." The State of Wisconsin argued "that its law places only a minor burden on the national party." The national party's counsel argued that the burden is substantial because it prevents the party from screening out those whose affiliation is slight, tenuous, or floating, and "that such screening is essential to build a more effective and responsible party." In deciding for the Democratic National Committee, Stewart said, "It is not for the courts to mediate the merits of this dispute. For even if the state were correct, a state or a court may not constitutionally substitute its own judgment for that of the party." While it is still too early to predict what the full impact of the Wisconsin open primary decision will be upon the national convention delegate selection process, some veteran party-watchers believe that the High Court's decision will halt the further proliferation of presidential primaries. Further speculation about the Court's decision on the delegation selection process and the shifting power balance between the national and state parties will be reserved for the final chapter.

The rapid spread of presidential primaries to more than two-thirds of the states has, it must be conceded, helped eliminate credentials challenges because the voters decide the issue in the primary. It becomes simply a matter of counting votes of the various contenders; all factions and groups supporting delegates within the party have a fair and open chance to win. As Louise Overacker noted more than half a century ago in her early study of the presidential primary system, after the voters have spoken on primary day, the competing delegates know that they have won or lost fair and square.[27]

Understandably, both parties try to resolve credentials disputes before they reach the convention floor—and the television cameras. Based upon past history, however, it seems safe to predict that we have not seen the last of the contested delegation fights as competing factions within a state continue to wage all-out battles for voting power—and ultimately the nomination—at national conventions. Credentials fights have been almost as much a part of the convention activity as the keynote speaker and platform-making.

Platform Committee Report

Toward the end of the second day or early in the third, the chairman of the Committee on Resolutions and Platform is asked to make his report. Party platforms are almost as old as the national convention itself. In May 1840, the Democratic convention "adopted a statement of party principles called a 'platform.' "[28] A short document of less than 1,000 words, the Democratic platform espoused a strict construction of the Constitution. The platform stated that the federal government did not have the power to finance internal improvements, assume state debts, charter a national bank, or interfere with the rights of states, especially the question of slavery. The rival Whig party, fearful of its fragile anti-Democratic coalition, chose not to adopt a platform. In 1844, the Democrats did not write a platform, but both major parties approved platforms in 1848.

The platform-drafting function, which soon became a normal part of the convention framework, was an early outgrowth of occasional party efforts to prepare "an address to the people." Early platform-drafting was usually deferred until after the nomination had been made. In 1852, however, both Democrats and Whigs adopted their platforms before acting on nominations. This calculated action reflecting the parties' deep concern over the slavery issue was an attempt to avoid widening the fissures between the northern and southern wings within each party. This shrewd reordering of the convention agenda set a precedent that, with few exceptions, has prevailed ever since.[29]

In recent years the platform report has frequently been submitted as a single package to preclude amendments. Then the chairman moves its adoption. Party leaders understandably try to minimize intra-party differences and maximize the positive features of the document. Sometimes it will be approved in routine fashion, particularly if a majority of the convention delegates has just about agreed informally on their nominee. In other years, faction fights over the platform have been remindful of rival armies girding for battle. In any case, the platform presentation represents the culmination of several months' labor by the committee members and their staff.

Political commentators often treat platforms as so much empty rhetoric. The low esteem that most American voters hold for platform-making, however, is generally exceeded only by their ignorance of the contents of these party documents. Nor do the party platforms generate much enthusiasm among the party faithful. This disinterest mirrors the general view that party platforms have little relationship to subsequent governmental policy-making. Gerald Pomper has summarized the charges as follows:

1. Platform statements are essentially unimportant, ambiguous, and often contradictory. . . .
2. No differences exist between the platforms of the major parties. They are therefore of no value to the voter in making his choice of party.
3. The party principles are not binding on party candidates. The principle object of the platform is, in the present day, as formerly, to catch votes by trading on the credulity of the electors. . . .[30]

Three decades ago, David Truman observed, "The platform is generally regarded as a document that says little, binds no one, and is forgotten by politicians as quickly as possible after it is adopted.... Considered as a pledge of future action, the party platform is almost meaningless and is properly so regarded by the voters."[31] In a number of cases, it has been pointed out, the presidential candidate has actually repudiated platform planks with which he disagreed.[32]

On the surface, these criticisms seem valid. But party platforms are not just so much rhetoric, as the critics claim. Polsby and Wildavsky have noted, "Party platforms written by the presidential parties should be understood not as ends in themselves but as a means of obtaining and holding public office."[33] The party platform is, first and foremost, a campaign document. The 1980 Republican platform, for example, mentioned tax cuts 46 times! The platform also offers a party the priceless opportunity to fire a heavy broadside of verbal missiles against the opposition party. In 1980, for example, the Republicans placed virtually all the blame for the nation's problems on Democratic politicians, especially President Carter: "Divided, leaderless, unseeing, uncomprehending, they plod on with listless offerings of pale imitations of the same policies they have pursued so long, knowing full well their futility."[34]

Equally important, the document is a meaningful statement of principles and issue positions. Platforms, according to one long-time observer, have been depicted as "a form of national planning" for the party documents are "taken very seriously by federal officials who occupy positions on the White House staff, the Bureau of the Budget and elsewhere."[35] Though the platform is not binding on the nominee, the platform has been over the years a reasonably accurate guide to what party officeholders will endeavor to accomplish in the future. Parties and presidential candidates both know, too, that parties must fulfill their pledges to a reasonable extent if they are to maintain their credibility. Party constituencies and interest groups take the language, as well as the substance, of the platform planks very seriously.

But during the platform-drafting sessions, two conflicting aims frequently surface. The presidential nominee and his managers are looking for a document that will help win the Presidency but will not alienate important constituent groups within the party or frighten away the large bloc of independent voters (approximately one-third of the electorate) who often hold the key to an election victory. The platform, as one commentator has noted, can indicate "program initiatives made by parties in anticipation of voter needs and demands."[36] To maximize voter appeal, the platform planks are often purposely ambiguous or vague, or filled with excesses of campaign rhetoric. Wendell L. Willkie, the 1940 GOP nominee, once characterized platforms as "fusions of ambiguity." Generally, the platform will contain a laundry list of promises offering something for almost everyone. Indeed, in the past two decades party platforms have become longer and broader in scope as each major party endeavors to meet the needs and fulfill the aspirations of its various constituent groups. The 1972 Democratic platform, Frank J. Sorauf reminds us, was 20 times the length of the Declaration of Independence![37] The 1980 Republican platform—nearly 40,000 words—has now become the longest in history.

How important is the platform to the party and the nominee? Platform-making for the party out of power is a negotiation process through which the various factions may receive their rewards or payoffs before the presidential nominations start. If the platform were to be approved after the Presidential nominee had been selected, it would generate much less interest and would lose much of its viability as a consensus-building instrument. Furthermore, the platform cannot dictate future action because American parties, unlike their European counterparts, are not centralized or disciplined organizations capable of implementing policy decisions by enforcing their positions on the President or members of Congress. Despite the trend toward party nationalization of the delegate selection process, parties are still confederations of state and local organizations that lack sanctions to enforce a specific position upon the candidate.

The separation of powers, which often inhibits close legislative-executive cooperation, also affects platform implementation. The President, if elected, has no assurance that he can impose the platform pledges on his party in Congress. This is especially true in view of the fact that during the past 30 years (1952-1982) party control of the Presidency and Congress has been divided for more than half of this period. But even if a President and a majority of Congress are from the same party, the congressional majority may repudiate the party pledges. This raises the basic question: Can parties consistently fulfill their campaign pledges?

ARE PLATFORM PLEDGES FULFILLED?

Platforms would be useless documents for the mass electorate in promoting their own specialized interests or concerns unless the party manifesto presaged action. In a comprehensive study of platforms for two periods, 1944-1966 and 1966-1978, Pomper and Lederman have concluded that pledges are, in a majority of cases, redeemed (see Table 4). During 1944-1966, over half the platform commitments were met by direct congressional or executive action. If similar actions or inactions are included, nearly three-fourths of all promises were kept. Only 10 percent of partisan pledges were totally ignored.[38] During the decade of 1968-1978, almost two-thirds of all promises were fulfilled to some degree, with 30 percent directly enacted through congressional or executive initiatives.[39] The record of platform fulfillment during the past decade, however, is less impressive—almost one-third of the promises were not acted upon. Part of the explanation for this downturn could be attributed to the political turmoil of the Vietnam War era and also to the fact that two Republican presidents had to contend with overwhelmingly Democratic Congresses. Also, the 1972 Democratic platform—the longest in history—promised, in great detail, many benefits that only a minority in Congress favored. Finally, President Jimmy Carter, despite solid Democratic majorities in Congress, lacked the experience and skills in forging legislative majorities for his programs. A political outsider, Carter also had the misfortune to face an increasingly independent Congress (with its recently reformed committee structure) bent upon flexing its legislative muscle in the post-Watergate era. Given the political upheaval of the 1968-1978 decade, it is probably remark-

TABLE 4
FUFILLMENT OF PLATFORM PLEDGES, BY POLICY TOPICS
(IN PERCENTAGES OF TOTAL ACTION)

Policy Topic	Democratic	Republican	Bipartisan	In-Party	Out-Party	Total
Foreign						
1944-66	76	47	96	76	53	79
1968-78	51	67	67	66	51	61
Defense						
1944-66	86	62	86	91	53	74
1968-78	66	77	100	67	75	73
Economics						
1944-66	68	66	95	84	53	73
1968-78	74	67	100	75	66	73
Labor						
1944-66	39	50	64	54	26	50
1968-78	45	48	100	49	44	48
Agriculture						
1944-66	69	76	100	91	57	81
1968-78	60	74	69	62	67	66
Resources						
1944-66	84	72	96	90	62	84
1968-78	64	70	77	74	61	69
Welfare						
1944-66	66	56	97	73	54	72
1968-78	51	59	83	65	49	58
Government						
1944-66	54	60	44	74	43	55
1968-78	60	58	76	62	58	62
Civil Rights						
1944-66	50	62	63	67	50	60
1968-78	59	69	50	68	58	61
N TOTAL						
1944-66	(517)	(418)	(464)	(432)	(503)	(1,399)
N TOTAL						
1968-78	(920)	(608)	(267)	(637)	(891)	(1,795)

Source: From *ELECTIONS IN AMERICA: Control and Influence in Democratic Politics*, Second Edition by Gerald M. Pomper with Susan S. Lederman. Copyright © 1968, 1980 by Longman Inc. Reprinted by permission of Longman Inc., New York.

able that the pledge fulfillment record was as high as Pomper and Lederman found it to be.

Bipartisanship on platform issues almost assures some action will be taken. During 1968-1978, three-fourths of the bipartisan pledges were fulfilled. The record on bipartisanship was even higher for the 1944-1966 period—85 percent of the bipartisan pledges were fulfilled.[40] Even the party out-of-power but controlling Congress has been able to redeem better than half its own pledges. During the first four years of the Nixon administration, for example, the Democrats slightly outperformed the Republicans in percentage of platform pledges fulfilled—almost two-thirds of the Democratic promises were carried out.

Winning the Presidency made an appreciable difference in fulfilling platform pledges during the 1944-1966 period. In all categories of pledges, the in-power party achieved about four-fifths of its program, half again as much as the losers. During the 1968-1978 decade, the difference in winning the presidency added an average of only ten percent to the record of pledge fulfillment.[41] Accomplishment of platform goals, it should be noted, varies considerably by policy topic. Promises relating to social security benefits have been consistently redeemed, in keeping with the nature of the parties' commitments to significant constituent groups and the parties' propensity to emphasize material benefits. Indeed, for either party to be against social security would be tantamount to political suicide. During the 1944-1966 period, however, platform pledge fulfillment was notably lower in three designated areas: labor, government, and civil rights. Issues involving labor or civil rights groups invariably produced conflicts between rival power groups, especially during 1944-1966, that reduced the platform fulfillment record. In other words, the nature of the issues and the distribution of political power often affect the record of platform pledge fulfillment. In the final analysis, the many checks and balances of the American governing system are a major barrier to platform fulfillment.

In view of a record that shows two-thirds to three-quarters of all platform pledges over the past four decades have been kept in some fashion would seem to belie conventional wisdom that platform pledges are empty promises. Indeed, the party manifesto drafted at each quadrennial convention deserves a far better reputation as a directional beacon for the party and the President than platform critics have been willing to concede over the years. As Michael J. Malbin reminds us, "The fact that people fight over platforms and that their pledges generally are fulfilled should be enough to dispel the myth that they are unimportant."[42]

PLATFORM BUILDING

The platforms of both parties usually are the results of candidate pressure and lobbying action by interest groups as well as the deliberations of platform committees. Interest groups at national conventions have two major goals: the nomination of a friendly presidential candidate and the inclusion of favorable planks in the platform. To achieve their goals, the interest groups may seek direct voice in picking the nominee by obtaining representation in state delegations (the Michigan Democratic party delegation, for example, will usually contain 20 or 25 trade unionists—at least one-quarter of the delegation). In the past few years the National Education Association—the chief voice of secondary and primary school teachers—has been extremely successful in electing its members as delegates to Democratic conventions. To illustrate the political "clout" of this group, President Jimmy Carter owed his renomination victory over Senator Edward Kennedy at the 1980 Democratic convention to the NEA delegates as much as any constituency within the party. (In 1980, the NEA elected 302 delegates and another 162 alternates to the Democratic conclave in New York City.) Interest groups usually receive a sympathetic hearing from the platform committee, for the political party and the presidential candidate need the support of organized groups as much as these groups need the party's backing. Mass membership organizations, for example, the United Auto Workers and the National Education Association, can encourage their members to turn out in force on election day. Also, these organizations can provide parties with the sinews of war in the form of direct mailings, phones, volunteers or trained workers to conduct registration drives, and other campaign activities.

Why do interest groups put such heavy emphasis upon obtaining desired platform planks? As explained by Michael J. Malbin:

Having such planks can help a group achieve its policy objectives in at least two different ways. If the group's presence at the convention, and therefore its ability to win concessions, is based on its campaign activities, those same activities in the fall may result in some administration appointments. If the candidate's reluctance to endorse the group's plank is based on electoral tactics rather than substance, an appointment might settle the issue. If the group fails to gain such power through appointments, however, or if the president remains dubious for substantive reasons, the platform's promises still retain some influence. Virtually every group able to win a plank will have congressional allies. Presidents may choose not to honor a pledge, but doing so will mean alienating somebody in Congress.[43]

In 1960, for example, the Democrat platform members endured four solid days of hearings and listened to more than 70 prominent witnesses (mostly from special interest groups) present testimony which, when printed or mimeographed, weighed over 13 pounds![44] The Democratic party now conducts extensive preconvention hearings across the land throughout the late spring, gathering political input from all types of special interest and pressure groups.[45] In 1976, Democratic National Chairman Robert Strauss prodded the Democratic Platform Committee's original chairman, Philip Noel, into starting work on the party document nine months before the convention. Anxious to give all interested individuals and constituencies the opportunity to present their views, the Committee heard more than 500 witnesses at the various regional meetings and at the New York City convention.[46] In contrast, the Republicans began work on their 1976 platform only two months before their party conclave. Draft copies of the GOP platform prepared by members of the staff were circulated among the full committee when it initially met in Kansas City only a week before the national convention. For most of the committee this was their first opportunity to view the document, much less discuss it. To counter criticism that the platform draft had been prepared in secret by the White House staff, Governor Robert Ray of Iowa, chairman of the GOP Platform Committee, opened a week's hearings to gather further testimony, mainly from high government officials.

Just how much influence these pressure groups and officials have upon the final draft of the platform has never been fully determined. Their success rate varies from year to year. Sometimes the policies and language, as suggested by certain groups, have been incorporated into platform statements. In 1960, for example, the Democratic resolutions committee adopted the civil rights position urged on it by the National Association for the Advancement of Colored People (NAACP) and obtained approval of the plank by the full convention with minimal debate after three previous conventions had been badly split over this issue.[47] Twenty years later, the conservative Republican platform of 1980 mirrored the pressure group stance of the Right-to-Life and anti-ERA groups on abortion and the proposed Equal Rights Amendment. In any case, by listening to a parade of witnesses the party can claim that it has heard from all sides before drawing up the platform. Also, the platform hearings help satisfy the internal demands of pressure groups on their leaders, that is, the hearings enable the pressure group leaders to give the impression to rank-and-file members that the leader has attempted to sell the organization's point of view to the platform committee.

The careful reader of the party platforms will be able to discern, over a period of time, long-term policy differences that accurately reflect significant distinctions between Democrats and Republicans on such issues as medicare, abortion, federal aid to education, civil rights, housing, and the economy. Gerald Pomper, however, in his study of platforms for the period 1944-1976, found that sometimes the two parties differed in emphases more than in fundamental disagreement on major issues.[48] Over two-thirds of the 3,194 pledges in the platforms were made by only one party; less than one-fourth were made by both parties; and in the remainder of the pledges (mostly on bread and butter issues), the parties were in basic disagreement (see Table 5).

More recently, however, the distinctions between Republican and Democratic platforms were plainly evident in 1980 when the GOP platform, drafted by pro-Reagan partisans, echoed the former California governor's conservative views. In contrast, the Democratic platform came out four-square in support of the Equal Rights Amendment and abortion-on-demand, while the Republican document opposed both of these actions. The Democratic platform pledged to seek a national health insurance program; the Republican document endorsed improvement of existing Medicare-private insurance programs. The Republican platform supported a tax reduction program of 10 percent cuts annually for three years in a row, while the Democratic document committed the party to "targeted tax reductions designed to stimulate production and combat recession as soon as it appears so that tax reductions will not have a disproportionately inflationary effect." The GOP platform pledged drastic cuts in government spending, whereas the Democratic document "supported the discipline of attempting to live within the limits of our anticipated revenues." Significant differences also appeared on election

TABLE 5
SIMILARITY AND CONFLICT IN PLATFORM PLEDGES
(IN PERCENTAGES OF PLEDGES AND DESIGNATED YEAR OR TOPIC)

Year or Topic	(N)	One-Party Pledge Only	Bipartisan Pledges	Conflicting Pledges
Election Year				
1944	(102)	70	28	2
1948	(124)	51	42	7
1952	(205)	52	29	19
1956	(302)	61	34	5
1960	(464)	51	39	10
1964	(202)	70	19	11
1968	(457)	77	16	7
1972	(698)	83	13	5
1976	(640)	76	17	7
Policy Topic				
Foreign	(509)	60	34	6
Defense	(166)	74	22	4
Economics	(397)	76	15	9
Labor	(180)	65	17	18
Agriculture	(243)	66	27	7
Resources	(338)	69	22	9
Welfare	(696)	71	19	10
Government	(441)	78	18	4
Civil Rights	(225)	63	35	2
All Pledges	(3,194)	69	23	8
N Total	(3,194)	(2,218)	(731)	(245)

Sources: From ELECTIONS IN AMERICA: Control and Influence in Democratic Politics, Second Edition by Gerald M. Pomper with Susan S. Lederman. Copyright © 1968, 1980 by Longman Inc. Reprinted by permission of Longman Inc., New York.

Note: Rows add horizontally to 100% for the three percentage columns.

reform. The Democratic platform supported public financing of Congressional campaigns and lower contribution limits for political action committees; the Republican document opposed these measures. More than any time since 1964, the two major party platforms offered American voters a genuine choice of policies, not an "echo," in a number of major policy areas.[49]

As for the charge that platforms are ambiguous, a reading of several party platforms will show that the party document is vague and imprecise when the party tries to resolve or reconcile basic conflicts between competing forces within the party. As Gerald Pomper has noted, "When the party seeks to appeal to a wide range of interests, vagueness results. When the party feels that its electoral chances will be improved by an uncompromising appeal to one group, platforms will become clearer."[50] For the individual voter and the interest groups concerned with the outcome of the election, knowledge of those political leaders responsible for drafting the platform is usually a tip-off on the future direction of policy changes.

Still, several presidential candidates elected to the White House have refused to be bound by platform provisions when it seemed expedient or unwise. Arch-critics of President Franklin D. Roosevelt, for example, never tired of reminding him that the 1932 Democratic platform pledged to reduce government expenditures during the bottom of the Great Depression; yet within six months after taking office, FDR launched the country on a vast government "pump-priming" program to stimulate the sagging economy—at the cost of a huge multi-billion-dollar deficit during his first term. Another more recent illustration will be found in the 1964 Democratic platform. This document pledged to limit American involvement in Vietnam, but within a year President Johnson had sent more than 250,000 American troops to block the attempted Viet Cong-North Vietnamese takeover of South Vietnam.

If platforms can be ignored, the question might be legitimately asked, why do parties go to such great length to quibble over specific provisions? Even more basic, why have platforms at all? Why not have the two rival presidential candidates delineate their own position on the issues during the course of the campaign?

The answer to these questions will be found within the internal dynamics of American parties.[51] Rarely, if ever, are American parties united on all major policy issues. Though factionalism is endemic to the American party system, it also undoubtedly produces much of the vitality found in our parties. From one election to the next the liberal and conservative wings within each party will be vying for control. Some veteran party-watchers are convinced that there is as much rivalry within parties as between the major parties. On the national level this factionalism is most likely to come to the surface at the quadrennial conventions. Factionalism between rival wings of the party, of course, can also be found on Capitol Hill as the liberal and conservative leaders within each major party seek to control legislative activity. But the high stakes of the Presidency and its domination of the national government make this office the focal point of a major tug-of-war between competing factions. At the national conventions, this rivalry is most likely to come to the surface during the consideration of the platform. That platform-making can throw a spotlight on intra-party power struggles has occurred frequently in modern party history. Seven times during the most recent 16 conventions (1952-1980) leaders of minority factions have felt that the stakes and issues were important enough to wage—though usually unsuccessful—floor fights.[52]

Probably the most famous platform fight in American political history took place at the marathon 1924 Democratic convention in Madison Square Garden, New York City. The 1924 Democratic platform fight centered on the two burning issues of the day—Prohibition and the Ku Klux Klan. These issues split the

Democratic party right down the middle. Democrats from the Eastern, urban, heavily Roman Catholic wing, led by Governor Alfred E. Smith of New York, supported repeal of Prohibition but bitterly opposed the Klan. The heavily rural, Southern Protestant, Prohibitionist wing, led by William G. McAdoo of California, contained many Klan members or sympathizers. So dramatically opposite in their views were these two factions it is a wonder that they could coexist under the same party banner—but they did. After an all-night debate the Platform Committee submitted two planks on the Klan: the majority report condemned "any effort to arouse religious and/or racial dissension," but named no names. The minority report pledged the party to "oppose any effort on the part of the Klan or any organization to interfere with the religious liberty or political freedom of any citizen."[53] When the minority plank was read, mention of the Klan triggered a torrent of booing from 13,000 guests and visitors, most of whom had been invited by the anti-Klan, anti-Prohibitionist, New York City Tammany Hall political machine. To quell the fist fights breaking out in the galleries, a call went out for 1,000 extra policemen. Finally, when the roll call was completed, the strong anti-Klan minority plank lost by less than one vote, 543 3/20 to 542 7/20—the closest vote in convention history![54]

The platform debate merely presaged the more acrimonious fight for the Democratic nomination, which required nearly two weeks and 103 ballots (under the required two-thirds rule) to pick the nominee: John W. Davis, a Wall Street lawyer and former Ambassador to Great Britain. The badly divided vote on the platform planks and the marathon balloting for the nominee signaled disaster for the Democrats in November. Even though the Republicans were reeling from the Teapot Dome oil lease scandals, the Democratic party in 1924 suffered its most shattering defeat since the Civil War. President Coolidge collected 15,719,921 votes (54.0 percent) to Davis' 8,386,704 (28.8 percent) and third party candidate Robert M. LaFollette's 4,832,532 votes (16.6 percent).

RECENT CONTROVERSIES OVER PLATFORMS

Both parties—the Republicans in 1964 and the Democrats in 1968—were badly divided by the bitterness of the platform debate. While the successful candidates—Senator Barry Goldwater and Vice President Hubert H. Humphrey—carried the day, the bitter exchanges during the platform debate left their parties hopelessly split and signaled their subsequent defeats in the general election.

In 1964, moderate Republicans Nelson Rockefeller and George Romney proposed platform amendments condemning the political extremism of the Ku Klux Klan and the John Birch Society (whose support Goldwater refused to disavow) and urged support for the 1964 Civil Rights Act (legislation which Goldwater had voted against), but they were shouted down by the Goldwaterites. When Goldwater's chief rival, Governor Nelson Rockefeller, mounted the rostrum to argue on behalf of one of the proposed amendments, he was met with a barrage of catcalls, jeers, and obscenities that drowned out many of his remarks. For several minutes Rockefeller could not be heard. Convention Chairman Thruston Morton finally restored sufficient order to enable Rockefeller to complete his statement. All of the amendments were quickly rejected by the pro-Goldwater majority, which then endorsed the full platform.[55] The next day the convention approved Goldwater as the nominee by a resounding majority. But the 1964 platform fight, which mirrored the deep rift within the GOP, foretold of an impending disaster—the GOP went down to defeat in November, losing by nearly 16 million votes.

Platform-making at the 1968 Democratic convention was not merely a parliamentary exercise either, for it revealed a deep schism within the Democratic party over the issue of the Vietnam War. Indeed, it was on this single issue that the leading anti-war challenger Senator Eugene McCarthy waged his courageous but losing battle for the Democratic nomination. By leading a floor fight over the minority proposal on Vietnam which called for an "unconditional end" to all bombing on North Vietnam, McCarthy had hoped to split the party ranks and attract enough support to capture the nomination from the front-runner, Vice President Humphrey. In an attempt to head off the McCarthy attack, the Humphrey forces initially tried to draft a Vietnam plank that would satisfy some of the "dove" delegates and play down the Vietnam issue. But the pro-Humphrey majority plank, drafted behind the scenes with some stern coaching from President Johnson, offered only a conditional cessation of the bombing and proposed to reduce military involvement "as the South Vietnamese forces are able to take over their large responsibilities." The minority proposal, on the other hand, pledged an immediate de-escalation, making possible "an early withdrawal of a significant number of our troops." Senator McCarthy, attacking the pro-Administration Vietnam plank, declared that the choice "was between those who want more of the same and those who think it is necessary to change our course in Vietnam."[56]

Thus, the battle lines between the Humphrey and McCarthy partisans were clearly drawn for the showdown platform fight over Vietnam. The Johnson Administration forces running the convention originally sought to schedule the platform proceedings during the late evening hours of the second day, after most TV viewers in the populous East had gone to bed. But as the session dragged on past midnight, delayed by the seating contests, the anti-Administration dissidents sought to postpone the platform discussion until the next afternoon with shouts of "Let's go home! Let's go home!" Amidst the pandemonium, Convention Chairman Carl Albert, taking a cue from Mayor Daley of Chicago, adjourned the session until the next afternoon. To the surprise of some observers, the two-hour platform debate on Vietnam offered an unusually open and high-level exchange of views by prominent party spokesmen. Senator Edmund Muskie of Maine, speaking for the majority and subsequently nominated for vice president, expressed the view that broad areas of agreement existed between the two opposing camps. Ted Sorenson, former aide to President John F. Kennedy, made the most eloquent plea for the minority: "If you cannot give our young people and the amateurs and the idealists the candidate of their choice, at least give them this plank to preserve their enthusiasm for the Democratic party."[57]

When the debate time limit expired on the Vietnam plank, the roll call showed the pro-Administration majority report prevailing 1,567.75 to 1,041.25 votes. The outcome of the platform debate signaled the collapse of the McCarthy candidacy (and a short-lived "boomlet" for Senator Ted Kennedy), thereby removing all doubt that Humphrey would be the Democratic standard-bearer. Some Democratic leaders had hoped that the public airing of the Vietnam issue in the platform debate would be a needed catharsis to bring the party together for the fall campaign. More pessimistic party leaders concluded that the rupture would cost the Democrats the presidency in 1968, and they were right. Vice President Humphrey lost the presidential race, as had been freely predicted by the party "doves"—though by the narrow popular margin of 517,777 votes.

Significantly, the 1968 convention's minority report position on the unilateral withdrawal of troops from Vietnam became within a year the prevailing position on Vietnam for a near majority of Democrats on Capitol Hill and by mid-1970 a majority of rank-and-file party members throughout the country. The impact of the "great convention debate" over Vietnam lived long after the delegates returned to their homes, and the country under a new Republican administration began a gradual American de-escalation of the war in Southeast Asia.

While the 1972 Democratic platform debate was less acrimonious than four years earlier, the platform proceedings reflected the deep schism between the McGovern majority and the ABM (Anybody but McGovern) minority faction. With the McGovern forces firmly in control of the 1972 Democratic convention, the South Dakotan obtained almost exactly the kind of platform he wanted to run against President Nixon—a 24,000 word document with a liberal populist tone. But many Democrats—blue collar workers, Roman Catholics, and Southerners—were turned off by the far-left positions espoused in the platform. Many sat on their hands during the general election campaign and then voted for the Republican incumbent, President Richard M. Nixon, in November.

What explains the increasing divisiveness and intensity of platform debate in recent years? Obviously, the unpopular Vietnam War was responsible for the schism within the Democratic ranks in 1968 and 1972. But other factors have also contributed to the expanding conflict over party platforms. Reforms in the delegate-selection process have produced many more issue-oriented delegates who are less dependent upon or loyal to the party leadership. The rise of special caucus groups within the Democratic party—some observers have called the Democratic party a federation of caucuses—has led to more minority demands for special recognition in the party platform. Women, blacks, and Hispanic-Americans have all insisted upon a larger voice in platform decision-making. United by their minority status and better organized, they have become far more adept in bargaining for their policy objectives. Network television, which thrives on intraparty confrontation, has also magnified the level of platform conflict by offering dissident elements the priceless opportunity to be heard "live" nationwide by millions of viewers.

Convention managers, cognizant of the severe damage that heated and unruly platform debate can have upon the huge television audience, have endeavored in recent years to minimize controversy over the platform proceedings. To halt the free-for-all platform debate, Democratic National Chairman Robert S. Strauss persuaded the Democratic National Committee in October 1975 to approve a proviso that minority platform reports must have the signatures of 25 percent of the platform committee's total membership before they can be considered on the floor. Moreover, under the new rules these minority reports had to be filed 24 hours before the platform discussion. If delegates to the 1976 Democratic convention did not like the majority reports, they had to suspend the rules by a two-thirds vote of *all* delegates, not just those present and voting. As the shrewd Strauss related after the 1976 conclave:

I decided the day I became chairman that I would pay any price for a 25 percent rule. I wasn't interested in having every little sliver of opinion presented on prime-time television. At 10 percent the gays and the abortion people and other weirdos could get together and sign each other's petitions—"You sign ours, and we'll sign yours." We cured the platform problems, and Carter cured the rest.[58]

As a result of this strict rule, only one minority proposal was offered at the 1976 Democratic convention, and it was accepted by a voice vote. But four years later, however, the Democratic 25 percent rule had become a hollow barrier to unrestricted debate. Because the Kennedy forces, the feminists, and environmentalists could easily mobilize 25 percent of the platform committee on any major issue, 23 minority reports were offered—and over half were either accepted by the Carter high command before the convention or approved on the floor in spite of the rule.[59] Indeed, the Democratic convention platform battle, one of the longest in history, filled 17 hours of debate and roll calls, including all of Tuesday and continued until four hours before nominations were opened on Wednesday evening, August 13.

Until 1976, the Republicans engaged in a closed-door platform drafting process in which most members of the Platform Committee did not see a copy of the draft until the first meeting of the Committee at the convention.[60] Consequently, the amount of time that platform dissidents had available to mount opposition to unwanted planks was extremely limited. Traditionally, the Republican party has been (with a few exceptions such as in 1964) more unified than the Democrats on platform matters. A more homogeneous and smaller party, the GOP has also been less pressured by organized interest groups. In 1976, President Ford's managers, faced with a strong platform challenge from the outnumbered Reagan partisans, chose not to beat down the Reagan challenge on foreign policy. The Reagan-sponsored resolution criticized President Ford and Secretary of State Henry A. Kissinger for losing public confidence, making secret international agreements, and discouraging the hope of freedom for those who do not have it— presumably the captive nations of Eastern Europe. Instead of opposing the

anti-Administration amendment, the pro-Ford majority on the platform committee (acting on directions from the Ford control center) conceded the point and
announced that there would be no opposition to the foreign policy resolution.
Approved by a voice vote, the Reagan amendment was added to the platform and
subsequently approved by the full GOP convention. Four years later, the 1980
GOP convention endorsed the Reagan-proposed platform in near-record time by
a voice vote. This action reconfirmed once again the relative ease with which a
party can approve a platform if it has general agreement on its nominee. How
much influence does the nominee have over platform drafting? Let's take a look
at the record under varying conditions.

Nominee's Influence on Platform-Writing

Over the years the party platform has reflected the strategic environment under
which it was written: whether the party occupied the White House, and if the
incumbent was seeking a second term, or whether the party was out-of-power.

INCUMBENCY

When a White House incumbent has sought a second term, platform-writing
has been, until recently, dominated by his preferences. The Democratic platform
of 1936, according to one former White House staffer, was written by President
Roosevelt and sent to the resolutions committee, which approved it after altering
one sentence.[61] In recent decades, the incumbent President standing for reelection has usually had the leading platform planks drafted by the White House staff
or key friends on the platform committee. This was certainly true for Presidents
Eisenhower in 1956, Johnson in 1964, Nixon in 1972, and Carter in 1980. In
1956, for example, White House aides superintended the platform-drafting under
"tight security conditions."[62] President Lyndon Johnson, in 1964, kept a close
rein on the platform-drafting through his trusted agents at the Atlantic City
convention; the Johnson-guided platform draft was approved by the delegates in
record time without dissent, by a voice vote. Eight years later, the 1972 Republican platform, written mostly in the White House and endorsed by the GOP
platform committee *pro forma*, was approved on the convention floor after two
hours of routine summarizing by seven platform sub-committees. This type of
platform charade prompted the late Paul Tillett to assert that platforms "are
prefabbed elsewhere and shipped in for election, display and ratification."[63]

With more intraparty challenges to presidential incumbents and the growth of
national candidate organizations and the intense commitment that convention
delegates have to these organizations, however, it will become increasingly
difficult, as Denis G. Sullivan and others have pointed out, "for losers to accept
the convention outcome and recommit their energies to the winner."[64] Platform-
writing can help keep supporters of losing contenders from bolting the party. To
placate the issue interests of defeated Reaganites at the 1976 GOP convention,
President Ford's campaign managers, as explained earlier, readily acceded to a

Reagan-endorsed platform plank sharply critical of the Ford Administration's foreign policy as the price to be paid to win over the disenchanted Reaganites. The willingness of the Ford team managers to accommodate the Reagan partisans on the platform demonstrated once again how successfully platform-writing at the national convention operates to mobilize the support of the losing faction for the upcoming general election.

President Carter, in a bid for party unity in 1980, granted a number of platform concessions to rival candidate, Senator Edward Kennedy and his die-hard supporters on such matters as an economic stimulus package and a $12 billion jobs program rather than risk an open split with Kennedy and the liberal wing of the Democratic party. Though this move did not save the Carter presidency in November, it shrewdly reflected Carter's awareness that he could not hope to remain in the White House without drawing strong backing from the liberal Kennedy wing of the party during the general election campaign. Although President Carter and Senator Ted Kennedy's battle for the 1980 Democratic nomination went down to the wire before Kennedy bowed out of the race, the disputes over the platform planks, according to one newsman, "seemed important more for their symbolic value than for any specific recommendation they contained."[65]

In his renomination acceptance speech, President Carter found himself in the embarrassing position of lending general, though somewhat vague, support to key provisions of the 1980 party platform sponsored by Senator Kennedy's supporters and originally opposed by the President. The chief cause of the President's predicament was a stirring speech by Senator Kennedy on platform night (second night of the convention) that led to a sudden voice-vote approval of three economic planks, including one which called for a new $12 billion jobs program to combat the current recession, and that contradicted Carter Administration policy. While President Carter had serious reservations about planks on economic policy and women's rights ("The Democratic party shall withhold financial support and technical campaign assistance from candidates who do not support the ERA"), he did not want to risk alienating the convention majority that voted for them. Feminist activists, for example, had threatened to walk out of the convention if President Carter tried to disavow the Equal Rights Amendment plank.

The new Democratic rule, adopted at the 1980 convention, requiring the nominee to state *in writing* his agreement or disagreement with specific platform planks is a significant innovation to the platform process that could take on greater importance in the years ahead.[66] In a bid to unify the party in his acceptance speech, Carter tightroped his way over this political minefield by not mentioning any of his disagreements with the convention platform; instead, he emphasized the major points of agreement among the various factions within the party. Knowledgeable delegates, of course, understood that the platform would not bind President Carter, if he were reelected, any more than did the 1976 Democratic platform, which contained a number of planks that the Carter Administration chose to ignore or downplay during its first three and one-half years in office.[67]

When an incumbent President decides not to seek another term, he usually shares authority on the platform-drafting with the front-running contender(s) in his party (or their managers), the platform committee chairman, and members of the committee. In 1952, for example, President Truman's White House staff prepared a series of draft planks, but a drafting committee, chaired by House Majority leader John W. McCormack of Massachusetts, made substantial revisions in the White House drafts without objections from President Truman. Skillful wording of the plank on civil rights avoided a floor fight and the full convention approved the platform report by a voice vote. In 1960, retiring President Eisenhower stayed above the platform battle between the conservative-oriented Platform Committee and New York Governor Nelson Rockefeller, who insisted on strong civil rights and defense planks. Privately, though, Eisenhower was reportedly incensed that Rockefeller successfully pressured Vice President Nixon into endorsing platform statements that were mildly critical of Ike's administration. In stronger terms, Senator Barry Goldwater, the leading spokesperson of the conservative wing of the party, termed the Nixon-Rockefeller pact the "Munich of the Republican Party."[68]

The 1968 Democratic platform, which generated more drama than the nomination itself, showed the maximum influence that a retiring president can exert on the drafting process. Indeed, the Vietnam platform plank became almost a referendum on President Johnson's handling of the Vietnam War. Determined to have a Vietnam plank that reflected a vote of confidence in his policies, Johnson masterminded the platform-writing from behind the scenes as if he were running for another term, instead of retiring. Drafts of the Vietnam plank were written and rewritten. According to one team of reporters, "draft planks were fluttering around like confetti."[69] Members of the Platform Committee worked frantically to come up with a statement that would be acceptable to both President Johnson and Vice President Humphrey (who feared that Johnson might change his mind and seek renomination) and to the McCarthy anti-war partisans. In the end, the strong-willed president carried the day, but his stubborn persistence on the Vietnam plank probably, in the view of many party experts, cost Humphrey the election.

Presidential candidates seeking the White House for the first time are usually far more occupied with winning the nomination than in platform-writing. Consequently, less centralized control of platform-writing sometimes exists in the out-of-power party during an "open" convention. Bargaining among the candidates, the platform committee and staff, and the major special interest groups takes place in the final days before the convention, especially after copies of the platform draft have been circulated. Unless a presidential contender has a clear road to the nomination before the convention, candidates will generally be preoccupied in nailing down the nomination, talking with the various state delegations, holding press conferences, and considering various vice presidential possibilities, not in putting the final touches on the party platform. Generally, when the front-running candidate turns his attention to platform matters, he delegates to trusted lieutenants the task of reviewing the proposed planks and refining the language. How does the experience of the two parties compare on these matters?

DEMOCRATS

Even a candidate renowned for his graceful writing style, Adlai E. Stevenson, took no leading role in drafting the 1952 and 1956 platforms. Yet, he opened his 1952 acceptance speech with the words, "I accept your nomination—and your program."[70] Eight years later, the front-running John F. Kennedy gave the draft platform "only a cursory glance," at the 1960 Democratic convention, according to his chief foreign affairs advisor, Chester Bowles, who also served as chairman of the 1960 Democratic Platform Committee. Robert Kennedy, his brother's campaign manager, read another platform draft more thoroughly the day before the document was presented to the convention but offered no suggestions.[71] In 1968, as explained earlier, Democratic nominee Hubert H. Humphrey proposed a statement on the key Vietnam plank, but his proposal was shunted aside by White House staffers in favor of a much stronger pro-Administration resolution personally endorsed by President Johnson. Four years later, Democratic nominee George McGovern's youthful cadre of supporters on the platform committee looked after his interests without involving the South Dakota senator, who was far more concerned with the crucial credentials fight and picking a suitable vice presidential running-mate. In 1976, the political unknown from Georgia who became the Democratic nominee, Jimmy Carter, relied on his issues chief, Stuart Eizenstat, to negotiate, cajole, and occasionally strong-arm opposition delegates to come up with a non-controversial platform. Carter deferred to big labor by supporting a watered-down national health insurance plan. His staffers won over black leaders with a limited welfare program and Southern acquiescence by side-stepping the volatile school-busing issue. Thus, during most of the final platform-writing proceedings Carter could remain preoccupied with narrowing the choice of a vice presidential running-mate. But at no time did he forget that he needed a liberal-oriented document, if he were to appeal successfully to all of the traditional Democratic constituencies during the general election campaign.

REPUBLICANS

Generally speaking, GOP presidential contenders have taken a more active interest in platform-drafting than their Democratic counterparts. In 1952, however, Eisenhower supporters concentrated on the credentials challenges and rules disputes, not the platform, because winning the credentials and rules fights was absolutely essential to capturing the nomination; the platform was not. This successfully executed battle plan prompted a leading political scientist to observe, "Taft got the platform and Eisenhower got the nomination."[72] But in 1960 and in 1968, as noted earlier, Richard Nixon intervened to obtain a platform that would be acceptable to the Rockefeller wing of the party as well as the more conservative elements. In 1964, Senator Barry Goldwater held such a dominant majority of delegates at the GOP convention that he obtained the type of platform he wanted without having to pressure the platform committee to conform to his wishes. Sixteen years later, California Governor Ronald Reagan obtained a tailor-made conservative platform from the 106-member GOP platform committee that he could not have personally drafted better himself.

The actual drafting in 1980, however, was handled by the executive director of the platform committee and the editor-in-chief (appointed by GOP Chairman William Brock) working under the direction of platform committee chairman, Senator John Tower of Texas and his six subcommittee chairmen—all members of Congress. The subcommittees, too, were staffed by congressional staff aides. In the formative stages the staff drafts were reviewed by an executive committee consisting of Senator Tower, his vice chairmen, subcommittee chairmen, their staffs, and two Reagan aides—Richard Allen for foreign affairs and Martin Anderson for domestic policy. In the final analysis, the platform remained a party statement, cleared by the Reagan staff aides, as opposed to a Reagan document.[73]

Liberal elements within the GOP had little voice in the formulation of the 1980 Republican platform. Delegates favoring the Equal Rights Amendment and free choice for women on abortion were steamrollered by the Reagan majority on the Platform Committee. As the full committee began its final markup of the 1980 platform, its pro-Reagan majority chose not even to vote directly on ERA and abortion issues. Instead, they substituted language acknowledging "the legitimate efforts of those who support or oppose the Equal Rights Amendment" in place of a proposal to restore traditional support for ERA (which previous Republican platforms had consistently endorsed since 1940). The Reagan substitute resolution carried 90 to 9. Then the pro-Reagan Platform Committee majority voted 75 to 18 to table, thus kill, a substitute amendment to tone down the abortion plan that favored a constitutional amendment banning all abortions.[74]

Not all political partisans, however, are satisfied with the present platform construction system. But what are the alternatives? Let's take a moment to explore some other possible approaches.

Alternatives to the Present Platform-Drafting System

NO PLATFORM

If the platform, as some critics argue, is not the solution for resolving intraparty policy differences, why not abolish it? This radical proposal has virtually no support among professional politicians or political scientists. Elimination of the platform would force the electorate to judge presidential candidates chiefly on the basis of their television "image," their public records, and public statements made during the campaign. If platform-writing were abolished, candidate rivalries and factional disputes would most likely be intensified. Instead of relaxing tension, abolition of the platform would shift factional disputes onto the nominating process. Without the platform-writing exercise, defeated presidential candidates would have virtually no opportunity to win consolation prizes in the form of their favorite platform planks. Without the solace of winning concessions on platform-writing the task of reconciling the winning and losing sides in the nomination race would be exacerbated. The nominee, in turn, would be deprived of the opportunity to extend the olive branch, in the form of concessions on the platform, such as President Ford extended to his defeated rival Ronald Reagan in the 1976 Republican convention, or President Jimmy Carter to Senator Ted Kennedy at the 1980 Democratic convention. In all likelihood, bargaining for the vice presidency would heat up because it would be the only consolation prize available to the defeated factions.

Without a party platform the presidential nominee would be deprived of a "buffer zone" on controversial issues that the platform presently affords the nominee during the general election campaign. No longer could the party nominee hide behind the platform that often contains cleverly drafted ambiguities that enable a candidate to appeal to a variety of constituencies without seemingly offending any of them.

CANDIDATE PLATFORMS

It has been suggested that the candidate, especially of the out-of-power party, have his own staff draft a candidate-sponsored platform. While this proposal might have some appeal, adoption of a candidate platform would eliminate platform-drafting as a separate object of bargaining among rival candidates or party leaders. If candidate platforms became the order of the day, conventions would focus almost exclusively on presidential and vice presidential nominations. Minority factions would probably view the vice presidential nomination as their only opportunity to win a consolation prize. Under this system the presidential nominee might have his freedom of action in picking a running-mate more circumscribed.

Candidate platforms would probably mean more programmatic campaigns with each major party candidate emphasizing his own sharply defined stand on major policy issues of the day. However, if the nominee took determined stands on controversial issues, it might have a divisive effect within his party, since those party members who disagreed with the candidate might abandon him during the general election campaign. Recent history provides one glaring example: many Republicans, dissatisfied with Senator Barry Goldwater's far-right posture on issues such as civil rights, social security, and foreign policy during the 1964 campaign, sat on their hands or lent tacit support to President Lyndon B. Johnson.

NATIONAL COMMITTEE PLATFORMS

Members of the party responsibility school would prefer to have the national committee or a party council draft the party platform, subject to amendment on the floor. Having a national party group draft a coherent party document delineating the party's stand on the major issues would, of course, be a big step in the direction of party accountability.[75] But it would make a non-incumbent presidential nominee the captive of the party. To win the support of a convention the nominee would have to agree to abide by the platform or risk alienating significant elements in the party. Or the prospective nominee might decide to make a fight over the platform planks on the convention floor—washing the party's linen in front of millions of television viewers. Once nominated, he might decide to disavow the platform, if he found certain sections unpalatable. While a national party committee-drafted platform would give a greater voice to party professionals, the increased tension generated by platform differences between the national committee and the nominee could weaken the party's chances of capturing the White House in November.

SUPERIORITY OF EXISTING METHOD OF CONSTRUCTING PLATFORM

All in all, the existing method of platform-drafting seems to be the best solution for welding together the disparate elements of 50 state parties and the colliding demands of numerous special interest groups, while simultaneously offering the maximum flexibility to the presidential candidate. Indeed, constructing the party platform is an effective means of achieving a majority coalition of factions and this helps accord recognition to the numerous power groups within a party.[76] During the convention and afterward, these diverse groups can point with pride to various planks in the party platform that specifically recognize their special concerns.

Platform-making helps strengthen the cohesiveness of the party by enabling minority factions that fail to nominate their Presidential candidate to win some measure of success. In other words, they do not leave the convention empty-handed. As Polsby and Wildavsky have observed: "The platform tests and communicates the ability of the many party factions to agree on something, even if on some crucial points major differences have to be papered over."[77]

A party platform cannot be quietly slipped under the rug whenever electoral circumstances change. Indeed, Gerald Pomper has reminded us that for a party to ignore consistently its pledges "confuses the voters and also results in distrust of the party, to its ultimate detriment."[78] Briefly, then, the platform is a campaign document. And it belongs to the party, not the presidential candidate. As a party manifesto, it is a reasonably predictable indication of the party's intentions. In Pomper's words, "Platforms indeed are to run on, not to stand on—but they also can reflect and affect the pace, direction, winner and meaning of the race."[79] The platform is also a type of road map indicating to interest group constituents what course of action the candidate and party would like to take, if successful in

November. But another convention-watcher reminds us, "Platforms can never be taken as *totally* reliable guides to future government action; nevertheless, they speak importantly to the question of what we generally expect in the way of executive leadership from the men who emerge from each convention as candidates for the office of President of the United States."[80]

One veteran team of political scientists has summarized the major function of the party's most important working document: "The platform defines the boundaries of intraparty agreement, and it does so with sufficient clarity to differentiate the parties and the interests they represent."[81] No wonder most serious students of American parties view the platform as a valuable mechanism for facilitating a degree of internal unity and for drawing a demarcation line between the major parties.

Looking ahead, however, platform-writing will probably come increasingly under the dominant influence of the national candidate organizations in the post-reform era. Most delegates elected to national conventions are now pledged by state law to specific candidates (or they may, if they choose, run uncommitted); indeed, the Democratic party rules now grant presidential candidates the right to approve or veto delegates running on their behalf. Consequently, convention delegates' basic loyalty no longer is tied to his or her home state, but to the presidential candidate. Under these circumstances delegate attitudes toward the platform and policy issues are going to be shaped more and more by the presidential candidates' preferences, not home state ties. As Christopher Arterton has cogently observed:

Although the platform and rules issues do provide real and symbolic prizes, useful for unifying the party around the nomination outcome, we need to consider the consequences of having all party business determined by the nomination struggle. Such a system is tantamount to parties being no more than areas for candidate competition.[82]

Once the party platform has been approved, the delegates are ready to settle down to the main item of convention business: nominating and selecting the party's presidential candidate—the subject of the next chapter.

Notes

1. *New York Times*, August 12, 1980.
2. The Democratic Platform Committee conducts regional hearings across the country during the spring months before preparing its final draft, which since 1972 has been published ten days before the convention opens and distributed to all delegates.
3. James A. Farley, Franklin D. Roosevelt's 1932 campaign manager, asked some years ago to compare the importance of the temporary and permanent chairman, remarked, "I think the temporary chairman in a sense is more important than the permanent chairman." In the many motions that have to be made the temporary chairman, Farley pointed out, can see over the heads of the delegates he doesn't want to recognize to the person he wants to put the motions, especially on crucial procedural matters. Richard L.

Strout, *Christian Science Monitor*, July 10, 1972. Mr. Strout began covering conventions in 1924, the year President Calvin Coolidge was nominated for a regular term.

4. Nelson Polsby and Aaron Wildavsky, *Presidential Elections*, 2nd ed. (New York: Charles Scribner's Sons, 1968), p. 96.

5. Paul T. David, Malcolm Moos, and Ralph M. Goldman, eds., *Presidential Nominating Politics in 1952*, Vol. 1 (Baltimore: The Johns Hopkins University Press, 1954), pp. 75-76.

6. *New York Times*, August 27, 1968.

7. Jules Witcover, *Marathon: The Pursuit of the Presidency, 1972-1976* (New York: Viking Press, 1977), pp. 456-503; *New York Times*, August 19, 1976.

8. *Washington Post*, August 12, 1980. Shortly before the 1980 Democratic convention opened, two new opinion polls—the *New York Times*/CBS poll and a Louis Harris survey—showed Democrats nationwide were roughly 2 to 1 in favor of an "open" convention rather than the proposed binding rule on convention delegates. *New York Times*, August 10, 1980.

9. *Washington Post*, August 12, 1980.

10. Ibid.

11. *Washington Post*, August 13, 1980.

12. As a result of this Democratic rule change, a special Commission on Presidential Nominations was appointed early in 1981 by the newly selected Democratic National Chairman Charles T. Manatt. Headed by North Carolina Governor James B. Hunt, Jr., the Democratic task force made a sweeping series of recommendations to the Democratic National Committee in late March 1982. These recommendations, designed to increase the power of party regulars and give the national convention more freedom to act on its own, were approved by the Democratic National Committee with a minimum of debate. See "Democrats' Rules Weaken Representation," *Congressional Quarterly Weekly Report*, Vol. 40 (April 3, 1982), pp. 749-51; See also *New York Times*, March 27, 1982.

13. Ibid.

14. Theodore H. White, *The Making of a President, 1964* (New York: Atheneum, 1965), pp. 334-35.

15. *New York Times*, August 28, 1968.

16. James W. Davis, *National Conventions: Nominations under the Big Top*, rev. ed. (Woodbury, N.Y.: Barron's, 1972), p. 101.

17. *New York Times*, July 9, 1972.

18. Ibid.

19. The vote on the California challenge was 1,618.28 votes for McGovern against 1,238.22 votes to uphold the seating of 151 anti-McGovern delegates. If the 120 pro-McGovern California delegates had been ineligible to vote, the pro-McGovern vote would have dropped to 1,498 votes (1,618.28 minus 120 = 1,498.28)—11 votes shy of the absolute majority of all convention delegates (1,509). Then, the Stop McGovern forces would have immediately gained the 151 anti-McGovern delegates that the Credentials Committee majority report recommended seating. With this setback the McGovern bandwagon—denied a clear majority of delegates on the first test of strength—might have broken down. See David S. Broder, *Washington Post*, July 10, 1972.

20. 14 Ill. App. 3d, N.E. 2d at 627,631, quoted by Charles D. Longley, "Party Reform and Party Nationalization: The Case of the Democrats," a paper presented at the annual meeting of the Midwest Political Science Association, Chicago, Illinois, 1976, p. 12.

21. 419 U.S. 475 (1975).
22. Ibid.
23. 101 S.Ct. 1010 (1981).
24. 419 U.S. 477.
25. Ibid., p. 490.
26. *Democratic Party of the United States et al. v. LaFollette* (1981), 101 S.CT. 1010.
27. Louise Overacker, *The Presidential Primary* (New York: The Macmillan Company, 1926), pp. 203-04.
28. Paul T. David, Ralph M. Goldman, and Richard C. Bain, *The Politics of National Party Conventions* (Washington, D.C.: The Brookings Institution, 1960), p. 19.
29. Ibid., p. 29. The last time that a platform was approved after the presidential nomination occurred at the 46-ballot 1912 Democratic convention. The Democrats approved their platform after Wilson had been nominated but before Governor Thomas Marshall of Indiana was selected as his running-mate. Eugene H. Roseboom, *A History of Presidential Elections*, 3rd ed. (New York: The Macmillan Company, 1970), p. 369.
30. Gerald Pomper, *Nominating the President* (Evanston, Ill.: Northwestern University Press, 1963), p. 68.
31. David Truman, *The Governmental Process* (New York: Knopf, 1951), pp. 282-83.
32. In 1928, for example, the Democrats pledged that their nominee would faithfully enforce the Eighteenth (Prohibition) Amendment. But Alfred E. Smith, after being nominated by the convention, announced that he believed that major changes were needed to deal with prohibition. V.O. Key, Jr., *Politics, Parties, and Pressure Groups*, 5th ed. (New York: Thomas Y. Crowell Company, 1964), p. 421.
33. Nelson Polsby and Aaron Wildavsky, *Presidential Elections*, 2nd ed., p. 252.
34. *New York Times*, July 16, 1981.
35. Paul T. David, "Party Platforms as National Plans," *Public Administration Review*, Vol. 31 (May/June 1971), p. 304.
36. Gerald M. Pomper, "Controls and Influence in American Elections (Even 1968)," *American Behavioral Scientist*, Vol. 13 (November/December 1969), p. 218.
37. Frank J. Sorauf, *Party Politics in America*, 4th ed. (Boston: Little, Brown, 1980), p. 284.
38. Gerald Pomper, with Susan Lederman, *Elections in America*, 2nd ed. (New York and London: Longman, Inc., 1980), pp. 161-65.
39. Ibid.; see also Fred J. Grogan, "Candidate Promises and Presidential Performance, 1964-1972," paper presented at Midwest Political Science Association meeting, Chicago, Illinois, 1977.
40. Ibid., p. 161.
41. Ibid., p. 165.
42. Michael J. Malbin, "The Convention Platforms and Issue Activists," in Austin Ranney, ed., *The American Elections of 1980* (Washington, D.C.: American Enterprise Institute, 1981), p. 139.
43. Ibid.
44. Paul Tillett, "The National Conventions," in Paul T. David, ed., *The Presidential Election and Transition, 1960-1961* (Washington, D.C.: The Brookings Institution, 1961), p. 35.
45. An excellent, concise summary of platform-drafting in 1976 for both parties will be found in Stephen J. Wayne, *The Road to the White House* (New York: St. Martin's Press, 1980), p. 134.

46. Denis G. Sullivan et al., "Candidates, Caucuses, and Issues: The Democratic Convention, 1976," in Louis Maisel and Joseph Cooper, eds., *The Impact of the Electoral Process* (Beverly Hills, Calif.: Sage Publications, 1977), pp. 84-90.

47. Ibid., pp. 32-33.

48. See Gerald Pomper with Susan Lederman, *Elections in America*, pp. 168-69.

49. See *The 1980 Republican National Convention Platform*, Washington, D.C.: Republican National Committee, 1980; *The 1980 Democratic National Platform*, Washington, D.C.: Democratic National Committee, 1980. For further comparison of the 1980 Democratic and Republican platforms, see Everett Carll Ladd, "More Than a Dime's Worth of Difference," *Commonsense*, 3 (Summer 1980), pp. 51-58.

50. Gerald Pomper, *Nominating the President*, p. 69.

51. The analysis of this section relies heavily on Karl O'Lessker, "The National Nominating Conventions," in Cornelius P. Cotter, ed., *Practical Politics in the United States* (Boston: Allyn & Bacon, Inc., 1969), p. 247.

52. The box score for these floor fights reads as follows: Republicans— 1952, 1960, 1964, and 1976; Democrats—1968, 1972, and 1980.

53. In this post-World War I era the Klan was not, Robert K. Murray reminds us, universally despised. Indeed, in many parts of the Midwest, as well as the South, the Klan shared membership and activities with several Protestant churches. Aspiring politicians joined this right-wing organization as routinely as they did the Elks. It was estimated that as many as 20 percent of the House of Representatives owed its election to Klan support. See Robert K. Murray, *The 103rd Ballot: Democrats and the Disaster in Madison Square Garden* (New York: Harper & Row, 1976), pp. 17-20.

54. Ibid., p. 161.

55. Theodore H. White, *The Making of the President, 1964*, pp. 200-02.

56. "Vietnam: The Dissidents Walk the Plank," *Newsweek*, Vol. 72 (September 9, 1968), p. 33.

57. Ibid.

58. Richard Reeves, *Convention* (New York: Harcourt Brace Jovanovich, 1977), p. 62.

59. Michael J. Malbin, "The Conventions, Platforms, and Issue Activists," pp. 124-25.

60. The 1976 GOP platform committee meetings, for the first time, were opened at the insistence of the Reagan delegates but over minor opposition from the Ford delegates. In 1980, Senator John Tower of Texas, chairperson of the platform committee, wanted to close the meetings again, but the Republican delegates voted to open them. However, the staff director of the committee, on orders from Senator Tower, refused to distribute draft copies to the press. Ibid., pp. 139-40.

61. Raymond Moley, *After Seven Years* (New York: Harper, 1939), pp. 346-47.

62. The discussion in this section follows closely the analysis of Judith H. Parris, *The Convention Problem* (Washington, D.C.: The Brookings Institution, 1972), pp. 116-24.

63. As quoted by Robert MacNeil, *The People Machine* (New York: Harper & Row, 1968), p. 116.

64. Denis G. Sullivan, "Party Unity: Appearance and Reality," *Political Science Quarterly*, Vol. 92 (Winter 1977-1978), p. 637.

65. Robert G. Kaiser, *Washington Post*, August 14, 1980.

66. Although supporters of Senator Edward M. Kennedy lost their rules fight for an "open convention," they won approval of a new rule requiring all presidential candidates to furnish delegates with a written report of their views on the party platform. Negotiators

for President Carter reluctantly accepted the rule (part of the Rules Committee report on Monday night) as one of their pre-convention compromises with the Kennedy camp. To the Kennedy backers the new rule was pushed through as a way to force candidates to take the platform seriously. But Carter's supporters regarded it as just one of a series of Kennedy ploys to help salvage his flickering hopes for capturing the nomination. Because the platform debate extended until four hours before nominations opened, the time for the distribution of President Carter's statement was changed from four hours before the nominating speeches to two hours. Actually, the Carter forces were unable to meet the extended deadline. Copies of President Carter's reaction to the platform reached the convention hall about the time the nominating speeches began. See, "Platform Views Required," *Congressional Quarterly Weekly Report*, Vol. 38 (August 16, 1980), p. 373.

67. Examples of the inconsistencies between the 1976 platform and Carter's performance in office included his failure to give strong support to national health insurance or the Humphrey-Hawkins full employment plan.

68. Theodore H. White, *The Making of the President, 1960* (New York: Atheneum, 1961), p. 239.

69. Lewis Chester, Godfrey Hodgson, and Bruce Page, *An American Melodrama: The Presidential Campaign of 1968* (New York: Viking Press, 1969), p. 594.

70. Adlai E. Stevenson, *Major Campaign Speeches of Adlai E. Stevenson, 1952* (New York: Random House, 1953), p. 7, as quoted by Judith Parris, *The Convention Problem*, p. 124.

71. Chester Bowles, *Promises to Keep: My Years in Public Life 1941-1969* (New York: Harper and Row, 1971), p. 21.

72. Austin Ranney, "The Platforms, the Parties, and the Voters," *Yale Review*, Vol. 42 (Autumn, 1952), p. 17.

73. Michael J. Malbin, "The Conventions, Platforms, and Issue Activists," p. 103.

74. *Washington Post*, July 19, 1980.

75. This proposal was suggested by the American Political Science Association Committee on Political Parties, "Toward a More Responsible Two-Party System," *American Political Science Review*, Vol. 44 (September 1950), Supplement, pp. 50-56. The 1980 Democratic National Convention created a Commission on Platform Accountability to recommend ways that will "yield an effective and disciplined effort to implement the platform of the Democratic Party." But the task of enforcing platform accountability, especially for an out-of-power party, is one that Democratic National Chairman Charles Manatt, during his first year in office, chose to side-step. The convention-ordained commission was not convened by Chairman Manatt until March 1982—a year behind schedule. In the charge given to the commission, Chairman Manatt spoke only of "using the platform and it processes to implement the Democratic legislative agenda" and "finding methods of evaluating accountability at all levels of the party." David Broder, *Washington Post*, March 24, 1982.

76. Paul T. David, Ralph M. Goldman, and Richard C. Bain, *The Politics of National Party Conventions*, pp. 407-09; Gerald Pomper, "If Elected, I Promise: American Party Platforms," pp. 318-52.

77. Nelson Polsby and Aaron Wildavsky, *Presidential Elections*, 2nd ed., p. 72.

78. Gerald Pomper, "If Elected, I Promise: American Party Platforms," p. 321.

79. Ibid., p. 349.

80. Karl O'Lessker, "The National Nominating Conventions," in Cornelius P. Cotter, ed., *Practical Politics in the United States* (Boston: Allyn and Bacon, Inc., 1969), p. 251.

81. Dennis S. Ippolito and Thomas G. Walker, *Political Parties, Interest Groups and Public Policy: Group Influence in American Politics* (Englewood Cliffs, N.J.: Prentice-Hall, 1980), p. 141.

82. F. Christopher Arterton, "Strategies and Tactics of Candidate Organizations," *Political Science Quarterly*, Vol. 92 (Winter 1977-1978), p. 671.

Presidential Contenders and the
Moment of Decision _____ 5

> Now the Lincoln men had to try it again, and as Mr. Delano of Ohio,
> on behalf "of a portion of the delegation of that State," seconded
> the nomination of Lincoln, the uproar was beyond description.
> Imagine all the hogs ever slaughtered in Cincinnati giving their death
> squeals together, a score of big steam whistles going (steam at
> 160 lbs. per inch), and you conceive something of the same nature.
> I thought the Seward yell could not be surpassed; but the Lincoln
> boys were clearly ahead, and feeling their victory, as there was a
> lull in the storm, took deep breaths all round, and gave a concen-
> trated shriek that was positively awful, and accompanied it with
> stamping that made every plank and pillar in the building quiver.
>
> Murat Halstead
> Cincinnati *Enquirer*, 1860

Officially, presidential nominees of the two major parties are still nominated by
delegates to national party conventions, just as they have been for more than 140
years. Over the past three decades, however, a gradual transformation of the
nominating process has taken place. Presidential primaries have preempted the
center stage of the nominating process, and during the past two decades they
have been gradually taking over the manifest functions of convention balloting,
outlined in the opening chapter.

In the traditional national nominating convention, multiple ballots served the
manifest function of informing the delegates about the relative delegate strengths
of the various contenders and of pointing to the likely nominee. In recent years,
however, this balloting or informing function has, in fact, been usurped by the
presidential primaries. Thus, while the formal selection of presidential nominees
takes place at the national conventions in mid-summer, the real selection process
generally occurs earlier during the springtime presidential primary season. Over
the past twenty years the chief winner of the primaries—at least in the out-of-

power party—has been able to lay claim to the nomination by the end of the primary season.[1]

Network television—the technology of instantaneous, pervasive communication—shares the major responsibility for changing the old rules of presidential nominating politics. Columnist Richard Reeves has noted among the new realities of television politics, "There is no such thing as a 'local' selection process in Iowa or New Hampshire or anyplace else. Television brings each caucus and each primary into every American living room. In the new nominating process, those early events are the equivalent of the first ballots in the old-time convention."[2] As a result, the national convention's chief manifest function in recent years has been not to choose the nominee from a group of presidential aspirants but to legitimize the voter's choice in the primaries. If no candidate wins enough delegates in the primaries, the national convention will, of course, resume its traditional manifest function—"broker" role of picking the "best qualified" candidate, with due consideration of all factions and group interests. This recent transformation of the nominating system, however, has not interfered with the other manifest functions of conventions listed in the opening chapter—platform-building, rallying the convention delegates and defeated contenders behind the national ticket, and governing the "national" party.

Growing Importance of Pre-Convention Activity

Formerly, the presidential campaign began in an active sense only after the national delegates had been selected throughout the country. Indeed, the drive for the nomination did not really heat up until the state party chieftains and delegates began arriving in the convention city. Consequently, the nation's political attention on presidential nominations in yesteryear was focused mainly on the national conventions, not the delegate selection process. But because in the present era presidential contenders know that the nomination can in most cases be won or lost during the primary season, pre-convention activity has taken on a crucial importance unknown during the heydey of the caucus-convention era. Unlike the typical four-day convention, presidential primary elections are spread over four months; unofficially, it begins for most presidential candidates at least a year before the convention. These springtime elections, now held in 35 states, select almost 75 percent of all convention delegates. The percentage is unusually high because all but one (Texas) of the twelve most populous states—constituting 40 percent of the nation's population—select the bulk of their convention delegates in presidential primaries. While winners of the first primaries are likely to be the nominee, winning a single primary, however, is not sufficient to sweep the nomination. Instead, candidates generally capture only a portion of the delegates in each state. Building a majority of delegates to win the nomination (approximately 1,650 in the Democratic party and 1,000 delegates in the GOP) is a slow, incremental process. Pledged delegates chosen over the 105-day period from the New Hampshire to California primaries are much less susceptible to the "bandwagon" psychology that sometimes in the past enabled a favorite-son or dark-horse candidate to stampede a convention. Under the present system there are fewer and fewer surprises at the national convention, since most delegates arrive at the convention pledged to a specific candidate. Indeed, with so many committed delegates, it seems improbable that future conventions will be stampeded by a "Willkie blitz" type of campaign that saw the dark-horse Hoosier-born Wall Street lawyer suddenly emerge as the nominee on the sixth ballot at the 1940 Republican convention.

Primaries Frequently "Select" Nominee Weeks before Convention

Within the out-of-power party, dramatic victories in the early primary and caucus states have, in recent years, catapulted a presidential contender into such a commanding lead that he, in effect, becomes the nominee before the primary season is half over. In 1980, for example, Ronald Reagan had, for all practical purposes, wrapped up the GOP nomination after the crucial Illinois primary—the ninth primary of the season—on March 18, 1980. By then, Senators Howard Baker and Robert Dole, and former Secretary of the Treasury John B. Connally had all raised the white flag of surrender. In addition, two Illinois presidential contenders—Congressmen Philip Crane and John Anderson—were also, in effect, knocked out of the race when they failed to carry their home-state primary. Crane's candidacy was moribund, although he refused to bail out of the race for another month. John Anderson, who had suddenly become a media favorite after his strong showings in the Vermont and Massachusetts primaries, was also staggering on the ropes. But instead of giving up the presidential chase, Anderson merely withdrew from the GOP sweepstakes and announced his independent presidential candidacy.

Four years earlier, Jimmy Carter had effectively locked up the Democratic presidential nomination by his decisive victory in the 1976 Pennsylvania primary—the seventh primary of the season—in late April. To be sure, Carter had by then collected only 500 of the 1,508 delegates needed to win a majority at the national convention, but he had effectively knocked out his leading rival Senator Henry "Scoop" Jackson, who withdrew from active campaigning after his Pennsylvania loss. Several other contenders—Bayh, Harris, Shriver, Shapp, and Sanford—had already thrown in the towel. Only California Governor Jerry Brown and Senator Frank Church—two late entrants in the race—and perennial second-place finisher, Representative Morris "Mo" Udall, remained in the Democratic race. But under the new Democratic rule of proportional apportionment of delegates, based upon the candidate's performance in the primaries, Carter needed merely to run down the clock while winning the remaining Southern state primaries in Kentucky, Tennessee, and Arkansas and breaking even in the delegate contests in the other nineteen primary states to claim the nomination in New York City.

In 1972 Senator George McGovern did not wrap up the Democratic nomination until the final-round California primary in early June, but five weeks before the convention there was little doubt in the minds of rival candidates, political professionals, and the national media that McGovern would be, barring unforeseen circumstances, the nominee at the Miami Beach convention in July.[3]

In 1968, former Vice President Richard Nixon drove one of his major rivals, Michigan Governor George Romney, out of the race ten days before the first-in-the-nation New Hampshire primary. By winning all of the major primaries against Ronald Reagan and John Ashbrook, Nixon built up such an insurmountable lead that New York Governor Nelson A. Rockefeller's last-minute national advertising "blitz" campaign effort to win the nomination by becoming the leader in the public opinion polls failed to erode Nixon's huge delegate lead. Nixon was selected as the 1968 Republican nominee on the first ballot.[4] Eight years earlier, John F. Kennedy had demolished his chief rivals, Senators Hubert H. Humphrey and Stuart Symington, by his impressive showing in the West Virginia primary in early May. Most political experts, though not his last remaining rival, Senate Majority Leader Lyndon B. Johnson, conceded the nomination to JFK before the primary season was over on the basis of his big victory in West Virginia and his strong delegate commitment from the caucus-convention states north of the Mason-Dixon Line.[5]

Despite the remarkable record of presidential primaries in singling out the future nominee in each of the major parties in recent years, not all nominating races are settled ahead of the convention. In the 1976 GOP nominating contest, for example, President Ford and Ronald Reagan were locked in a neck-and-neck race that was not decided until the first ballot had been completed at the Kansas City convention. President Ford emerged victorious 1,187 delegates to 1,070—the narrowest margin since the Eisenhower-Taft photo finish in 1952.

In the 1980 Democratic nominating race President Carter clearly out-pointed Senator Ted Kennedy in the primaries, but Kennedy refused to bow out of the race until he lost a rules change floor fight over the binding mandate of delegate pledges on the first ballot. But, for the most part, convention decisions have become, in one observer's words, "a symbolic culmination of a process that began much earlier and whose decisive stages occurred long before."[6] Since 1956, all nominees, including incumbents, have been chosen on the first ballot (see Table 6).

Unofficial Delegate Counts and the Convention Outcome

Since 1952, the Associated Press wire service and, more recently, the *New York Times*/CBS News have conducted national delegate polls on a state-by-state basis in an effort to determine how many committed delegates each presidential contender can lay claim to throughout the primary season and to predict, if possible, the future nominee. These delegate head counts have been remarkably accurate—and a growing factor in pre-convention candidate strategy. In recent years the steady proliferation of presidential primaries has, of course, simplified the task of counting delegates, since most delegates now run committed to a

TABLE 6
NUMBER OF PRESIDENTIAL BALLOTS IN NATIONAL PARTY CONVENTIONS, 1928-1980

Year	Democrats	Republicans
1928	1	1
1932	4	1*
1936	1*	1
1940	1*	6
1944	1*	1
1948	1*	3
1952	3	1
1956	1	1*
1960	1	1
1964	1*	1
1968	1	1
1972	1	1*
1976	1	1*
1980	1*	1

Note: First Ballot Total:
Democrats   12/14 (6 incumbents)
Republicans   12/14 (4 incumbents)
First Ballot Nominations:
Non-incumbents   14/18
Incumbents   10/10
*Incumbents renominated.

specific presidential candidate and because Democratic primary rules require that all delegate votes be proportionately apportioned according to the percentage of votes captured by each presidential candidate. (If state primary laws require proportional allocation of delegates—sixteen states had proportional primaries in 1980—the Republican delegates are also allocated proportionately.)

Before 1968, when only fifteen or sixteen states used presidential primaries and because approximately half of these states used advisory (instead of mandatory) primaries, delegate counting was a much more complicated operation. Even so, the Associated Press wire service poll in 1952 predicted within thirty votes the number of delegates Senator Robert A. Taft, the early front-runner, would receive on the first ballot in his losing battle against General Dwight D. Eisenhower. The wire service delegate count on Eisenhower was slightly less accurate because there were a large number of uncommitted delegates in Michigan and Pennsylvania and challenged delegates in Georgia, Louisiana, and Texas. However, when the bulk of these uncommitted and challenged delegates jumped on the Eisenhower bandwagon, they brought his first ballot total to within twenty delegates of his actual first ballot count of 595.[7] During the 1960 Democratic pre-convention race the Associated Press delegate poll provided an accurate inning-by-inning scorecard of John F. Kennedy's successful drive for the nomination. Two days before the national convention opened, Kennedy was credited by the Associated Press with 546 votes (761 needed to nominate). On the second night of the convention the Associated Press scorecard listed Kennedy with 736 delegates, just 25 votes shy of a majority. When the convention roll call on the first round was completed, Kennedy's delegate count was 806 votes—45 more than necessary for the nomination.

In recent years, the *New York Times*/CBS delegate polls have surpassed the accuracy of the old Associated Press delegate poll. The chief explanation for the increased precision of this poll is the greater willingness of the *Times* and CBS to invest large amounts of staff time and money in contacting and, if necessary, recontacting the 3,000-plus delegates in the Democratic party and the 1,900-plus delegates in the Republican party.[8]

In 1976, for example, the *Times*' delegate count of the hotly contested GOP nominating race, taken immediately after the final round of primaries in California, New Jersey, and Ohio, showed President Gerald Ford leading challenger Ronald Reagan, 958 committed delegates to 863 (1,130 needed to nominate) with slightly more than two months to go until the GOP convention in Kansas City. On the weekend of the final set of state conventions in mid-July 1976—one month before the GOP convention— the *New York Times* delegate count gave President Ford 1,102 committed delegates, 28 short of the nomination; and Reagan 1,063 or 67 short; with 94 uncommitted. As convention time approached and with time running out for his candidate, Reagan's manager John Sears futilely sought to discredit the newspaper's head count by claiming a majority of delegates.[9] Still, Reagan struggled in vain to overcome the Ford lead, and subsequent delegate counts taken right up to convention time showed that Ford maintained his 80-plus delegate lead. One day before convention balloting the *New York Times* delegate count showed President Ford with 1,118 committed delegates, twelve short of an absolute majority. Reagan had 1,039 delegates, and 90 remained uncommitted.[10] The convention vote reconfirmed what all of the major unofficial delegate counts had been showing throughout the final six weeks of the race—Ford winning by a margin slightly over 100 delegates.

In the 1980 Democratic race Carter was the conceded winner of the nomination by early June in all of the major unofficial delegate counts. Thus, on June 5, 1980—more than two months before the Democratic convention—the *New York Times*' delegate scorecard showed President Carter leading Senator Kennedy by 1,964 delegates to 1,239, with only 1,666 needed to win.[11] While these totals were based in part on projections of final delegation allocations from caucus-convention states that had not all held their state conventions, the *Times*' box score was within a handful of votes of Carter's delegate count two months later on the convention showdown test of strength on the binding delegate rule change. Kennedy's delegate count was within 140 delegates of his convention vote count on the crucial rule change vote. Once again, the delegate counts proved to be remarkably accurate.

The growth in credibility of these television network, news service, and newspaper delegate counts, along with the presidential primaries, have removed much of the suspense from most national conventions. Changes in the nominating process—mandatory primaries in most states and Democratic rules requiring delegates in the caucus-convention states to announce upon their initial candidacy their pledged or uncommitted status—have resulted in fewer and fewer boss-controlled delegates and more grass-roots true believers. This means that delegates are likely to hold firm to their pledges and not jump on a dark-horse's bandwagon, as sometimes occurred in yesteryear. Consequently, the precision of the delegate counts has given them more believability and impact in recent years. It is noteworthy that as early as 1960 Paul T. David and his associates detected the growing significance of the wire service polls:

Advance polls of delegates (like those conducted by the Associated Press)...may themselves influence the outcome. When they reveal that sentiment is turning strongly toward a single outstanding candidate, they accelerate a development that would otherwise take place more slowly.... When one candidate is showing strength in delegate polls, other candidates are under pressure to make a similar showing by urging supporters to become publicly committed.... Open contests thus tend to develop more openness of information and the stage is set for bandwagon movements even before the actual voting in the convention. [12]

Theodore H. White, the chronicler of presidential races since 1960, recently noted that in 1968, Martin Plissner, the CBS delegate counter (who is still in charge of the network's count) "knew more about the delegates at the 1968 Republican convention than the campaign staffs did."[13] But head counts by news organizations were not readily accepted then as authoritative because they were relatively new. But now, because they have an established track record on accuracy, these counts are given widespread credence. Since neither nominating race was close in 1980, the unofficial delegate counts were less important as a factor in affecting pre-convention strategy. But in the tight Republican race of 1976, both the Ford and Reagan campaign managers watched them intensely—even though they had their own private counts—because of the potential damage they could do or the special advantage that they could give to their candidate. Losers in the delegate count deplore their influence; winners understandably try to exploit their delegate head count at every opportunity. In the years ahead it can be anticipated that these unofficial delegate counts—they are almost the equivalent of early ballots—will play an increasingly vital role in pre-convention strategy.

Decline of Party Power Brokers

Over the past thirty years one of the most significant changes at national conventions has been the steadily declining influence of state party leaders and party professionals. Formerly, two-thirds of the national convention delegates were selected in the caucus-convention states. Under this old system presidential contenders relied on an "inside strategy" to try to capture these delegates, sending out their agents or "drummers" to the caucus-convention states to sell their candidacies and strike up deals with state party leaders in return for their delegate support. Promises of a cabinet post, federal judgeships, or location of a defense plant in the state concerned were the political currency for reaching bargains between the presidential contender and the state (or big city) leader. Before the widespread election of delegates by primary voters, state party leaders could "deliver" the bulk of their state's delegates to the presidential candidates because the leaders controlled the delegate-selection process from the precinct level through the state convention.

Whenever political veterans gather to discuss the politics of yesteryear and the role performed by party power brokers at national conventions, the first name that usually comes to mind is Mark Hanna—William McKinley's campaign mentor. Hanna's consummate handling of McKinley's 1896 nominating campaign remains today the model for comparing performances of all power brokers in the pre-reform era. A wealthy businessman-turned-politician, Hanna masterminded McKinley's nomination with a degree of professionalism that has rarely been matched. Hanna's adroit handling of rival political bosses, Matthew Quay of Pennsylvania and Thomas C. Platt of New York, his early nurturing of Southern Republican delegates, his careful attention to detail, his efficient fundraising and budget control all simplified McKinley's task of winning the GOP nomination on the first ballot.[14] Since then, party leaders have gathered from time to time in "smoke-filled rooms" in the convention city to cut deals on presidential nominations—Warren Harding's selection on the tenth ballot at the 1920 Republican convention in Chicago is a classic example of a brokered nomination.[15] Indeed, state party and big city leaders continued to exert a major influence on the selection of party nominees as recently as 1960. Most party observers would probably agree that John F. Kennedy could not have won the 1960 Democratic nomination without the heavy backing of Mayor Richard J. Daley of Chicago (who delivered 61½ out of Illinois' 69 votes) and Pennsylvania Governor David Lawrence (who produced 68 out of his state's 81 votes) on the first ballot. Although both of these party leaders had earlier thought Kennedy's Roman Catholicism and relative youth were too serious a handicap, they jumped on Kennedy's bandwagon after his decisive victory in the West Virginia primary. Since 1960, however, the influence of party leaders and power brokers has been on a steady decline.

Several explanations can be given for the demise of state party leaders and power brokers at national nominating conventions. As a result of the rising pressure and demands for more participatory democracy in American politics state parties and their leaders have been largely pushed out of or have abdicated their role in the national convention delegate selection process. Faced with new and complex rules for the selection of delegates, some state party organizations have simply left the choice and mandate of national convention delegates to the state primaries. Clearly the spread of presidential primaries to 35 states has taken power to select delegates away from party leaders and given it to rank-and-file voters in states with a grand total population of 175 million people. Partly as a result of the McGovern-Fraser party reforms in the Democratic party after 1968, the presidential selection process (mostly in the Democratic party) moved from a system that mixed primary elections and the caucus-convention, consisting of one-third primary states and two-thirds caucus-convention states (with party elites still dominating the selection process) to a reformed system in which nearly three-quarters of all national convention delegates were chosen by the primary electorates.

With the decline in the number of caucus-convention states, party leaders have been deprived of much of their former operating turf. Under the traditional "closed" caucus-convention system, leaders could exert their control on the levers of power by dominating delegate choice at the precinct caucus, city ward, and county levels. These boss-controlled delegates attended the congressional district and state conventions which selected all of the delegates sent from these states to the national conventions. But once the primary laws put the selection of most delegates in the hands of the party electorate, party leaders lost control of the selection process. Deprived of this gatekeeping power and influence, state party leaders began gradually withering on the vine. Even in the remaining fifteen caucus-convention states, the new Democratic party reform rules also opened up the caucus system. Under the reformed selection rules, the caucus-convention system has become almost as open as the primary system itself. Caucus rules now require that meeting places and time of the precinct caucus be publicized. Delegates must announce their pledged or uncommitted status at the time of their candidacy, and this status cannot be shifted beyond the caucus level. Thus, party leaders can no longer switch or trade delegate votes, as was formerly done at national conventions. Proxy voting, which formerly enabled party bosses to control the outcome of many precinct caucuses, is now banned. Indeed, veteran convention-watchers and the national press can discern little real difference between, say, the Iowa caucus-convention delegate selection process and the first-round New Hampshire presidential primary.[16]

The declining influence of traditional party groupings—state party leaders, county chairpersons, and big state delegation power blocs in presidential nominating races—has also been hastened by the fact that the prime means through which most voters derive their information about candidates are the mass media. Television enables the presidential candidate to communicate directly via the TV screen with the individual voters in their own homes. As a result, candidate dependence on state and local party organizations for electoral success has been reduced to nearly zero. Even when state parties cast aside their traditional neutrality during the primary race to support a specific presidential candidate, the pervasive reach of television has virtually eliminated presidential candidate dependence upon the party to serve as intermediary between the candidate and the electorate.

National Candidate Organizations Supplant Party Elites

In the past two decades, national candidate organizations—one critic has called them temporary national parties—have gradually usurped the role of state party elites in the presidential candidate selection process. As described by Jeane J. Kirkpatrick, "The modern candidate organization is an arsenal replete with all the skills and weapons of modern political combat: speech-writers, advance men, pollsters, public relations specialists, media consultants, fund raisers, computerized voter lists, and a general staff with lieutenants in every state."[17] In a sense, the emergence of powerful candidate organizations is a necessary by-product of popular participation in the presidential nominating process. When presidential nominees were selected by a congressional caucus or by national conventions dominated by state and local party "bosses," an independent candidate campaign organization was, of course, not needed or required. Once nominated, the candidate relied on state and local leaders to mobilize party support, raise money to support the general election campaign, and to get out the voters on election day. But with the massive growth of the electorate (the population of the United States more than doubled between 1920 and 1980—105 million to 225 million persons), the rapid proliferation of presidential primaries, and the need to reach millions of voters in the primary states, presidential candidates can no longer plan or rely heavily on state party leaders for delegate support or part-time party volunteers to ring doorbells to reach the voting public.

As a result, presidential candidates have turned increasingly to a corps of experienced aides, notably media specialists, pollsters, and fundraisers, dedicated completely to winning the nomination, and hopefully the presidency, for their leader. These political technicians, skilled in dealing with the national media, experienced in purchasing television time to reach the most voters within the major market areas of key primary states, and masters of computerized fund-raising, constitute the elite cadre that make up the national candidate organization. Indeed, in this era of participatory democracy and the mass media, no presidential candidate can entertain serious hopes of winning the nomination without a highly efficient personal candidate organization. As explained by Kirkpatrick, "The rise of multifaceted, multifunctional candidate organizations is a direct consequence of changes in the nominating process that make it necessary for a candidate to win primaries and capture 'open' caucuses in many states and do well in opinion polls to qualify for matching funds."[18]

Federal matching subsidies of up to $5 million to presidential contenders have further weakened the political "clout" of state and local party leaders, because the subsidies are given to the individual presidential candidate, not the party. Also, the 1974 Federal Election Campaign Act limit on contributions ($1,000 per contributor) has restricted the ability of both presidential candidates and state party leaders to raise large sums in big denominations during the nominating campaign. Especially, this contribution ceiling puts a heavy premium on a presidential candidate's ability to generate huge sums from large numbers of small contributors. Faced with this low contribution limit, national candidates and their campaign managers have been forced to depend heavily on their direct-mail experts to reach thousands of potential contributors on computerized lists—usually persons who have contributed to candidates in previous elections and to specific causes.

Recently, the emergence of organized interest groups who now want to elect their own members as delegates to national conventions has also undermined state and local party leadership. In 1980, the National Education Association concluded that NEA members would be far more reliable representatives of teachers' interests at the national conclave than state or local politicians. Also, these organized interest groups prefer to deal directly with the national candidate organization—in 1980 the pro-Carter NEA leaders negotiated directly with the President's campaign advisers rather than work through their individual state party organizations.

All in all, the continuing spread of presidential primaries to more and more states, the combined forces of party reform, revamped delegate selection rules, the dominance of the mass media, independent candidate organizations, the growing number of single interest group delegates, and recent federal campaign fund reform legislation have all helped reduce state party elites to little more than party custodians in most states. It is unlikely, barring wholesale reform of the presidential nominating process, that decision-making power will be returned to them.

Candidate Floor Strategy and Organization

Over the past two generations candidate convention strategy and organization have shifted, especially as a result of the delegate-selection reforms adopted in the Democratic party and the powerful impact of nationwide television. Not since the days of Franklin Delano Roosevelt, for example, has a campaign manager had to trade the vice presidential nomination for delegate votes. Nor will recent convention-watchers detect one state delegation chieftain lending some of his delegate votes to another candidate to stave off the front-runner (as the Harding kingmakers did in 1920) to buy time while bargaining over the nomination with other state leaders. No longer can blocs of appointed or hand-picked delegates be used as pawns in the nominating chess game. Pledged delegates elected in presidential primaries have obviously halted such old-fashioned practices of the smoke-filled room era.

Even though most recent conventions have been transformed into ratification assemblies, merely giving the final stamp of approval to the winner of the primaries, front-running candidates still do not leave the management of their convention operations to chance. With the nomination no longer in doubt, managers of the established favorite, for example Jimmy Carter in 1976 or Ronald Reagan in 1980, have normally focused on transforming the convention into a huge campaign rally to demonstrate to the huge national television audience, especially the political independents, that the nominee is a competent, experienced leader who can be depended upon to manage the nation's business with a sure hand and keep cool in the face of continuing international crises. Also, the national convention affords the prospective nominee the opportunity to mend some political fences with defeated contenders with the view toward uniting the party for the fall campaign.

The key to final victory is, of course, organization. Recent nominees have all relied on maximum utilization of staff organization and modern technology. John F. Kennedy's convention staff organization is still regarded as the archetype of successful convention management. Prior to the 1960 Democratic convention, Kennedy's aides compiled extensive files on all delegates, listing their occupation, role in the state organizations, wife's name, issue positions, and candidate preferences. Kennedy loyalists were assigned to each state delegation (author Theodore H. White called them "delegate shepherds") to monitor all their activity and report daily on any shifts in candidate sentiment. Top Kennedy staffers evaluated all of these reports and prepared daily summaries for the candidate and his top advisers. To coordinate all floor activists the Kennedyites set up a command post next to the convention center and installed a private telephone system, with walkie-talkies held on standby basis if the phones failed.[19] (Four years earlier, the Kennedy communications system had broken down between the floor lieutenants and the off-floor command post during the tumultuous balloting for the vice presidency between Kennedy and Kefauver, and the Kennedys were determined not to repeat that error.) Since then, computerized lists have replaced the Kennedy card files and television monitors have been added to the list of electronic gadgetry used by the leading contenders to nail down the nomination. But the floor organization and communications channels differ little from that of the young Massachusetts Senator's convention organizational plan of 1960.

The only recent close contest for nomination, the Ford-Reagan battle in 1976, sheds additional light on winning strategy.[20] President Ford's superior convention management team—the Ford committee even had telephone repairmen standing by to replace sabotaged phone lines—served him well in dealing with vitally-important undecided delegates. With three tiers of floor leaders, the Ford organization maintained close vigilance over these delegates to keep them from straying into the Reagan camp. In a tight nomination race most party experts are in general agreement that, other things remaining equal, superior organization will determine the nominee. President Ford's victory reaffirmed this view. Conversely, weak floor organization put Governor Reagan at a strategic disadvantage, for example, when his managers needed mobility and rapid communication in dealing with the wavering Mississippi delegation before a crucial vote.

As the underdog candidate, Governor Reagan's convention strategy was to maximize uncertainty over the nomination and to bring additional wavering and undecided voters under his banner. To accomplish this, Reagan's organizers sought to find important issues that could be won on their merits. If successful, these actions would expose President Ford's vulnerability and create doubt in the minds of delegates about Ford's ability to win the nomination. One major ploy used by Reagan's managers was to propose a convention rule change to force President Ford to name his running-mate (as Reagan had already done before the convention), with the hope that any choice would alienate all of the disappointed aspirants and their supporters. This rule change failed by 111 votes and with it the last hope of Reagan winning the nomination in 1976. Reagan's strategists resorted to still another desperation tactic to stave off defeat; they offered a minority platform plank strongly criticizing President Ford's foreign policy. To the surprise of the Reaganites, the Ford top command conceded the issue and instructed all of their floor lieutenants and supporters to vote for the minority plank, preferring to accept this wrist slap from the Reagan forces rather than a divisive vote on foreign policy that might foster party disunity in the fall campaign.

Four years later, Senator Edward Kennedy, the underdog candidate at the 1980 Democratic convention, resorted to similar tactics. Kennedy bet all of his chips on an effort to undermine President Carter's huge delegate lead by challenging the "faithful delegate rule," which required convention delegates to vote in accordance with their original vote pledge. When Kennedy and his supporters lost this rule change vote, he immediately withdrew from the race and, in effect, conceded the nomination to President Carter. But Kennedy, as explained in the previous chapter, did not give up the fight to obtain a liberally oriented platform. Though President Carter and his staff privately opposed planks supporting an economic stimulus package and a $12 billion jobs program, the Carter high command passed the word to their partisans not to oppose the Kennedy-sponsored planks for fear of driving away many Kennedy backers from the Democratic party during the general election.[21]

Since Ronald Reagan, unlike President Carter, had locked up the 1980 GOP nomination by late May, his convention strategy was devoted chiefly to making the Republican convention a festival of unity and a well-orchestrated demonstration to the huge national television audience that only the Republicans could bring back prosperity and return the country to a respected place in the international community.

Picking the Presidential Nominee

Even though the interaction of presidential primary victories, public opinion polls, and the mass media are generally turning national conventions into decision-registering assemblies instead of deliberative bodies, these power influences still have not preempted one aspect of the conventions (especially within the out-of-power party) that never ceases to fascinate the delegates and observers alike: the tension and uncertainty over the outcome. Though the front-runner and his managers may have cross-checked his delegate count and tabulated the scorecard totals down to the last confirmed vote, an air of uncertainty usually hangs over the convention hall until the balloting has been completed.

With almost 75 percent of the delegates now selected by mandatory primaries and pledged to specific candidates, the managers of leading candidates have substantially less room to maneuver during the convention itself than in those earlier years when no strategic options could be ruled out in the final hours before (or during) the balloting. No longer can a large bloc of uncommitted delegates be stampeded into voting for a "dark horse" candidate who suddenly emerges from the pack. Indeed, it seems extremely doubtful if delegates at future national conventions will ever again be stampeded to support a dark horse candidate as were the Democrats at their 1896 Chicago convention by William Jennings Bryan, the Boy Orator of the Platte. Bryan, a political unknown, 36 years old and only one year beyond the constitutional minimum for the presidency, delivered his famous "Cross of Gold" speech—generally considered the most electrifying speech ever made at a national convention—the day before nominations opened. (Bryan, who was chosen to make the closing speech on the platform debate over the silver question, was the last presidential contender to deliver a prenomination speech until Senator Edward Kennedy addressed the Democratic delegates on the second night of the 1980 convention in New York City.) Front-running Senator Richard P. (Silver Dick) Bland of Missouri, Governor Robert E. Pattison of Pennsylvania, and former Governor Horace Boies of Iowa, his chief rivals, were simply overwhelmed by Bryan's peroration. The next day the euphoric Democrats (though badly divided over the silver issue) selected Bryan, the youngest man ever to win the presidential nomination, on the fifth ballot. *Washington Post* reporter, Harry West, who was covering the Chicago convention, telegraphed the following account of Bryan's mesmerizing oratory:

[Bryan's] dramatic and theatrical entrance to the hall yesterday was but a part of a well laid plan to stampede the convention for him, and this program was carried out today to its fullest development.... He was inspired with the possibilities which the occasion meant for his future, he knew his subject, he had the popular side of the controversy, he felt himself among friends. Combined with this, he had the rhythm of language, grace of oratory, and picturesqueness of presence.

Certain it is that his speech was the only one of the convention to thrill, electrify, stir, and sway the throng. He struck fire with every word. Earnest as Savonarola, eloquent as Ingersoll, burning with fiery conviction, able enough to emphasize the points which would stick like burrs, artfully modulating his musical voice until it played like the wind upon aeolian strings, he stimulated and swelled the enthusiasm until the great audience was absolutely under his persuasive, yet powerful, domination.

Of his speech... it is enough to say that demagogic and full of sophistry as it was, it suited the sentiment and temper of his audience, and nearly every sentence was wildly cheered.... The peroration, memorized with studied care, flowed from his lips with syrupy ease. "You shall not," he exclaimed in conclusion, stretching out his arms as if in benediction and voice trembling with passionate thrill, "place a crown of thorns upon the brow of Liberty or sacrifice mankind upon your cross of gold."[22]

This speech, delivered before the age of radio, network television, mandatory presidential primaries, public opinion polls, and press surveys of delegates' candidate commitment, would probably be listened to courteously by convention delegates during the present age of party reform but in all likelihood would not sway more than a handful of pledged delegates to change their votes.

Still, rumors continue to sweep through the delegations; the hotel lobbies are filled with talk and gossip about last-minute switches; and television network reporters' efforts to spotlight controversies within or between delegations may even threaten to upset the front-runner's carefully-mapped strategy. All these factors help keep the candidates and delegates on a high emotional pitch as the convention moves toward its climax. Within the out-of-power party the average delegate's lack of confirmatory information and absence of a personal intelligence network—even though he or she may have heard that the delegate counts compiled by the television network and the wire services show that the front-runner has an insurmountable lead—often heightens the uncertainty about the convention's choice for president. Under the new ground rules of the extended primary system, even with an incumbent president seeking reelection, an air of uncertainty can sometimes hang over the convention—witness the cliff-hanger finish at the 1976 Republican National Convention which saw President Gerald Ford beat down Ronald Reagan's strong nomination challenge.

Once all the contenders have been nominated, the drama and suspense of the national convention reaches a peak when the convention chairman declares, "The clerk will read the roll call:. . . Alabama, ——votes; Arkansas, ——votes. . .". The roll call within the Democratic party since 1972, however, reads differently. The 1972 Democratic convention approved an O'Hara Commission rule (VI-C2) change that establishes the roll call list of states by lot, rather than alphabetically.[23]

Balloting is conducted state-by-state by an oral vote. Each state delegation chairman announces the vote of his delegates. Though it has not been necessary to go beyond the first ballot in either party since 1956, successive ballots will be taken until a majority (not a plurality) is obtained by one of the candidates. (The all-time record number for balloting was set in 1924 when the Democrats required 103 ballots to pick their nominee: John W. Davis, a New York corporate lawyer.) Before the official results of each ballot are announced, state delegations may request the convention chairman to change their vote. One of the most memorable delegate shifts occurred at the 1952 GOP convention when the Minnesota delegation leader wigwagged his standard to attract Convention Chairman Joseph Martin's attention. Martin recognized Minnesota Delegation Chairman, Senator Edward Thye, who announced that Minnesota wished to change all of its 28 votes to General Eisenhower. Since Eisenhower had 595 votes and needed only 605 for a majority, the additional 19 votes from the Minnesota delegation were more than enough votes for the General to win on the final, first-round count.[24] As soon as a candidate goes over the top, pandemonium breaks loose. When the chairman finally restores order (since the advent of television, this takes only ten minutes or so) spokespersons for the rival candidates usually move that the rules be suspended and that the nomination be made unanimous.

As indicated earlier, the potent forces of mass democracy affecting the nominating process now usually single out the pre-convention front-runner for the nomination weeks before the convention opens. As a result, the nominee is generally selected on the first ballot (see Table 7). With the trend toward nomination on the first ballot, the convention's action becomes rather anticlimactic—but one would not think so in viewing the hectic, carnival-like proceedings on the convention floor.

The "nationalizing" forces in American political life—television, opinion polls, and jet aircraft—also would seem to have ruled out, if the impatience of millions of viewers in the nation's television audience has not, the marathon conventions of yesteryear. In this rapidly moving age it is sometimes forgotten that in earlier periods of our history multiple ballots (especially at Democratic conventions) were not uncommon before a clear-cut winner emerged from the field (see Table 7). In 1880, for example, the Republicans took 36 ballots to select James A. Garfield as their nominee. In 1912 the Democrats could not agree on their winning candidate—Woodrow Wilson—until the 46th ballot. In 1920 it took the Democrats 44 ballots before they settled on Governor James Cox of Ohio as their standard-bearer. The chief explanation for prolonged balloting at Democratic conventions was, of course, the historic two-thirds rule—a topic that merits brief elaboration.

TABLE 7
YEARS OF MULTI-BALLOT CONVENTIONS

Democrats		Republicans	
Year	*Number*	*Year*	*Number*
1924	103	1880	36
1860	57	1920	10
1852	49	1888	8
1912	46	1876	7
1920	44	1940	6
1868	22	1884	4
1856	17	1860, 1916, 1948	3
1844	9	1856	2
1896	5		
1848, 1932	4		
1952	3		
1876, 1880, 1884	2		

Source: Richard C. Bain and Judith Parris, *Convention Decisions and Voting Records*, 2nd ed. (Washington, D.C.: The Brookings Institution, 1973), appendix C.

The Democratic Two-thirds Rule

For more than a century (1835-1936) the Democratic party—but not the Republicans—adhered to the "two-thirds rule," that is, the requirement that a two-thirds majority of the delegates voting was needed to nominate a presidential candidate. Adopted at the 1835 Democratic convention (party conventions were then held a year ahead of schedule due to poor transportation and communication), the final clause of the formal resolution states "that two-thirds of the whole number of votes of the convention shall be necessary to constitute a choice."[25] This rule was the outgrowth of the first Democratic convention of 1832. President Andrew Jackson's renomination was assured, but the delegates agreed that a two-thirds majority would be needed to nominate the vice presidential candidate.

From the 1835 convention onward, the two-thirds rule was adopted at each quadrennial convention on motions that were passed by simple majorities. From time to time, the two-thirds rule was debated, but as a leading team of scholars has commented: "Over the years it developed its own body of powerful supporters, strongly wedded to states' rights, party federalism, and the Calhoun doctrine of concurrent majorities."[26] Supporters of the two-thirds rule (mostly from the South) were determined that no candidate would be nominated without the assent—or at least acquiescence—of most major factions within the party.

As mentioned earlier, the two-thirds rule twice blocked the nomination of candidates who actually had gained a majority of delegate votes. In the aftermath of the 1924 marathon Democratic convention, deadlocked nearly two weeks by the two-thirds rule, further proposals for its abolition were heard. Nothing was done about repeal in 1928, however, because Governor Al Smith, one of the losing contenders in 1924, appeared to have the nomination wrapped up before convention time. In 1932, Governor Franklin D. Roosevelt and his managers, recognizing that they might not be able to corral the two-thirds majority needed for the nomination, had sent up a trial balloon urging repeal of the historic two-thirds rule. But the FDR partisans soon ran into a hornet's nest of opposition. When rumors of the proposed change reached the ears of Southern delegates, and it became evident that they might bolt from Roosevelt if he persisted in pushing the rule change, Roosevelt quickly told his managers to pull back this proposed reform rule. Instead, Roosevelt's campaign manager, James A. Farley, appeared before the rules committee to oppose any change in the convention ground rules.[27] But the Roosevelt supporters did not give up the fight entirely. They persuaded the rules committee to offer the following resolution, which was adopted by a voice vote.

We recommend to the next National Convention of the party that it shall consider the question of changing the two-thirds rule now required for the nomination of President and Vice President of the United States so as to make the nomination by a majority vote of the delegates to the convention with a further declaration that the convention is to be the sole judge of its own rules.[28]

Four years later, the famous two-thirds rule was abolished by the Democratic National Convention that renominated FDR for a second term.[29] With its repeal came a decline in the number of Democratic favorite sons nominated at conventions (see Table 8). This is understandable, since previously under the two-thirds rule it was the standard practice of state party organizations to put up favorite-son candidates to block the front-runner candidate—until major promises on patronage or other concessions had been extracted from him. Failing that, the tough-minded state party leaders usually turned to other more sympathetic candidates.

TABLE 8

FAVORITE-SON CANDIDATES POLLING FIFTEEN VOTES OR MORE AT NATIONAL CONVENTIONS (FIRST BALLOT ONLY) WHEN PARTY HAS BEEN OUT-OF-POWER OR WHEN AN "OPEN" CONVENTION RACE HAS EXISTED, 1920-1980

Year	Number of Favorite-Son Candidates	
	Democrats	*Republicans*
1920	11	7
1924	10	—
1928	10	—
1932	6	—
1936	—	*
1940	—	6
1944	—	*
1948	—	4
1952	5	2
1956	5	—
1960	3	—
1964	—	2
1968	—	1
1972	—	—
1976	—	—
1980	—	—

* Only one candidate nominated at the convention.

Repeal of the Unit Rule

Some critics of the two-thirds rule believed that another historic voting rule at the Democratic conventions—the unit rule—should also have been abolished in 1936 when the two-thirds rule was dropped. The unit rule, by which a majority of a state delegation could cast all the votes of its delegation (if instructed by its state convention or if the delegation agreed to abide by the rule), was first adopted by the Democratic party in 1836. Though occasionally criticized, it was not repealed until the 1968 Democratic convention—132 years later.[30]

The chief objection to the unit rule in 1968 was the same as that made in 1936, and earlier: namely, the unit rule, theoretically at least, permitted an embattled convention minority to frustrate the will of the majority whenever it was used. (The GOP, for this reason, has never used the unit rule.) Indeed, under the unit rule prior to repeal of the two-thirds rule in 1936, a presidential nomination could have been blocked, theoretically at least, by a cohesive minority faction with considerably less than one-third of the voting strength of the entire convention, if these votes were distributed in such a way as to form working majorities within delegations that comprised a total of one-third plus one of the voting delegates of the national convention.

The unit rule, as explained above, was not imposed upon the states by the Democratic convention; rather, the conventions merely enforced the instructions imposed upon a state delegation by a state party convention. In the case of delegates chosen in presidential primaries, the national convention recognized state laws that excluded these delegates from the operation of the unit rule.[31]

Prior to its repeal, the unit rule had been losing its popularity. Only ten states were bound by the unit rule at the 1964 Democratic convention. It had been a common assumption that the unit rule was retained, as the two-thirds rule before it, only to placate the Southern Democrats. However, a perusal of the list of the states that were still using the unit rule when they arrived at the 1968 Democratic National Convention indicated that while it was used most frequently in the South (Arkansas, Mississippi, South Carolina, and Texas), the other five states that still adhered to the rule (Alaska, Maryland, Massachusetts, Kansas, and Oregon) were scattered across the map.

Vice Presidential Nomination

The last major substantive item of convention business is the selection of the vice presidential nominee. In the words of one veteran commentator, "The only real suspense in the modern nominating convention is that associated with selecting a vice presidential candidate."[32] If a candidate has had to fight for the nomination right through to the convention, as General Dwight D. Eisenhower did in 1952 or President Gerald Ford in 1976, the nominee has had, of course, little time to devote to screening candidates in advance. During the tense prenomination maneuvering and the presidential balloting, especially in the out-of-power party, the delegates are usually so deeply engrossed with who is to be the nominee that there is scarcely a moment to reflect on the party's choice for the number two spot on the ticket. Yet, in view of the fact that four vice presidents have succeeded to the presidency upon the death of the incumbent thus far in the twentieth century, and one has succeeded a resigning president— Ford replaced

Nixon in 1974—the selection of the vice presidential candidate who may unexpectedly be elevated to the presidency is not a superficial task. No longer do the scornful remarks about the office by the first vice presidential incumbent John Adams apply—"the most insignificant...that ever the invention of man contrived." Indeed, as one perceptive convention-watcher has noted, "In times of constant national peril most of us would agree that vice presidents can hardly afford to be men of substantially less stature than those whom they might have to succeed in the White House."[33]

Generally, the choice of the president's running-mate is held over until the day following the presidential balloting. Meanwhile, it is customary for the nominee to sound out key party leaders on their recommendation for vice president—even though the nominee may have already made up his mind on his own choice. Indeed, it is almost universally accepted that the presidential nominee's choice for running-mate will be approved by the convention by a routine roll call vote, whether the vice presidential candidate is a popular favorite or a surprise choice. This is the main reason why so little formal campaigning is done for the vice presidency. As Gerald Pomper explains, "public preferences are either unavailable or unsolicited, party leaders have few commitments other than tepid enthusiasm for a favorite son, and strategy to gain the second position is undeveloped."[34] Also, it is difficult to campaign openly for the vice presidency, as former Massachusetts Governor Endicott "Chub" Peabody soon discovered when he unsuccessfully attempted to mount a sustained drive to win the number two spot on the 1972 Democratic ticket. (Peabody received 107.3 votes out of 3,016 on the first and only ballot, which saw the Democrats select Senator Thomas Eagleton, Senator McGovern's choice for running-mate.) Stephen J. Wayne has summarized well the dilemma of vice presidential contenders, "There are no vice presidential primaries and no government matching funds for vice presidential candidates. Only one 'vote' really counts—the presidential nominee's."[35]

Throughout the years most candidates have preferred to aim their sights for the top job in the White House. Only after this hope has been dashed by other candidates in the caucuses and primaries have they been willing to settle for the vice presidential consolation prize.

Both the Democratic and Republican parties have flirted with the idea of changing the method of selecting the vice presidential nominee. Actually, the complaint has not been so much that the vice presidential running-mate is hand-picked by the newly selected presidential nominee, but rather that a spur-of-the-moment decision is made by a tired nominee and wearied advisers in the early pre-dawn hours after the presidential balloting has been completed.[36] (The newly selected nominee must, of course, come up with a vice presidential choice for the delegates to vote on the next evening.) Four different men who were presidential candidates from 1960 through 1980 (Humphrey, Muskie, Mondale, and Bush) have subsequently been chosen as vice presidential candidates in the hectic early morning hours following the presidential balloting. The abrupt withdrawal of the initial Democratic nominee in 1972 (Senator Thomas Eagleton) and the eventual resignation one year later of Republican Vice President Spiro Agnew in the face of possible impeachment proceedings spawned new concern over the vice presidential selection process. But this uneasiness has not led to a new method of selection.

In 1976, however, presidential challenger Ronald Reagan, involved in a tight uphill nominating race against President Gerald Ford, announced his own choice for vice presidential nominee, Senator Richard S. Schweiker of Pennsylvania a week before the GOP convention opened and dared President Ford to follow suit. But Reagan's desperate gamble, aimed at putting President Ford on the defensive, was an obvious attempt to shake loose pro-Ford delegates who would be alienated by any vice presidential choice Ford might make.[37] But the stratagem failed when President Ford refused to tip his hand before the convention. When the convention Rules Committee offered its pro-Ford report, Reagan's supporters introduced an amendment to Rule 16 requiring presidential candidates to name their vice presidential choices before the presidential balloting the next night. Under this proposal, failure of a candidate to comply would have freed all of his delegates from any commitments to vote for him. This proposed amendment, however, was voted down by the pro-Ford majority at the convention by a margin of 111 votes. Clearly, the Reagan forces had lost their first, and probably the most important, roll call of the convention.[38] Indeed, this was virtually the same margin that he lost the nomination to Ford two nights later. Understandably, Reagan's concern about his prospective vice presidential nominee was motivated far more by presidential nominating strategy than a fundamental desire to reform the method of picking vice presidential candidates. In 1980 Reagan quietly dropped this selection approach for choosing his running-mate and reverted to the traditional method of handpicking his choice.

In the past, balancing the ticket geographically has been an important consideration in both parties: if the GOP presidential nominee was from the East, a Midwesterner or Pacific Coast candidate would most likely be selected for the number two spot. Within the Democratic party a Southern or Border State vice presidential candidate has frequently been picked to balance the ticket.[39] (Nor should it be overlooked that in 1920 a young Assistant Secretary of the Navy from New York state by the name of Franklin D. Roosevelt was chosen as the Democratic vice presidential nominee to help balance the ticket. The Democratic presidential nominee was Governor James M. Cox of Ohio.) Another consideration that is often taken into account by the presidential nominee is to choose a vice presidential candidate from another wing or faction of the party.

Occasionally, the choice for vice president may be the result of a trade whereby a rival contender or faction gives its votes to the front-runner in exchange for the "consolation prize." Franklin D. Roosevelt clinched his first nomination in 1932 by just such a horse trade. After failure to capture the nomination in three ballots (even though he received over a majority of votes on each of these ballots), and when his drive to win a two-thirds majority appeared to be losing steam, Roosevelt authorized his managers to offer the vice presidency to Speaker John N.

Garner, a conservative Southerner from Texas, in return for his Texas and California votes (Garner had won the California primary). Garner's 90 delegate votes from these two states were more than enough to give FDR the two-thirds majority then needed to win the nomination.[40] In the Republican convention of 1944, a similar sequence of events occurred when Governor John Bricker of Ohio yielded the presidential nomination to Thomas E. Dewey without a fight and subsequently was given second place on the ticket.

The Democratic nominee in 1956, Adlai Stevenson, tried to inject some "grass roots" democracy into the vice presidential selection process by permitting the convention, without any guidance from him, to choose his running-mate in an open contest. Senator Estes Kefauver, his chief opponent in the primaries, was nominated by the convention, barely edging out a young senator from Massachusetts, John F. Kennedy. The Stevenson action, however, did not set a precedent. In 1960 Senator Kennedy reverted to the standard practice of the nominee hand-picking his own running-mate. Kennedy chose a Southerner, Senate Majority Leader Lyndon B. Johnson of Texas, to help keep most of the Southern states in the Democratic column—a strategy that paid off handsomely in November. Nixon, then a resident of California, chose Henry Cabot Lodge, Jr. of Massachusetts—United States Ambassador to the United Nations, an avowed internationalist with a more liberal viewpoint on domestic issues than Nixon. Four years later, Johnson leaned toward geographical balance, though Johnson's running-mate, Senator Humphrey of Minnesota, was also considerably to the left of the President. Congressman William Miller of New York, Senator Goldwater's vice presidential choice, was a fellow conservative. In 1968 Nixon selected a Border State governor, Spiro Agnew of Maryland—a concession to Southern Republicans who had played a major role in Nixon's nomination. Humphrey, the Democratic nominee, chose a fellow Northern Liberal, Senator Edmund Muskie of Maine.

In 1972 the Democrats held, in effect, two nominating conventions to resolve a special problem with their vice presidential nominee. The second Democratic convention refers to the "mini-convention" held in Washington, D.C., August 8, 1972, that selected R. Sargent Shriver as a new vice presidential running-mate to replace Senator Thomas F. Eagleton. This almost unprecedented action was taken after it was disclosed by two enterprising reporters, less than two weeks after the Miami Beach convention, that Senator Eagleton had undergone extensive psychiatric therapy—including electric shock treatment—for nervous exhaustion three times during the 1960's. Actually, the Democrats' second convention was a special meeting of the 278-member Democratic National Committee, in which each state's representatives cast the same number of votes as the state did at the regular Democratic convention in Miami Beach. At this "extraordinary" session the Democratic National Committee members voted overwhelmingly to endorse McGovern's choice for vice president— R. Sargent Shriver, a former director of the Peace Corps and brother-in-law of the late President Kennedy.[41]

In recent years there has been a notable trend toward the nomination of prominent individuals as running-mates. And as the prestige of the office has grown and its political influence seemingly increased, major public figures (frequently leading U.S. senators) have been willing to accept nomination for vice president. Formerly, the prestige of the office was so low that offers for the nomination were usually brushed aside by prominent governors and senators. In 1924, for example, Governor Frank O. Lowden of Illinois flatly turned down the vice presidential nomination offer from President Coolidge, even though it was a near certainty that if he accepted, he would be elected Vice President of the United States. It is noteworthy that in the past four decades, defeated aspirants for the presidency have later been chosen as the vice presidential nominee or replacement on seven occasions.[42] But there are few convention defenders who urge that this method become mandatory. Otherwise, this requirement in 1960 would have made Nixon's running-mate Arizona Republican Senator Barry Goldwater; Senator Robert Taft would have been Eisenhower's vice presidential candidate in 1952; Senator Richard Russell of Georgia, Truman's running-mate in 1948; and except for a constitutional ban on presidential electors voting for two members of the ticket from the same state, Alfred E. Smith of New York would have been Franklin Delano Roosevelt's vice presidential nominee in 1932.[43] Clearly, the wide policy differences between these presidential nominees and their mandatory running-mates under this arrangement would have been too wide for the party to present a united front against the opposition.

Critics of the traditional vice presidential selection process have attempted to assure that no longer can the presidential nominee's choice of a running-mate be imposed upon an unwilling convention. But despite numerous proposals to change the present system, no clearly superior method has yet been devised. Nothing stands in the way of preventing nominees from making their preferences known ahead of time, if they wish to divulge them. Among the suggested reforms, having an announced presidential and vice presidential candidate team run on the same ticket would mean that the runners-up in the presidential sweepstakes would be removed from consideration for the number two spot. Picking the vice president first would restrict the field to those who had no hope for the presidential nomination. Limiting the choice to the top three runners-up for the presidential nomination would constrain the convention and the nominee in their attempts to field the strongest possible national ticket. Having the party designate someone holding another high office as vice president would involve the risk that the designee would be insufficiently informed to assume the presidency, if necessary. Eliminating the office of vice president or reshuffling the line of succession to the presidency has also been suggested, but they do not necessarily resolve the leadership succession problem.

Another vice presidential selection proposal drafted by state GOP chairpersons from Arkansas and Maryland in 1979 would have authorized the victorious nominee to submit a sealed list of three to five names of prospective running-mates to the convention chairman and then have the convention vote for a vice presidential candidate from this list.[44] Critics of this proposal claim that the outcome would be the same with or without the list in the sealed envelope, since it could be expected that the presidential candidate would simply pass the word along about which name on the list is his first choice. Advocates of the plan also did not have the answer to the problem that might arise if a president's choice were rejected by the convention. Although this vice presidential selection proposal enjoyed varying degrees of support from GOP presidential contenders, Reagan, Senator Howard Baker (R.-Tenn.), and former Secretary of the Treasury John B. Connally in the early stages of the 1980 nominating race, the Republican National Committee took no positive action on the proposal at its January 1980 meeting. Like proposed changes in the Electoral College, reform of the vice presidential selection process is discussed frequently after the general election but then nothing happens until the next general election, when the discussion cycle begins anew.

The year 1980, marked by one of the most bizarre episodes in the history of national nominating conventions, almost resulted in the selection of former President Gerald Ford as Ronald Reagan's vice presidential running-mate. This "near-miss," which would have been the first time in American history that a former President had taken the number two spot on a party ticket, occurred during the final hours before Reagan's almost unanimous nomination (1,939 out of 1,994 votes) at the 1980 Detroit convention.

Described as a "dream ticket" by some leading Republicans, the proposed Reagan-Ford ticket reportedly fell apart in the final hours before the presidential nominations were scheduled to begin. It collapsed when former President Ford insisted that former Secretary of State Henry Kissinger be reappointed to his old post in a new Reagan Administration and that Alan Greenspan, Ford's economic adviser, be given the Secretary of the Treasury slot. This inflated asking price that Ford laid on Reagan was, according to party insiders, too much for Reagan. The soon-to-be-nominated Reagan was astounded to hear some of Ford's exorbitant demands publicly aired during a "live" televised interview between Ford and CBS anchorman Walter Cronkite in the network booth high inside the Joe Louis Convention Hall, as the milling delegates began taking their seats preparatory to the presidential balloting. By 9 P.M. Ford reportedly had scaled down his demands, but his insistence on veto power over two Cabinet appointments—State and Defense—further soured Reagan's attitude toward the former president.[45] Instead, two hours later amidst rampant convention rumors that Ford would be Reagan's choice as vice presidential nominee, Reagan abruptly selected George Bush—his chief rival during the hard-fought primary season. In retrospect, Ronald Reagan apparently concluded that presidential power could not be shared. Though former President Ford would probably have strengthened the GOP ticket— at the time of the Republican convention the impending race between President Carter and Reagan was thought to be extremely close—the former California governor was clearly unprepared to deal away the powers of the presidency to improve his chances of winning in November. Thus, the dream ticket of Reagan and Ford, with its potentially numerous constitutional ramifications, never came to pass. But historians and political scientists will be talking and writing for years about the "might-have-beens," if a former President of the United States, Gerald Ford, had run and been elected Vice President in a subsequent presidential election.

By carefully selecting his running-mate, the presidential nominee cannot only score political points, but he can also protect his flanks from attack. For example, both Jimmy Carter in 1976 and Ronald Reagan in 1980 faced criticism at the time of their nomination of being an outsider without "Washington experience." Critics said that they would be handicapped in dealing with Congress and the bureaucracy. To blunt this criticism Carter selected a popular member of the U.S. Senate—Walter F. "Fritz" Mondale. Four years later, Reagan neutralized these complaints by selecting as his running-mate George Bush—who had held five different national party and government posts in the previous ten years.

Legitimation and Consensus-Building Functions

In 1976 (for the Democrats) and 1980 (for the Republicans) several of the most important manifest functions (listed in Chapter 1) of the national conventions—selecting the nominee, framing the platform, and agreeing on party rules—were in fact carried out in the weeks preceding the convention. If these functions can be fulfilled in the pre-convention period when a single candidate dominates the field, one might logically ask, "Why do we really need a convention at all?" The simple response would seem under the circumstances to be to cancel the quadrennial party gathering. But this hasty action would overlook other important latent functions (also listed in Chapter 1) performed by national conventions. Even when the choice of nominee is a foregone conclusion, the holding of a national convention can, for example, still be important in facilitating legitimation. Generally, the following factors contribute to legitimation: (1) the willingness of delegates to detach themselves from commitment to defeated candidates, (2) the existence of multiple prizes (for example, platform planks, vice presidential nomination) at the convention, (3) the expectation of victory in the general election, (4) the low level of issue polarization, (5) multiple group identifications, and (6) a moderately high level of party loyalty.[46]

It should not be forgotten that most of our recent Presidents—and many of the earlier Chief Executives—were the choice for nominee of only slightly more than 50 percent of the convention delegates of the out-of-power party. General Dwight D. Eisenhower finished only 95 votes ahead of Senator Robert Taft on the first ballot at the 1952 GOP convention before a decisive number of delegates shifted to his winning banner. Eight years later, the youthful John F. Kennedy collected only 46 votes more than a majority (53 percent) at the 1960 Democratic convention. In 1968, former Vice President Nixon captured the GOP nomination with a wafer-thin majority of 25 votes (slightly less than 52 percent). Though Governor Jimmy Carter won a one-sided victory at the 1976 Democratic National Convention (because most of his opponents dropped out of the race long before convention time), he was the choice of only 39 percent of the voters in the primaries. Within the incumbent party, President Gerald Ford nosed out challenger Ronald Reagan in 1976 by only 111 votes out of 2,259—a margin of approximately 52.2 percent of the convention. In all five cases cited, the convention victory—all on the first ballot—helped to legitimate the nominee as the chosen leader of the party. All four nominees of the out-of-power party went on to capture the White House in November, but President Ford, badly bruised in a tough nominating race, was unsuccessful in his bid to win a first full term.

Failure to be accepted as the legitimate standard-bearer by a solid majority of the convention delegates and members of the party at-large usually spells defeat for the presidential nominee in November. In 1912, for example, anti-administration charges that the majority of convention delegates supporting President William Howard Taft had "stolen" the nomination from Teddy Roosevelt by the seating of more than 200 challenged delegates, mostly from the "rotten borough" districts in the South, wrecked Taft's chances for reelection. More than a half century later, Vice President Hubert H. Humphrey learned, ultimately to his dismay, that a nomination won with delegate votes that the McCarthy anti-Vietnam War delegates claimed had been selected in violation of "fair play" rules doomed his chances for winning the White House. (The McCarthyites charged that over 600 delegates to the 1968 Democratic convention— approximately half the number needed to win the nomination—"were selected by processes which included no means (however indirect) of voter participation since 1966.")[47] In other words, if the nominee cannot obtain reasonable consensus from the convention delegates, the dialogue between the new standard-bearer and various party constituencies and interest groups within the party usually breaks down. By and large, though, national conventions have usually induced divergent elements in the party to close ranks behind the newly appointed leader, at least to the extent of refraining from actively opposing the nominee.

Generally, national conventions provide an arena in which major elements bargain not only with each other, but they also serve as a site for negotiations between the party nominee and the leaders of various party groups—trade unions, Black and Hispanic caucuses, the National Organization of Women, the Moral Majority, teachers' organizations, environmental groups, and so on. These negotiations, it has been pointed out by Denis G. Sullivan and others, serve two purposes: "They place constraints on the nominee, who must make himself acceptable to groups; and they serve to reassure groups by allowing them to become familiar with the candidate."[48] While these constraints could be applied in the absence of a convention, the convention environment serves to increase the group's strength as negotiators and, generally, the nominee's euphoria over his victory makes him more amenable to compromise. The ready accessibility of hundreds of television and press media at the convention strengthens the interest group's negotiating position, since they can easily call a press conference, if they feel short-changed, to air their complaints. In this manner, the unique convention setting contributes to the ability of party groups to bargain with, and to constrain, the policy choices of the nominee.

If the convention can perform these legitimating and consensus-building functions effectively when a single candidate dominates the scene, these "fringe benefits" are even more valuable when the convention is divided in its support among numerous candidates. For these reasons alone, one can rightfully conclude that there is no substitute for this venerable political institution, especially for integrating defeated factions within the party.

The Convention as a Campaign Rally

The growing role of conventions as a campaign rally mechanism to kick off the presidential election campaign has not escaped the attention of convention managers and political professionals alike. Prior to 1940, both parties held their conventions before July 1. As a rule, another ten days or two weeks elapsed before the candidate was "officially" notified that he had been nominated—even though the entire country had been informed by press, telegraph, and radio (after 1924) about the nomination. Before the emergence of presidential primaries, opinion polls, and television as major factors in the nominating process, conventions also served more as deliberative bodies than campaign launchers. During this early modern era the general election campaign extended over a four-month period, marked by the usual summer doldrums. This leisurely pace did not pick up until Labor Day, or shortly thereafter, when the whistle-stopping rail tours got underway.

But since the age of television, especially from 1952 onward, national conventions have served as an indispensable rallying mechanism for the party faithful and the mass electorate. With the nationwide television audience numbering upwards of fifty million viewers during prime evening time, the convention managers quickly recognized that conventions offer a priceless opportunity to appeal to millions of potential voters. Not only the party loyalists but the uncommitted independents (who constitute approximately 30 percent of the electorate and the balance of power) and even some wavering opposition party members can be reached—and influenced—by the cost-free network telecasts. So important are the conventions as a campaign launching pad that both parties hire professional TV consultants to advise and direct the handling of the televised proceedings in order to achieve maximum impact upon the millions of home viewers.

In the 1950's one observer predicted that in twenty years conventions would be held primarily to ratify previous decisions and "to stage a rally for the benefit of the national television audience."[49] This prediction about the growing role of the "campaign rally" function of national conventions has been remarkably accurate. Indeed, in light of the transformation of the presidential nominating process, which now usually finds the out-party's national favorite singled out in the presidential primaries and the national polls and, in effect, "nominated" before the convention, the campaign rally function of the national convention has assumed vital importance. Even if presidential nominations were to be handled through national primaries, and even if party platforms were written by a special team of experts, the need for the campaign rally would still be a vitally important step toward capturing the White House.

In discussing the campaign rally function of conventions, we are not talking merely about the cheerleading atmosphere and delegate euphoria. The authors of the leading study of national conventions two decades ago summarized the campaign rally activity as follows: "The conventions have the effect of projecting an image of the parties in their collective, corporate identity. They provide a setting within which the major-party leaders and eventual candidates can be subjected to an intense form of public scrutiny."[50] It is no wonder, then, that the growing campaign rally role for the conventions prompted the same authors to conclude: "Political strategists of both parties have thus been compelled to recognize that the campaign begins at the convention, not afterwards, and that it should therefore be conducted as a major segment of the campaign."[51]

In short, while the convention managers are anxious to send the hundreds of delegates home in a festive mood so that they will work actively during the general election campaign, the real target of campaign rally activities is the mass electorate watching the proceedings on television.

Since the advent of national television, convention rally activities have indeed been altered and streamlined in order to project a more favorable party "image" upon television land's millions of viewers. Among the first convention casualties have been the long "spontaneous" demonstrations for presidential contenders that sometimes took days to organize. At first, all leading candidates were urged by the convention managers to restrict the demonstrations to a reasonable length, that is ten or twelve minutes. In 1968, however, the Democratic National Committee banned all floor demonstrations at the Chicago convention. One of the reasons for the ban was, of course, to help preserve "law and order" among the badly divided Democrats, but the convention managers were well aware that the national television audiences have grown tired of the "highjinks" and contrived attempts to persuade delegates and the TV audiences alike that a specific candidate enjoys massive grass roots support. Subsequently, more than a year before the 1972 Democratic National Convention, the National Committee's Commission of Rules (O'Hara Commission) voted to ban all floor demonstrations and lengthy speeches, and make the nomination of favorite-son candidates all but impossible.[52] These recommendations, which were accepted by the Democratic National Committee, became the rules of the 1972 convention. Opponents of floor demonstrations echoed one O'Hara Commission member's comments that "the American people seemed to have become estranged from the parties, partly because of 'some of the foolishness' at the conventions."[53]

The Republicans soon followed suit, banning all floor demonstrations at their national conclaves. But in 1976, disappointed supporters of former California Governor Ronald Reagan, who lost the GOP nomination to President Ford, ignored the ban and staged their own noisy, hour-long demonstration on behalf of Reagan before President Ford delivered his acceptance speech on the final night of the Kansas City convention. The lengthy demonstration, as Ford's managers recognized, served as excellent therapy for the Reaganites to work off frustrations over their nomination loss. Consequently, no effort was made to shut off the horn and cowbell ringing, even though it wasted over an hour of precious network prime time. The 1980 Republican convention, by contrast, was a model of decorum—no floor demonstrations and no interruptions in a tightly orchestrated schedule—as it moved toward a grand finale of party unity. In the final minutes, fifty million televiewers saw Presidential nominee Ronald Reagan, his running-mate George Bush, and former President Jerry Ford, who had been passed over for the number two spot, all locked arm-in-arm smiling and waving to the throng below and to the millions of potential voters in televisionland. Reagan, the former Hollywood star, could not have maximized the campaign rally function of the national convention more effectively if he had written the entire script himself.

To fully appreciate the campaign rally function, one has only to contrast the spectacular Republican convention send-off for the Reagan-Bush team with John Anderson's lonely kick-off of his 1980 third-party fall election campaign. Lacking the ready-made nationally televised forum of a nominating convention, Anderson was forced to invent a substitute. Instead of holding a national convention, with its millions of dollars worth of free televised publicity, he merely called a press conference and announced in late August 1980 that his running-mate would be Patrick Lucey, former governor of Wisconsin, ambassador to Mexico, and more recently, Senator Ted Kennedy's deputy campaign manager. Announcing the choice of a running-mate solely to members of the traveling press is somewhat comparable to attending a festive homecoming celebration in which only the former cheerleaders show up. Over the Labor Day weekend the Anderson-Lucey office released its 317-page equivalent of a party platform for their "National Unity Campaign."[54] Excerpts were published in the *New York Times* and other leading dailies, but unlike the Republican and Democratic platforms adopted on prime-time network television, this carefully drafted document received less attention from daily newspaper readers than the daily stock market quotations. As columnist David Broder observed, "the document was dropped into the newspapers on the Labor Day holiday weekend, when few voters were paying attention. And after one day it disappeared."[55] Third-party candidates like John Anderson can only dream about reaping the tremendous publicity dividends of a national convention. Inability to capitalize on the valuable campaign rally function of the national convention will continue to plague third-party presidential candidates until they, too, hold their own conclaves before the television cameras and persuade their party faithful "to rally round the flag."

In a sense, televised national conventions also perform an "educational" function for the party and its nominee. The national convention allows millions of television viewers to see non-incumbents in a new role—as head of a political party. Indeed, for many of these viewers the conventions offer a first glimpse into the makeup of the nominee, his family, staff, style of operation, and his decision-making ability in choosing a running-mate. In addition, a smooth and well-run convention offers the public evidence of the party and the candidate's capacity to manage the government.[56]

Before the age of television, the final action of the convention did not culminate with the presidential and vice presidential nominee acceptance speeches and the farewell ceremony at the podium but rather with the appointment of a special party committee to "notify" the candidate formally of his nomination and another committee to inform the vice presidential candidate of his nomination. During the month of August, usually on dates spaced a week or so apart, these two committees performed their official notification duties at elaborate ceremonies in the candidate's home town. The chairman of the committee would make a speech notifying the candidate of his nomination. The nominee would, in turn, follow with a speech accepting the nomination, explaining his general views on the issues and committing himself to the platform adopted at the convention, unless he specifically wanted to ignore or repudiate some planks. This notification ceremony, which provided a forum and served as a campaign document for the candidates after their nomination, was abruptly changed by Governor Franklin D. Roosevelt in 1932, when he dramatically flew to Chicago to make his acceptance speech at the Democratic convention. Roosevelt took special delight in this precedent-shattering action to break, as he called it, "the absurd tradition that the candidate should remain in professed ignorance of what has happened for weeks until he is formally notified."[57] Also, this adroit move enabled FDR to obtain free nationwide radio time in the depths of the Great Depression to address the American people. The Democrats have continued to follow this quadrennial custom set by Roosevelt. The Republicans used the traditional notification ceremonies for the last time in 1940, when a GOP committee journeyed to Elwood, Indiana, to notify Wendell L. Willkie of his nomination. Four years later, however, the Republicans adopted the Roosevelt method of having the candidate make his acceptance speech in person at the convention.

Both parties now, of course, receive millions of dollars of free TV network coverage of the acceptance speeches. One of the most memorable acceptance speeches of the television era was made by the late Senator John F. Kennedy in 1960 at the Democratic convention when he concluded:

We stand today on the edge of a New Frontier—the frontier of the 1960's.... Are we up to the task? Are we equal to the challenge? Are we willing to match the Russian sacrifice of the present for the future?...That is the choice our nation must make...between the public interest and private comfort—between national greatness and national decline.[58]

For the out-of-power party the nominee's acceptance speech also marks the end (at least officially) of intra-party candidate squabbling, as attention is shifted from the nominating process to the arena of two-party competition.

In the years ahead convention managers will undoubtedly continue to deemphasize the conduct of party business and endeavor instead to capitalize on the party rally function (as exemplified by the acceptance speeches) to persuade the national electorate—via the free television network coverage of the conventions—to vote for their party nominee in November.

As the presidential nominees stand poised for the final stretch drive to capture the Grand Prize, it seems appropriate to ask several questions: Who are the serious presidential possibilities? How did they become contenders for the highest office in the land? Have the conditions for a presidential incumbent seeking a second nomination changed? Has the recent transformation in the presidential nominating system produced a new type of nominee?

In the next chapter we will seek to find an answer to some of these perplexing questions.

Notes

1. See James W. Davis, *Presidential Primaries: Road to the White House*, 2nd ed. (Westport, Conn.: Greenwood Press, 1980).

2. Richard Reeves, Universal Press Syndicate, quoted in *Bellingham Herald* (Bellingham, Wash.), February 2, 1982.

3. Theodore H. White, *The Making of the President, 1972* (New York: Atheneum, 1973), pp. 96-133.

4. Lewis Chester, Godfrey Hodgson, and Bruce Page, *An American Melodrama: The Presidential Campaign of 1968* (New York: Viking Press, 1969), pp. 454-75.

5. Theodore H. White, *The Making of the President, 1960* (New York: Atheneum, 1961), pp. 115-79.

6. Donald R. Matthews, "Presidential Nominations: Process and Outcome," in James David Barber, ed., *Choosing the President* (Englewood Cliffs, N.J.: Prentice-Hall, 1974), p. 39.

7. See James W. Davis, *Presidential Primaries: Road to the White House*, pp. 77-78.

8. The techniques of delegate counting, however, are not uniform. The wire services depend most heavily on their bureau chiefs in the state capitals. The television networks use a different combination of techniques: talking directly to delegates via phone, calculations from the raw results of caucus selections of delegates, and comparing the estimates of the state and national campaign leaders. The *New York Times* relies more heavily on the national campaign staffs of various candidates. Adam Clymer, *New York Times*, May 17, 1980.

9. Sears explained to newsmen four years later why he tried to stop a perception of delegate drift to President Ford by claiming a majority of delegates for Reagan one day in July, a month before the 1976 GOP convention. "It introduced an element of confusion," he said, "because the minute delegates and politicians believe a race is over, it is over." *New York Times*, May 17, 1980.

10. Ibid., August 17, 1976.

11. Ibid., June 5, 1980.

12. Paul T. David, Ralph M. Goldman, and Richard C. Bain, *The Politics of National Party Conventions* (Washington, D.C.: The Brookings Institution, 1960), pp. 319-20.

See also James W. Davis, *Presidential Primaries: Road to the White House* (New York: Thomas Y. Crowell, 1967) for additional discussion of the crucial importance of the week-by-week reports of the Associated Press delegate count in pinpointing the convention winner. For a more critical analysis of the impact of Associated Press delegate count on convention outcome, see Donald S. Collat, Stanley Kelley, Jr., and Ronald Rogowski, "The End Game in Presidential Nominations," *American Political Science Review*, Vol. 75 (June 1981), pp. 426-35.

13. *New York Times*, May 17, 1980.

14. Herbert Croly, *Marcus Alonzo Hanna* (New York: Macmillan, 1912).

15. Harding's campaign manager confidently described the process to two reporters several weeks before the 1920 GOP convention. "I don't expect Senator Harding to be nominated on the first, second, or third ballot, but I think about eleven minutes after two o'clock on Friday morning (the fifth day) of the convention, when fifteen or twenty men, bleary-eyed and perspiring profusely from the heat, are sitting around the table some of them will say: "Who will we nominate?" At that decisive time the friends of Senator Harding can suggest him and can afford to abide by the result. I don't know but what I might suggest him myself." Harry M. Daughtery, in collaboration with Thomas Dixon, *The Inside Story of the Harding Tragedy* (New York: Churchill Company, 1932), pp. 341-42; see also Mark Sullivan, *Our Times: The United States, 1900-1925* Vol. 6 (New York: Scribner's, 1935), pp. 37-38.

16. Leon D. Epstein, "Political Science and Presidential Nominations," *Political Science Quarterly*, Vol. 93 (Summer 1978), p. 187.

17. Jeane J. Kirkpatrick, *Dismantling the Parties: Reflections on the Role of Policy in the Decomposition* (Washington, D.C.: American Enterprise Institute, 1978), p. 14.

18. Ibid., p. 15.

19. Theodore H. White, *The Making of the President, 1960* (New York: Atheneum, 1961), pp. 157-58.

20. The material in this section closely follows the analysis in Stephen J. Wayne, *The Road to the White House* (New York: St. Martin's Press, 1980), pp. 135-38.

21. Jack W. Germond and Jules Witcover, *Blue Smoke and Mirrors: How Reagan Won and Why Carter Lost the Election of 1980* (New York: The Viking Press, 1981), pp. 202-4. If the Carter organization had wished to block approval of these platform planks, they certainly had the manpower to do so. According to one floor reporter, the Carter forces had divided the convention floor into 14 areas and assigned a "cluster whip" to each. These area whips supervised the whips assigned to the delegates from each congressional district. In delegations that seemed restless the Carter chieftains assigned a special whip to each row of seats to keep an eye on the delegates. "The Carter people have incredible control over their delegates," said Representative Don Edwards of California, a Kennedy supporter. "They're hardly allowed to go to bed alone." Terence Smith, *New York Times*, August 12, 1980.

22. Chalmers M. Roberts, *The Washington Post: The First 100 Years* (Boston: Houghton Mifflin Company, 1977), p. 54.

23. *Call to Order*, Commission on Rules of the Democratic National Committee, Rep. James G. O'Hara, Chairman (Washington, D.C.: Democratic National Committee, 1972), p. 90.

24. Paul T. David, Malcolm Moos, and Ralph M. Goldman, *Presidential Nominating Politics in 1952*, Vol. 1 (Baltimore: The Johns Hopkins University Press, 1954), p. 94.

25. Paul T. David, Ralph M. Goldman, and Richard C. Bain, *The Politics of National Party Conventions*, p. 208.

26. Ibid.

27. Ibid., p. 211.

28. *Democratic National Convention Proceedings* (1932), p. 140. See also Richard C. Bain and Judith Parris, *Convention Decisions and Voting Records*, 2nd ed. (Washington, D.C.: The Brookings Institution, 1973), p. 241.

29. The report of the 1936 Democratic Committee on Rules recommending repeal of the two-thirds rule was presented to the convention by Bennett Clark, whose father had lost the Democratic nomination in 1912 because of the operation of the two-thirds rule.

30. *New York Times*, August 28, 1968.

31. V.O. Key, Jr., *Politics, Parties, and Pressure Groups*, 5th ed. (New York: Thomas Y. Crowell Company, 1964), p. 428.

32. Charles O. Jones, "Nominating 'Carter's Favorite Opponent': The Republicans in 1980," in Austin Ranney, ed., *The American Elections of 1980* (Washington, D.C.: American Enterprise Institute, 1981), p. 94.

33. Karl O'Lessker, "The National Nominating Conventions," in Cornelius P. Cotter, ed., *Practical Politics in the United States* (Boston: Allyn & Bacon, Inc., 1969), p. 264.

34. Gerald Pomper, *Nominating the President* (Evanston, Ill.: Northwestern University Press, 1963), p. 155.

35. Stephen J. Wayne, *The Road to the White House*, p. 122.

36. Jimmy Carter, by wrapping up the 1976 presidential nomination during the primary season, avoided the typical frantic, last-minute choice of a running-mate. Instead, he invited all six prospective vice presidential nominees to his Plains, Georgia, home for a careful screening and then waited until the morning after his formal nomination before announcing his personal choice—Senator Walter F. Mondale of Minnesota.

37. Jules Witcover, *Marathon: The Pursuit of the Presidency, 1972-1976* (New York: The Viking Press, 1977), p. 458.

38. See *National Party Conventions, 1831-1976* (Washington, D.C.: Congressional Quarterly, Inc., 1979), p. 124.

39. Since 1932, the Democrats have chosen seven Southern or Border State vice presidential candidates: Garner (Texas), 1932 and 1936; Truman (Missouri), 1944; Barkley (Kentucky), 1948; Sparkman (Alabama), 1952; Kefauver (Tennessee), 1956; Johnson (Texas), 1960; and Eagleton (Missouri), 1972, who resigned from the ticket two weeks after the convention when it was disclosed that he had been under psychiatric care on several occasions.

40. James A. Farley, *Behind the Ballots* (New York: Harcourt, Brace and World, Inc., 1938), p. 151.

41. The balloting, however, was not unanimous. Shriver received 2,936 votes. Missouri, remaining loyal to its home state senator, cast its 73 votes for Eagleton. Oregon split its votes, giving 30 votes to Shriver and 4 votes to former U.S. Senator Wayne Morse—presumably to give Morse a little extra national television publicity in his election bid to recapture his former U.S. Senate seat. Guam's 3 votes were not cast because their national committee members could not make it to the mini-convention.

42. Warren (1948), Kefauver (1956), Johnson (1960), Humphrey (1964), Rockefeller (1974), Mondale (1976), and Bush (1980).

43. Gerald Pomper, *Nominating the President*, p. 179.

44. *Seattle Post Intelligencer*, November 29, 1979.

45. "Inside the Jerry Ford Drama," *Time*, Vol. 116 (July 28, 1980), pp. 16-19. See also William Greider, "Republicans," in Richard Harwood, ed., *The Pursuit of the Presidency, 1980* (New York: Berkley Books, 1980), pp. 174-77. Theodore H. White, *America in Search of Itself: The Making of the President, 1956-1980* (New York: Harper & Row, Publishers, 1982), pp. 320-27.

46. Denis G. Sullivan, et al., "Candidates, Caucuses, and Issues: The Democratic Convention, 1976," in Louis Maisel and Joseph Cooper, eds., *The Impact of the Electoral Process* (Beverly Hills, Calif.: Sage Publications, 1977), p. 128.

47. Alexander M. Bickel, *The New Age of Political Reform: The Electoral College, the Convention and the Party* (New York: Harper & Row, 1968), p. 40.

48. Denis G. Sullivan et al., "Candidates, Caucuses, and Issues: The Democratic Convention, 1976," p. 129.

49. William G. Carleton, "The Revolution in the Presidential Nominating Convention," *Political Science Quarterly*, Vol. 72 (June 1957), p. 237.

50. Paul T. David, Ralph M. Goldman, and Richard C. Bain, *The Politics of National Party Conventions*, p. 495.

51. Ibid.

52. *Call to Order* pp. 56-60.

53. *New York Times*, June 12, 1971.

54. *New York Times*, August 31, 1980.

55. *Washington Post*, September 7, 1980.

56. Cliff Zukin, "A Triumph of Form over Content: Television and the 1976 National Nominating Convention." Paper presented at the Midwest Political Science Association meeting, Chicago, Illinois, April 1979.

57. *Nothing to Fear*, The Selected Addresses of Franklin Delano Roosevelt, 1932-1945, edited by B.D. Zevin (Cambridge, Mass.: Houghton Mifflin Company, 1946), p. 2.

58. Wilfred E. Binkley, *American Political Parties*, 4th ed. (New York: Alfred A. Knopf, 1962), p. 415.

The Dynamics of Convention Choice ___ 6

> All is over. As you step out of the building you inhale with relief
> the gentle breeze which tempers the scorching heat of July; you
> come to your self; you recover your sensibility, which has been
> blunted by the incessant uproar, and your faculty of judgment,
> which has been held in abeyance amid the pandemonium in which
> day after day has passed. You collect your impressions, and you
> realize what a colossal travesty of popular institutions you have just
> been witnessing. A greedy crowd of officeholders, or of office
> seekers, disguised as delegates of the people, on pretense of holding
> the grand council of the party, indulged in, or were victims of,
> intrigues and maneuvers, the object of which was the chief magis-
> tracy of the greatest republic of the two hemispheres—the succes-
> sion to the Washingtons and Jeffersons. . . . Yet, when you carry your
> thoughts back from the scene which you have just witnessed and
> review the line of Presidents, you find that if they have not all been
> great men—far from it—they were all honorable men; and you
> cannot help repeating the American saying: "God takes care of
> drunkards, of little children, and of the United States."
>
> M. Ostrogorski

The game of presidential candidate roulette has longer odds than any game of
chance in Las Vegas or Atlantic City. Sidney Hyman, in his thoughtful study of
the Presidency almost three decades ago, pointed out that although almost 100
million voters in the United States at the time met the formal qualifications for
the Presidency, not more than a handful could entertain serious hopes of reaching
the White House.[1] Typically, presidential nominees have been governors, vice
presidents, and U.S. senators. But not every political leader who becomes a
governor or United States senator is regarded as tall presidential timber. To
differentiate between the public figures who are potentially serious presidential

candidates and those who are not, professional politicians long ago developed the concept of "availability."

Presidential "Availability"

By "availability" we do not mean a person who merely aspires to high office, since many small-bore politicians have their sights set high. Availability means that one is capable of being elected President of the United States. A number of factors contribute to a candidate's availability, but the chief factor is evidence that the candidate can convince the party leaders and national convention delegates that he, the candidate, has enough vote-getting ability to reach the White House. Almost a century ago, Lord Bryce, the British observer, commented on the pragmatic aspects of availability: "Plainly, it is the man most likely to win. . . . What a party wants is not a good President but a good candidate. The party managers therefore focus on the person likely to gain most popular support and at the same time generate the least opposition."[2]

Availability criteria have been classified under the following general headings: political background, personal life and characteristics, geography, religion, a combined category of age-sex-race, and ethnicity (preferably English stock). More than two decades ago, Sidney Hyman refined the concept of availability into nine conventional criteria that, in many respects, are now outdated:

1. He must first have had some official connection with the governmental process in an elective or appointive post.

2. Nominating conventions show a clear preference for state governors.

3. A candidate is preferred who comes from a pivotal state which has a large electoral vote and which does not have a one-party voting pattern.

4. Candidates have been favored who come from the big Northern states to the exclusion of Southerners.

5. Conventions will choose only men who are in fact, or who can be made to appear acceptable to the claims of many economic interests in the nation.

6. Presidential candidates, like the English Crown, are expected by nominating conventions to present an idealized version of all that is virtuous in home and family life.

7. Even though the majority of Americans live in great urban centers, candidates are preferred who come from small towns.

8. Candidates are preferred who come from Western European stock.

9. Nominating conventions have, in effect, an extra-Constitutional religious test by their decisive preference for Protestant hopefuls.[3]

From the beginning of the twentieth century to the present no serious aspirant for the Presidency has ever scored 100 percent in all these categories. But the nominees of both parties have usually scored above average in most categories.

Since the age of television, however, the standard criteria of availability listed in Hyman's study have been eroded to a point that the term has lost much of its viability. The history of the past three decades offers ample documentation that the availability concept has been seriously undermined by the open politics of presidential primaries in building the stature of the popular favorite.

Since John F. Kennedy's nomination and election in 1960, for example, being a Roman Catholic has not been a bar to the nomination. Also, the former taboo against a divorced man was broken by Adlai E. Stevenson's nomination twice (1952 and 1956) and further eroded by the recent nomination and election of another divorced candidate, Ronald Reagan, in 1980.

Readers will also note that Mr. Hyman did not include women among those "available" for the Presidency. But in 1972, for the first time in history, a black woman presidential candidate—Representative Shirley Chisholm of New York—was nominated for the highest office in the land. (She received 151.95 votes on the first and only ballot.) When Mrs. Chisholm declined to be nominated for vice president, saying that she thought she had achieved enough for one national convention, a coalition of women's groups nominated Mrs. Frances Farenthold of Texas for the second highest office. Surprisingly, she received the second highest number of votes (400), outdistancing all the candidates except Senator Thomas F. Eagleton, McGovern's original choice for running-mate.

For almost 130 years Southern candidates, no matter how well qualified, were almost totally ignored by both major parties (except for Lyndon B. Johnson who originally had been elevated to the Presidency upon President Kennedy's assassination in 1963). General Zachary Taylor, elected in 1848, was the last Southerner—Taylor was from Louisiana—to be nominated and then to occupy the White House, until Johnson. Southerners were passed over for two major reasons: First, the Republicans, as a result of their harsh Reconstruction policies toward the South after the Civil War, wrote off the South as a lost cause—at least until the 1960's, although Herbert Hoover carried five states of the Confederacy in 1928. Secondly, the Democrats felt that they could carry the Solid South, irrespective of their candidates; hence, they preferred to pick candidates from the large, pivotal, swing states of the North. In 1976, however, an unknown Southerner, former Georgia Governor Jimmy Carter, surprised the odds-makers by winning the Democratic nomination and the Presidency.

Dwight D. Eisenhower in 1952 and, earlier, Wendell Willkie in 1940 both won the Republican nomination despite their lack of elective office experience. Nor is residency in a small electoral vote state any longer a political barrier to the nomination. Arizona Senator Barry Goldwater, for example, became the 1964 GOP standard-bearer, though his home state in the "Sun Belt" had only four electoral votes at the time. Four years later, the home state of the 1968 Democratic nominee, Hubert H. Humphrey, Minnesota, had only ten electoral votes. In 1972, the five leading contenders for the Democratic nomination were from South Dakota, Minnesota, Maine, Alabama, and the State of Washington—all small electoral vote states. Senator McGovern, the nominee, came from South Dakota—a state with only four electoral votes.

Before 1928, Matthews and Keech found that three-quarters of the nominations were won by contenders who met most of the availability qualifications. Since then, considerably less than half have fitted them.[4] "Availability," according to Pomper, "applied most completely when conventions were controlled by state party organizations."[5] But state party organizations can no longer dominate the presidential nominating process in face of the challenges of mass democracy as reflected in the primaries, polls, and media. Indeed, Gerald Pomper has explained, "As the capacity to deal with the ultimate questions of peace and war become the principal test of Presidential ability, less consideration will be given to the state of origin, the domestic economic policy, the political experience, and even the family life of the aspirants."[6] This is not to say that specific tests of availability will be entirely discarded. Women and other minority candidates, for example, will continue to face extremely heavy odds against winning the nomination. Candidates who have never held elective office and with no previous experience in government will also find it hard going to capture the nomination. But these odds, it must be cautioned, are not insurmountable. Indeed, in this era if a candidate has a moderate record of accomplishment, a favorable "image" on television, and adequate financial backing to mount a hard-hitting preconvention campaign, he can be considered to be "available." Beyond that, it is impossible to tell where political lightning may strike. Sometimes the fate of a candidate may rest upon factors unforeseen or uncontrollable. And no systematic analysis has been found that entirely rules out luck or the "breaks of the game."

Availability, according to Gerald Pomper, has been replaced by new criteria which might be termed "prominence."[7] More than two decades ago William Carleton also argued that in order to win the Presidency the candidate first needed to be a national "name" or "celebrity."[8] While Carleton may have overstated his case, the experience of recent conventions indicates that to become a serious contender a prospective nominee must soon build up his political "visibility" in the primaries by winning or finishing a strong second or third in the early rounds or risk political oblivion. Recent nominees McGovern and Carter, who were both political unknowns at the outset of the nominating race, can attest to this point. Representative John Anderson, though he failed to win the 1980 GOP nomination and who was unsuccessful in his independent quest for the Presidency, is another recent example of an unknown presidential contender being transformed by the TV networks into a celebrity almost overnight. Indeed, the Gallup polling organization announced some years ago that in "trial heat" polls of various presidential contenders, a candidate needed to be recognized by 80 percent of the electorate in order to give the candidate a fair chance in the poll ratings. In this fast-moving era a presidential candidate can utilize presidential primary contests, the public opinion polls, and the mass media to pyramid himself from nowhere into front-runner contention and thereby "force himself on the attention of the convention."

Availability Criteria Eroded by Transformation of Nominating System

The shift away from the standard availability criteria reflects the steady transformation of American nominating politics over the past three decades from the traditional "closed" system of party controlled decision-making to the "open" participatory politics of presidential primaries. No longer does the Democratic party nominee owe his nomination to the coalition of big state party leaders or big city mayors who formerly controlled large blocs of uncommitted delegates, nor the Republican nominee to the party leaders of the big Eastern states, state leaders representing the Southern rotten boroughs, or key farm state chieftains with their smaller blocs of uncommitted delegates. The party nomination in the out-party now goes to the winner of the primaries, whether the victor comes from South Dakota, Georgia, California, or, for that matter, almost any state in the Union. Since almost 75 percent of all the national convention delegates are now chosen in states that use some form of the primary, and run as pledged to specific candidates in these springtime elections, it is absolutely imperative that contenders perform well in the primaries. Unlike yesteryear when less than 40 percent of the delegates were selected in the primaries—and many of these delegates still remained unpledged at convention time—the successful contender must win a majority of the primaries and pick up a sizeable chunk of delegates in those states using proportional representation.

The television revolution has also encompassed the presidential nominating process. Indeed, the emergence of nationwide television now enables a political unknown to come from out of nowhere to become a serious challenger. In 1968, for example, Senator Eugene McCarthy did not win the 1968 Democratic nomination, but he drove an incumbent President, Lyndon B. Johnson, out of the race and became an instant television celebrity as a result of his giant-killer role in the New Hampshire and Wisconsin primaries. Four years later, network television coverage aided a relatively unknown Senator from South Dakota, George McGovern, to outduel five leading Democratic contenders—Humphrey, Muskie, Wallace, Jackson, and Lindsay—in the primaries to become the party frontrunner and party nominee. Translated into more direct political terms, McGovern defeated a former vice president, the vice presidential nominee on the 1968 Democratic ticket, a powerful Southern governor, one of the five most influential senators in Washington, and a former mayor of New York City. In 1976, an obscure former Georgia governor, Jimmy Carter, became the popular hero of the television networks and the national news magazines, *Time* and *Newsweek*, soon after his plurality victories in the Iowa Democratic precinct caucuses and the early round primaries in New Hampshire and Florida. Millions of viewers across the land no longer asked "Jimmy Who?" when the evening television newscasts showed the smiling Georgian shaking hands with prospective voters in the primary states. Without this massive amount of cost-free publicity generated by the mass media, it seems doubtful that Carter could have overcome his earlier low-name recognition problem to become the party nominee.

Public opinion poll standings now overshadow most traditional availability criteria. Next to victories in the primaries, presidential contenders must show a steady rise in the Gallup polls during the pre-convention period if they wish to remain in serious contention. It's not necessary that the presidential aspirants enter the race with high poll ratings—indeed, the early ratings of both George McGovern and Jimmy Carter did not exceed four or five percent at the time of the Iowa precinct caucuses in mid-January—but the contenders must register substantial gains in the opinion polls during the primary season. Failure to run well in the polls is fatal to any serious candidacy. Senator Henry "Scoop" Jackson in 1976 was a prime example of this failure. In three years of heavy pre-convention campaigning for the Presidency, Jackson was never able to push his Gallup poll rating above 15 percent—despite plurality victories in the early round Massachusetts and New York primaries and his early lead in the Democratic delegate count before his fateful loss to Carter in the Pennsylvania primary.

Looking ahead, political availability will probably continue to be used as one measuring stick for evaluating those attributes deemed necessary for a winning candidate. But unless a candidate registers an impressive record in the primaries and moves up steadily in the Gallup (and other) opinion poll standings, the aspirant can forget about meeting the traditional availability criteria, for the nomination will, in effect, already have passed him by.

Serious "Presidential Possibilities" Limited to Select Few

Matthews and Keech found that between 1936 and 1972 only slightly more than 100 men (and one woman) emerged as "presidential possibilities"—serious candidates—for the Presidency. Using the criterion of one percent or more public support in the Gallup poll, Matthews and Keech calculated that 62 Democrats and 47 Republicans met this "presidential possibility" criterion during this period.[9] The recent plethora of candidates in the 1976 Democratic and 1980 Republican races (using the same Gallup criterion) would expand this number of presidential possibilities by 16. Other similar criteria probably would not enlarge this entire list of presidential possibilities by more than a dozen or so. Indeed, this working list probably errs on the side of including too many potential candidates rather than too few. It is also noteworthy that no one between 1936 and 1972 was nominated for the Presidency who was not on this list. Moreover, with the exception of Wendell Willkie, no one has been nominated who had not been on this list for a substantial period of time. Undoubtedly, a more realistic rule-of-thumb for developing a "short list" of presidential possibilities would be to exclude all candidates who fail to become the choice of at least 15 percent of their fellow partisans in the Gallup poll sometime during the pre-convention campaign.

During the 1928-1980 period, almost 85 percent of all nominees were elected officeholders—the only exceptions being Herbert Hoover (1928), a cabinet member in the Harding and Coolidge administrations; Wendell Willkie (1940), a businessman-lawyer; and retired General Dwight D. Eisenhower (1952). The record during this period also shows that all presidential nominees who have held public office have been either vice presidents, governors, or U.S. senators at the time of their nomination or formerly held one of these offices (see Table 9). The exact travel route followed by each of the nominees for the period 1928-1980 is depicted in Figure 3.

TABLE 9
**LAST OFFICE HELD BEFORE PRESIDENTIAL
NOMINATION IN TWO MAJOR PARTIES, 1868-1980**

	1868-1892		1896-1924		1928-1956		1960-1980	
	%	(N)	%	(N)	%	(N)	%	(N)
Vice President succeeded to Presidency			18.1	(2)	11.1	(1)	44.4	(4)
Senate	10.0	(1)	9.1	(1)			33.3	(3)
House of Representatives	10.0	(1)	9.1	(1)				
Governor	40.0	(4)	27.3	(3)	55.6	(5)	22.2	(2)
Federal appointive	20.0	(2)	27.3	(3)	11.1	(1)		
Statewide elective			9.1	(1)				
None	20.0	(2)			22.2	(2)		
	100	(10)	100	(11)	100	(9)	100	(9)

Source: Robert L. Peabody and Eve Lubalin, "The Making of Presidential Candidates," in James I. Lengle and Byron E. Shafer, eds., *Presidential Politics* (New York: St. Martin's Press, 1980), p. 55, for the period 1868-1956. The more recent calculations have been made by the present author.

One of the most significant trends in twentieth-century nominating politics has been the electoral success of vice presidents winning the White House outright after moving up to the presidency upon the death of the incumbent. This represents a complete reversal from the nineteenth century pattern.[10] Four twentieth-century vice presidents—Theodore Roosevelt, Calvin Coolidge, Harry Truman, and Lyndon Johnson—have all been subsequently nominated and elected president on their own. Only Gerald Ford, who won nomination to a full term after taking over the presidential duties from the deposed President Nixon (who had also previously served two terms as vice president), failed to retain his office. Of the four nineteenth-century presidents who succeeded automatically to the presidency—Tyler, Fillmore, Johnson, and Arthur—all four sought renomination and none achieved it. Why? This complete reversal from the nineteenth-century experience can probably be explained by the twentieth-century presidents' ability to capitalize on the expanded role of presidents as world leaders, the persistence of international crises, and continuing domestic problems. (Coolidge, however, should be excluded on these counts.) The power and expanded prestige of the White House also helped the incumbents keep potential challengers at a distance—at least for one term. Also, it might be noted that all four of these incumbents won office before the recent age of party reform and the rapid spread of presidential primaries.

More recently, the vice presidency has become an important stepping-stone to the nomination for president in yet another way. Since 1956, each time an incumbent president has stepped down, the incumbent vice president—Nixon in 1960 and Humphrey in 1968—has received the nomination of the party in power. Even serving as the party nominee for vice president in an unsuccessful venture or seeking the number two spot can sometimes have future payoffs. It should not be forgotten that Franklin D. Roosevelt was the Democratic vice presidential nominee in 1920—12 years before he won the presidency. In 1956, John F. Kennedy narrowly missed being selected the Democratic vice presidential nominee, but four years later he moved into the White House.

In recent years the U.S. Senate has been depicted as the "incubator" of presidential candidates.[11] But this recent emergence of the Senate as a major source of presidential candidates should not hide the fact that from 1878 to 1960 only two members of the U.S. Senate—Benjamin Harrison and Warren G. Harding—were nominated for President. Why? Several reasons have been advanced to explain senatorial failures to win nomination contests. First, presidential duties were considered largely administrative and, unlike the governors, the legislative experience of senators was not seen as directly relevant to the skills required of the President. Second, governors usually had more influence than senators over state party organizations and therefore frequently controlled state party delegations at national conventions. Consequently, governors were usually in a better position to launch their own candidacies. Third, senators were not popularly elected until 1914 (after passage of the Seventeenth Amendment in 1913). Consequently, senators usually lacked first-hand campaign experience and popularity testing in their own states. Without established political track records in an era of closely contested national elections, especially when special importance was attached to carrying one's own state, senators were viewed as riskier candidates than governors fresh from one or more recent election victories. More recently, however, the reasons formerly advanced for picking governors as presidential nominees have now come to be regarded in some instances as liabilities, and the former liabilities of senators have been transformed into political assets.

As a result of the nationalization of American politics and the growth of the mass media centered in Washington, senators have found that they can become

FIGURE 3
HIGH PUBLIC OFFICES HELD BY MAJOR PARTY
PRESIDENTIAL NOMINEES, 1928-1980

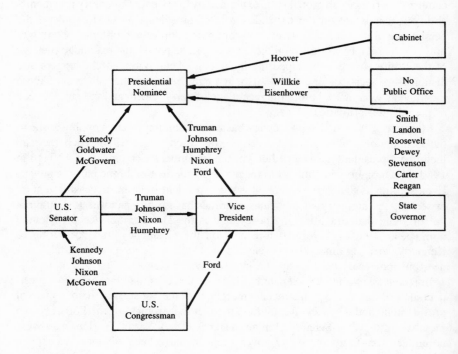

Source: John A. Crittenden, *Parties and Elections in the United States*, (Englewood Cliffs, N.J.: Prentice-Hall, Inc., 1982), p. 213.
Adapted from William Keech and Donald R. Matthews, *The Party's Choice* (Washington, D.C.: The Brookings Institution, 1976), p. 20, reprinted by permission of Brookings Institution.

nationally known as experts on foreign affairs, energy, and military affairs, even in their first term, by appearing frequently on national television news and the regular news interview panels, such as "Meet the Press" and "Face the Nation." Indeed, the rise of the mass media has made it possible, unlike earlier times, for relatively junior senators to use their subcommittee chairmanships to build up their national standings in the opinion polls. Meanwhile, the purely administrative aspects of the president's job have been overshadowed by global diplomacy and pressing domestic issues. Moreover, the longer six-year senatorial term means that those members infected with the presidential virus have more free time to advance their presidential ambitions than, say, governors who often face almost insolvable fiscal problems with inadequate sources of revenue.

In the century between 1868 and 1968, more governors were selected as presidential nominees than any other category of nominees listed in Table 9. Before the era of the mass media and jet aircraft, support of state and local party organizations and the ability to carry a large doubtful state were often more important for winning the presidency than personal candidate appeal. As a result, the criterion of "winability" dictated that national convention delegates find a candidate acceptable to most, if not all, party factions who would help carry the state and local tickets. Also, convention deliberations were dominated by the search of a safe "available" candidate, possessing most of the qualifications listed earlier in the chapter.

Typically, the candidates who met most closely these availability criteria were governors of a large swing state, for example, New York or Ohio. Governors also enjoyed the luxury of evading the difficult decisions on national policy. More importantly, governors from the big states formerly controlled large blocs of delegates. In the days when state parties dominated the selection of delegates, the governor of a big state such as New York could be assured upon arrival at the convention of at least 15 percent of the delegates needed to win the nomination. Small wonder, then, that governors from New York, whether Democratic or Republican, were frequently nominated for President. But as Peabody and Lubalin have observed, "The patterns in the nominating process, patterns that obtained as recently as 40 years ago, seem almost quaint in light of contemporary preconvention campaigns.[12] Clearly, the rapid expansion of the mass media, especially television, the decline of sectionalism, the proliferation of two-party competitive politics to a relatively large number of pivotal states, and the spread of presidential primaries to two-thirds of the states have all drastically changed the political landscape and the conditions under which candidates for the highest office have sought the nomination.

National convention delegates are now looking for candidates with national appeal who have successfully campaigned in the presidential primaries, enjoy a high standing in the opinion polls, and evoke a favorable television "image." As a result of this transformation of the nominating process, governors have been, for the most part, passed by in favor of vice presidents and U.S. senators. Frequently, the governors have had to work with antiquated state constitutions, independent administrative agencies, and, until the mid-1960's, malapportioned, hostile state legislatures. Asking state legislatures to increase taxes became the chief preoccupation of many state chief executives. Consequently, incumbent governors found themselves increasingly vulnerable politically, often failing to win reelection. Thus, the relative short tenure of many governors is another compelling explanation for recent gubernatorial failures in nominating contests. Another set of liabilities that have plagued contemporary governors is "their relative anonymity and the public's image of them as parochial figures."[13] Network television producers rarely find reason to cover state capital politics or to invite governors to appear on "Meet the Press" and the other news panel programs. What happens in Springfield, Columbus, Lansing, or Madison is of minimal concern to network decision-makers. No wonder state chief executives have been perceived, at best, as marginal presidential candidates. However, another category of state executives—former governors—should also be added to our list of presidential possibilities. Indeed, the two most recent White House occupants, Presidents Jimmy Carter and Ronald Reagan, both received their political apprenticeship in the state executive mansions, though they had stepped down from the governorship before launching their successful presidential drives. It remains to be seen, of course, if this recent phenomenon represents the emergence of a new category of nominees, or is merely a political aberration.

In reviewing recent nominating history, another fact also stands out: incumbent presidents are no longer automatically assured renomination. Let's take a few moments to explain why.

Incumbent Presidents No Longer Guaranteed Renomination

From the post-Civil War era to the end of World War II, it was axiomatic that any incumbent President who wanted renomination could have it for the asking. To be sure, President Chester Arthur, who was elevated to the White House following President Garfield's assassination, was denied renomination by the Republicans in 1884, and President William Howard Taft had a close call in winning the GOP renomination in 1912, after throwing back a heroic challenge by former President Theodore Roosevelt. But no other incumbent in either major party experienced serious opposition in seeking renomination for almost a century. Indeed, a serious challenge from inside the party ranks to an incumbent President—a rare event prior to the 1960's—was tantamount to a party's open admission that its nomination in the first place had been a mistake.

The resurgence of the presidential primary movement after World War II, however, provided a rediscovered weapon—presidential primaries—for an ambitious candidate to challenge an incumbent president. In the early months of 1952, Senator Estes Kefauver (D.-Tenn.) decided to challenge President Truman for the Democratic nomination by entering the primaries. Even before President Truman had announced his intentions, Kefauver upset the President in the first-round New Hampshire primary. (Truman, who had already served nearly two full terms following President Roosevelt's death in April 1945, was specifically excluded from provisions of the recently passed Twenty-second Amendment, limiting a President to two terms.) Though President Truman depicted presidential primaries as just so much "eye-wash," he suddenly announced on March 31, 1952, that he would not be a candidate for renomination—the first incumbent casualty to the new presidential primary competition. Kefauver, however, did not win the nomination because most of his 12 primary victories were in advisory (not mandatory) primary states, meaning that delegates in these states were not pledged to the winner of the primary. Less than half of these delegates voted for Kefauver on the first ballot at the 1952 Chicago convention. As a result of recent Democratic party nominating reforms, however, most of the 30-plus primary states now have mandatory primary laws (which in most cases also cover the Republican party as well).[14] With most delegates pledged in advance, the opportunity for national convention bargaining that characterized most conventions under the old system has now been sharply curtailed. Mandatory primaries seriously reduced the influence of the traditional "power brokers" in the large states who formerly controlled sizeable blocs of uncommitted delegates that could be moved from one candidate to another.

Sixteen years later, President Lyndon B. Johnson decided to withdraw his candidacy for renomination two days before the important Wisconsin primary, after eking out a narrow victory (49.6 percent) over Senator Eugene McCarthy (42 percent) in the first-in-the-nation New Hampshire preferential primary. Johnson, according to most on-the-scene observers, faced almost certain defeat in the impending Wisconsin contest against McCarthy before he bowed out of the race. One of the major lessons of the 1968 "dump Johnson" movement was that henceforth no incumbent President would be safe from an in-party challenge whenever the incumbent appeared even slightly vulnerable. In 1972, President Nixon easily brushed aside two weak challengers, Representatives Paul N. "Pete" McCloskey, California, and John Ashbrook, Ohio, in the GOP nominating race. But four years later Nixon's successor, President Gerald Ford (who had taken over as Chief Executive after Nixon's forced resignation), came within an eyelash of losing the GOP nomination to former California Governor Ronald Reagan. In the early stages of the 1976 pre-convention race Ford moved out in front quickly by winning the first five primaries, but Reagan mounted a strong counterattack and, for a time in early May 1976, jumped ahead of Ford in the delegate count. Ford, however, regained the lead, thanks to the overwhelmingly favorable support from the huge party-controlled New York state delegation (Ford received 133 delegates to 20 for Reagan) and then managed to hang onto his narrow delegate lead to edge out Reagan at the Republican convention.

Once again, in 1980, President Jimmy Carter faced a heavy challenge from Senator Edward M. Kennedy in the Democratic nominating sweepstakes. Starting out in the unusual position, for an incumbent at least, of being an underdog in his renomination campaign (President Carter's public approval rating in the Gallup poll at the time was near an all-time low), Carter managed to overtake Senator Kennedy's long-time lead in the Gallup poll in early December 1979. Aided by the Iranian hostage crisis and Kennedy's disastrous performance on a CBS-TV network interview, Carter rebounded to clearly outdistance Kennedy in the first-round Iowa precinct caucuses and the early primaries. Kennedy mounted a strong comeback in the late primaries—but his victory in five out of eight primaries on the last day of the season was still not enough to overcome Carter's big early lead. Still undaunted, the Kennedy forces made a last-ditch fight at the 1980 Democratic convention, challenging a new Carter-sponsored rule change, requiring all delegates mandated in the primaries to vote for the candidate they ran pledged to on the first ballot. Kennedy lost this historic battle, as indicated earlier, and with it any hope of thwarting Carter's renomination. While the

Kennedy forces saved some "face" by winning approval of several platform planks dear to their hearts on full employment and social welfare, the remainder of the 1980 convention more closely resembled a coronation than a deliberative assembly. Even though President Carter won renomination, he had been badly wounded by the long months of campaigning for a second nomination. In retrospect, President Lyndon B. Johnson's bitter observation about his own plight in the early months of 1968 before he renounced seeking another term seems ever closer to the mark: "The old belief that a President can carry out the responsibilities of his office and at the same time undergo the rigors of campaigning is, in my opinion, no longer valid."[15] The extremely close 1976 GOP nominating race—the *New York Times* delegate count did not show Ford with the needed 1,130 delegates until the first night of the convention—forced President Ford to push aside his duties as Chief Executive and travel to Kansas City on the eve of the convention to meet with his campaign staff and to importune uncommitted delegates, one-on-one, for their support in his showdown battle with Governor Reagan. For the first time in modern convention history an incumbent President was cast in the unceremonious role of actively hustling delegates at the convention just like any other presidential aspirant seeking the top office in the land. During a recent round-table forum on the presidential nominating process, former President Gerald Ford estimated that he had to spend 20 percent of his time in 1976 seeking the GOP nomination.[16] Unless the existing presidential nominating system is overhauled and shortened, future presidents can be expected to echo this same complaint.

The Convention's Choice

Nominating decisions of American party conventions require an absolute majority—50 percent, plus one, of the delegates must agree on a single choice—before this candidate becomes the nominee. No possibility exists for a minority candidate to win by a plurality (more votes than any competitor but less than a majority), as often occurs in the nomination of U.S. senatorial and congressional candidates or state and local officeholders. (Until the 1936 Democratic convention, the party of Jefferson and Jackson required a two-thirds delegate majority to select a nominee.) Perhaps one of the amazing wonders of the national convention, comprising delegates from 50 separate state parties, 435 congressional districts, 3,000-plus counties, and 175,000 precincts, plus several territories, has been the ability of the convention to coalesce and agree on a single candidate, despite intense candidate rivalries and competing state interests. To claim the nomination the winner must enlist the support of more delegates than all of his opponents combined. Finding a candidate upon whom more than half the convention can agree and who also has an excellent chance to win the election is indeed a powerful incentive for consensus-building.

Our next task will be to classify nominations on the ease with which the party has achieved agreement on a candidate for the period 1936-1980. To simplify our work we have borrowed three categories of nominations developed by Keech and Matthews: consensual, semi-consensual, and non-consensual.[17] A quick review of the record of the 24 conventions held by the two parties since 1936 shows, as we shall see, a fairly even distribution among the three categories.

CONSENSUAL NOMINATIONS

Despite the numerous obstacles to achieving consensual agreement on a nominee, nine of the 24 conventions can be characterized as consensual. The percentage of delegate votes reflects the high level of consensus the nine nominees received:

Roosevelt (1936)	100.0	Nixon (1960)	99.2
Landon (1936)	98.1	Johnson (1964)	100.0
Roosevelt (1944)	92.3	Nixon (1972)	99.9
Dewey (1944)	99.7	Reagan (1980)	97.2
Eisenhower (1956)	100.0		

Six of the high consensus nominations occurred in the Republican party. Only three of these consensual nominations—Landon, Dewey, and Reagan—were made by the party out-of-power. Generally, the single provisional leader moved into the front-runner spot before the formal process of choice began and maintained this lead until he was formally chosen. To include the Reagan nomination in 1980 in this category might be stretching the point, for when the GOP nominating race opened, Reagan faced six formidable opponents—Bush, Baker, Crane, Connally, Dole, and Anderson. But by the day after the Illinois primary (March 18) most of Reagan's opponents had departed the field of battle. Bush continued the fight through most of May until, like General Robert E. Lee at Appomattox, he ran out of troops and ammunition. Thus, six weeks before the GOP convention, all six of Reagan's opponents had bowed out of the GOP race, leaving the road wide open for the Californian's nomination. While Reagan may not have been preferred by all of the delegates, the bright prospects for a GOP return to the White House soon led the party dissidents to cast aside their objections to the former movie star.

SEMI-CONSENSUAL NOMINATIONS

Each of the six semi-consensual choices survived the primaries, entered the convention as a front-runner, and won on the first ballot with the following vote percentages:

Roosevelt (1940)	86.0	Kennedy (1960)	53.0
Truman (1948)	75.0	Nixon (1968)	51.9
Stevenson (1956)	66.0	Carter (1976)	74.4

Roosevelt and Truman were, of course, incumbents seeking reelection; the other four represented the party out-of-power. Each of the nominees was stronger than any of his opponents, but all of them were vulnerable on some point. That no other candidate on the scene had the votes to block their nomination, however, can be adduced from their ability to win the nomination on the first ballot. It is noteworthy, however, that President Kennedy, viewed now as one of the most popular presidents of the twentieth century, barely squeaked through with a paper-thin majority on the first round of balloting. Kennedy was the only one of the semi-consensual nominations, it might be noted, in which the second strongest candidate (Lyndon B. Johnson) had as much as half as many votes as the nominee—Johnson had 409 votes to Kennedy's 806. But Johnson, a southerner, lacked a formidable coalition of allies needed to halt Kennedy's nomination.

NON-CONSENSUAL NOMINATIONS

This category of nominations ranges from a wide open field of candidates in some years to a bifactional battle royal between two candidates, for example, Eisenhower and Taft in 1952 or Ford and Reagan in 1976, fighting down to the wire. In any case, agreement on a nominee was not easily achieved, even though five of the nine non-consensual nominations came on the first ballot. Only one non-consensual nominee, Eisenhower in 1952, reached the White House. The percentages gained by the non-consensual nominees were as follows:

Willkie (1940)	sixth ballot	65.5
Dewey (1948)	third ballot	100.0
Eisenhower (1952)	first ballot after shift	70.1
Stevenson (1952)	third ballot	50.2
Goldwater (1964)	first ballot	67.5
Humphrey (1968)	first ballot	67.1
McGovern (1972)	first ballot	56.8
Ford (1976)	first ballot	52.5
Carter (1980)	first ballot	63.7

Significantly, the two incumbent Presidents who managed to win non-consensual nominations subsequently lost in the general election. This phenomenon seems to suggest that any incumbent who has to wage a major battle to win renomination (or nomination for a first full term) enters the fall campaign in a badly weakened condition. It is significant that during the recent era of first ballot nominations (1956-1980) that four out of seven of the nominees who won the Presidency have been consensual nominees; three have been semi-consensual nominees; none of the non-consensual nominees was successful in winning the Presidency for the first time or returning to the White House (see Table 10). Three of the consensual nominees who won in November were incumbents. Keech and Matthews have also called attention to another significant aspect of non-consensual nominations, "Political amateurs, not routinely active in presidential nominating politics, were active on behalf of one of the contenders in most of the non-consensual races."[18] In only one case out of six—General Eisenhower's nomination in 1952—did the amateur involvement in the nominating race result in a presidential victory in November. Indeed, non-consensual nominations, with the exception of Eisenhower, have been ominous indicators

TABLE 10
FIRST BALLOT NOMINATIONS, 1956-1980

	Consensual Nominees	Semi-Consensual Nominees	Non-Consensual Nominees
1956	Eisenhower (R)* (incumbent)	Stevenson (D)	
1960	Nixon (R)	Kennedy (D)*	
1964	Johnson (D)* (incumbent)		Goldwater (R)
1968		Nixon (R)*	Humphrey (D)
1972	Nixon (R)* (incumbent)		McGovern (D)
1976		Carter (D)*	Ford (R)
1980	Reagan (R)*		Carter (D)
	(4 R) (1 D)	(1 R) (3 D)	(2 R) (3 D)

* Elected

that the party faces an uphill fight in the general election. While some observers may think that there's nothing like a good fight at the convention to put the nominee and the party in tip-top shape for the general election campaign, the evidence presented in Table 10 suggests the contrary.

It is noteworthy that no President since former General Dwight D. Eisenhower has completed two full terms. Why? Some observers attribute this rapid turnover of presidents to the influence of national television which seems to grow tired of the same White House occupant and his supporting cast; instead the American viewing public wants a "new season" almost every term. Don Hewitt, CBS-TV producer of the top-rated show *Sixty Minutes*, has put it this way: "We may be in for a series of one-term Presidents. The Presidents are overexposed, become targets, they get taken apart. They're like a TV series—four years and the people get bored; they tune out. They want a new show every four years."[19] Also, the complexity and intractability of domestic and international problems and the inability of our presidents to come up with satisfactory solutions suggests that the American public soon becomes disenchanted with the White House incumbent. In addition, the record shows that the various "availability" criteria developed by party professionals, especially in their search for a candidate likely to gain the most popular support with the least number of negative attributes, have been, in retrospect, probably better yardsticks for measuring the capability of "presidential possibilities" than the enthusiasm of the current generation of political amateurs and newly involved activists sent to the national conventions by primary voters.

Recent bipartisan proposals to reserve at least one-third of the convention delegate seats for coalition-minded and compromise-oriented party leaders and elected officeholders would seem to indicate that the "post-reform" reformers are particularly cognizant of the dangers that non-consensual nominations pose for a party, especially for the out-of-power party. More will be said about the role of party professionals as delegates in the final chapter. In the meantime, let's take a moment to examine the best single early indicator of the convention nominee— the pre-primary poll leader.

Convention Nominee is Often Pre-Primary Poll Leader

Convention choices usually have been foreshadowed early by Gallup preference polls, often in the first poll of the campaign, taken up to three years before the conventions. In 14 of 23 campaigns (61 percent) the most popular candidate in the first poll went on to receive the nomination (see Table 11). Even excluding the seven cases in which incumbent presidents won renomination, the first poll predicted the nominee 50 percent of the time (8 of 16 cases).

As shown in Table 11, both the mid-term November elections and the early state primaries have sometimes produced temporary leaders who rapidly fell from favor in the polls (for instance, George Romney after the election of November 1966; Henry Cabot Lodge after the New Hampshire primary in 1964). Nevertheless, as the conventions draw nearer, national public opinion—as reflected in the polls—has tended to shift to the eventual nominees.

This raises an even more basic question, one which speaks directly to the success of the party nominating system as a democratic process: Do presidential nominations go to the candidates most preferred by party voters? This has indeed been the case in 22 of 23 nominations for which Gallup polls are available.[20] Only once in the last 24 nominations has the leader of the party rank-and-file preferences in the final pre-convention Gallup poll failed to be the convention's choice—the exception was Senator Kefauver in 1952. In the 1964 Republican race, nominee Barry Goldwater tied with Richard Nixon (at 22 percent) in the final pre-convention poll; they finished in a virtual dead heat with two other candidates, Henry Cabot Lodge (21 percent) and William Scranton (20 percent). In a third case, the 1972 Democratic race, nominee McGovern trailed both Humphrey and George Wallace until the month before the convention; the final pre-convention poll produced no statistically significant differences between McGovern at 30 percent, Humphrey at 27 percent, and Wallace at 25 percent.

These three exceptions or near-exceptions, nominees Stevenson (in 1952), Goldwater, and McGovern, rank among the period's five weakest candidates (along with Alfred M. Landon and Stevenson in 1956), as measured by percentage of popular vote in the presidential election. This suggests that conventions have generally been prudent in abiding by the preferences of their own party's voters.

Several years ago, James R. Beniger concluded that "there is no greater advantage than strength in the early polls for winning the presidential nomination."[21] But thanks to the rapid proliferation of primaries and nominating reforms in both parties no longer will presidential nominations fall routinely to sitting presidents, long-established party leaders, and early front-runners in the opinion polls. In future campaigns we can expect from time to time relatively obscure candidates—like McGovern and Carter—to use the state primary system to capture in a matter of weeks public support that has traditionally taken several years and even several nominating campaigns to build. We can also expect serious challengers—like Ronald Reagan in 1976 and Teddy Kennedy in 1980—to mount all-out nomination campaigns against sitting presidents. Barring major reforms in the primary system, it is unlikely that any future candidate, including incumbent presidents, can be nominated without a string of state primary victories. If that candidate does well in the primaries, he (or she) can expect to see his standings automatically skyrocket in the Gallup polls as well as in the pre-convention delegate count. Under these favorable circumstances the primary-opinion poll leader's nomination is virtually assured.

Within the out-of-power party the failure of the pre-primary opinion poll leader to win the presidential nomination in 1972 and 1976, however, produced a new outbreak of skepticism about the viability of using pre-primary polls to predict presidential nominees. Let's take a moment to review some alternative methods of nominee prognostication.

Sophisticated Indicators for Predicting the Nominee

Recently, a team of veteran political scientists—Donald S. Collat, Stanley Kelley, Jr., and Ronald Rogowski—analyzed various alternative procedures for predicting the party nominee for President. They categorized these five methods into rules, four of which are fairly well known and have enjoyed varying degrees of success. The fifth method, the newly developed gain-deficit rule, yielded surprisingly good results. All five procedures, or rules, can be summarized briefly as follows:

1. The *polling majority rule* (candidate who first wins the support of a majority in press polls of delegates will become the nominee).

2. The *threshold rule* (candidate who first receives the support of delegates with 41 percent of a convention's votes will become the nominee).

3. The *rule of second-ballot gains* (candidate whose gain in votes from the first to the second test of support is greatest will become the nominee).

4. The *front-runner rule* (candidate who has a plurality on the first test of support will become the nominee).

5. The *gain-deficit rule* (candidate who registers a critical value increase of 0.360 between the first and second test of strength— before or at the convention—will become the nominee).[22]

TABLE 11

MOST POPULAR CANDIDATES AMONG PARTY VOTERS, AS MEASURED BY LAST GALLUP PREFERENCE POLL, AT CRUCIAL POINTS IN PRESIDENTIAL NOMINATION CAMPAIGN, 1936-1980

Election Year and Party	First Poll of Campaign	First Poll after Mid-term Nov. Elections	First Poll after First Major Primary	Final Poll of Campaign	Nominee
1936 D*	—	—	—	—	ROOSEVELT
R	Landon	Landon	Landon	Landon	Landon
1940 D	ROOSEVELT	ROOSEVELT	ROOSEVELT	ROOSEVELT	ROOSEVELT
R	(Dewey)	(Dewey)	(Dewey)	Willkie	Willkie
1944 D	ROOSEVELT	ROOSEVELT	ROOSEVELT	ROOSEVELT	ROOSEVELT
R	Dewey	Dewey	Dewey	Dewey	Dewey
1948 D	TRUMAN	TRUMAN	TRUMAN	TRUMAN	TRUMAN
R	Dewey	Dewey	(Stassen)	Dewey	Dewey
1952 D	(TRUMAN)	(Eisenhower)	(Kefauver)	(Kefauver)	Stevenson
R	Eisenhower	Eisenhower	Eisenhower	Eisenhower	Eisenhower
1956 D	Stevenson	Stevenson	Stevenson	Stevenson	Stevenson
R	EISENHOWER	EISENHOWER	EISENHOWER	EISENHOWER	EISENHOWER
1960 D	(Kefauver)	(Stevenson)	J. Kennedy	J. Kennedy	J. Kennedy
R	Nixon	Nixon	Nixon	Nixon	Nixon
1964 D	JOHNSON	JOHNSON	—	JOHNSON	JOHNSON
R	(Nixon)	(Rockefeller)	(Lodge)	Goldwater & (Nixon) (tie)	Goldwater

1968 D	(R. Kennedy)	(R. Kennedy)	(R. Kennedy)	Humphrey	Humphrey
R	Nixon	(Romney)	Nixon	Nixon	Nixon
1972 D	(Muskie)	(Muskie)	(Humphrey)	McGovern	McGovern
R	NIXON	NIXON	—	NIXON	NIXON
1976 D	(E. Kennedy)	(E. Kennedy)	(Humphrey)	Carter	Carter
R	(Agnew)	FORD	FORD	FORD	FORD
1980 D	(E. Kennedy)	(E. Kennedy)	CARTER	CARTER	CARTER
R	Reagan	Reagan	Reagan	Reagan	Reagan
% Predict Nominee (all races)	61% (14/23)	61% (14/23)	67% (14/21)	96% (22/23)	
% Predict Nominee (Presidents excluded)	50% (8/16)	47% (7/15)	53% (8/15)	93% (14/15)	

Source: The Gallup Poll, *Public Opinion 1935-1971*, Vols. 1-3 (New York: Random House, 1972); *The Gallup Opinion Index*, various numbers (Princeton, N.J.: Gallup International, 1971-1980).

Note: Presidents in capital letters, unsuccessful candidates in parentheses.

*The index of *The Gallup Poll, Public Opinion 1935-1971* does not list any Democratic voter preference polls on President Franklin Roosevelt's renomination in 1936.

Looking briefly at each of these prediction rules, the record shows the following results:

1. The polling majority rule pinpointed the winner in four out of nine contested nominating races between 1952 and 1976; the outcome in the other five was inconclusive (see Table 12). The influence of delegate polls in shaping the outcome of the convention was also discussed in chapter 4.

2. The threshold rule predicted the nominee in seven out of eight cases between 1952 and 1976 and erred only once (the 1952 GOP races between Eisenhower and Taft). For conventions in the century from 1848 to 1948 the threshold rule yielded seven predictions in eleven cases (see Table 12).

3. The rule of second-ballot gains (developed originally by Eugene B. McGregor, Jr.) yielded a record of seven correct and two incorrect predictions between 1952 and 1976.[23] First ballot nominations during all but one of the races in this period complicated the operation. To overcome the methodological problem of the one-ballot conventions since 1956, the Collat-Kelley-Rogowski team treated the press polls (Associated Press, *New York Times*, and *Washington Post*) as equivalent to convention ballots. In recent races the success of this rule is, the authors concede, affected considerably by which surveys or polls are regarded as the first and second "ballots."[24] For 18 conventions from 1848 to 1976 in which the rule of second-ballot gains permits prediction, the record shows 13 correct predictions out of 18 contests. McGregor's second ballot gain hypothesis, for example, enabled him to pinpoint Woodrow Wilson as the eventual nominee at the 1912 Democratic convention, even though Wilson did not win the nomination until the 46th ballot.

4. The front-runner rule predicted the nominee correctly seven times out of nine and erred only twice during the period 1952-1976. But for the century between 1848 and 1948, the front-runner rule was much less successful—seven errors in eleven cases (see Table 12).

5. The gain-deficit rule accurately predicted all nine winners of contested nominations between 1952 and 1976.[25]

Even though multi-ballot conventions have virtually disappeared in the past 30 years, Collat-Kelley-Rogowski discovered that the use of the Associated Press wire service (or *New York Times* or *Washington Post*) delegate polls as substitutes for convention ballots in calculating the gain-deficit rule enabled the authors to predict correctly the outcome of all contested presidential nominations since 1952 before any candidate had achieved majority support in the Associated Press polls of delegates (see Table 13). An empirically derived rule, the gain-deficit ratio takes into account (1) where a specific candidate ranks among the various contenders on a specific ballot (or since the onset of single ballot nominations, the candidate's ranking among the press poll delegate preferences), (2) how close victory is for the candidate, and (3) how fast the candidate is moving toward the nomination.[26]

To forecast the outcome of a convention using the gain-deficit ratio, it is necessary to compare the amount of support that each candidate still needs to win after the second test of support (the candidate's "deficit") with the change in that candidate's support between the first and second test. If the gain deficit ratio does not reach a critical value, the process is repeated until it does. If a candidate makes a small gain when close to the nomination, or a large gain when not, the "gain-deficit" ratio will be large and positive. The more impressive the candidate's showing between ballots (or press poll delegate preferences) the larger will be the gain-deficit ratio. When that ratio reaches a critical value—0.36 or slightly more than one-third—of one set of conventions (the 11 majority rule conventions of three or more ballots held before 1952) and this ratio is used to predict the more recent set of conventions (contested conventions since 1952), the results have been uncannily accurate (see Table 13).

The gain-deficit ratio performed almost as well in predicting the outcome of multi-ballot, majority rule conventions in the period 1848-1948. Of the 11 majority rule conventions prior to 1952, the gain-deficit ratio enabled the Collat-Kelley-Rogowski team to predict the nominee at nine conventions. In the remaining two conventions, Collat-Kelley-Rogowski were unable to make a prediction because no candidate's gain-deficit ratio reached 0.360.[27] Development of a reliable rule for predicting the presidential nominee was simplified by the Collat-Kelley-Rogowski research team's discovery that "no candidate who led on the first ballot of a majority-rule convention ever lost votes thereafter—*any* number of votes on *any* ballot—and then won the nomination."[28] Clearly, the Collat-Kelley-Rogowski gain-deficit ratio nominee prediction system represents a genuine breakthrough in national convention politics. No other method of nominee prognostication approaches the accuracy of the Collat-Kelley-Rogowski gain-deficit ratio system. Unless the results of the next two or three national conventions upset this new prediction system, it seems fair to say that much (but not all) of the mystery will have been taken out of the crystal ball used for predicting party nominees for the highest office in the land.

Since uncertainty of outcome is still the hallmark of the presidential nominating process, it seems worthwhile to explore still another new type of party nominee that has recently emerged in the out-of-power party—the "unemployed" presidential candidate.

Has a Reformed Nominating System Produced a New Type of Nominee?

David S. Broder, the highly respected *Washington Post* columnist and reporter, in a recent panel discussion, differentiated the types of presidential candidates

TABLE 12
FIVE PROCEDURES FOR PREDICTING THE OUTCOMES OF MAJORITY-RULE CONVENTIONS

Front-Runner Rule		Threshold Rule[a]				Rule of Second-Ballot Gains			Poll Majority			Gain-Deficit Rule[b]	
C	E	C	E	N-UP	NP	C	E	N-UP	C	NP	NA	C	NP
1848W	1852W	1848W	1880R	1852W	1876R	1848W	1876R	1880R	1964R	1952R	1848W	1848W	1876R
1884R	1860R	1860R	1952R		1888R	1852W	1888R		1968R	1952D	1852W	1852W	1880R
1916R	1876R	1884R			1916R	1860R	1920R		1968D	1956D	1860R	1860R	
1948R	1880R	1940R			1920R	1884R	1952R		1972D	1960D	1876R	1884R	
1956D	1888R	1948R			1952D	1916R	1976R			1976R	1880R	1888R	
1960D	1920R	1956D				1940R					1884R	1916R	
1964R	1940R	1960D				1948R					1888R	1920R	
1968R	1952R	1964R				1952D					1916R	1940R	
1968D	1952D	1968R				1956D					1920R	1948R	
1940R		1968D				1960D					1940R	1952R	
1952R		1972R				1964R					1948R	1952D	
1976R		1976R				1968R						1956D	
						1968D						1960D	
						1972D						1964R	
												1968R	
												1968D	
												1972D	
												1976R	

182

C	= Correct Prediction	N-UP	= Non-Unique Prediction	D	= Democratic
E	= Incorrect Prediction	NA	= Data for Prediction Not Available	R	= Republican
NP	= No Prediction Possible			W	= Whig

Source: Donald S. Collat, Stanley Kelley, Jr., and Ronald Rogowski, "The End Game in Presidential Nominations," *American Political Science Review,* Vol. 75 (June 1981), p. 434. Their sources were: Richard C. Bain and Judith H. Parris, *Convention Decisions and Voting Records,* 2nd ed. (Washington, D.C.: Brookings, 1973); *New York Times,* June 22, 1852; *Official Proceedings of the Republican Convention of 1880;* Associated Press surveys of delegates reported in the *New York Times* and *Washington Post,* supplemented by Associated Press releases; and a report of a *New York Times* survey, published July 29, 1956.

[a]Threshold = 41.0%.   [b]Critical value = 0.360.

TABLE 13
PREDICTING THE OUTCOMES OF CONTESTED
PRESIDENTIAL NOMINATIONS, 1952-1976 (CRITICAL
VALUE OF GAIN-DEFICIT RATIO = 0.360)

Convention[a]	Winner Predicted	Gain- Deficit Ratio	No. of Tests of Support	Test No. at Predic- tion	Prediction Was Possible
1952 R	Eisenhower	0.602	16[b]	13	One day before balloting
1952 D	Stevenson	0.364	11	9	First ballot (of 3)
1956 D	Stevenson	12.654	8	7	Just before balloting
1960 D	Kennedy	0.672	8	2	2½ weeks before convention
1964 R	Goldwater	1.568	11	2	4½ weeks before convention
1968 R	Nixon	0.519	12[c]	11	Day before balloting
1968 D	Humphrey	1.169	15	13	Day before balloting
1972 D	McGovern	1.113	9	2	3 weeks before convention
1976 R	Ford	0.431	18	4	5¾ weeks before convention

Source: Donald S. Collat, Stanley Kelley, Jr., and Ronald Rogowski, "The End Game in Presidential Nominations," *American Political Science Review,* Vol. 75 (June 1981), p. 432. Their sources were: Richard C. Bain and Judith H. Parris, *Convention Decisions and Voting Records,* 2nd ed. (Washington, D.C.: Brookings, 1973); Associated Press surveys of delegates reported in the *New York Times* and *Washington Post,* supplemented by Associated Press releases; and a report of a *New York Times* survey, published July 29, 1956.

Note: 1980 data have not been included in the table because neither Republican nor Democratic nominations were seriously in doubt at the end of the primary season. Personal communication with Dr. Stanley Kelley, Jr., August 5, 1982.

[a]R = Republican, D = Democrat.

[b]The first ballot in which there was shift in votes after the roll call has been counted as two ballots, since Eisenhower fell short of a majority before the shift.

[c]A shift after the roll call has not been counted as a separate ballot, since a majority was attained before the shift.

that emerged in both parties under the traditional pre-reform nominating process and those that have been spawned, indirectly at least, by the post-1968 Democratic party reforms.

In the old way, whoever wanted to run for president of the United States took a couple of months off from public office in the year of the presidential election and presented his credentials to the leaders of his party, who were elected officials, party officials, leaders of allied interest groups, and bosses in some cases. These people had known the candidate over a period of time and had carefully examined his work.

In the new way, the first thing a candidate does is to get out of public office so he has nothing to do for two, three, four, or in some cases, six years, except run for president of the United States. The candidate takes his case not to the professionals who know him or to his political peers, but to the amateurs who meet him only briefly in their living room or in the town hall [or on a television set] and have very little basis on which to make that screening.[29]

Two swallows do not maketh a summer either, but the recent phenomenon of "unemployed" presidential candidates capturing the nomination and then the Presidency in 1976 and 1980 may forecast a trend that Broder's commentary hints at. Jimmy Carter, the Democratic nominee in 1976, left the Georgia governorship after one term at the end of 1974 (under the Georgia constitution he was ineligible to seek reelection) to begin his full-time pursuit of the Presidency. Carter, of course, was not technically unemployed—he still held a major interest in the family peanut warehouse business. But he had no public office demands on his time nor, unlike other candidates, did he have to respond to political complaints that he was neglecting his official duties while on the campaign trail. As a result, he could devote the entire year of 1975 to building up grass-roots support in Iowa, New Hampshire, and Florida—three states in which he scored key early round victories in the 1976 delegate hunt. Meanwhile, his chief rivals, Senators Jackson, Bayh, and Church, Representative Udall, and Governors Wallace and Brown had to juggle and rejuggle their campaign schedules in order to spend substantial portions of their time on Capitol Hill or in the governor's mansion. Freed from official duties, Carter devoted nearly 300 days traveling the byways of these early caucus and primary states, meeting prospective delegates, cultivating local media representatives, and engaging in low-profile fund-raising. This heavy investment in time and energy obviously paid off for Carter in 1976.

Similarly, the "unemployed" former California governor, Ronald Reagan, was free to devote almost unlimited blocks of time during the period 1977-1980 to give speeches at various business conventions and party fund-raising events throughout the country. Reagan was also not unemployed in the ordinary sense of the term. Since leaving the governorship in Sacramento, he continued to earn a lucrative income from taped five-minute radio commentaries for a chain of stations across the country; he also published a syndicated weekly newspaper column for conservative newspapers. In fact, Governor Reagan postponed formal announcement of his 1980 presidential candidacy until the last possible minute to avoid a potential conflict with the Federal Communications Commission's equal-time rule on political candidacies. In other words, Reagan had a relatively free schedule during most of this three-year period—or more accurately, since he left the governor's chair in January 1975. This extensive, long-term unofficial campaign for the White House finally paid off on his third try (Reagan first tried for the Presidency in 1968 against former Vice President Nixon) at the 1980 GOP convention in Detroit. Nor should it be forgotten that Adlai E. Stevenson gained renomination in 1956 while he held no political office, and former Vice President Richard M. Nixon won a second nomination in 1968, while politically unemployed—but affiliated with a Wall Street law firm.

Being an "unemployed" presidential candidate, of course, is not a sure-fire guarantee of the nomination. Vice President George Bush, too, was "unemployed" during this same 1977-1980 pre-convention period. Month after month, Bush cultivated the GOP nationwide "knife-and-fork" circuit during this long interim period but failed to walk off with the grand prize at the 1980 GOP convention. But Bush did collect the consolation prize—the vice presidential nomination—and as a result of the Republican 1980 sweep, Bush is now "only a heartbeat away from the Presidency." Former Treasury Secretary John B. Connally, on the other hand, was totally free of the demands of public office for several years before he announced his candidacy for the GOP nomination in January 1979, but he, too, came up empty-handed. Connally's expensive ($11 million) two-year campaign for the Presidency had yielded exactly one delegate when he pulled out of the race after his disastrous setback in the South Carolina party-sponsored Republican primary in early March 1980.

Presidential candidates who are unable to leave public responsibilities or private jobs to devote many months to campaigning will find it increasingly difficult to compete effectively for the highest office in the land. Also, the onerous demands of the present marathon nominating system have, in effect, eliminated many well-qualified aspirants from serious consideration by the national convention because they are forced out of the race early for want of delegate support. Senator Howard Baker, who failed to mount his 1980 presidential campaign early because of his pressing duties as Senate GOP Minority Leader, learned this harsh lesson well in 1980. After withdrawing from the race, Senator Baker lamented that running for President "requires you to be unemployed to be a successful candidate."[30]

With the emergence of the "continuous presidential campaign" that extends virtually from one presidential election campaign to the next, there are probably going to be fewer and fewer high elective officeholders who can afford to neglect their official responsibilities for at least the 24-month period preceding the next national convention. Possibly it's only coincidence, but former Vice President Walter F. Mondale, a potential leading aspirant for the 1984 Democratic nomination, announced in early 1981 that he would not seek to regain his old U.S. Senate seat from Minnesota in 1982—the seat he relinquished in 1976 when he was elected Vice President. Instead, he gave the go-ahead signal to his key supporters to form an "exploratory" political action committee to probe, unofficially at least, his prospects for the 1984 Democratic nomination. Previously, Mondale had withdrawn from the 1976 pre-nominating race two weeks after the 1974 fall election stating, "Basically, I found that I did not have the overwhelming desire to be President which is essential for the kind of campaign that is required."[31] By the time Mondale had a change of political heart six years later, he had obviously absorbed some of the valuable lessons Jimmy Carter and Ronald Reagan learned from their long months of pre-convention campaigning while officially "unemployed."

Other unemployed presidential aspirants can also be expected to obtain a special tactical advantage from the present nominating system, unless the length of the presidential primary season is drastically curtailed by legislative or party action. It would be unfortunate—and indeed a sad commentary on our political system—if the foremost qualification for winning the party nomination for the highest office in the land is the amount of unencumbered time that the candidate has available for pre-convention campaigning. This topic will be discussed further in the final chapter.

Television coverage of national conventions has become such an integral part of these quadrennial conclaves that it, too, deserves special treatment. For this reason, the next chapter will be devoted to the crucial interrelationships of television and national conventions.

Notes

1. Sidney Hyman, *The American President* (New York: Harper & Brothers, 1954), p. 183. According to the Constitution of the United States, Art. 2, Sec. 1, Presidents must be native-born citizens, 35 years old, and have spent at least 14 years of their lives residing in the United States. Children of American nationals who were born abroad also qualify, although some ambiguity remains on the matter. The 14 years of residence need not immediately precede election to office.

2. James Lord Bryce, *The American Commonwealth*, 3rd rev. ed. (New York: Macmillan, 1914), Vol. 2, p. 187.

3. Sidney Hyman, "Nine Tests for the Presidential Hopeful," *New York Times Magazine* (January 4, 1959), p. 11.

4. William R. Keech and Donald R. Matthews, *The Party's Choice* (Washington, D.C.: The Brookings Institution, 1976), p. 7.

5. Gerald Pomper, *Nominating the President* (Evanston, Ill.: Northwestern University Press, 1963), p. 133.

6. Ibid.

7. Ibid., p. 129.

8. William G. Carleton, "The Revolution in the Presidential Nominating Convention," *Political Science Quarterly*, Vol. 72 (June 1957), pp. 224-40.

9. William R. Keech and Donald R. Matthews, *The Party's Choice*, p. 15.

10. The discussion in this section relies heavily on Robert L. Peabody and Eve Lubalin, "The Making of Presidential Candidates," in James I. Lengle and Byron E. Shafer, eds. *Presidential Politics* (New York: St. Martin's Press, 1980), pp. 50-68.

11. Ibid.

12. Ibid., p. 59.

13. Ibid., p. 61.

14. See James W. Davis, *Presidential Primaries: Road to the White House*, 2nd ed. (Westport, Conn.: Greenwood Press, 1980), chapter 3.

15. As quoted by Cyrus R. Vance "Reforming the Electoral Reforms," *New York Times Magazine* (February 22, 1981), p. 16.

16. Jack L. Walker, "Reforming the Reforms," *Wilson Quarterly*, Vol. 5 (Autumn 1981), p. 98.

17. William R. Keech and Donald R. Matthews, *The Party's Choice*, pp. 157-67.

18. Specifically, the amateurs or enthusiasts were especially active in the Democratic nominations in 1952, 1968, and 1972 and the Republican nominations of 1964, 1952, and 1964. Ibid., p. 166.

19. Theodore H. White, *America in Search of Itself: The Making of the President, 1956-1980* (New York: Harper & Row Publishers, 1982), p. 187.

20. The index of *The Gallup Poll, Public Opinion 1935-1971*, Vols. 1-3 (New York: Random House, 1972) does not list any Democratic voter preference polls on President Roosevelt's renomination in 1936; hence the figure is 23, not 24, nominations for the 12 presidential elections held since 1936.

21. James R. Beniger, "Winning the Presidential Nomination: National Polls and State Primary Elections, 1936-1972," *Public Opinion Quarterly*, Vol. 40 (Spring 1976), p. 38.

22. See Donald S. Collat, Stanley Kelley, Jr., and Ronald Rogowski, "The End Game in Presidential Nominations," *American Political Science Review*, Vol. 75 (June 1981), pp. 427-35. The authors derived the critical value of the gain-deficit ratio from one set of conventions—and 11 majority-rule conventions of three or more ballots held before 1952—and they then used that value to predict the outcomes of another set, contested conventions from 1952 onward. The critical value that maximized the accuracy of predictions for the conventions before 1952 turned out to be 0.360. Ibid., p. 428.

23. Eugene B. McGregor, Jr., "Rationality and Uncertainty at National Nominating Conventions," *Journal of Politics*, Vol. 35 (May 1973), pp. 459-78.

24. Donald S. Collat, Stanley Kelley, Jr., and Ronald Rogowski, "The End Game in Presidential Nominations," p. 433.

25. Theoretically, it is possible that the gain-deficit ratios of more than one candidate might reach the critical value figure of 0.360 simultaneously. But in none of the races examined did this happen. Nor was this purely accidental, since a big gain for one candidate naturally depletes the pool of votes from which big gains for another candidate must come. The perfect batting average of the Collat-Kelley-Rogowski team was maintained, in part, because the credentials challenges at the 1952 GOP convention and the 1972 Democratic convention turned out in favor of the victorious candidate. Had these contests come out differently, the Collat-Kelley-Rogowski predictions would, the authors acknowledge, probably have been wrong in each case.

26. Ibid., p. 426.

27. Ibid., p. 428.

28. Ibid., footnote 3.

29. *Choosing Presidential Candidates: How Good Is the New Way?* (Washington, D.C.: American Enterprise Institute, 1980), pp. 2-3.

30. *New York Times*, August 30, 1980.

31. Jules Witcover, *Marathon: The Pursuit of the Presidency, 1972-1976* (New York: The Viking Press, 1977), p. 126.

The National Convention in the Age of Television _____ 7

Presidential politics today, it is reasonably fair to say, is television. Party politics in America has given way to media politics.

                                                    —Tom Wicker

National nominating conventions and network television are made for each other. Until 1952, the year that the coaxial cable made possible coast-to-coast network telecasts, most Americans had only a passing acquaintance with national conventions. Mr. and Mrs. Citizen could turn on their radio sets to hear broadcasts from convention hall, read briefly about conventions in the daily newspapers, or catch a glimpse of convention activity on the Pathe News or Fox Movietone newsreels while attending the local movie theater. In the nineteenth century, convention information was understandably far more restricted; only a handful of professional politicians and a limited audience of daily or weekly newspaper readers were familiar with convention activities. All of this, of course, has been changed by the network camera. As veteran reporter Neil Hickey has commented, "What were once relatively private exercises in intramural politics are now monster pageants choreographed for the benefit of the whole nation."[1] Television has become the middleman between the parties' selection of presidential candidates and the American electorate. Furthermore, television networks have altered the character of national conventions by their demands for fast-paced action and a not-so-subtle insistence that the cameras be in the midst of or near all decision-making parleys.

Prime-Time Political Pageantry

Thirty years have passed since the television networks first aimed their new cameras at the Republican and Democratic conventions, both held in Chicago, and ushered in a new era of national politics. Middle-age convention-watchers can now recall the infectious smile of General Dwight D. Eisenhower as he accepted the GOP nomination at the historic 1952 convention after vanquishing "Mr. Republican"—Senator Robert A. Taft. Presidential chronicler Theodore H. White has also reminded us of television's crucial role in conveying the white-heat tension of the rancorous 1964 GOP convention battle between the dominant forces of Senator Barry Goldwater, the nominee, and Governor Nelson A. Rockefeller, his chief rival:

> . . . as the TV cameras translated [the Goldwater hecklers'] wrath and fury to the national audience, they pressed on the viewers that indelible impression of savagery which no Goldwater leader or wordsmith could later erase.[2]

Television's most famous convention hours were recorded at the strife-torn 1968 Democratic convention in Chicago when television screens across the land flashed pictures of phalanxes of helmeted Chicago policemen, their clubs raised, advancing upon hundreds of youthful anti-Vietnam War demonstrators in Grant Park, across from the convention hotels in downtown Chicago. Millions of viewers were shocked to see the excessive overreaction of Chicago police clubbing the young demonstrators. The introduction of color television in 1968 heightened viewer reaction to the violence. Nor will viewers of the 1968 Democratic convention ever forget the armed camp atmosphere existing around Chicago's International Amphitheatre, site of the convention. A security ring several blocks wide guarded the convention arena itself, surrounded by a high barbed wire fence and multiple security checkpoints for delegates, media personnel, and guests. Never before in the 125-year history of national conventions had the party conclave resembled a military encampment—11,900 Chicago police, 7,500 U.S. Army regulars, 7,500 Illinois National Guardsmen, and 1,000 FBI and Secret Service personnel were on duty to keep vociferous Vietnam War protesters away from convention headquarters and the Amphitheatre. Most over-30 voters will also recall Senator Abraham Ribicoff's directed remarks to Mayor Daley, in which he referred to the "Gestapo tactics" of the Chicago police and the Mayor's fist-shaking response. No wonder millions of TV viewers concluded that if the Democratic party could not manage its own internal problems, then the party should not be entrusted with running the government for the next four years. As much as anything else, these televised convention pictures wrecked the hopes of the Democratic party and its nominee, Hubert H. Humphrey, of retaining control of the White House. Presidential chronicler Theodore H. White has contended that the network's intercutting of film of Chicago's street riots with the proceedings on the convention floor "created the most striking and fake political picture of 1968—the nomination of a man for the American Presidency by the brutality and violence of merciless police."[3] Since the tumultuous Democratic convention of 1968, no political analyst will ever underestimate the powerful role of television's instantaneous reporting of national conventions. National conventions are now dominated by the three major television networks.

TV Networks' Huge Convention Investment

The three TV networks spend far more on the national conventions than do the two major parties. Indeed, network coverage of national conventions has become a big business. Preparations for covering a national convention begin almost as soon as the clean-up crews have finished their work on the last conclave. News divisions at all three television networks have special year-round convention and election units. Dozens of staff members devote their time exclusively to the business of presidential nominations, starting with the presidential primaries and then capping off the season with the quadrennial extravaganzas. Advanced planning proceeds at a regular pace until the party national committees announce the selection of their next convention city and site—usually about 18 months ahead of the convention date. Then, the network units move into high gear. First of all, each network reserves 600 to 700 hotel rooms in the convention city. Technical and logistics units then commence charting their plans, much like the military quartermaster corps.

Network outlays for the national conventions far exceed the number of dollars spent by the parties (and the $2.5 million federal subsidies to help defray the cost of each party's national convention, as provided by the Federal Election Campaign Act of 1974). To cover the 1980 Republican and Democratic conventions, the three commercial television networks shelled out more than $30 million collectively to provide the public cost-free, gavel-to-gavel coverage of these political pageants. The three networks sent nearly 2,000 journalists, technicians, and support troops to the convention cities, along with 500 tons of office and technical equipment, including an entourage of huge tractor-trailers crammed with electronic gear, TV monitors, and miles of black, python-like cable used to connect the intricate combination of 30-plus camera stations set up by each network and the jointly operated "pool" cameras. "Covering a convention", said a CBS News executive, "basically entails building a completely operational radio and television network."[4] NBC News President William Small reviewed his 600-member team at a special "pep rally" before the 1980 GOP convention opened and quipped, "If King George had an army this large, we'd all be working for the BBC."[5]

Covering national conventions is not a money-making venture for the networks, however, since television commercials produce less than one-quarter of the revenue needed to underwrite the massive costs. But network executives, locked in a gigantic battle with their competitors, are prepared to write off more than $10 million each as an investment in building their prestige with advertisers and generating public goodwill. The networks have a certain element of self-interest, too. The higher the share of the national viewer audience during the national conventions the higher the rate the networks can charge their advertisers for their regular programs, starting in the fall season, thus netting returns several times the cost of each national convention. Each percentage point increase in viewership for, say, the evening news show is worth at least $7 million more in annual advertising revenue. High viewer ratings and convention coverage also boost the network's chances of winning top bill for the fall season viewer sweepstakes. In short, network competition for audience share is the cardinal rule of electronic journalism.

In the continuous head-to-head confrontations among the three national television networks, no area of competition exceeds the network rivalry over coverage of the national conventions. The battle royal, especially between CBS-TV and NBC-TV, begins during the primary season and reaches its peak during the national conventions. NBC, for example, beat CBS by less than one minute on balloting night at the 1980 GOP convention when its young star reporter Chris Wallace dramatically announced on the air that George Bush, not former President Gerald Ford, would be Ronald Reagan's vice presidential choice. Earlier in the same evening, CBS anchorman Walter Cronkite had also collected a gold medal by obtaining a special late-round interview with former President Ford in the network booth high above the milling delegates in the Joe Louis Sports Arena. During the course of this interview, conducted less than two hours before the presidential balloting started, Ford laid down a number of conditions that would have to be met by Ronald Reagan before the former President would be willing to serve as the number two member on the GOP ticket. Cronkite, sensing the importance of this issue, suggested that perhaps Ford might be thinking of a "co-Presidency." The former President did not object to the use of the term. Reagan, however, as mentioned earlier, was so shocked and incensed to see and hear about this public bargaining and breach of confidentiality on a national telecast that he abruptly dropped Ford from further vice presidential consideration. For the first time in convention history, a single television interview may have been the decisive factor in the vice presidential selection process—indeed, may have determined the next person in line to occupy (or, in this case, reoccupy) the White House. The other high point of the televised presidential sweepstakes occurs, of course, on general election night in November when the networks vie with each other to be the first to project the "winner" of the presidential race— sometimes before the polls close on the West Coast.

The 1980 GOP convention also produced another distinctly new press story on another aspect of televised coverage of the party conclaves—local station coverage. Only a handful of local television stations have covered the conventions in the past. But in 1980, more than 150 local stations reported to the folks back home. With new lightweight "minicams" and the latest transmission technology, the local television stations made hot competition for the network affiliates in the home city. With their small cameras, the local stations can highlight their coverage with repeated interviews with the local politicos, spiced with plenty of human interest stories, lots of footage of the Motor City or the "Big Apple," and detailed reports on what local delegates are doing in their spare moments.

Similarly, the newly established Cable News Network (CNN), which inaugurated nationwide service via satellite in June 1980, beamed convention coverage to 2.5 million cable subscribers. Cable television may well be the wave of the future. The first major alternative to network coverage since coast-to-coast coverage in 1952, the cable network telecasts 24 hours a day—via a portable satellite transmit Earth station—selective highlights of the national conventions as well as other news and sports events. With this round-the-clock flexibility, the CNN reporters and analysts have even greater latitude than the big three networks. Cable TV, local and decentralized, can appeal to more selective audiences; indeed it may represent a bigger threat to network television than their executives are willing to concede. (By 1982 the flagship station of the Cable News Network, WTBS-TV, Atlanta, reached 22.5 million viewers via satellite links.) Nor should the topical coverage of the national conventions by the Public Broadcasting System (PBS) be ignored. With a loyal audience in the four to five million persons range, the government-subsidized television network now offers high-quality commentary, notably the award-winning "MacNeil-Lehrer Report," on the convention proceedings.

That television offers political parties and their national conventions an unparalleled opportunity to reach almost every American of voting age is beyond dispute. Only one American household in 100 has no working television set, according to results of a *Washington Post* survey in late February 1979.[6] A majority of householders own two or more sets. The survey, which produced fresh evidence that television consistently holds the biggest audience in the history of communication, also revealed that the average adult watches television for three hours each weekday and three hours and 25 minutes on Saturdays and Sundays.

Television has become such a popular national institution that at the 1980 GOP convention in Detroit television luminaries were frequently better known than the people they were covering. TV personages have become bigger stars than leading politicians. CBS's Dan Rather and NBC's Tom Brokaw, for example, were besieged by autograph seekers everywhere they went—even on the convention floor. One *New York Daily News* reporter at the Motor City convention polled the curiosity seekers in the lobby of the Detroit Plaza Hotel, Reagan's convention hotel, and discovered that CBS anchorman Walter Cronkite was the main attraction, ahead of former President Ford, Reagan, and movie star Elizabeth Taylor.[7]

National conventions are the greatest media events in the political world, and the convention hall is the world's biggest TV studio. The TV networks thrive on filmable ritual, the waving candidate placards, the red-white-and-blue streamers, the exuberant delegates and their silly hats. Executive producers, facing great walls of TV monitors carrying separate pictures from 30 or more strategically placed cameras throughout the convention hall, at the major convention hotels, and even at the city's airport, decide minute-by-minute which monitor becomes the network's "live" picture. Throughout the proceedings these producers decide which floor reporter gets on the air next and how much time he or she will be given. Time must, of course, also be reserved for network commercials, without disrupting the continuity of convention coverage. Special-breaking stories on a

rumored choice for vice president, or a threatened walk-out from a dissident group may upset the normal coverage, but this is the type of excitement that the executive producer is looking for.

To add an extra dimension to their coverage, the networks hire nationally known writers and columnists—Theodore H. White, Bill Moyers, James Kilpatrick, and George Will—to work with the anchormen.Occasionally, defeated presidential contenders—and even former Presidents— have sometimes been hired as special commentators. In 1964, for example, ABC hired former President Eisenhower as a "special on-the-air consultant." This network coup made news on and for ABC. The other two networks and media had to tune to ABC to hear the retired President and former Supreme Allied Commander reaffirm his belief in civilian control over the military state, observe that the GOP vice presidential nominee, Representative William Miller of New York, would not have been his choice for the number two spot on the ticket, and recall that he hadn't understood the politics of the 1952 GOP convention that first nominated him. (Former President Harry Truman declined to serve in a similar capacity at the Democratic convention.) In 1980, NBC's "Today Show" aired pretaped interviews with independent presidential candidate John Anderson, but the interviews failed to generate much enthusiasm from the network executives or the general public. As a result, his time slot soon dwindled to two to three minutes a day.

Impact of Conventions upon Voter Attitudes

Voting studies have found that many voters review their party preferences most actively at the time of the conventions, with the plan of deciding for whom they will vote in the November election. Indeed, the composition of the attentive electorate changes significantly during the convention period. Whereas interested voters during the primary season in 1976 tended to be strong party identifiers, during the convention period the interested electorate expanded to include a greater proportion of weak partisans.[8] According to one leading authority, Thomas Patterson, "Interest was particularly likely to increase among weak identifiers who happened to see parts or all of the conventions. Apparently convention coverage helps to arouse latent partisanship, in the process enlisting people's interest in the campaign."[9] Similarly, the political impact of convention coverage appeared to be greater than that of presidential debate coverage, perhaps because the conventions come at a time when interest is at a lower level and the potential for media impact is higher.[10] A significant fact about television coverage of national conventions is that it helps activate interest at a point early in the campaign, generating interest months before the voters must make their final decision on presidential choice in early November. As Patterson, in his study of network viewing during the 1976 campaign, concluded, "People who watched the conventions were more likely, by August, to have formed the judgment that some aspect of policy or leadership was the campaign's most significant feature."[11]

National conventions represent the turning point in the presidential race when competition within parties is replaced by competition between parties. Indeed, the national conventions mark the beginning of the general election campaign.

EFFECT OF CONVENTIONS ON REPORTED TIME OF VOTE DECISION

When do voters make up their minds on the choice of presidential candidates? According to data from the early trail-blazing study on partisan choice, *The American Voter*, approximately one-third of the voters sampled in 1952 and 1956 reported that their vote decision on nominees crystallized when General Dwight Eisenhower and Adlai E.Stevenson became candidates or at the time of the national conventions.[12] Another large segment of the survey (30 percent in 1952 and 44 percent in 1956) reported that they "knew all along how they would vote." Roughly, the final third decided after the conventions, during the fall campaign, or decided on election day. How the American electorate came to a decision on presidential choice in 1952 and 1956 is reported in Table 14. Since 1960, the Center for Political Studies of Michigan's Institute for Social Research has asked the following question on the timing of voter decision: "How long before the election did you decide that you were going to vote the way you did?" (see Table 15).

As the reader will note, these data show a sharp increase in 1976 in the proportion of the electorate making a late decision on presidential choice. Recent Gallup survey data also show that American voters are not, by and large, making up their minds about their presidential choice as early as formerly. In 1976, for example, approximately one-quarter of the persons surveyed reported their vote decision crystallized between two weeks before the November election and election day (see Table 16). The influence of convention-watching upon voter attitudes should not be underestimated. In a survey of 400 San Francisco respondents in 1976, Cliff Zukin found that one-quarter of those who followed the Democratic convention and almost a fifth of those who followed the GOP conclave said they changed their views about the candidates (see Table 16).

Both Democratic and Republican partisans were more likely to change views of their own candidate than of the opposing candidate. Twenty-eight percent of the Democrats changed their feelings (in either direction or intensity) toward Jimmy Carter, as did 17 percent of the Republican viewers. Approximately 25 percent of the Republicans changed their impression of President Ford, as did 14 percent of the Democrats who watched the Republican proceedings. As Table 16 indicates, both candidates registered impressive "change ratios"—the proportion of favorable to unfavorable changes of view was about three-to-one for the entire sample. Ten percent of the Democrats looked more favorably on Ford as a result of exposure to the convention, while only two percent reported a less favorable view toward Ford. For Republican viewers approximately 16 percent looked more favorably on Ford (rather remarkable in view of the bitter nominating battle between the Californian Reagan and President Ford), and only six percent had a negative attitude toward Ford. Jimmy Carter's change of viewer attitude ratio

TABLE 14
REPORTED TIME OF VOTE DECISION ON PRESIDENT, 1952-1956

	1952	1956
Knew all along how they would vote	30%	44%
Decided when Eisenhower or Stevenson became a candidate or at time of conventions	35	32
Decided after conventions, during campaign	20	11
Decided within two weeks of election	9	7
Decided on election day	2	2
Do not remember	1	1
Not ascertained	3	3
Total	100%	100%
N	1,195	1,291

Source: Angus Campbell, Philip E. Converse, Warren E. Miller, and Donald E. Stokes, *The American Voter* (New York: John Wiley & Sons, 1960), p. 78. Reprinted by permission of John Wiley & Sons, Inc.

TABLE 15
REPORTED TIME OF VOTE DECISION ON PRESIDENT, 1960-1980

	1960	1964	1968	1972	1976	1980
Knew all along, always vote same party, pre-convention	31%	41%	35%	44%	33%	41%
At time of conventions	31	25	24	18	21	18
After conventions	26	21	19	22	22	15
Within 2 weeks of election, on election day	12	13	21	13	24	26

Sources: "Opinion Roundup," *Public Opinion* (December/January 1981), p. 26. Reprinted by permission of American Enterprise Institute for Public Policy Research. Data for 1980 supplied by Institute for Social Research, University of Michigan, and reprinted by permission.

Note: The responses above were made to the standard question asked quadrennially by interviewers from the University of Michigan's Institute for Social Research: "How long before the election did you decide that you were going to vote the way you did?"

was more limited in a partisan sense. He registered a five-to-one positive change in ratio among Democrats (20 percent positive and four percent negative), but among Republicans the shift in attitude was evenly divided—seven percent viewed Carter more favorably and six percent were less impressed with the Democratic nominee. Thus, for the most part, convention-watching among this 400-person San Francisco survey in 1976 reinforced partisan predispositions toward the candidates.[13]

TABLE 16
MEDIA EXPOSURE TO CONVENTIONS AND CANDIDATE IMAGERY, 1976 SURVEY

	Carter[a]	Ford[b]	By Partisanship			
			Carter		Ford	
			DEM.	REP.	DEM.	REP.
Change of Views						
No Change	75%	83%	72%	83%	86%	75%
Favorable	15	11	20	7	10	16
Neutral	4	3	4	4	2	3
Negative	5	4	4	6	2	6
Total	99%	101%	100%	100%	100%	100%
(N)	(319)	(343)	(204)	(69)	(215)	(81)

Source: Cliff Zukin, "A Triumph of Form over Content: Television and the 1976 National Nominating Convention." Paper presented at the Midwest Political Science Association annual meeting, Chicago, Illinois, April 1979.

Note: Taken from a telephone survey of 400 San Franciscans, conducted in the week following the 1976 Republican National Convention.

[a]This was asked only of those who followed the Democratic convention.

[b]This was asked only of those who followed the Republican convention.

While one can only speculate about the time sequence of voter decision-making, it may be that the re-establishment of presidential debates in 1976 (the only previous debates were held between Kennedy and Nixon in 1960) offers prospective voters two or three additional opportunities to "size up" the presidential nominees before making a final choice. As Table 17 indicates, at least eight percent of the voters surveyed made up their minds during or immediately after the three Ford-Carter debates.

In 1980, the Gallup organization reported in mid-September that while 89 percent of the voters stated a candidate preference, more than one-third of the persons interviewed could be considered "soft" on their preference. ("Soft" voters are those who qualify their presidential choice by indicating that they only moderately support their candidate and at the same time are only moderately opposed to his opponents.)[14] Similarly, an NBC/Associated Press poll among "likely voters," conducted October 22-24, 1980, showed that 25 percent of the respondents had not yet made up their minds or were not sure about their presidential choice.[15] These polls would seem to suggest that the national conventions of 1980 were less successful than previous conclaves in reinforcing existing voter loyalties. It is noteworthy, however, that in 1976 approximately the same percentage of voters (27 percent) as in 1952 and 1956 made up their minds on presidential choice before the conventions or when the candidate started

TABLE 17
REPORTED TIME OF VOTE DECISION ON PRESIDENT, 1976
(GALLUP POLL)

Election day/last minute	12%
On last two or three days	6
Between two weeks and several days before the election	7
After the debates (general)	2
After the *third* debate	3
After the *second* debate	2
After the *first* debate	1
Between conventions and two weeks before the election	15
When candidate was nominated	11
As soon as *other* candidate was nominated	5
Before conventions/when candidate started to campaign	27
After heard candidate speak	1
Miscellaneous	3
Can't remember	5
	100%

Source: *Gallup Opinion Index*, No. 137 (December 1976), p. 8.

to campaign. According to a 1980 post-convention Gallup poll, nearly two-thirds (64 percent) of the American public of voting age said that they watched the Democratic convention at one point or another. What effect did the convention proceedings have upon voter attitudes toward the Democratic party and its nominee? Prior to the convention, network newscasts were filled with dire predictions about the possible negative impact that the bitter Carter-Kennedy nominating contest would have upon the voters. To find out if this were true, the Gallup organization asked a 1,500-person national sample of those who watched the convention: "Did watching the convention give you a more favorable or less favorable impression of the Democratic party?"

Approximately 39 percent of those sampled who watched the convention responded that their opinion had not been changed. Of those who reported that their opinion had indeed changed, less favorable versus more favorable impression nearly counterbalanced one another. Approximately 28 percent of those who viewed the convention looked more favorably upon the Democrats in the aftermath of the conventions; 31 percent had a less favorable image; and another two percent had no opinion.[16] Reinforcement of existing partisan loyalties appeared to be the chief by-product of the viewer's television exposure to the convention. Political independents (36 percent), however, were less favorably impressed with the 1980 Democratic conclave, and only 19 percent more favorably impressed.[17]

EFFECT OF CONVENTION ON CANDIDATE'S STANDING IN OPINION POLLS

After three or four days of nationally televised coverage of conventions, newly selected presidential nominees—whether they be incumbents or challengers—have generally enjoyed a short, rapid surge in the leading opinion polls. Gallup polls have shown that the candidate's strength is measurably increased by national conventions. Thus, even though President Carter's job rating in the Gallup poll reached a record low of 21 percent shortly before the 1980 Democratic convention, he nevertheless enjoyed a temporary lift in the polls. Like every major party candidate in the past 20 years, except George McGovern in 1972, Carter got what one member of the Gallup organization called a "bump" from his nomination convention. Picking up seven percentage points in the first two weeks immediately following the Democratic convention while his November rival, Ronald Reagan, lost six points, the President trailed the former California governor only 39 percent to 38, with 14 percent going to Representative John B. Anderson, the independent candidate. Among the other national polls, Carter went up 13 points in the CBS poll, 12 points in the NBC poll, and 9 points in the ABC poll.[18]

Governor Reagan also enjoyed a post-convention surge in his poll standings after his unchallenged nomination at the 1980 Republican convention. Just before the GOP conclave opened, Reagan moved into a narrow 47 to 41 percent lead over Carter. But with a strong show of unity at the Republican convention, Reagan spurted ahead to a 14 percent lead in a post-convention Gallup poll. Polling experts in both parties, however, are aware of this "artificial advantage" that accrues to a nominee shortly after his selection, but this advantage frequently vanishes in subsequent polls. In 1976, for example, Democratic nominee Jimmy Carter saw his huge post-convention 33 percentage point lead over President Ford gradually melt away in the face of Ford's dramatic post-convention comeback in the fall campaign. Carter's post-convention euphoria began to turn to gloom. Carter, however, did succeed in holding off Ford, eking out a 1.5 percent vote margin in the November 1976 election. Likewise, former Vice President Richard Nixon, with a post-convention 43 percent to 25 percent Gallup poll lead in 1968 over Democratic nominee Hubert H. Humphrey, barely nosed out the "Happy Warrior," who had regrouped his forces after a badly split Democratic convention, by one percent of the voters in November. Small wonder, then, that party nominees do not rest too long on their post-convention laurels. As the record shows, post-convention polls can sometimes be misleading as an omen for predicting the outcome of the November presidential election.

Party and Nominee's Use of Convention as a Campaign Tool

Veteran political managers have long recognized that national conventions can be skillfully exploited to strengthen their party's chances of electoral victory in

November. Party professionals also are painfully aware that an unruly and divided convention can, in effect, forfeit the presidential election. Consequently, both major parties, whether occupying the White House or not, always attempt to maximize the conventions's four evenings of prime television time to generate a favorable "image" in the minds of millions of the American electorate. As one GOP convention official has put it, "The whole idea is to make the event into a TV production instead of a convention.[19]

The classic case of a stage-managed convention, it is generally agreed, was the 1972 GOP conclave in Miami Beach. Careful planning minimized confusion and the minute-by-minute scheduling created a general impression of harmony and unity. To the average television viewer, noncontroversial conventions are terribly boring. But President Nixon's convention planner, Peter Dailey, in 1972 knew what he was doing when he asserted that: "It was... very important that the Republican convention was run with a degree of precision and organization that added to the impression that the President was a man who was able to control his own destiny and therefore control the destiny of the country."[20] Just how tightly planned the Republican convention was organized came to light when a GOP staff messenger mistakenly delivered mimeographed copies of a detailed convention script to the British Broadcasting Corporation outlining minute-by-minute the unfolding of the proceedings, including time allotted to introductions, "spontaneous" demonstrations, applause, and even the release of colored balloons. Other copies of the script were also inadvertently sent out, and they, too, soon fell into the hands of network correspondents. One excerpt from the nomination night script read:

9:39-9:43
(4 minutes)   Introduction of Nominator

Chairman Ford: At this time, the state of New York having requested recognition for the purposes of nominating the next President of the United States, the Chair recognizes the spokesman for that state. Will the spokesman for the state of New York please come to the podium.

(Delegates from Floor): Mr. Chairman, our spokesman is following your request and is going to the podium.

(If necessary Chair may request music while spokesman is approaching podium.)

And, at 10:33 p.m., according to the convention script, the President would be nominated and there would be a "ten-minute spontaneous demonstration with balloons." Though revelation of the convention script made hot news copy briefly for the national media, it apparently had no lasting negative effect upon the convention outcome, the party, or the nominee. As author Timothy Crouse commented, "The script simply confirmed what everybody already knew, the convention was a totally stage-managed coronation of Richard Nixon."[21]

In 1980, Republican convention planners, especially GOP Chairman William Brock, orchestrated their thirty-second quadrennial conclave to reassure independent voters, wavering Democrats, and doubting Republicans watching the show that their nominee, Ronald Reagan, wasn't—as his critics claimed— "a shallow, irresponsible hip-shooter." Reagan's convention managers, looking ahead to the general election campaign, were especially anxious about retaining the support of liberal Republicans and fence-sitting independents who might opt for independent candidate John Anderson, who then was the choice of—according to the Gallup poll—upwards of 21 percent of the American electorate.[22] To demonstrate his abiding concern for minority rights (and faced with a threatened walkout of black delegates), Reagan personally insisted that Benjamin L. Hooks, the Executive Director of the National Association for the Advancement of Colored People, be included among the list of speakers to be heard after the keynote speech. Nor did Governor Reagan miss the opportunity in his own acceptance speech to make elimination of "discrimination against women" a high priority in his planned new administration, even though the GOP platform openly avoided endorsing the Equal Rights Amendment. Not by accident, a special biographical film (which preceded Governor Reagan's acceptance speech) stressed his early ties with labor unions while he worked in Hollywood. Showing these candidate films has become standard operating procedure at national conventions. Briefly, then, the Republican nominee used his convention appearance and acceptance speech to reassure millions in the electorate that his future administration would be responsive, if elected, to the aspirations and needs of minorities, women, and blue-collar workers. Thanks to instantaneous communication via an electronic screen, Governor Reagan's cost-free convention speech reached more than half of the adult Americans who would vote in November.

Both major parties, as indicated above, now utilize a standard stratagem— special films—to monopolize network convention coverage during part of the prime viewing time. As described by one newsman, "The convention house lights dim, a big screen appears and filmed images of personalities arise with messages as urgent as any television commercial, messages laced with canned laughter to prime the seated conventioneers"—and, it should be added, the millions of home viewers watching the proceedings on television.[23] By turning down the convention hall lights for the films, the convention managers have virtually forced the networks to carry the films because network floor reporters cannot conduct special floor interviews in the darkened convention hall. Free access to prime time television has prompted both major parties to rely heavily on motion picture films to extoll the manifold accomplishments of an incumbent (for example, President Nixon's visit to Communist China and the Soviet Union in 1972), to celebrate the nomination of an early first ballot winner (for example, Jimmy Carter in 1976), or to honor fallen heroes (for example, President John F. Kennedy and Robert F. Kennedy). Extensive use of films can serve two manifold objectives: propagandize the viewing electorate about the many accomplishments and the laudatory goals of the sponsoring party, and entertain the delegates and inspire them to return home and work harder than ever for the party ticket.

TV Reshapes Convention Schedule

Television coverage of national conventions, beginning in 1952, marks the dividing line between the old-style and modern national nominating conventions. Gone forever are the old-fashioned party conclaves with the longwinded keynote speech, numerous hour-long "spontaneous" snake-dance demonstrations, long lines of favorite-son nominations lasting for hours, the interminable seconding speeches for each of these candidates, and frequent multiple-ballot conventions.[24] All this has been consigned to the archives of history. Television has forced convention managers to streamline their quadrennial meetings. Before each national convention network executives and party officials work jointly to plan the convention coverage. The party's convention manager and his staff and the network executives deal with such matters as convention site facilities and schedule, network space location and credentials, access and camera coverage, and sponsors. The average living-room viewer is probably unaware of the immense amount of advanced planning that the networks invest in each convention. In the year before the 1976 Democratic convention, for example, officials of CBS, NBC, and ABC traveled across the country with the Democratic National Committee's site-selection committee during the eight-month process that led to the selection of New York. And at the convention, network producers and executives met with DNC officials and Jimmy Carter's representatives "to exchange their plans for the day—game plans so that politicians and cameras would be in the same places at the same time."[25]

Convention scheduling has been drastically altered to maximize the party's use of prime-time network coverage. Keynote and nominating speeches, balloting, and acceptance speeches have been trimmed and scheduled for the choice prime-time viewing hours between 7 p.m. and 10 p.m. In marked contrast, Senator Henry Cabot Lodge, Sr.'s keynote speech at the 1920 GOP convention in Chicago lasted one hour and twenty minutes.Four years later, the 1924 GOP keynoter, Senator Theodore Burton of Ohio, spoke for one hour and fifty minutes! His Democratic counterpart Senator Pat Harrison of Mississippi, the Democratic keynoter at the 1924 marathon convention and one of the Senate's finest orators, entertained the delegates and excoriated the opposition party for one hour and fifteen minutes. Author Robert K. Murray has provided a colorful description of Harrison's performance:

Keynoters are usually selected for their oratorical ability and Harrison was no exception. He could talk on anything. As one political commentator assessed him, Harrison could in Detroit give so effective a campaign talk on Kosciusko that it would "cause all the livers of all Poles to tremble" yet the next day could deliver a speech on Lee in a Confederate cemetery that would "melt the tombstones themselves." Wearing a bow tie and a soft collar, and having a high forehead which belied the fact that he was the second-youngest member of the Senate in 1924, Harrison gave the convention a gourmet sampling of his forensic talents. Rolling his words about in his mouth to give them both an Irish and a southern coating, Harrison engaged in hyperbole so extravagant that even the most militant delegate was satisfied. Calling his colleagues "Dimmicrats" and the Republicans the "innimy," he expressed "utter amazemunt" at the degradation of the government in Washington. As he zeroed in on the Teapot Dome oil scandal the Georgia delegates in the front rows, who had been interjecting "Atta boy, Pat, give it to em!" fell temporarily quiet, but rediscovered their voices as soon as he returned to safer ground. New Yorkers, amused at the obvious discomfort of the McAdoo men during Harrison's recital of the oil corruption in Washington, were themselves embarrassed a short time later when the galleries met Harrison's call for a new Paul Revere with much cheering in the mistaken notion that he had said, "What this country needs [is] real beer."[26]

Television executives would, of course, shudder in horror if they had to accommodate the networks to the convention schedules of yesteryear. Nominations alone at the 1924 Democratic convention in New York City took three full days![27] Credentials and rules committees now meet as *de facto* bodies the week before the convention to eliminate (as much as possible) the "dull Tuesday" of waiting for these two committees to meet and make their long (and frequently boring) reports. If there are serious challenges, the convention managers will try (but not always successfully) to get them cleared up before the evening session. To streamline platform proceedings, the committees in both parties meet initially several months ahead of the conventions and conduct hearings in major cities throughout the land so that they (at least the Democrats) can have a final draft in hand before the convention opens.

To speed up the convention proceedings, the Democrats (in 1972) virtually ended "favorite-son" nominations by requiring that each person put in nomination have the written support of at least 50 delegates from at least three different delegations, with no more than 20 supporters coming from any one delegation.[28] (Formerly, favorite-son nominations sometimes consumed most of a full day's session.) Both parties have stiffened the requirements for roll call votes, and if a roll call of a state delegation is requested and in order, the convention chairman may send a designated representative to conduct the poll and continue the state-by-state roll call without waiting for the results from the undecided states. No longer can a state stall the convention for half an hour or more by slowly polling each delegate and verifying the uncertain count. Furthermore, the polling must be done at the state's place on the convention floor to avoid disrupting the proceedings (as was formerly done) by moving a delegation into a corridor or special meeting room. To avoid driving the home viewers away from their TV sets, the number and length of seconding speeches has been drastically curbed.

Strenuous efforts have been made to trim the major sessions to three or four hours during the prime evening hours, especially if there is no conflict over the nominee or platform. In 1972, however, the marathon Democratic platform session, which began during prime time, lasted until 6:26 a.m., Eastern Daylight Time, well after sunrise in Miami Beach. Also, two nights later, the Democratic vice presidential balloting delayed the start of Senator George McGovern's acceptance speech until 2:53 a.m. in the heavily populated Eastern Time zone. By and large, though, convention time has been reduced substantially since the advent of television. Judith Parris reports that the 1952 Democratic convention totaled ten sessions that lasted over 47 hours, while the 1968 Democratic convention—despite the street riots and bitter debate over the Vietnam War platform plank—consisted of only five sessions that ran less than 29 hours.[29] While two of the major networks (CBS and NBC) pride themselves on "gavel-to-gavel" coverage of the quadrennial conventions, their air time does not always measure up to this norm. In 1980, for example, CBS and NBC covered the Democrats for the most part only after their regular half-hour evening news programs. Network executives chose to skip carrying the lengthy afternoon sessions devoted to intense debate over convention rules and the party platform during the first two days of the New York City convention.

If parties try too openly to control their conventions and exploit the presence of the television cameras, they, of course, run the risk of being accused of stage managing. But a subtle game goes on continuously between the convention director and the networks on the management of the convention.

All in all, the network and party trade-offs are fairly well equalized. The networks have ample time to concentrate on providing the home viewing audience with a combination pageant-like television drama, and the parties obtain a priceless bargain of four full days of cost-free advertising to tell their political story to the American electorate. Asked how much each of the parties would have had to pay the television networks if they were charged standard advertising rates for coverage of the 1980 conventions, one network executive frowned, rolled his eyes, and muttered, "about $10 million."[30]

The national conventions also offer another valuable "fringe" benefit to the parties. The convention can serve as a "test market" for new stars in the party—young governors, upcoming leaders in the U.S. Senate or House of Representatives, and popular big-city mayors. Who knows, an impressive convention speech may transform one of these officeholders into a future nominee.

Concern over the party "image," as related to the appearance of its convention officers on television, led the Republican party in 1964 to break tradition and not name House Minority Leader Charles Halleck of Indiana as convention chairman. Some party insiders felt that Halleck's resemblance to the late comedian W.C. Fields was too close to risk projecting an unwanted image across televisionland. Instead, the Republican National Committee sought to emphasize the image of a "young and modern party," with the youthful, photogenic Governor Mark Hatfield of Oregon as keynote speaker and temporary chairman and the handsome Senator Thruston Morton of Kentucky as permanent chairman. Printed instructions to platform speakers urged them to be brief in their remarks, to rehearse their lines for effective television delivery and consider the use of appropriate TV dusting powder "make up." So eager were the Republican convention managers in 1968 to be seen at their best by the network cameras that they hired a firm of TV consultants to drill them on how to act at the podium, what to wear, and how to read the TelePrompTer. As the president of the firm explained, "We are responsible for the 'presentation'—that is, how the convention appears in color. We advise on the rostrum design, the selection of colors, lighting, background, make-up, prompting, and so forth."[31] The TV consulting firm sent over 30 staffers to Miami Beach to work with the convention speakers, setting up orientation courses and studying photographs of the leading convention personae so that when each arrived at the podium he or she would be bathed in the most flattering cosmetic lighting possible. Delegates were urged by their state chairpersons to act decorously to prevent the millions of home viewers from getting an unfavorable impression about the party's decision-makers. In 1976, the Republicans took their advice on lighting, color management, and TelePrompTer usage from the same Madison Avenue firm hired by the Democrats. This consulting agency—called TNT Communications— had previously contracted to provide coaching on the use of TelePrompTers, wardrobe advice, and make-up artists for 60 speakers at the Democratic convention.[32]

Network executives have not been modest about claiming credit for reforming national conventions. As one veteran convention analyst has observed: "Television has been given and has taken credit for initiating improvements in convention procedure, purging politics of the phony and the charlatan, slaying the wild orator and one-speech politician, ending the reign of cabals in smoke-filled rooms, creating a better informed electorate, transforming the national convention into a 'national town meeting'."[33] Some years ago, former CBS President Dr. Frank Stanton modestly claimed, "Television has made the convention more than an organizational device to select candidates and frame a platform. It has become the major forum through which voters all across the land come to know the personality of the party and its leaders, to get a sense of values, to judge them, their characters and their capacity for leadership."[34] Perhaps this is a self-serving statement from an insider, but most can agree with Walter Cronkite that television coverage of national conventions provides a valuable "civics lesson" for any potential voter willing to turn the dial to his/her favorite network station.

Criticism of Network Coverage

As the prime means of communication in the modern world, television not only reports events but it sometimes creates news. Criticism is frequently directed at the capriciousness of the network's coverage of the convention proceedings. Speeches are sometimes interrupted in mid-sentence for commentaries from roving floor reporters that may be even less exciting or significant— or for commercials. Indeed, the viewer who is intent upon following the convention agenda—for example, the platform debate—will be hard-pressed, with all the interruptions, to maintain sustained concentration on the floor debate. For all the network boasting about "gavel-to-gavel" coverage, the executive producers focus their cameras most of the time on their anchor "stars." Occasionally something of major importance will be said at the podium relating to a party rule or a platform plank, but the millions of television viewers will never hear it because Walter

Cronkite or John Chancellor are commenting on some convention history or talking with their floor reporters. Dial switching to a rival network simply yields more of the same disjointed coverage. Fortunately, the Public Broadcasting System and the cable networks now offer most viewers some options.

Convention television has also been blamed repeatedly for concentrating on competition and controversy, instead of basic policy issues and national leadership. Network producers, for example, hope and pray for a platform fight, especially if the primaries have "selected" the nominee. Otherwise, covering the convention is like "covering a football game when the score is announced in advance."[35] Critics also complain that television focuses far too heavily on the telegenic qualities of candidates. One critic has accused the networks of ignoring the significant "in favor of the inconsequential and inscrutable."[36] Another close observer, Judith Parris, has commented on the undesirable repercussions of this allegedly "hit-or-miss" strategy in convention interviewing and covering speeches: "Not only may the frivolous or irrelevant get as much time as the significant; they may be made thereby to appear equally important."[37]

On the television screen national conventions often appear more disorderly and confused than they actually are. Television journalism dictates the avoidance of visual monotony. There must always be the illusion of action, even when there's a lull in the proceedings. The rapid switching of cameras from the booth, to the podium, to the floor, to a special network reporter interviewing a political personality or celebrity, to a scene at a convention hotel, and back and forth among these camera sites creates a sense of constant action. Indeed, the cameras rarely rest on any of these locations for more than two or three minutes without a cutback to the anchorman. As a result, the constant shifting of pictures creates "an impression of many different activities occurring simultaneously in a rather confused indistinct relation to each other."[38] Consequently, one team of writers has noted, "the viewer's impression is that the confusion is a function of the nature of the convention not an artifact of television coverage."[39] Also, the contrast of the cool, detached commentary of the anchorman in his booth high above the convention floor with the milling throng of delegates in the crowded aisles on the convention floor creates an additional impression of confusion and general disorder.

Over the years veteran convention-watchers have also detected a countervailing media bias in favor of drama, conflict, and uncertainty. Indeed, the probable outcome of the convention nomination is frequently presented as more uncertain than it really is in order—at least according to these critics— to create a sense of drama and suspense for the millions of TV home viewers. Part of this impression derives from the nature of television reporting. Whenever television reporters and their cameramen do portray any confrontations, they do not always do so in ways to suggest that it represents a healthy discussion of partisan issues, but rather that it symbolizes deep cleavages and fissures within the convention itself. During a convention, whether it is dull or not, the networks—unlike newspapers— must fill every moment of their time schedule throughout every session. Sometimes in their haste to generate excitement, they may seize upon a wild rumor or inconsequential story and blow them all out of proportion. At the strife-torn 1968 Democratic convention, for example, NBC television newsmen Sander Vanocur and John Chancellor were responsible for a Teddy Kennedy-for-President "boomlet" that momentarily electrified the convention. But the story was just a rumor. Kennedy made it clear that he had no intention of running—his brother, Senator Robert F. Kennedy, having been assassinated only 11 weeks earlier.[40] In 1972, the television network reporters misinterpreted a South Carolina delegation credentials challenge at the Democratic convention, which led the TV anchormen to conclude erroneously that the McGovern candidacy was in trouble when exactly the opposite was the case.[41]

Countervailing media bias generally works against the front-running candidate and in favor of his challengers, even though their chances may be almost nil. The 1964 GOP convention, which nominated Senator Barry Goldwater by a one-sided margin, and the 1980 Democratic convention, which renominated President Carter by a wide margin, are two cases of built-in media bias that immediately come to mind. It is noteworthy that the network's effort to generate suspense, even though little doubt existed about Goldwater's nomination and Carter's renomination among the delegates and party professionals, had no significant impact on the convention outcome.

Television Cameras—Public Watchdogs or Barriers to Compromise?

Television, most party professionals concede, has helped make the convention more public. One convention authority has noted that "because of television, conventions must not only be fair, they must also *look* fair.[42] During the post-mortems of the 1952 conventions, party professionals in both parties became aware for the first time of television's powerful impact on national conventions. As one veteran authority on presidential elections noted:

Both conventions came in for a good deal of criticism from watchers at TV sets. The noisy inattention of delegates, the artificial demonstrations (the Republicans even had paid performers), the banal oratory, the parliamentary tangles and public quarreling, the mysterious deals and shiftings of votes behind the camera's eye, the "show-off" delegates who demanded polls of their delegations just to give themselves a brief television appearance, the hectic carnival atmosphere—all were disillusioning to citizens who, before the television era, had thought of a convention as a kind of deliberative assembly. Radio had revealed unlovely aspects, but the camera was devastating.[43]

With the knowledge that the television camera eyes are constantly focused on all of the convention proceedings, national and state, politicians are now far more conscious of the appearance of their actions and, consequently, much more sensitive to the issues of fairness in procedure than in the pre-TV era. Highhanded rulings by the convention chairman, for example, would cast an unwanted image in front of millions of viewers in televisionland. Television has also led the way toward opening up more private meetings at the convention to all of the national press. Most observers would agree that the amount of secret activity has been substantially reduced. Television cameras serve as public watchdogs portraying the smoke-filled room meetings from the hallways as underhanded attempts to exclude the viewing public from important convention business. During the first nationally televised convention in 1952, Republican National Committee officials sought to exclude the TV cameras from the credentials and platform committee hearings. But network officials complained so vociferously that the pro-Taft convention officials finally relented and let the camera crews in. Since then, convention officials have been reluctant to exclude the television cameras from crucial meetings, though Senator Barry Goldwater and his lieutenants waged a small, undeclared war against the television networks at the 1964 GOP convention in San Francisco. Goldwater's managers battled with the television networks over the plan to keep network reporters and portable cameras ("creepie peepies") off the convention floor, but ultimately surrendered to the wishes of the television industry. But the Goldwaterites did not lose every round to the networks. Shortly before the convention opened, NBC and CBS installed camera pick-up points and telephones near the Goldwater suite in his San Francisco hotel, but Goldwater aides simply removed them and declared the area "off limits," except by special invitation.[44]

Open politics is the rule of the day in the age of television. It seems doubtful, for example, that a Warren G. Harding smoke-filled room nomination could be pulled off by party power brokers in the present era. In retrospect, one may wonder, too, if the supporters of General Dwight D. Eisenhower could have, without television, stampeded the 1952 GOP convention to grab the nomination away from Senator Robert A. Taft, son of former President William H. Taft. Twice denied the nomination in 1940 and 1948, Taft was considered the front-runner for the 1952 Republican nomination when the 1952 GOP nominating sweepstakes opened. One of the most influential members of the U.S. Senate, Taft had spent many years grooming himself for the Presidency and cultivating party professionals across the country. With majority control of the Republican National Committee, Taft's team had carefully selected all of the convention's temporary and permanent officers. Until the famous "fair play" resolution was introduced by Eisenhower's floor leaders as a substitute for part of the Rules Committee report, some professional observers felt that Taft enjoyed a slight advantage in the nip-and-tuck nominating race.

As in 1912, when Teddy Roosevelt's Bull Moosers stormed out of the Taft-dominated convention hall to stand with the Rough Rider at Armageddon, the crucial fight in the 1952 GOP convention centered on who would control the contested Southern delegations in several states. But there was one difference—Teddy Roosevelt had no television cameras to help wage his battle to sway uncommitted delegates and to influence public opinion.

Forty years later, supporters of General Eisenhower, recognizing the crucial importance of television, argued that the Republican National Committee hearings of the Rules and Credentials Committees should be broadcast and televised. Although Senator Taft said he was agreeable to live broadcasts, his followers on the national committee took a different view. They insisted that broadcasts were not conducive to a judicial atmosphere. By a vote of 60 to 40 the GOP National Committee originally voted to ban televising the committee sessions. But it was a different story once the rules and credentials disputes reached the convention floor. Unlike previous conventions, the Taft partisans for the first time found themselves under the intense scrutiny of the network television cameras, playing before a national audience of 20 million viewers. When the Taft forces attempted to seat the pro-Taft delegation from Texas, the Eisenhower leaders labeled this move— once again before 20 million viewers—the "Texas steal." General Ike's supporters insisted instead that the rival pro-Eisenhower Texas delegation should be seated. During the critical credentials floor debate on the seating of the competing Texas delegations (and the disputed rival delegations from Georgia and Louisiana) the Eisenhower floor leader warned the Taftites before the national television audience, "Thou Shalt Not Steal."[45] This televised show of force appeared to sway enough uncommitted delegates to join the Eisenhower bandwagon and tip the balance in Ike's favor on the key credentials challenges. In retrospect, if Taft had won the credentials challenges in the three states, he would have picked up 61 additional delegates (only 46 short of the nomination)—and probably won over enough uncommitted delegates to go over the top on the first ballot. But this is merely replaying history. Unlike his father's successful steamroller tactics in the pre-television era against Teddy Roosevelt in 1912, Robert Taft seemed to lose his nerve and early tactical advantage while operating before a national television audience. Almost overnight, television had become the single most important force affecting a candidate's convention strategy.

Probing cameras also make it more difficult to hammer out convention compromises. Television thrives on controversy. Indeed, television makes classic negotiations at a national convention virtually impossible. The unsuccessful negotiations surrounding former President Gerald Ford as a possible choice as Ronald Reagan's running-mate at the 1980 GOP convention demonstrated how difficult it is to carry on sensitive political discussions in this era of open conventions. As Gerald M. Pomper has commented, "'open covenants openly arrived at' are as difficult to achieve domestically as internationally. Parties do not want to present a messy picture of bargaining to their cost-free television audience."[46] Consequently, party leaders generally meet privately to try and work out satisfactory compromises on key questions because any willingness to modify one's stand before network cameras is generally interpreted as a sign of weakness, not wisdom. No candidate or party wishes to be accused in public of selling out their principles for short-term gain.

Looking back to the 1952 Democratic nominating race, it seems unlikely also that President Truman, meeting in a smoke-filled room, would have been able to persuade key delegations to switch from Senator Estes Kefauver, the popular favorite in the primaries, to the still-uncommitted Adlai E. Stevenson and thus break a deadlock if all of the network cameras had been peering over Mr. Truman's shoulder. By the same token, Senator Kefauver and his key advisers did not fully appreciate the powerful influence of television or capitalize on it during the 1952 Democratic convention to claim that the big city and state party bosses were unfairly denying him the nomination since he was the popular winner in 12 out of 14 (mostly uncontested) primaries.

In this era of "open" politics, most citizens feel that the public interest is better served if the important work of the convention can be reported before the cameras. The national convention has been likened to a national "town meeting." Consequently, any attempts by the parties or candidates to restrict public access to convention business is frowned upon. Private meetings for "cutting deals" are incompatible with the open democracy of the current presidential nominating process; consequently, candidates who engage in back room bargaining may risk alienating a sizeable portion of the multi-million viewing audience. But this may be a risk they are prepared to take.

Television coverage of national conventions has also given minority elements within a party a powerful weapon to extract concessions from the prospective nominee and other party leaders. By threatening to make statements before the network cameras criticizing the majority faction, minor coalition leaders know that party leaders must bargain with them—or risk widening party rifts and possibly increasing the chances of electoral defeat in November. Feminist demands upon President Carter for a tough pro-ERA platform plank and support for funding of abortions by the Women's Caucus at the 1980 Democratic National Convention are a recent case illustrating this point. In assessing the overall record of conventions, before and since the advent of television, it seems fair to say that television has, on balance, made the national convention a more democratic institution, more attuned to the open politics of the post-Vietnam War era.

Media Impact on Candidate Selection

Has television coverage influenced the choice of the convention nominee? Does television promote the success of candidates with "telegenic" personalities? Given the paucity of research on media impact on candidate selection, no definitive answer can be given as yet to these questions. In a pioneering study on the influence of television over voter choice in the 1972 presidential election, however, Patterson and McClure concluded that, contrary to the prevailing view that television had become the most important medium for persuading and communicating with the electorate, television's influence on political decision-making has been seriously overestimated. Three main conclusions emerged from the Patterson-McClure in-depth study: (1) political commercials, considered by political professionals since 1964 as a potent weapon, have almost no power to overcome a voter's preexisting view of a candidate and his party; (2) 30- and 60- second spot commercials, frowned upon by the intelligentsia as too short and clever to provide an honest basis for political choice, actually provide the voter with a considerable amount of serious information about the candidates; and (3) television network news coverage of the campaign, long touted for its impact, was no more influential than newspaper coverage in affecting the voter's attitudes toward the candidates.[47] Patterson and McClure have also criticized the television networks' failure to cover candidates' qualifications to be President in these words:

Instead of analyzing characters and examining backgrounds, the networks simply parade faces. ABC, CBS, and NBC offer few penetrating reports on the candidates and their personal qualifications for President. They seldom discuss the candidates' personal fitness for office—their moral codes, personal habits and private behaviors, personal reactions to past political stresses, or leadership styles. Likewise, the networks avoid intimate interviews that would provide viewers themselves with a chance to study closely presidential candidates.[48]

These criticisms, based upon extensive hour-long panel interviews with 2,000 voters over the course of the 1972 general election campaign and close monitoring of network television news and televised political advertising during the regular presidential campaign, could also be directed against the networks for their pre-convention and convention analysis of the candidates, since the television coverage and advertising techniques used on television in the primary and general election campaigns do not differ significantly.

Because television provides the viewer with almost a face-to-face view of political candidates, it would appear to be a powerful medium for informing the electorate about the leadership and personal qualities of the various contenders. But it has fallen far short of the mark. Still, a favorable public image has never hurt a candidate. John F. Kennedy certainly relied on his photogenic profile and his war-hero record in his drive for the White House. More recently, former movie star Ronald Reagan, described as the most telegenic personality to be elected President since the advent of television, used the electronic medium throughout his arduous 12-year drive to gain the White House. But a telegenic public image has not in itself been a guarantee of the nomination. None of the following candidates—all adjudged photogenic—have ever been selected as their party's standard-bearer: Henry Cabot Lodge, Jr., William Scranton, George Romney, Mark Hatfield, Eugene McCarthy, and George Bush. Obviously, it takes more than good looks to become a party nominee. John Anderson, who suddenly became the new matinee idol of the 1980 campaign, also discovered that while his white hair and rugged good looks attracted heavy attention from the national media after his strong second-place finishes in the 1980 Massachusetts and Vermont primaries, it still failed to persuade much more than five percent of the national electorate to cast their ballots for him in November. Senator Edward Kennedy, despite his political charisma, can attest to the potent negative effect that network television can have on a leading contender's chances for the nomination. Kennedy's disastrous performance during a CBS-TV documentary interview with Roger Mudd shortly before his candidacy announcement for the 1980 Democratic nomination nearly finished him off right then. Later, one Kennedy aide testified that the Mudd interview, more than anything else except the Iranian hostage crisis, was responsible for Kennedy's ultimate failure to wrest the Democratic nomination from President Carter.[49] Not many political professionals or media experts would disagree with this assessment. Even more significant, Ronald Reagan's consummate skill on television and his startling success in sweeping aside all opposition in the primaries to win the 1980 GOP nomination and then the Presidency, may cause some students of the presidential selection process to reassess the influence of television on candidate choice. In any case, friends and foes alike of national conventions are generally in agreement that the television coverage of the national party conclaves has made the American public far more aware than ever before of the leadership selection process for the highest office in the land.

Network television, however, has seldom probed below the surface of the continuing controversy of whether or not national conventions should be abolished and replaced by a national primary or series of regional primaries. Or should the existing mixed system of primaries and caucus-conventions, topped with a national nominating convention, be retained? These are some of the issues and questions that we will examine in the final two chapters.

By way of summary, television coverage of conventions, it seems clear, has changed profoundly the way parties and politicians operate in selecting their presidential nominees, even though its long-term impact on voter attitudes is often unpredictable. It is probably accurate to conclude that television doesn't influence convention choice and elections so much through its effect on vote decisions as it does through the way parties run conventions and politicians conduct campaigns. In other words, politicians believe that television has a significant influence on voter choice and therefore they act differently than they did in the era before television cameras appeared on the scene.[50]

Future Convention Coverage

In the wake of the two 1980 national conventions that served as little more than ratification assemblies for Governor Reagan's and President Carter's nominations, unconfirmed reports began circulating with increasing frequency in the television industry that we have seen the last gavel-to-gavel network coverage of the four-day national conventions. Finally, in October 1981, CBS President Thomas H. Wyman announced that his network would henceforth carry only convention highlights and revert to standard summer programming (which usually consists chiefly of reruns of the regular season's most popular shows).[51] The executive explained his reasons for the network's planned cutback of convention coverage as follows:

The real action has shifted to the primaries, and for the most part the choices already have been made by the time the midsummer gatherings occur. The conventions can be anticl mactic exercises in horn-blowing and hat-wearing. We must ask ourselves whether the public is well served by the availability of long hours when the political process is embarrassed by triviality. The viewers say no; they are watching other programs.[52]

If networks cut back on convention coverage, it will, of course, be interesting to see how the political parties respond to retain as much air time and exposure for their quadrennial conclaves.

Notes

1. Neil Hickey, "The Men Who...," *TV Guide*, August 3, 1968, p. 6. Actually the first TV coverage of national conventions occurred shortly before America's entrance in World War II. In 1940, the infant television industry carried filmed excerpts of the GOP convention, held in Philadelphia, to 100,000 local and New York viewers. World War II interrupted the growth of this embryo industry. By 1948, however, an estimated 10 million people, mostly in the eastern section of the country, saw parts of the Dewey and Truman conventions on television. Robert MacNeil, *The People Machine* (New York: Harper & Row, 1968), p. 99.

2. Theodore H. White, *The Making of a President* (New York: Atheneum, 1965), p. 201.

3. Theodore H. White, *The Making of the President, 1968* (New York: Atheneum, 1969), p. 243. But a nationwide Louis Harris poll, taken shortly after the Chicago convention, revealed that a substantial majority of respondents supported the strong countermeasures taken by the Chicago police against the young demonstrators. The poll showed:

REACTION TO 1968 DEMOCRATIC CONVENTION (HARRIS POLL)

	Agree	Disagree	Not Sure
Mayor Daley was right the way he used police against demonstrators.	66	20	14
Anti-Vietnam demonstrators had protest rights taken away unlawfully.	14	66	20

Source: Richard M. Scammon and Ben J. Wattenberg, *The Real Majority* (New York: Coward, McCann and Geoghegan, 1970), pp. 161-62.

4. United Press International wire service story in *Seattle Post Intelligencer*, August 4, 1980.

5. "A Convention Hall of Mirrors," *Time*, Vol. 116 (July 28, 1980), p. 54.

6. *Seattle Post Intelligencer*, March 1, 1979.

7. "A Convention Hall of Mirrors," *Time*, p. 55.

8. Thomas E. Patterson, *The Mass Media Election* (New York: Praeger, 1980), pp. 72-73.

9. Ibid., p. 73.

10. Ibid., p. 72.

11. Ibid., p. 103.

12. Angus Campbell, Philip E. Converse, Warren E. Miller, and Donald E. Stokes, *The American Voter* (New York: John Wiley and Sons, 1960), p. 78.

13. Cliff Zukin, "A Triumph of Form over Content: Television and the 1976 National Nominating Convention." Paper presented at the 1979 Midwest Political Science Association annual meeting, Chicago, Illinois, April 1979.

14. *Gallup Opinion Index*, No. 181, (September 1980), p. 3.

15. "Opinion Roundup," *Public Opinion* (December/January 1981), p. 26.

16. *Gallup Opinion Index*, No. 180 (August 1980), p. 23.

17. Ibid.

18. "The Major Election Polls," *Public Opinion* (December/January 1981), p. 19.

19. "TV's Rush to Judgment," *Newsweek*, Vol. 96 (July 28, 1980), p. 72.

20. Ernest R. May and Janet Fraser, eds., *Campaign '72: The Managers Speak*, Cambridge, Mass.: Harvard University Press, 1973), p. 174.

21. Timothy Crouse, *The Boys on the Bus* (New York: Ballantine Books, 1973), p. 176.

22. Anderson's mid-summer public support, however, faded during the fall campaign, and he barely qualified for federal election funds with slightly over 5 percent of the vote, as required by the Federal Election Campaign Act of 1974. Anderson reached his highwater mark in the Gallup poll "trial heats" in mid-June 1980, when he was the choice of 24 percent of the respondents. In the same poll Carter received 35 percent, Reagan 33 percent, and 8 percent were undecided. *Gallup Opinion Index*, No. 183 (December 1980), p. 13.

23. Francis X. Clines, *New York Times*, July 16, 1980.

24. The all-time record for seconding speeches was set in 1936, when 52 seconding speeches were made on behalf of President Franklin D. Roosevelt, then seeking a second term.

25. Richard Reeves, *Convention* (New York: Harcourt Brace Jovanovich, 1977), pp. 86-87.

26. This speech was given, of course, during the Prohibition era. Robert K. Murray, *The 103rd Ballot: Democrats and the Disaster in Madison Square Garden* (New York: Harper & Row, 1976), p. 119.

27. Ibid., p. 123.

28. *Call to Order*, Report of the Commission on Rules of the Democratic National Committee (O'Hara Commission), Washington, D.C.: Democratic National Committee, 1972, p. 56.

29. Judith Parris, *The Convention Problem* (Washington, D.C.: The Brookings Institution, 1972), p. 150.

30. Neil Hickey, "It's a $40 Million Circus," *TV Guide*, July 13, 1980, p. 4.

31. Neil Hickey, "The Men Who. . . .," pp. 6-7.

32. Joseph Lelyveld, *New York Times*, August 16, 1976.

33. Herbert Waltzer, "In the Magic Lantern: Television Coverage of the 1964 National Conventions," *Public Opinion Quarterly*, Vol. 30 (Spring 1966), p. 54.

34. Frank Stanton, "The Case for Political Debates on TV," *New York Times Magazine* (January 19, 1964), p. 16.

35. Tom Shales, *Washington Post*, May 13, 1980.

36. Marvin Barrett, ed., *The Politics of Broadcasting* (New York: Thomas Y. Crowell, 1973), p. 123.

37. Judith Parris, *The Convention Problem*, p. 169.

38. David L. Paletz and Martha Elson, "Television Coverage of Presidential Conven-

tions: Now You See It, Now You Don't," *Political Science Quarterly*, Vol. 91 (Spring 1976), p. 126.

39. Paletz and Elson, in 1972, made one of the few systematic analyses of what aspects of the convention television actually emphasizes. Although their quantitative analysis of the National Broadcasting Company's coverage of the Democratic Convention showed that the network did not give undue emphasis to the "hippie" protesters nor display any bias for or against Senator McGovern, the nominee, their qualitative analysis of NBC revealed a different conclusion. Paletz and Elson concluded that the predominant impression left by television of the 1972 Democratic convention was one of conflict and disorder. Ibid.

40. James M. Perry, *Us and Them: How the Press Covered the 1972 Election* (New York: Clarkson N. Potter, 1973), p. 171. For a different version of the Kennedy "boomlet," indicating that the last surviving son in the Kennedy clan seriously considered a presidential "draft" at the 1968 convention, see Lewis Chester, Godfrey Hodgson, and Bruce Page, *An American Melodrama: The Presidential Campaign of 1968* (New York: Viking Press, 1969), pp. 564-76.

41. For an insightful and hilarious account of this misunderstood, crucial, early-test vote by an iconoclastic journalist, see Hunter S. Thompson, *Fear and Loathing: On The Campaign Trail '72* (New York: Fawcett Popular Library, 1973), pp. 295-310.

42. Judith Parris, *The Convention Problem*, p. 142.

43. Eugene H. Roseboom, *The History of Presidential Elections*, 3rd ed. (New York: The Macmillan Company, 1970), p. 517.

44. Robert MacNeil, *The People Machine*, p. 115.

45. For a detailed report of this action-filled convention, see Paul T. David, Malcolm Moos, and Ralph M. Goldman, *Presidential Nominating Politics in 1952: The National Story* (Baltimore, Md.: The Johns Hopkins University Press, 1954), Vol. 1, pp. 67-100.

46. Gerald M. Pomper, "The Decline of Partisan Politics," in Louis Maisel and Joseph Cooper, eds., *The Impact of the Electoral Process* (Beverly Hills, Calif.: Sage Publications, 1977), p. 26.

47. Thomas E. Patterson and Robert D. McClure, *The Unseeing Eye: The Myth of Television Power in National Politics* (New York: G.P. Putnam's Sons, 1976).

48. Ibid., p. 31.

49. Jack W. Germond and Jules Witcover, *Blue Smoke & Mirrors: How Reagan Won & Why Carter Lost the Election of 1980* (New York: The Viking Press, 1981), p. 78.

50. For further discussion of this point, see Doris A. Graber, *Mass Media and American Politics* (Washington D.C.: Congressional Quarterly Inc., 1980), chapter 6.

51. Thomas H. Wyman, President, CBS, Inc., "Electoral Reform—It's Time to Move," an address to the International Radio and Television Society, Waldorf Astoria Hotel, New York City, October 7, 1981. Copy of the speech furnished to the author by CBS News.

52. Ibid. Recently, Leonard Goldenson, chairman of ABC, has recommended that the Public Broadcasting System assume sole responsibility for gavel-to-gavel coverage of the 1984 political conventions. Under the Goldenson proposal, ABC, CBS, and NBC would jointly pay the full cost of the PBS continuous "pool" camera coverage of the convention. Then, the three networks would be free—free at last! (according to one critic)—to telecast only selective coverage of the conventions, maintain most of their more profitable commercial programming schedule, and save a major chunk of the estimated $10 million outlay each network made to cover the eight nights of live television during the two 1980 conventions. See Sally Bedell, *New York Times*, December 25, 1982.

The National Nominating Convention under Attack _____ 8

> There is nothing inherently undemocratic about a national convention
> . . . its weaknesses are the product of inertia and indifference,
> rather than structure . . . with meaningful reform, it is a contribution
> well worth preserving.
>
> Governor Harold Hughes, Iowa, (1968)

Because the nominating process occupies such a central position in a party system, it is not strange that the screening process that narrows the choice down to one presidential candidate in each major party should be the object of frequent, vitriolic criticism. As one veteran convention-watcher has noted commenting on the defeated McCarthy anti-Vietnam War Democrats in 1968, "It is not uncommon for the losers in a political struggle to propose the structural reforms of the institution that denies them victory."[1] But neutral observers have also found a number of flaws in the national convention system. Indeed, over the years the convention has had far more detractors than defenders.[2] In December 1979, for example, a Gallup poll reported that 66 percent of the American electorate favored abolishing the parties' national nominating conventions altogether and choosing the nominees by a one-day national primary election, while only 24 percent of the respondents favored the present convention system; 10 percent had no opinion or were undecided. (See Table 18.)

In the early years of the twentieth century, Progressive Republican leaders, such as Robert M. LaFollette of Wisconsin and others, charged that the national conventions were controlled by a dual oligarchy of political bosses and privilege-seeking business interests. In 1912, the charges of "steal" reverberated throughout the Republican National Convention hall when several dozen contested delegates favorable to Theodore Roosevelt were denied seats by the Taft-controlled credentials committee. As a result of this cavalier treatment, Roosevelt and his delegates bolted the GOP convention and formed a new party, the Progressive Party—or the Bull Moose Party, as it was popularly called. In his acceptance speech Roosevelt advocated a nationwide presidential primary law to take the power of presidential nominations out of the hands of the party leaders and give the decision-making authority to delegates elected by the rank-and-file voters in each party. As mentioned earlier, President Woodrow Wilson, in his first message to Congress in 1913, also called for a national presidential primary law. But this suggestion had low priority on his legislative agenda and was soon pushed aside by more pressing domestic legislation and mounting international crises in Europe and Mexico.

TABLE 18
PROPOSED NATIONAL PRESIDENTIAL PRIMARY
(GALLUP POLL)

	Favor	Oppose	No Opinion
1979 (Dec.)	66%	24%	10%
1976	68	21	11
1968	76	13	11
1964	62	25	13
1956	58	27	15
1955	58	27	15
1952 (Sept.)	73	16	11
1952 (Feb.)	73	12	15

Source: Gallup Opinion Index, No. 174 (January 1980), p. 19.

Since then, proposals to replace the convention with a nationwide presidential primary have been offered from time to time. In the 1950's, three Democrats—the late Senator Estes Kefauver of Tennessee, the late Senator Paul Douglas of Illinois, and Senator William Proxmire of Wisconsin—all introduced legislation to establish a national presidential primary to replace the national convention.[3] These proposals received only sporadic attention in the press. Sometimes they were accorded the dignity of a Congressional committee hearing, but then the proposals were left to die in committee at the end of the session. None of these reform proposals, however, quieted the complaints against the convention during the 1950's and 1960's.

Major Arguments against National Conventions

Over the years complaints against national conventions remained essentially the same. National conventions were assailed by critics as "unwieldy, unrepresentative, and irresponsible." The party conclaves were criticized because the conventions were reportedly "rigged," thus blocking an honest, open vote. These complaints, heard since the Progressive era, echoed more loudly than ever across the land in the aftermath of the tumultuous 1968 Democratic National Convention in Chicago. The vicious encounters between the Chicago police and the pro-McCarthy youthful convention demonstrators—witnessed by millions of television viewers—provoked a torrent of criticism against the convention. Led by anti-war students, journalists, intellectuals, and various minority spokesmen, these critics charged that the convention choice of Humphrey as the nominee was manipulated by the pro-Administration forces, especially those in the caucus-convention states, supporting Vice President Humphrey. The McCarthyites charged that the delegates in some states were handpicked by party committees, and exclusively by the governor or his designated aides in two states (Georgia and Louisiana). In other states the outnumbered McCarthy forces complained that many delegates were selected by a process in which closed slate-making, secret caucuses, and widespread proxy voting were all too common. More than a third of the Democratic convention delegates, the McCarthy people charged, were selected, in effect, prior to 1968 (for example, national committee members automatically became delegates when they were elected to these four-year positions in 1964). However, after the adoption of the McGovern-Fraser reforms in the Democratic nominating process for the 1972 convention, these complaints about procedural violations were seldom heard any longer. The proliferation of presidential primaries in the aftermath of the anti-war protest movement (between 1968 and 1980 the number of primaries more than doubled—from 16 to 35 states) also removed another major source of criticism about the insufficient representativeness of national conventions.

Most critics (and many supporters) agree that the conventions are too large—so large, in fact, that it is virtually impossible to conduct the proceedings with any meaningful rank-and-file participation.[4] Most students of politics believe that conventions should be substantially reduced in membership in order to foster a more deliberative environment and diminish the carnival-like atmosphere of the proceedings. This subject is discussed in greater detail in the final chapter.

National conventions have been likened to a combination of circus, medicine show, and revival meeting. How in the name of common sense, the critics ask, can a meeting of hundreds of delegates milling through the aisles, visiting with neighboring state delegations, talking with newsmen, or collecting autographs be called a deliberative assembly convened for the solemn business of nominating a candidate for the Presidency of the United States? Former President Dwight D. Eisenhower, twice nominated by GOP national conventions, depicted the convention as "a thoroughly disgraceful spectacle which can scarcely fail to appall our own voters and create a shockingly bad image of our country abroad."[5]

Other critics charge that the national conventions are concerned only with picking a "winner," who will help carry state party tickets, instead of choosing "the best-qualified" candidate. To the party ideologues who have occupied more and more delegate seats in recent years, the traditional convention practice of picking the so-called winning candidate at the price of the ideological purity is unacceptable. These critics, it would appear, prefer to have their candidate "be right rather than be President," even though the ideologically pure candidate rarely possesses popular appeal and the qualifications to attract enough votes from the moderate, middle-of-the-road American electorate to win the White House. In the past, critics have also pointed out that vice presidential nominations— the second most important decision to be made by the convention— have often been made too hastily, largely on the basis of political payoffs, and with little regard to the grave possibility that the man selected may be called upon unexpectedly to assume the Presidency.[6]

Until the recent expansion of the presidential primary system, anti-convention critics asserted that all the major decisions on the eventual nominee, the vice presidential running-mate, and the platform were made by "kingmakers"—a handful of professional political leaders in "smoke-filled rooms." Meanwhile, hundreds of delegates sat by passively, accepting these verdicts without a whimper. As J. K. Galbraith, the economist whose long-standing attachment to liberal Democratic politics has often brought him close to the political arena, cynically observed some years ago, "The delegates have about the same power of self-determination as a carload of prime steers at the Kansas City yards."[7] Conventions, said the critics, were also too exclusively concerned with making presidential nominations; consequently, they did not serve as the national governing organs and deliberative assemblies for the major parties.

Another major argument against the national convention is that the nominating machinery is susceptible to capture by a well-organized, disciplined extremist faction of the party, working in the primary states or behind the scenes in the caucus-convention states. This militant minority may select a party nominee who is the darling of the far-out activists, but who enjoys only limited national voter appeal. The takeover of the GOP nominating machinery in 1964 by the conservative Goldwater faction is cited as a classic example. In defying the usual custom of selecting a nominee of moderate views, the right-wing Goldwater faction brought down upon the GOP one of the most crushing general election defeats that the party has ever suffered—Goldwater lost by nearly 16 million votes.

Similarly, the successful takeover of the Democratic nominating machinery in 1972 by a well-organized minority of youthful anti-war activists proved to be a disaster for the Democrats in the general election campaign. McGovern's anti-Vietnam War partisans discovered that it was much easier to capture the Democratic nomination by winning plurality victories against three middle-of-the-road Democrats—Edmund Muskie, Hubert H. Humphrey, and Henry M. Jackson— and right-wing Democrat George Wallace than to run a general election campaign against an incumbent Republican president. By excluding many party veterans from delegate seats, including Chicago Mayor Richard J. Daley and several key senators and congressmen, and by espousing numerous far-left causes, including platform planks on amnesty for Vietnam War draft evaders and abortion-on-demand, the McGovernites alienated a large number of traditional Democrats— blue-collar workers, Roman Catholics, and so forth. As a result, McGovern lost the presidential election to President Richard Nixon by the biggest landslide in

American history. McGovern captured only one state (Massachusetts) and the District of Columbia.

Some long time critics have also charged that the conventions are not representative, that is, they do not properly reflect the number of party voters in the various states. This has long been true of Republicans in the South, though less so today. It will be recalled that the 1912 Republican convention was deeply split over contested rival Southern delegations, largely self-appointed, who represented little more than themselves and their close associates. Subsequent reapportionment plans over the years reduced the overrepresentation of Southern Republican delegations, but it continued until the rise of the two-party system in the urban, industrialized areas of the South, and especially those congressional districts with huge communities of transplanted Northern Republican retirees in Florida. Prior to World War II, the Democratic delegations from Republican-dominated Midwestern states were also overrepresented at the national conventions in terms of party vote within their congressional districts, since each rural district with a light Democratic vote enjoyed the same representation as urban districts with a heavy Democratic vote. After 1968, however, the Democrats used a weighted formula (based upon 53 percent population and 47 percent popular vote—changed to a fifty-fifty basis before the 1980 convention) that gives greater representation to those congressional districts with a heavy Democratic vote. Thus, for example, Michigan urban districts in the Detroit area with a heavy Democratic vote have been allocated seven delegates to the national convention, whereas in Republican-dominated out-state rural districts the Democrats will be allocated only two or three national convention delegates.

Because both major parties have selected all of their presidential nominees on the first ballot since 1956, some critics have depicted the national conventions as orchestrated coronations, convened merely to ratify the victor of the presidential primary race. As one irreverent critic has commented:

The modern political convention stands in the same relationship to the already chosen nominee as the Roman Senate did to Emperor Augustus. The delegates don't come to deliberate but recreate, they don't come to designate a candidate but to celebrate him.[8]

If national conventions have degenerated into ratification assemblies, these critics ask, why bother to convene them? The simple solution, if these critics are right, would seem to be that the parties would save themselves a lot of money and grief if they were to abolish these quadrennial gatherings and declare the nominee to be the winner of the primaries. But this superficial answer belies a serious misunderstanding of the multiple functions performed by national conventions, earlier discussed in the opening chapter. Still, many critics insist that the national convention should be replaced by a single national primary. Let's take a few moments to discuss this proposal that has been advocated off and on since the Teddy Roosevelt era.

Proposed National Direct Primary

In the past decade proposals for a national direct primary have been heard with increasing frequency. This resurgence of interest has been spawned, in part, by the widespread belief that the present presidential primary system, which now includes almost three dozen states, has gotten out of hand. The hectic five-month, sixteen-hour-a-day primary campaign, preceded by a year or more of a pre-nomination campaign—Arthur T. Hadley calls this period "The Invisible Primary"—has exhausted the candidates, the press, and the public alike.[9] Critics say that this unending string of primaries, held nearly every Tuesday (and sometimes on Saturday) between late February and early June, has changed the nominating race into a political marathon. Added to the endurance contest are the early caucus-convention states, such as Iowa and Maine, which now attract almost as much media attention as the early primary states. Enough is enough, say the critics. Instead, they argue, let's have a national direct primary.

In the halls of Congress, the national primary movement has been pushed along by a twin drive for a constitutional amendment to abolish the Electoral College and substitute direct election of the president without regard to state lines. As explained by Austin Ranney, "Most of the arguments against the Electoral College and in favor of direct national elections can also be made against the national party convention and in favor of a direct national primary."[10] Both the Electoral College and the national convention, the critics insist, are artificial devices thrust between the sovereign voters and their choosing of a president. Both of these time-honored institutions make possible the selection of a president by a minority of voters, whereas direct election of the president and a national presidential primary will always reflect the popular will, the equally weighted votes of individual citizens.

Both reforms—direct election of the president and a national primary to select the party nominee—enjoy broad public support as measured by the Gallup poll. Over the past decade polls have consistently shown that well over two-thirds of the general population also favor direct national election of presidents. With increased popular attention and interest focused on the presidential nomination and election process, the need to examine carefully the existing system and proposed alternatives takes on growing importance.

While the proposal for a national presidential primary continues to be a popular topic of political reform on Capitol Hill, congressional action on elimination of the Electoral College—an institution that has operated in the same manner since the 1804 election—came to an abrupt halt in March 1979 in the U.S. Senate. By a vote of 51 to 39—15 votes short of the required two-thirds majority—the Senate failed to adopt a proposed constitutional amendment to eliminate the Electoral College and substitute direct election of the President.[11] A curious combination of small- and big-state liberal senators from both parties, allied with conservative Southern Democrats, voted against the fundamental change in presidential election procedure. Especially black and Jewish spokespersons in the big

Eastern states pressured their Senators to block the elimination of the Electoral College because in a close presidential race these ethnic groups believe (and many agree) that their votes can sometimes tilt the outcome. This turndown by the U.S. Senate, after years of off-and-on hearings, effectively throttled any serious hope of abolishing the Electoral College for several years—or at least until another serious crisis occurs in a close presidential election, such as a president being elected by a minority of the popular vote.

Under most national direct primary proposals the national nominating convention would be abolished and replaced by a one-day national direct primary held in all 50 states. Federal legislation to establish a national presidential primary, as indicated earlier, dates back to the Progressive era. The first bill to federalize the legal machinery for nominating presidential candidates was introduced in 1911 by Representative Richard P. Hobson (D. Ala.).[12] Under his plan presidential candidates were to be nominated by direct national primaries regulated by federal law instead of by the traditional national convention governed by party rules. One of the most frequently introduced electoral reforms on Capitol Hill, approximately one-half of the 250-plus presidential primary bills introduced since 1911 have called for some version of a national direct primary election.[13]

Probably the best-known model is the Mansfield-Aiken bill, introduced in March 1972.[14] The jointly sponsored proposal would establish by constitutional amendment a single national primary in early August for any party whose candidate received at least ten percent of the national vote in the previous presidential election. Candidates would become eligible for the primary by submitting petitions signed by voters numbering at least one percent of that party's total vote in the previous national election. Another provision would establish a minimum level of support in at least 17 of the 50 states, presumably to prevent a candidate with only regional popularity from gaining a spot on the primary ballot. Each party's nomination would go to the candidate with the most primary votes, with the following condition. If no candidate received 40 percent of the vote, a run-off between the top two would be held four weeks later. Under the Mansfield-Aiken bill, national conventions still would be held to select vice presidential candidates and presumably to adopt a platform.

More recently, proposals to establish a direct national primary were introduced in 1977 by Representatives Joseph Gaydos (D. Ohio), Albert Quie (R. Minn.), and Senator Lowell Weicker (R. Conn.).[15] Typical of the most recent bills put in the legislative hopper is the Quie plan, which provides that "the official candidates of political parties for President and Vice President shall be nominated at a primary election by direct popular vote." Under the Quie plan all intermediaries between the voters and the nomination—in other words, state party leaders and national convention delegates—would be eliminated in the selection process. Held in all 50 states on the same day, the Quie plan sets the national primary date as the first Tuesday after the first Monday in August of presidential election years.

Like most of the direct national primary bills, the Quie proposal calls for a closed primary, though no provision is made for federally supervised party registration. Senator Weicker's bill, however, permits persons registered as independents to vote in either party's primary.

Candidates acquire positions on the ballot by filing with the president of the Senate petitions bearing a number of signatures equal to at least one percent of the total number of popular votes cast in the nation for all candidates in the most recent presidential election. Candidates for vice president would be required to petition separately and appear on the ballot in a separate group. No person would be allowed to run for both the presidential and vice presidential nominations.

To win nomination a presidential candidate would have to receive a majority of popular votes. (The Gaydos bill allows a candidate to win the first primary with 45 percent or more of the votes.) If no candidate received an absolute majority on the first ballot, the two top vote-getters would face each other in a run-off primary four weeks later. The winner of the run-off would be the party nominee. The same conditions would prevail for the vice presidential primaries.

ADVANTAGES

The main advantages of a national primary are its directness and simplicity. Former Senate Majority Leader Mike Mansfield (D. Mont.), a major sponsor, insists that even with a run-off election, the national primary would come closest to the Democratic ideal of citizens choosing their nominees on a one-person, one-vote basis. Proponents of a national primary avow that it would be the choice preferred by most rank-and-file identifiers. Nominations would be done in the voting booths of America and not in the circus-like, mass rally atmosphere of the national convention.

Advocates of the national primary assert that this election could be understood much more easily by the rank-and-file voter. If the selection rules are simplified and made the same in all 50 states, proponents argue, more rank-and-file members of the electorate will understand the nominating process and therefore participate in the primary, instead of waiting until November to vote. Further, the national primary would eliminate the chance for a presidential hopeful to manipulate the existing primary system by picking and choosing certain primaries and skillfully avoiding strong opponents on their own turf.

Robert Bendiner has argued that the national primary would cut down the "bandwagon" effect, the process whereby a candidate can move from a victory in one primary to make a strong showing in another carefully selected state.[16] The national direct primary would, of course, eliminate early front-runner heavy media attention and help attract organizational and financial support.

Proponents of a national primary insist that it would shorten the pre-nomination season, thus helping lessen the physical strain on the candidates. Over and above these advantages, candidates in a national primary would probably be unable to campaign personally in all 50 states; instead, they could take their campaign to the voters via television. Thus, in place of the present hit-or-miss system of primaries, the national primary would give the voters in every state a chance to judge the qualifications of every candidate. Candidates could focus their campaigns on issues instead of jetting from one primary to another in frantic search of votes.

Still another argument has been advanced by James W. Ceaser, "The national primary would focus the greatest attention on the candidates and stimulate the average citizen, whose attitudes are less ideological than those of the amateur organizational participant to turn out and vote. The people, in short, would be used to circumvent the parties for the explicit purpose of moderating the selection process."[17]

DISADVANTAGES

Deceptively appealing, the national primary would have revolutionary implications on the presidential nominating process and would probably shatter our already weakened two-party system. Indeed, adoption of a national direct primary would constitute as great an alteration in the American party system and in our way of choosing a president as did the changes in the early 1800's, when the rise of political parties transformed the Electoral College into an instrument for popular election of the President.[18] On paper, the national primary concept appears eminently sensible. All 50 states would hold a national primary on a single day and choose their favorite as the party nominee for president. If no candidate received a majority of the votes—or 40 percent of the votes under some plans—then a second or run-off primary between the top two candidates would be held to pick a winner to head the ticket in the November general election. What could be more simple? But a closer examination of the national primary reveals that it is filled with political booby traps. Several of the worst features of the national primary warrant a detailed review.

The single national direct primary would abolish the sequential nature of presidential nominating contests. Unlike the present five-month, extended "candidate review" process in 35 primary and 15 caucus-convention states, the party nominee would be selected during a one-day, twelve-hour election. Delegates, the parties, the national media, and the public would be denied the present opportunity to defer final judgment on prospective nominees until convention time while they assess the candidate's appeal in a variety of electoral settings and over several months of intense scrutiny. Although the initial delegate selection process begins with the mid-January caucuses in frosty Iowa, the final list of delegates is not picked until June. As a matter of fact, almost 50 percent of the delegates nationwide were selected or apportioned during the last six weeks of the 1976 and 1980 primary seasons and the final-round district and state party conventions. Under the present system all interested constituencies have ample opportunity to assess the early front-runners, the political unknowns, the favorite sons, the late entries, and the strong finishers before the opening gavel is sounded at the national convention. This deferred decision-making—the strongest feature of the existing nominating system—would all be lost if a national primary were adopted.

National primaries would most likely favor candidates with the best-known names—Eisenhower, Kennedy, Reagan. A single national primary would make it next to impossible for relatively unknown candidates, such as Eugene McCarthy in 1968, George McGovern in 1972, or Jimmy Carter in 1976, to capitalize on early victories in state primaries to attract a growing number of supporters in the latter stages of the nominating campaign. With all the chips riding on a single national primary, the best-known names would enjoy a tremendous advantage over the political unknowns, since voters generally prefer to vote for someone they know something about over someone unknown. Political visibility or name recognition, party professionals readily concede, is an important factor in any successful local, state or national campaign. The first task of any aspiring presidential contender is to become better known. Table 19 shows how well known various Democratic hopefuls for the 1976 nomination were nine months before the New York City convention. It stretches the imagination to conclude that the eleventh-ranked Jimmy Carter, without the benefit of his victories in the Iowa caucuses, the New Hampshire, Vermont, Florida, North Carolina, Wisconsin, and 12 other primaries, would have been able to build his name recognition high enough to compete on even terms with a Kennedy or a Humphrey in a single national primary contest. Carter needed more than four months of intensive media coverage to become an established national political figure. Fortunately for him also was the fact that four of the five best-known candidates—Kennedy, Humphrey, McGovern, and Muskie—chose not to enter the 1976 Democratic sweepstakes.

The national direct primary would appear to favor extremist candidates with strong ideological ties to the far left or right wings of the party, at the expense of middle-of-the-road candidates. Since these extremist candidates would have little to lose by engaging in demogogic appeals or absurd promises, the Huey "Kingfish" Longs' and Joe McCarthys' of this era would have a field day in a wide-open national primary.

TABLE 19
NAME RECOGNITION OF DEMOCRATIC PRESIDENTIAL HOPEFULS IN OCTOBER 1975 (IN PERCENTAGES)

Candidate	Recognition	Candidate	Recognition
Kennedy	96	Bayh	50
Wallace	93	Udall	47
Humphrey	91	Shapp	31
McGovern	89	Carter	29
Muskie	84	Bentsen	24
Shriver	76	Harris	22
Jackson	64	Sanford	21

Source: *Gallup Opinion Index*, No. 125 (November-December 1975), p. 98.

It seems likely a national primary would attract a sizeable field of entrants in the out-of-power party, though the number of entrants would clearly depend upon the type of law and the various prevailing circumstances.[19]

Indeed, even with three or four candidates, the prospects of a run-off primary would be high. With a large field of candidates drawn mostly from the moderate wings of the two parties, it is more than likely that one or two candidates from the extreme wings of the party would be in the run-offs because the centrist candidates would cancel each other out in the primaries. Also, as the Republicans learned in 1964 and the Democrats in 1972, a Goldwater- or McGovern-type candidate attracts a strong, committed activist following which can be mobilized for the primary campaign, while the moderate, low-key candidate encounters serious problems in arousing support among the apathetic rank-and-file electorate. These voters invariably prefer to stay home and wait until November before going to the polls. Thus, the ideologically oriented candidate can turn out his factional supporters in large numbers on primary day to defeat middle-of-the-road candidates. But, paradoxically, this extremist candidate, who can carry the primaries with his enthusiasts, lacks the broad-based support among rank-and-file party members and fence-sitting independent voters needed to win the general election.

If there were a large field of candidates, such as in 1972 and 1976—and presidential primaries generally encourage more entrants—the winner of the national primary could conceivably be a divisive personality unacceptable to a majority of his party. Theoretically, a presidential candidate could win the nomination with 40 percent of the primary vote, even if he were the last choice of the remaining 60 percent. Nevertheless, his party would be forced to accept him as the nominee. As a vehicle to democratize nominations, the national primary would probably have the opposite effect.

The national primary also lacks the "safety-valve" feature of the present mixed system which permits a last-minute "draft" should the rapid turn of events—strategic considerations, a personal scandal, or health reasons—require a switch in candidates.

Another drawback sometimes overlooked is that a national primary would probably discourage some of the best-qualified candidates from undertaking the presidential quest, considering the high risk of a one-day primary in all fifty states. In 1952, for example, all available evidence shows that neither General Eisenhower nor Governor Adlai E. Stevenson—both "reluctant dragon" candidates— would have been willing to seek the nomination if a national primary had existed at that time.[20]

The cost of running in a national primary in 50 states would be almost prohibitive, even with the new federal matching-fund feature of the 1974 Federal Election Campaign Act. Assuming that no candidate received 40 percent of the votes (Jimmy Carter, despite his one-sided victory—17 primary wins—in the 1976 Democratic nominating race, won only 39 percent of the total primary vote), a run-off national primary would have to be held between the two top contenders. Thus, two or more national elections would escalate the original cost to the candidates and the 50 states conducting the elections. With three national elections the cost of television time, radio commercials, airline tickets, billboards, computerized direct mailings, organization, and headquarters costs would reach an all-time high. For the candidates the task of soliciting primary campaign contributions would be a mammoth job requiring a large staff of fund raisers and accountants (who are now as important as campaign managers) to assure full compliance with the new 1974 Federal Election Campaign Act.

To reduce the general election campaign period, sponsors of national primary legislation have scheduled (in those bills listing a specific date) the election for the last half of August or at the end of the first week of September, just after the Labor Day holiday weekend. Thus, the national primary would be held at the end of the summer "political dog days," when voter interest is generally considered at its lowest ebb by most professional politicians. Voter turnout would probably be extremely light—the 1976 primary turnout averaged 29 percent. With the anticipated large field of contenders—a dozen or more in the out-of-power party would not be surprising—voters would be less likely to be familiar with the candidates' relative merits, policy positions, and shortcomings.

Though holding the national primary in late August-early September would obviously shorten the general election campaign, the late primary date would most likely result in a longer national primary campaign—probably longer than the present ten-month primary-general election campaign. In the past two nominating campaigns the trend for presidential aspirants has been to make their official announcements earlier than ever. By February 1975, sixteen months before the 1976 Democratic convention, five Democratic hopefuls, including Jimmy Carter, had tossed their hats into the ring. The first candidate to announce his entry in the 1980 primaries (Representative Philip Crane, R.-Ill.) entered the presidential sweepstakes in August 1978, nearly two years before the next GOP national convention and almost 27 months before the 1980 presidential election. Under a national primary the intense desire of relatively unknown candidates to become nationally recognized would likely lead to even earlier announcements and consequently a longer primary campaign.

Although the informal nominating campaign would probably start at least two years before the primary election day, the successful candidate for the presidency and his opponent would have to face three national elections (assuming a run-off primary) within approximately 70 days. The thought of three elections within a ten-week period makes most political scientists and campaign managers shudder. For the average citizen, three trips to the polls within three months might begin to overtax his or her patience with the democratic process. Voter reaction might well take the form of lower voter turnout, which now averages less than 55 percent in presidential elections—the lowest among the Western democracies.[21] While high voter participation is not necessarily a sign of robust political health for a nation, the likelihood of 70 to 80 million or more potential voters sitting on the sidelines in an election to pick the highest officeholder in the land does not bode well for the nation's future.

A national primary would further weaken the party structure, and as indicated earlier, lead to intensive factionalism within each major party. Leading contenders would probably seek the endorsement of state organizations, creating further divisions within the party. This disruptive influence would become especially serious every time two major candidates became involved in a run-off primary. The result would be a bitter collision between candidates of opposing philosophies, with party wounds deepened and moderates forced to move to one extreme wing of the party or the other. This factionalism, usually slow to dissipate, would undermine the party throughout the general election campaign. It might lead to a multi-faction or multi-party system, instead of the present, viable two-party system. The existing nominating system, haphazard as it may sometimes be, nevertheless allows minority factions to have more bargaining power for seeking concessions from the nominee—for example, in the choice of vice presidential nominee, platform changes, political appointees, or support for legislation favorable to the minority group. These give-and-take negotiations usually enable the nominee to approach the general campaign with a more united party behind him. A presidential candidate selected in a national primary could ignore the party apparatus, preempt the party label for his personal campaign organization, and capture the nomination with minimal communication with or dependence upon the party leadership. Any national primary would enhance the importance of candidate organizations at the expense of the parties.

More fundamentally, a one-day national direct primary would effectively shut out national and state party organizations from any active role in the sifting and winnowing nominating process that narrows down the theoretical list of millions of potential presidential candidates who meet the constitutional qualifications to a manageable "short list" of, say, five to ten serious possibilities. The growing trend toward personalist politics and individual candidates' organizations, fostered by the emergence of television as a universal form of communication between the candidates and voters, would come to dominate presidential nominating machinery as the parties lose their ability to influence and control the selection process. With the "dismantling" of the party organizations, the national news media would continue to expand their already pervading influence and perhaps tilt the outcome of presidential nominating contests. By shaping most voters' perceptions of how the various contenders stand in the race, the national television and radio networks, major newspapers, and wire services not only could tip the outcome of the nominating races but heighten tensions between candidates and rival campaign organizations. Instead of the moderating influence of a political party that strives to facilitate bargaining, consensus, and reconciliation in the presidential selection process, the national news media focus their coverage on the conflicts and rivalries between candidates to stimulate viewer and reader interest.[22] While these headline-producing stories make good entertainment, they are a poor substitute for the balancing role parties have generally performed in the nominating process.

Adoption of a national direct primary, one can predict with confidence, would turn political parties into little more than "flags of convenience" with only the covering labels of Democrat and Republican visible to the electorate. Presidential nominating races would consist almost exclusively of competition among rival entrepreneurial candidate organizations as reported by the national news media. These conditions would not be unlike the one-party—indeed, no-party—politics of the Old South, typified by intense factionalism and demagogic politicians. National primaries would most likely resemble traditional Southern Democratic gubernatorial primaries, depicted by the late V.O. Key, Jr., as gigantic popularity contests based on personalities rather than issues and characterized by the office seeker's lack of accountability to organized party electorates.[23] As Jeane J. Kirkpatrick has observed, ". . . any national primary would accelerate the trend toward personalist politics, exacerbate intraparty divisions, increase the likelihood of selecting unrepresentative candidates and an unrepresentative President, render the parties still more irrelevant to the presidential contest, and enhance the importance of candidate organizations.[24]

Passage of a national direct primary or mandatory regional primary would also signal the end of experimentation with various types of primary or caucus-convention systems within the states. Since the Progressive era, states have served as "laboratories" for testing various kinds of primaries and caucus systems.[25] In some cases, states have adopted the primary for a time and then switched to the caucus system, only to return to the presidential primary system again later on. A national primary would mean that one and only one set of rules would govern the selection process across the nation. Uniformity seems too high a price to pay for the replacement of a confederate political system that has operated with only limited failings in selecting presidential candidates over the past 140 years.

Because so many objections have been raised against the traditional caucus-convention system, against the existing crazy quilt presidential primary structure, and against the proposed national direct primary, Senator Robert Packwood (R.-Ore.) in March 1972 came up with a compromise proposal: regional primaries.[26]

Regional Primaries

PACKWOOD PLAN

Under the Packwood plan the national nominating convention would be left intact, but a system of five regional primaries would be held, one a month from March to July.[27] The states would be grouped in clusters generally corresponding to the following geographical areas: the Northeast (ten states); the Midwest (six states); the South (nine states, plus the District of Columbia and three territories); the Great Plains (twelve states stretching from the Canadian border to the Gulf); and the Far West (thirteen states and one territory). The order of the primaries would be determined by lot by a five-member federal elections commission. The time sequence of the primaries for each of the five regions would be released only 70 days before the primary date, with the view of cutting down heavy campaigning in the "early bird" primaries.

No state would be allowed to conduct its own primary. Each regional primary ballot would include the names of all candidates judged to be serious contenders by the federal commission. Candidates not chosen by the commission could win a place on the ballot by petition. To have his or her name removed from the ballot, a candidate would sign a statement that he or she was not and did not intend to become a candidate. The candidate would have to withdraw separately from each regional primary. Under the Packwood proposal a presidential candidate would be authorized to select delegates in proportion to the vote he received in that state. In other words, the Packwood plan would be based on proportionality and eliminate "winner-take-all" primaries. Candidates receiving less than five percent of the vote in a state would not be entitled to any delegates. Each delegate would be committed to support the candidate who appointed him for two ballots, or until the candidate's total fell below 20 percent of the convention total—or until he released them.[28]

The chief advantage of the Packwood plan is that it reduces the number of primary races to a manageable number of five, while retaining the staggered time sequence of the present system. By spreading the regional primaries over five months the Packwood plan would give the less well-known, inadequately financed candidates an opportunity to gain national recognition through strong showings in an early round regional primary, such as was done in individual primaries by Senator McGovern in 1972 and Jimmy Carter in 1976. Regional primaries would also cut down travel time, the wear and tear on candidates, and allow weaker candidates some prospects for winning the nomination. If a candidate failed to attract favorable voter support in the early primaries, he could withdraw gracefully. The Packwood plan would permit each state to decide for itself whether or not to hold a primary, but the state would have no choice of dates; it would have to use the same date stipulated for all states of the region.

The Oregon senator's plan, however, is not a panacea. Although Packwood's regional primary system would preserve the national nominating convention, the proportional allocation of delegates on the basis of each state's primary vote might well lead to a return of the bitter, multi-ballot conventions of yesteryear. Unlike the present convention system, which usually contains several hundred unpledged or uncommitted delegates willing under certain circumstances to shift their preferences, a national convention under the Packwood plan would consist almost entirely of pledged delegates ideologically loyal to the candidate who appointed them—and probably much less willing to compromise and shift their choices of candidates, even in face of a convention deadlock. In short, the Packwood plan lacks an easy mechanism to allow state party leaders to negotiate and switch their choice toward a compromise candidate. Under the present convention system uncommitted delegates perform this role. Undoubtedly, Packwood's provision for the release of delegates after two ballots or after a candidate's support falls below 20 percent of the convention total would help reduce the possibility of convention stalemate, but the threat of deadlock would frequently hover over the convention.

The Packwood plan would not cut down the length of the primary season. It would still be long and expensive, though the regional concept might cut down travel costs. Candidates from minor parties could qualify for entry. The major departure from the existing system would be the introduction of a congressionally approved, presidentially appointed national primary election commission to act as a certification body and administrative manager of the nominating campaign—a radical departure in U.S. nominating politics. More will be said about the threat of greater federal intervention in the presidential nominating process later in the chapter.

UDALL PLAN

Several other presidential nominating proposals—variations on the Packwood plan—were also put forward in 1972. Congressman Morris Udall (D.-Ariz.), a candidate for President four years later, offered a plan that would not require states to hold primaries but would compel those states holding them to do so on one of three dates in April, May, or June. No regional groupings of primaries would be required, and each state could select any date it wanted.[29] As in the Packwood plan, the names of presidential candidates would be put on the ballot by a candidate designation committee; Udall would have national party leaders serve on this committee. Under the Udall plan delegates would be awarded to candidates in proportion to the votes they received—but with two important differences from Packwood's proposal. First, a presidential candidate winning a majority of the vote in a state would be entitled to all its delegates. Second, a contender receiving less than 10 percent of the vote would *not* be entitled to any delegates.

Udall's 50 percent winner-take-all provision (which violated the 1980 Democratic delegate selection ground rules) would permit a candidate to gain momentum with a series of convincing victories and thus reduce the chances of a deadlocked convention. But it would also preserve proportional representation in states where the vote was rather evenly divided. Thus, in the 1972 California Democratic presidential primary, for example, the Udall plan would have wiped out Senator McGovern's clean sweep of 271 delegates and given him only 45 percent (121 delegates), with 40 percent (108 delegates) going to Humphrey and the remainder to Governor George Wallace and other candidates.

Similar to Packwood's plan, the Udall proposal would virtually force each presidential contender to compete seriously for a portion of the delegation in every state. The Udall plan would probably encourage the proliferation of minor candidates who, although they could not win many delegates themselves, would hope to block any rivals from gaining a majority of delegates and thereby force the return of the nomination to the convention floor. Udall, a perennial second-place finisher in the 1976 presidential primaries, believes that his system is better than others because it does less violence to the existing nominating system.[30]

Several other objections to the optional regional primary plan immediately come to mind. To establish an equitable sequence of regions holding primaries would not be easy. An impressive candidate performance in the first regional primary might have the same powerful impact on subsequent primaries as the New Hampshire primary has under the existing system. The outcome of a regional plan could vary greatly depending upon which states were included within a region. The arbitrary division of the country into regions, some critics argue, could heighten regional tensions or sectional rivalries. For states without presidential primaries the regional plan, even if it did not mandate that states must have primaries, would probably have the effect of pressuring states—even against their best judgment—to move to primaries.[31] In a close nominating race decided at a "brokered" convention, outsider states might feel left out of key decision-making if they were not a member of the regional primary coalition.

Time zone primaries are another modified form of regional primary. Under this plan all state primaries in the eastern time zone would be required to be held on the same Tuesday (or another day of the week), all of the states in the central time zone would be held on another Tuesday, and so on. Each four years the sequence of the time zone primaries would be rotated to avoid giving undue media and political influence to the early, first-round set of states. The same objections raised about optional and mandatory regional primaries would generally apply to either type of time zone primaries. Let's take a moment to analyze several proposals for holding mandatory regional primaries.

MANDATORY REGIONAL PRIMARIES

In 1976, Representative Richard Ottinger (D.-N.Y.) introduced a mandatory regional primary bill.[32] Although the Ottinger bill resembles the Packwood regional primary plan it has one major difference: the Ottinger bill *requires* every state to hold a presidential primary; the optional Packwood plan leaves the decision to each state. The Ottinger compulsory regional primary assigns each state to one or another of five regions (the same regions designated in the Packwood bill). Primaries are to be held simultaneously in all states of the region on the first Tuesday of April and on Tuesdays of the third, sixth, ninth, and twelfth succeeding weeks, ending in June. As in the Packwood plan, the Federal Election Commission (FEC) would determine by lot which region votes first. Then, the FEC would hold a drawing 20 days prior to the next scheduled date to determine by lot which region would hold the next regional primary.

Ballots in each state must include the names of all candidates whom the FEC had declared eligible for federal matching funds. Other presidential aspirants may also get their names on the ballot in particular states by submitting petitions to the secretaries of state or equivalent officers. State election officials would probably scream at the idea of not knowing when an election was to be held until 20 days before the date. If this mandatory primary were approved, it would mean in all likelihood that the presidential primary would have to be separated from all other primary elections, and even then, 20 days does not seem long enough to be practical in printing a long ballot with the appropriate rotation of names from district to district.

The Ottinger bill requires that in all states each party's primary must be closed to all but registered members of the party and directs the FEC to prescribe a system of party registration for any state that does not already have it.

Ottinger's plan for proportional allocation of delegates, binding the delegates' votes at the convention, selection of vice presidential candidates, and reimbursement of the states for the costs of holding primaries are identical to those in the Packwood plan.

The major difference, then, between the Ottinger and Packwood plans is that the former requires all states to hold primaries under conditions stipulated by federal law, while the Oregon senator's plan imposes these conditions only on those states that decide to hold a presidential primary.

Most of the objections to the voluntary regional primary apply as well to the compulsory regional primary: lack of an adequate "brokering" mechanism for shifting delegate support at conventions, determining the order of the sequential regional primaries, and the potential heightening of tension between regions supporting different candidates.

Though the Packwood plan and, to a lesser extent, the Ottinger mandatory regional primary have attracted the attention of party reformers, none of the bills have been reported out of committee.

The regional primary concept, designed as a middle ground between the present 30-plus primaries and a single national primary, can be expected to remain one of the major alternatives to the existing "mixed" primary-convention system.

National-Regional Threat to Contemporary Parties

Establishment of regional or national primaries could have many unintended consequences that would be harmful to the national political process. Expansion of the primary to include all, or virtually all, of the 50 states would further weaken the already shaky national and state party structures. Nationwide or mandatory regional primaries would lessen the capacity of parties to articulate, aggregate, and represent voter concerns. Instead, the mass communications media, especially the television networks, would become—some critics insist they already have—the chief agencies for sorting out the candidates, designating the front-runner candidate, and discarding the "also-rans" from further serious consideration. As a result of this rank-ordering of candidates, the national media would, in effect, be defining the voters' choices.[33]

Most of the regional and national primary proposals contain provisions for a federal committee to certify candidates to compete in elections and to establish common procedural standards. Most proposals would also establish rigid delegate commitment rules. This would inhibit political "brokering" at the conventions and effectively block the type of state delegate shifts (even from pledged delegates) that in recent years have helped put Dwight D. Eisenhower, John F. Kennedy, and Jimmy Carter over the top on the first ballot. Some of the measures also reimburse the states for their expenditures in primary elections, a carrot-type inducement to encourage states to adopt this method of delegate selection. Overall, the thrust of these bills would eventually leave little discretion to the states or the national parties. As William J. Crotty has observed, "Regardless of intention, they would insinuate the federal government into a process that despite its serious faults is best left to the states."[34] By and large, these proposals tend to introduce more severe difficulties into the Presidential selection process than currently exist. In Crotty's words, "The present system is preferable to what is likely to evolve from a national specification of rules for nominating operations no matter how benevolent the goal of its creators."[35] Another well-informed observer also warns that nominating reforms initiated by the federal government:

would alter fundamentally the status of parties and change, probably permanently, the decisionmaking authority for the nominating process. Furthermore, such a shift in authority is filled with possibilities for unforeseen consequences, including the spectacle of quadrennial struggles among political factions in Congress to change the law to favor particular candidates. Finally, it is impossible to overlook the contradiction that, if strength and independence of parties are the objectives, basing that strength on a "prop" of federal support would leave the parties hostage to a change in congressional sentiment.[36]

Under the proposed Mansfield-Aiken national direct primary, national conventions would still be held to select vice presidential candidates and a platform. But the basic function of selecting the nominee would be taken away from the national convention and put in the hands of voters within the 50 states. If no candidate in the field received 40 percent of the primary vote, a run-off election (similar to the double primary held in many Southern Democratic primaries) would be held among the two top vote-getters. The damage to the national convention would be less severe than under the Quie national direct primary, which would consist of a direct popular vote without regard for state party lines. In the minds of some observers this plan would probably lead to the complete abolition of national conventions. All intermediaries between the voters and the nomination—in other words, state party leaders and national convention delegates— would be totally eliminated. The national parties would become little more than advertising agencies pasting labels on the candidates. Under these conditions the future survival of the national parties would be seriously in doubt.

If the major parties were to disappear under the waves, what agency would replace them for aggregating, moderating, and building consensus among the divergent power groups within our democratic society? The answer is almost too frightening to contemplate.

Regional primaries do not pose quite the life-threatening danger to parties that the national primary does. The Ottinger regional primary proposal would require all delegates to be elected in the primaries, but this proposal would still invest the national convention with the power to make the final selection of the party nominee, pick the vice presidential candidate, and hammer out the platform. The original Packwood regional primary bill (later co-sponsored by Senators Mark Hatfield, R.-Ore., and Ted Stevens, R.-Alaska) leaves each state free to decide for itself on whether or not to hold a presidential primary. Thus, the states retain much wider latitude in the management and selection of their national convention delegates.[37] And the viability of the national convention would be less seriously threatened than under the national direct primary reform.

Recent Plans for Reforming the Presidential Nominating System

In the continuing debate over reform of the presidential nominating process, especially within the Democratic party, three more new plans have recently surfaced. Two of the plans seek to combine the strongest features of the national direct primary and traditional party decision-making machinery into a more effective instrument for choosing presidential nominees. The third plan seeks to establish a fully deliberative national convention, consisting exclusively of uninstructed delegates. Each plan merits close study.

THE LADD PLAN

Formulated by political scientist Everett C. Ladd, the Ladd pian is based upon a national convention in which two-thirds of the delegates to the national convention would be elected in a national primary, with the other third chosen by the parties.[38] The other main features of the Ladd proposal are:

- All states would hold their primary on the same day, for example, the third Tuesday in June. Delegates would be allocated within the states on the basis of proportional representation for candidate preference. A low threshold, for example 10 percent, would be used as a guarantee for a share of the votes.

- Delegates chosen in the primaries would be bound to their candidate for one—and only one—ballot, regardless of whether the candidate withdrew or shifted his support to someone else.

- Candidates would qualify for the ballot through: (a) certification by the party's national committee, based on a candidate's intentions and support; or (b) by petition or a specified number of enrolled party members from at least twelve states.

- One-third of the delegates would be selected by the party and consist almost entirely of ex officio delegates. Most of this total would consist of U.S. senators and representatives, governors, the national chairman and co-chairman, members of the National Committee, and the chairman and co-chairman of each state party. These delegates, numbering on the order of 1,000 to 1,200, would not be bound to any candidate. (Parties would adjust the total number of delegates to conform roughly with the proportion allocated as ex officio delegates.)

- The federal government would give each national party committee $15 million to spend in accordance with its designated purposes. This sum would be in addition to the present federal subsidies currently given to presidential candidates.

While the Ladd plan does not constitute as radical a departure from the existing primary and caucus-convention system as the straight national direct primary, it does nevertheless entail a major restructuring of the present decentralized system of delegate selection. A strikingly ingenious plan, the proposed Ladd national primary constitutes a major step toward plebiscitary democracy—but tempered with a heavy mix of party decisionmaking in the form of 33 percent of the national convention delegates being designated *ex officio* members from among elected officeholders and organizational leaders. Ladd's plan would thus offer a broad mixture of delegates chosen in the primaries and elected officeholders and party officials selected by virtue of their standing within the party. The popularly elected delegates would, of course, provide a broad base of support from the party rank and file. At the same time, the *ex officio* delegates would offer a special dimension to the assessment of presidential candidates, furnishing a careful evaluation based not only on the candidates' popular appeal but also on how they are viewed by their peers. Under Ladd's plan a popular favorite winning, say, 60 percent of the delegates in the primaries would probably encounter little difficulty in attracting enough support from the uncommitted professional politician delegates to secure the nomination.[39]

Inherent in the Ladd plan, however, are many of the major defects of the national direct primary: high cost to candidates, favors the well-known candidate, overturns the sequential nature of the existing delegate selection process, lacks some of the "safety valve" features of present system, and insinuates the federal government ever more deeply into the presidential nominating process. Do we need, it seems fair to ask, such a drastic overhaul of the existing nominating system to achieve the desired (and elusive) goal that produces both good candidates and effective presidents? Might it not be possible to attain this same laudable goal by a less extreme approach? Before we offer a number of modest recommendations for improving the existing convention system in the final chapter, let's take a moment to examine two other major convention reform plans that have recently appeared—the national preprimary convention plan and the Sanford plan.

NATIONAL PREPRIMARY CONVENTION PLAN

Perhaps the most imaginative presidential nominating plan advanced in recent years to revitalize national conventions and to bridge the gap between the participatory democracy and party responsibility (or decision-making) doctrines is the national preprimary convention plan, recently advocated by Thomas E. Cronin and Robert D. Loevy.[40]

Unlike the existing system, the national preprimary convention plan would reverse part of the traditional order or schedule in the presidential selection process. National conventions would be held *before*, not after, a national presidential primary. The Cronin-Loevy plan would replace the present nominating system dominated by nearly three dozen presidential primaries with a caucus-convention system in all states, to be followed by a national convention in July, which in turn would be followed by separate national presidential primaries in both major parties, to be held on the same day in September. The general timetable for the Cronin-Loevy plan would read as follows:

May 1st	Local precinct caucuses throughout the nation
May 15th	County convention day nationwide
May 22nd	Congressional district caucuses nationwide
June 1st	State conventions nationwide
July	National conventions
September 10th	National primary day

Although the national preprimary convention plan runs counter to present established thinking that presidential primaries should occur before the party conventions rather than afterwards, there are a number of working precedents at the state level. For example, Colorado, Connecticut, Utah, and New York all hold preprimary caucuses and conventions before the state primary.

Under the national preprimary convention plan any citizen would be eligible to attend a particular party caucus, but all of those who participated and voted at the party caucus would have to first register at the caucus as members of that political party. Once the citizen registered in that party he or she would be required by national law to vote only in that particular party. Any caucus participant would be eligible to run for delegate to the county congressional district, state and national conventions. Delegate candidates for president could do so, and they could be bound (for one ballot only) to vote for that candidate when they attended subsequent conventions. After the first ballot, convention delegates would be free to exercise their personal judgment. The national preprimary convention plan would permit state conventions to select twenty-five percent of the state's delegation to the national convention as uncommitted delegates. These delegates would consist mostly of elected public officials and party leaders. States would be prohibited by national law from holding any form of official preconvention presidential primary election. The structure, organization, and scheduling of the Democratic and Republican conventions would be the same as they are now, except that both national conventions would be held in July, instead of one convention in July and the other in August, as is presently the case.

The major task, as always, of the national convention would be to nominate candidates for the national party primary the following September. Two ballots would be held. On the first ballot committed delegates would vote for their declared choice and uncommitted delegates would vote for any candidate. After the first ballot all candidates except the top three finishers would be eliminated. The top three candidates would then run off against each other on the second ballot, at which time all delegates would be uncommitted and free to vote their individual preference. Only two—or possibly three—of the top remaining candidates (so long as each received a minimum of 25 or 30 percent of the vote from the convention) would be placed on the September primary ballot.

On the first ballot, Cronin and Loevy point out, a number of delegates will have voted for candidates who did not finish among the top two or three candidates. On the second ballot, however, these delegates will have the opportunity to vote their preference for the party nominee front-runners. As Cronin and Loevy observe, "The system thus allows delegates to vote their first choices, no matter how weak, on the first ballot, but it also allows all of the delegates to participate in the final ranking of the strongest party candidates on the second ballot.[41] (On the state level, candidates running in a preprimary convention system work generally hard at state conventions to receive the preferred "top-line" designation because political research has shown and candidates believe that the first name on the ballot enjoys an electoral advantage.) In the September national primary, the candidate who captures the most votes would of course be the party nominee in the November general election. In other words, a plurality of votes rather than a majority would be sufficient to declare the nominee. If the winning candidate should become functionally disabled or die after the primary, the party national committee would select a new nominee.

In certain presidential years, if history tells us anything, one candidate may be so strong at the convention that it would not be necessary to hold a national primary election. This would occur if, on the second ballot, one candidate is so popular that neither of the second or third place candidates garners 25 percent of the convention vote (or if a three-candidate field is used, when the second of the top two finishers has less than 30 percent of the delegate vote). At present some states that use a preprimary convention system also declare that the front-running candidate for state office who receives 70 percent of the convention vote automatically receives the party's nomination. This same rule could sensibly apply at the national level. Also, this arrangement would enable a popular incumbent president with heavy support within his party to avoid the strain of a September national primary.

Another major duty of the national convention would be to create a pool of acceptable vice presidential candidates from which the eventual presidential nominee could make the final choice following the national primary in September. All of the presidential candidates who qualify for the second convention ballot would automatically be included in this vice presidential pool (although one of them would, of course, be eventually removed by winning the party's presidential nomination). Cronin and Loevy propose that the convention add three more vice presidential candidates to the pool. Immediately following the national primary in September, the party's presidential nominee would select his vice presidential running-mate from the candidate pool. While the presidential nominee would thus make the final selection of his running-mate, all of the vice presidential eligibles in the pool would, as Cronin and Loevy explain, have received "party approval" at the national convention. It will be noted that the presidential nominee would have considerable latitude in selecting his running-mate. If it appears politically expedient to select one of his defeated opponents, he would be free to do so. If he has another candidate in mind, he might arrange to have his supporters at the national convention include this person among the list of three officially approved by the convention.

To prevent party voters from jumping from one party to the other after they see which candidates are going to be nominated or which parties are going to have national primaries, party registration deadlines would be July first. The objective here would be to prevent partisan voters whose party is not having a presidential primary in a particular year from switching their registration in order to vote for the weakest opposition candidate.

The chief advantages of the national preprimary convention plan, as viewed by its sponsors, are:

- It shortens the formal election season and neutralizes the predominant heavy influence of small, unrepresentative states, such as Iowa and New Hampshire, the major beneficiaries of massive national media coverage.

- It tests the coalition-building skills of serious contenders, those skills needed to win the general election and to govern effectively.

- It would promote responsible parties that at the same time are subject to popular control.

- It would facilitate and encourage the best possible candidates, including busy officeholders, to run for the presidency.

- It would eliminate the artificial regional advantages for those state candidates who are fortunate enough to have strong support in states that just happen to have early primary elections.

- It would encourage broad participation by all elements within the party and foster greater voter interest and accordingly higher turnout.

- It would once again help transform the national convention from a ratifying assembly into a deliberative body.[42]

On the negative side, the national preprimary convention plan contains most of the shortcomings inherent in the straight, national presidential primary: it would mean two national elections within a sixty-day period; its high cost would require candidates to hire a huge corps of fund-raisers and accountants to assure compliance with the 1974 Federal Election Campaign Act; it would favor well-known candidates over their lesser known competitors; and it would most likely lead to intense factionalism within each party.

Further, both parties would be required to follow a lock-step timetable in all fifty states with no deviation for traditional practices within certain states. The national preprimary convention plan would destroy many unique regional qualities as well as the remarkable diversity found in the political cultures of the fifty states. Indeed, it's difficult to visualize, for example, the states of New Hampshire and Texas conducting their convention delegate and presidential candidate selection process in the same standardized manner. Also, it should not be overlooked that a substantial number of states conduct their primaries for state and local offices simultaneously with their presidential primary–national convention delegate selection. The national preprimary convention plan would obviously put an end to this efficient election management at the state level. Clearly, national uniformity seems too high a price to pay for the replacement of a decentralized presidential nominating system that has operated with only limited failings for almost 150 years.

But the national preprimary convention plan, on paper at least, does possess a number of attractive features that cannot be easily dismissed. Especially for strengthening the party's role in presidential nominations, it is to be applauded. For the present, however, it would seem preferable for the major parties, particularly the Democrats, to digest carefully the most recent presidential nomination reforms, notably the provision for a sizeable increase in the number of uncommitted delegate seats, before launching into additional experimentation with the presidential candidate selection process. If the remaining presidential nominating contests in the 1980's continue to lead to mounting dissatisfaction with the existing machinery and the choice of candidates in the two major parties, it will be time enough to take the national preprimary convention plan off the shelf and give further consideration to this rather unique method of picking presidential nominees.

SANFORD PLAN

Another plan to improve the nominating process has been offered by Terry Sanford, a former presidential candidate and chairperson of the Democratic commission that drafted the 1974 Democratic Charter.[43] Sanford would rely upon national party rules to implement his plan to make the national convention a fully deliberative body, consisting entirely of uninstructed delegates. It is his expectation, whether realistic or not, that both parties would accept the same basic rules on delegate selection and that this compact would quickly bring state legislatures and state parties into compliance. The main thrust of the Sanford Plan is to increase the discretion of the delegates. Sanford's goal, as he states it, is to "send thinking delegates to the national convention."[44] The main features of his plan are:

- All delegates would be chosen individually without any kind of formal commitment.

- Delegates would be chosen from single-member districts (i.e., one member per district), whether by popular election or in a caucus. (Selection of a smaller number of *ex officio* delegates by state conventions or other processes also would be permitted.)

- Presidential primaries would still be permitted, but only "beauty contest" presidential primaries. Delegates would be chosen separately but not mandated by the primary results. Primaries would be held on any one of six dates in March or April, with each state selecting its own date. No attempt would be made to achieve regional groupings.

- Incumbent presidents would not, unless they so chose, need to involve themselves in primary campaigns, since they have already proved their campaigning abilities.

Under the Sanford plan, each delegate would become, in essence, an unencumbered representative or agent free to vote as he or she chooses. Sanford believes that delegates should represent the voters and party members of their constituencies, not presidential candidates, as is presently the case. Sanford abhors "messenger (committed) delegates," who, in effect, belong to the candidates. Sanford feels that it is essential that delegates have discretionary authority—but that they use it wisely. Moreover, Sanford argues, "With elected representative delegates sitting out there two months in advance [of the convention], we would have an institutionalized system for deeper analysis, more thorough examination, and ample contemplation."[45] Presumably, a sizeable number of delegates would be party officials who would be fairly knowledgeable about the presidential contenders. But it is Sanford's view that we have not known very much about several recent candidates until after they have had the nomination in hand. In Sanford's words: "The intense examination of candidates, their views and peculiarities, their strengths and weaknesses, is not part of the presidential scenario."[46] To provide a closer look at the contenders, Sanford proposes to hold a series of state forums where the candidates would go before the chosen delegates to answer questions, debate the issues, and be cross-examined. Thus, in the closing weeks of the preconvention period the uninstructed delegates would be able to look over the full field of candidates instead of the one or two late primary season survivors "who have run a crazy obstacle course."[47]

Obviously, Sanford's plan would require extensive surgery with the current nominating process. Whether the national parties would use their authority to implement such an ambitious plan—it seems highly doubtful, for example, that Republican leadership, which views our party system as a confederation of state parties, would buy it—the Sanford plan would, it seems fair to predict, generate widespread controversy. To obtain the willing cooperation of legislatures in the three dozen primary states would be a big, perhaps impossible, order. It also seems questionable that Sanford's uncommitted delegates would be able to withstand the intensive pressure of a front-running candidate's national campaign organization to remain uncommitted—even though Sanford's plan would impose a ban on presidential candidates spending money on behalf of prospective or elected delegates without full disclosure. Fear of missing the probable victor's preconvention bandwagon and future presidential favors would most likely convince many uncommitted delegates to cast aside their neutral status in favor of pledging their vote to the winner's team. In that case, Sanford's attempt to build a convention system of uncommitted delegates would collapse from its own internal weakness. Only if delegates were to behave as near-saints does it seem possible that Sanford's uninstructed delegate plan would operate successfully.

If the various national and regional primary proposals, the Ladd plan, the national preprimary convention plan, and the Sanford plan are all rejected as unsuitable prescriptions for healing the real and imagined ills of the existing presidential nominating process, what corrective action is needed? Most supporters of the national convention, including this author, are agreed that some reform of the existing system is needed.

In the final chapter, several recommendations will be offered to make the national convention more responsive to party leadership and to avoid the dangerous aspects of plebiscitarian democracy lurking in the existing three dozen presidential primaries. Indeed, the participation of more than 32 million voters (1980 figures) in the presidential nominating process threatens to totally undermine the major parties' prerogative to nominate, after careful consideration of the various contenders, their "best-qualified" candidate for the highest office in the land.

Notes

1. Herbert McClosky, "Are Political Conventions Undemocratic?" *New York Times Magazine* (August 4, 1968), p. 62.

2. James Reston, "The Convention System: A Five-Count Indictment," *New York Times Magazine* (July 11, 1948), p. 7.

3. See Estes Kefauver, "Why Not Let the People Elect Our President," *Colliers*, Vol. 131 (January 31, 1953), pp. 34-39; Senator Paul O. Douglas, "Let the People In," *New Republic*, Vol. 126 (March 31, 1952), pp. 14-15; and Senator William E. Proxmire, "Appeal for the Vanishing Primary," *New York Times Magazine* (March 27, 1960), pp. 22, 82-83.

4. At the 1976 Democratic convention, for example, there were usually between 5,000 and 7,000 people on the convention floor during the sessions at Madison Square Garden. Many of them walked under a sign, hung on the podium camera platform, stating that under various New York City codes, the maximum safe occupancy of the area was 2,476 persons! Richard Reeves, *Convention* (New York: Harcourt Brace Jovanovich, 1977), p. 29.

5. Dwight D. Eisenhower, "Our National Nominating Conventions Are a Disgrace," *Reader's Digest*, Vol. 89 (July 1966), p. 76.

6. Austin Ranney and Willmoore Kendall, *Democracy and the American Party System* (New York: Harcourt, Brace and World, Inc., 1956), p. 315.

7. Quoted in Robert MacNeil, *The People Machine* (New York: Harper & Row, 1968), p. 116.

8. Nicholas von Hoffman, *Washington Post*, July 13, 1980.

9. Arthur T. Hadley, *The Invisible Primary* (Englewood Cliffs, N.J.: Prentice-Hall, 1976).

10. Austin Ranney, *The Federalization of Presidential Primaries* (Washington, D.C.: American Enterprise Institute, 1978), p. 4.

11. *New York Times*, July 11, 1979. This bipartisan issue produced such strange bedfellows as Senator Strom Thurmond, conservative Republican from South Carolina, siding with Senator Edmund G. Muskie, liberal Democrat from Maine, to defeat the proposed constitutional amendment. No vote was taken in the House of Representatives because the one-sided Senate vote effectively killed any hope of passing the proposed amendment.

12. Austin Ranney, *The Federalization of Presidential Primaries*, p. 1.

13. Ibid., p. 7.

14. U.S. Congress, Senate, *Senate Journal*, 92nd Cong. 2nd sess., 1972, 118, pt. 7: 8014-16.

15. Austin Ranney, *The Federalization of Presidential Primaries*, pp. 7-8.

16. Robert Bendiner, "The Presidential Primaries Are Haphazard, Unfair, and Wildly Illogical," *New York Times*, February 17, 1972.

17. James W. Ceaser, *Presidential Selection: Theory and Development*, p. 351.

18. Austin Ranney, *The Federalization of Presidential Primaries*, pp. 39-40.

19. Paul T. David, a leading authority on national conventions, is less convinced that a national primary would attract a large field of candidates. Whatever the rules, candidates would find it difficult to qualify. The Mansfield plan, David points out, would call for upward of a million names on petitions spread evenly through most of the states—an organizing job that would disqualify many contenders. If there were a requirement to raise a large sum of money, such as under the present federal matching fund rules, David believes that this, too, would probably eliminate a number of presidential aspirants. Letter from Professor David to author, dated September 2, 1981.

20. Paul T. David, Malcolm Moos, and Ralph M. Goldman, *Presidential Nominating Politics in 1952* (Baltimore: The Johns Hopkins University Press, 1954), Vol. 1, pp. 218-19.

21. Voter turnout in the 1980 presidential election, according to the Federal Election Commission, was 53.95 percent—the lowest since President Truman's victory over Dewey in 1948, when only 51.1 percent of eligible voters cast ballots. The 1980 figure was just below the 54.5 percent voter turnout in 1976. *New York Times*, January 3, 1981.

22. Austin Ranney, *The Federalization of Presidential Primaries*, pp. 36-37.

23. V. O. Key, Jr., *Southern Politics* (New York: Alfred A. Knopf, 1949), especially chapters 18-22.

24. Jeane J. Kirkpatrick, *Dismantling the Parties: Reflections of Party Reform and Party Decomposition* (Washington, D.C.: American Enterprise Institute, 1978), p. 27.

25. Austin Ranney, *The Federalization of Presidential Primaries*, p. 38.

26. For a discussion of the Packwood plan, see U.S. Congress, Senate, *Congressional Record*, 92nd Cong., 2nd sess., 1972, 118, pt. 12: 15231-42.

27. Ibid.

28. "Presidential Primaries: Proposals for a New System," *Congressional Quarterly Weekly Report*, Vol. 30 (July 10, 1972), pp. 1653-54.

29. Ibid.

30. Senator Walter F. Mondale also introduced a regional presidential primary bill in 1976, which would have established six closed regional primaries, to be held at two-week intervals on specified dates during the spring. To qualify for federal campaign matching funds, a candidate would have been required to contest at least one state per region. But once Mondale became involved with his vice presidential election campaign, he did not pursue the issue further. See, *The Presidential Nominating System: A Primer* (Cambridge, Mass.: Institute of Politics, John F. Kennedy School of Government, Harvard University, 1979), p. 36.

31. See Democratic National Committee, *Openness, Participation, and Party Building: Reforms for a Strong Democratic Primary*, Report of the Commission on Presidential Nomination and Party Structure (Washington, D.C.: Democratic National Committee, 1978), pp. 33-35.

32. U.S. Congress, House, *Regional Presidential Primaries Act of 1979*, 94th Cong., 2nd sess., H. Report, 12161, pp. 4653-54.

33. Austin Ranney, *The Federalization of Presidential Primaries*, p. 37.

34. William J. Crotty, *Political Reform and the American Experiment* (New York: Thomas Y. Crowell, 1977), p. 232.

35. Ibid.

36. James W. Ceaser, *Reforming the Reforms*, p. 184.

37. Significantly, all recent primary bills introduced since 1977 rely on acts of Congress, not constitutional amendments, to federalize the presidential nominating system. Whether Congress has the power to overhaul the presidential nominating system without use of a constitutional amendment has never been clearly established. But it is significant, as Austin Ranney has pointed out, that none of the challengers to the constitutionality of the Federal Elections Campaign Act of 1974 argued that Congress lacked the power to regulate presidential primaries. Austin Ranney, *The Federalization of Presidential Primaries*, pp. 9-12.

38. Everett C. Ladd, "A Better Way to Pick Presidents," *Fortune*, Vol. 101 (May 5, 1980), pp. 132-42.

39. This analysis of the Ladd plan relies heavily on James W. Ceaser, *Reforming the Reforms*, pp. 143-46.

40. The plan is outlined in Thomas E. Cronin and Robert D. Loevy, "Putting the Party As Well As the People Back in Presidential Picking" (Paper presented at the 78th annual meeting of the American Political Science Association meeting, Denver, Colorado, September 2-5, 1982).

41. Ibid., p. 15.

42. Ibid., pp. 28-29.

43. Terry Sanford, "Picking the Presidents," *Atlantic Monthly*, Vol. 246 (August 1980), pp. 29-33.

44. Ibid.

45. Ibid., p. 33.

46. Ibid.

47. Terry Sanford, *A Danger of Democracy* (Boulder, Colorado: Westview Press, 1981), p. 141.

National Convention Reform ⎯⎯⎯⎯⎯ 9

> No civilization since time began has ever devised a perfect system
> for the choosing of its leaders; all have ultimately collapsed ei-
> ther because the success of the system undermined its virtues, or
> failures of the system exposed its people to disaster.
>
> Theodore H. White, *The Making of A President, 1968*

In the past fifteen years the unanticipated consequences of Democratic party
reforms and the heavy candidate reliance on television have widened the gap
between the ability to get elected and the ability to govern the country. As one
British commentator has observed, "A disjunction seems to have developed in
the United States between the qualities required to win the presidential nomination of one's party and the qualities required to be a good president."[1] Further,
the presidential candidate who may be good at running a nominating and election
campaign may not prove to be a successful incumbent. Indeed, one critic of the
present nomination system has complained: "Our selection procedures place a
higher premium on the ability to campaign than on the ability to govern."[2] In this
concluding chapter we will explore some suggested reforms of the national
convention that would make this huge deliberative assembly more effective
during this era of participatory democracy and mass media politics in selecting
presidential candidates capable not only of winning the nomination but also of
providing strong national leadership.

Nominations in the Reform Era

Candidates' heavy reliance on party professionals within the individual states
to secure the presidential nomination came to an end with the 1968 conventions.
Subsequently, the rapid spread of presidential primary legislation—the number
of primary states more than doubled between 1968 and 1980 (from 15 to
35)—virtually destroyed the last vestiges of state and local party organizational

control of national conventions. By 1980, 9 out of 10 of the largest states in the Union had adopted primaries and the number of popularly-elected delegates (most of them pledged, rather than uncommitted) approached 75 percent of the national convention total in each of the major parties. Even in most caucus-convention states, delegate candidates, especially in the Democratic party, now run pledged to specific presidential contenders. Formerly, delegate control exercised by the party regulars enabled the dominant leadership factions in most states to bargain as cohesive units at the national conventions. But all this came to a halt when the rules were changed, making most convention delegates popularly-elected and pledged to a specific candidate. As a result, most delegates became far more interested in furthering the nomination of their pledged candidate at the national convention than in representing their state party and its long-term goals. Confronted with basically a new set of selection rules, presidential candidates switched their nominating strategies. Instead of courting state party leaders, presidential candidates shifted their heavy attention to developing their popular appeal with the mass electorate. Other developments—the overpowering influence of national television and federal campaign finance reform legislation—also have had a powerful effect on the presidential nominating process.

To win the nomination in the age of party reform a presidential candidate, above all else, must be able to attract the attention of the national television media and the working press and project a favorable "image" on the television screen. Indeed, the momentous shift toward media politics has seriously eroded the traditional function of parties to recruit presidential candidates capable of working with Congress, to develop party programs, and, if successful at election time, govern the country. No longer do the candidates have to bargain with or build coalitions with members of Congress, big-state governors, big-city mayors, or leaders of major interest groups—those political entrepreneurs that the nominee will have to work with, if he is successful in reaching the White House. Instead, presidential aspirants now bypass party and congressional leaders and seek the nomination by appealing directly via television to the voters, who will elect delegates in the presidential primaries instructed to vote the electorate's preferences at the national convention. Television, in short, enables a candidate to elude all controls of the party and present himself directly to the electorate. Voters, in turn, see far more of candidates via television than they ever did under the old-style system.

The diminution of party influence in the political process—especially the presidential nomination process—has been hastened by passage of the Federal Election Campaign Act of 1974, pushed through Congress in the aftermath of the Watergate scandals. Revelations that President Nixon's reelection committee had raised vast sums (over $60 million) in 1972, including substantial amounts under the table, prompted Congress to pass a new complex federal subsidy matching scheme for presidential candidates in the primaries and to underwrite the full cost of the candidate's general election campaign. All of this legislation was passed to "take the money out of politics." But the chief casualties of this Congressional venture into campaign finance have been the major parties themselves because Uncle Sam's subsidies are given to the candidates, not the parties. Thus, candidates are less dependent than ever on the parties. As a result of the unanticipated consequences of this legislation, parties have been seriously undermined in their ability to screen presidential contenders, help elect the party nominee, and to hold the President-elect accountable to the various constituencies within the party.

Have the recent party reforms "opening up the system" and the federal matching subsidies in the primaries, coupled with the magnified influence of television, really turned the presidential nominating system upside down? Has the injection of too much democracy and too many of Uncle Sam's dollars thrown the presidential nominating system into disarray? Most thoughtful observers would answer these questions in the affirmative.

National columnist David S. Broder's criticism of recent conventions is typical: "What began after 1968 as an effort by the Democrats to make their conventions more 'representative' has ended by straitjacketing what had been a spontaneous engrossing assembly with a vital political function to perform." Broder continues: ". . . the 'reforms' of recent years have reduced the delegates to the status of computers on which the results of the primaries and caucuses are imprinted."[3]

Equally significant, the recent reforms have fostered a further separation of the presidential nominating process from the rest of the activity of a political party. Jesse "Big Daddy" Unruh, California state treasurer and long-time Democratic activist, speaking of this problem at the 1980 Democratic convention complained, "These delegates feel no responsibility for anything but the presidential candidate they're backing. Twenty-five percent of the Carter delegates and 55 to 65 percent of the Kennedy delegates, we'll never see again."[4] In the process, absolute control of the nominating process has been turned over to the presidential candidates and their staffs; pledged delegates merely follow the orders of the prospective nominee on party rules, the platform, and other party business.

Since the 1980 elections, numerous students of politics—practitioners, academics, and journalists—have begun reassessing the emergent plebiscitarian system that, in effect, selects presidential candidates by mandating convention delegate votes in almost three dozen primaries and fosters the separation of presidential nominating machinery from other important party activity. Most are agreed that a "reform of the reforms" is now needed if we are to save the two-party system as we know it, and to prevent the total usurpation of the presidential nominating process by the further proliferation of binding presidential primaries, the ubiquitous television camera, and by candidates (whether they are qualified or not) using this electronic instrument to springboard themselves into the presidential nomination and possibly the White House itself. To be sure, there is no necessary distinction between a candidate's ability to capitalize on a popular television "image" to pyramid himself (or herself) into the nomination and the ability to govern successfully after election. But the main thesis of this study is that final judgment on the type of presidential choice the party wishes to offer the electorate in November should be left to the party delegates assembled in the national convention, not rank-and-file voters or the mass media.

Senator Alan Cranston (D.-Calif.), an unannounced candidate for the 1984 Democratic nomination, has advanced several persuasive reasons why presidential nominees should be carefully selected by popularly elected or party designated delegates meeting in a national convention, not exclusively by the millions of voters in the primaries or the mass media.

Participation in primaries can tell us something about a candidate's electability—his or her fund-raising or organizational talents—and how a candidate comes across in a television commercial. On the other hand, it may well tell us only that a candidate has been willing to quit work and devote two full years or more to full-time campaigning for the Presidency.[5]

Senator Cranston also reminds us that victory in a primary doesn't necessarily tell the party whether a candidate can appeal to a larger constituency—party identifiers, some weak identifiers of the opposition party, and independents—that will determine ultimate victory in the general election. Primaries, Senator Cranston points out, do not tell the party how well a candidate will delegate authority. Nor do they demonstrate his ability to choose the best people for top government posts—everything from the Cabinet and the White House staff to the Supreme Court. Primaries also don't tell the party how well a candidate will conduct our foreign policy or interface personally with the heads of foreign nations. Primaries don't tell the party how effective a candidate will be in dealing with Congress, nor how capable a candidate will be at moving the national power structure, nor how good an "educator" of the American public a candidate would be as President. And, most important, primaries don't tell us how good a candidate would be at presidential decision-making—the ultimate test of a good President.

Rather than leaving this final choice exclusively to the millions of voters in primaries, the author shares with Senator Cranston the view that we should not fall into the trap of an "irrational Lockianism" that holds that every decision affecting presidential candidates or public policy must be decided by the voters.[6] Since party activists and ideologues are more likely to vote in primaries than the typical rank-and-file voter and because the absolute determination of the democratic will is well nigh impossible to achieve if more than two candidates contest the nomination, there is no special reason, in the view of some critics, to suppose that national convention delegates selected in primaries or by an open process in the caucus-convention states will more accurately represent the party's will than delegates chosen in a closed nominating system heavily populated with elected officeholders or party professionals.[7] In short, the nominating process does not require full participation of the voters, only that the voters have the opportunity to make their preferences known in the general election. In the final analysis it is the responsibility of the national nominating convention—after fully assessing all the results in the primaries and caucus-conventions and evaluating all the pluses and minuses of each presidential candidate—to make the final judgment about the "best qualified" candidate for the Presidency.

Presidential nominations by national conventions are, of course, not a panacea for leadership selection problems in contemporary America. Nor will party organizations necessarily represent every new current of opinion in the exact proportion to its general electoral strength. But unless the role of the party is partially restored in the presidential nominating process and the national convention is reconstituted as a deliberative body to pick presidential nominees (instead of merely becoming a ratification assembly to approve the victor in the primaries), presidential candidates will continue, as they have for the past two decades, to be selected chiefly on the basis of their favorable television image and their ability to run a successful nominating campaign, not their ability to govern the country. Moreover, if the trend toward the plebiscitarian democracy of the primary-dominated system continues, national conventions may well become purely ceremonial gatherings to observe the coronation of the primary winner. Under these conditions conventions would come to be viewed as just another series of ritualistic rites that we now associate with the quadrennial meeting of the Electoral College's presidential electors in mid-December to declare officially the winner of the presidential election—previously decided, of course, by the voters and announced across the land six weeks earlier.

No set of reforms will, of course, solve all the problems or meet all the objections of the existing nominating system. But the underlying thesis of this study has been that the quadrennial national conventions, despite their shortcomings, have on the whole performed their nominating function remarkably well for almost 150 years—better than any alternative system could have under the circumstances. Consequently, suggestions for reform of this long-established quadrennial conclave must be carefully scrutinized before any serious consideration can be given to them. National conventions have also exhibited an extraordinary resilient quality that has made them noticeably adaptive to their environment, especially the growing pressure from reformers in the past fifteen years to make the giant party conclaves more responsive and open to rank-and-file influence. It is with these thoughts in mind that the suggested reforms sketched in this chapter are offered to the reader.

Reduce Convention Size

National conventions of both major parties should be limited in size to approximately 1,500 delegates and an equal number of alternates. Almost all convention observers are in agreement that national conventions, especially the Democratic conclaves, are too large. As the late Alexander Bickel commented at one point, "What we now have is a mass meeting in a bull ring." The growth in the size of national conventions has been largely the result of the desire of party chieftains to include as many diverse elements in the party as possible, especially those previously underrepresented, while taking pains not to exclude any deserving member of the party. At the 1980 Democratic National Convention in New York there were more than 5,500 delegates and alternates, a figure that had nearly doubled in the previous twenty years as pressure has mounted to accord this form of recognition for party officials and workers, contributors, single interest groups, and minorities. The importance and prestige attached to attending a national convention should not be underestimated. As put by one reporter, "The sophisticated wisdom these days is that the convention is an obsolete bore where nothing of much substance happens. But to the insurance salesman, teachers, housewives, bankers and others who populate this arena the nominating convention remains an American ritual, and it is their porthole to history."[8]

While these conclaves are so huge that they have ceased to be deliberative bodies, no responsible public official in this age of plebiscitarian politics wishes to go on record in favor of reducing the size of national conventions. Indeed, recommending a reduction in the size of national conventions is not unlike recommending a cutback on the number of automobiles on our highways. On paper, the idea seems eminently sensible, but few elected officials are prepared to sacrifice themselves on the barricades fighting for fewer automobiles on the highway or for smaller national conventions.

Party leaders, recognizing that the prestige of attending a national convention has grown steadily in recent years and aware that a huge convention hall full of delegates can be an impressive display of party strength and popularity to the 90 million TV viewers watching portions or all of the national conventions, have been reluctant to slap a delegate lid on the size of their conclaves. Party officials have also learned that once "bonus" delegates are given to a state, it's excruciatingly painful to deny the state these same bonus delegates at future conventions, even after the state party's poor electoral performance dictates a reduction in its delegate allocation. As a result, conventions continue to grow in size, and the end is not in sight.

In 1950, the American Political Science Association's Committee on Political Parties recommended that a national convention be limited to 500 to 600 members. This recommendation, it might be noted, was made when national conventions were approximately half their present size. In the words of the Committee:

Much better results could be attained with a convention of not more than 500-600 members, composed mostly of delegates elected directly by party voters on a more representative basis (300-350 members), a substantial number of ex-officio members (the National Committee, state party chairmen, congressional leaders—probably about 150 altogether), and a selected group of prominent party leaders outside the party organizations (probably 25).[9]

A modification of a proposal first put forward by President Woodrow Wilson in 1913, the proposed "downsized" national convention was expected to achieve several goals. It would provide a manageable convention more representative of the party voters and of the party organization—national and state. The smaller convention would afford "opportunity for expressing and harmonizing the views and interests of the different elements of the party." Also, it would be a small enough body to make possible more responsible deliberation and action on program matters. The Committee also recommended that the national convention meet more frequently (at least biennially) and hold longer sessions in order that, as the highest representative assembly of the party, it could deliberate and transact business on all major policies and issues.[10]

This proposal for a smaller convention turned out to be nothing more than an academic exercise. It fell on deaf ears in both the Republican and Democratic parties and failed to generate any enthusiasm in the halls of Congress or the state capitals. Some critics have labeled attempts to reduce the size of conventions as "elitist," a move to deprive deserving rank-and-file party workers of the opportunity to attend a national convention. Other critics have argued that any gathering of more than a few hundred makes it impossible, in any case, to function as a deliberative body, so why worry if national conventions continue to balloon in size. In any large-scale meeting, these critics argue, decision-making shifts to smaller bodies—convention committees, state delegations, and, of course, to the "smoke-filled" (or air-conditioned) rooms of party leaders.

Other proposals to reduce the size of conventions have been received with the same lack of enthusiasm. In 1969, Mr. J. Leonard Reinsch, a radio and television executive who helped direct Democratic conventions for a quarter of a century, proposed to the O'Hara Commission on Rules that there be no more than 1,500 voting delegates and 500 alternates at future conventions. To mollify those would-be delegates who would be denied a seat at the convention, Mr. Reinsch suggested listing them as "honorary delegates" in the official program and giving them souvenir convention badges.[11] The broadcasting executive's proposal, however, was soon forgotten. In fact, the number of delegates approved for the 1972 convention by the O'Hara Commission and the Democratic National Committee was increased from 2,599 delegates in 1968 to 3,016 delegates.

To limit conventions to the five or six hundred delegates recommended by the APSA Committee on Political Parites would appear to be illusionary. Among most convention observers, however, there is agreement that the two parties should set an upper limit of approximately 1,500 delegates—a ceiling that the Republicans adhered to until 1976. Over the past two decades, however, the Democrats have been concerned more about "grass roots" representation at their national conventions than manageable size. Also, the Democrats appear to view the convention rally function as more important than making the convention into a deliberative body. Now the Republicans have joined them. But the GOP has not been dazzled by the numbers game to quite the same degree as the Democrats. The 1980 GOP convention delegate count was 1,994—down 265 delegates since 1976. Gerald Pomper has commented, "Limiting the size of the convention ...can contribute to more rational decisions within the state delegations and to more careful bargaining between these delegations."[12] But party officials have more important convention goals in mind. Nevertheless, both parties, in the interest of improving the deliberative and bargaining processes and playing down the "mass rally" emphasis of national conventions, should reduce the size of the quadrennial conclaves to 1,500 delegates—and even a smaller number if the party decision-makers can agree to make this hard choice.

Reduction in the number of alternate delegates to national conventions is the only area in which the Democrats have made slight progress in recent years. Under changes made in Democratic convention rules for 1972, the number of alternates was reduced by more than one-half for large state delegations and by smaller percentages for middle-sized states, but with no reduction for the least populous states.[13] The Republicans, with smaller conventions, however, have thus far displayed no interest in moving from their one-vote, one-delegate, one-alternate plan.

Long-time convention scholar Paul T. David, in 1969, urged the Democratic party to reduce the size of its convention committees as well as the convention itself. He suggested that convention committees be limited to a maximum of forty members.[14] Smaller committees, representing the party not individual states, David said, would facilitate better deliberation. But the small states objected vehemently to this proposal. Professor David then suggested that the committees be put on a fair apportionment basis with the smallest states restricted to one member and the other states represented in proportion to the size of their convention delegation. The two largest states—New York and California—were to be given a maximum of ten or so seats on these committees. The O'Hara Commission bought this idea, and it has since been in effect at the Democratic conclaves. The same voting formula was carried over into the reconstruction of the Democratic National Committee after the 1972 convention. Republican reformers on the GOP Delegate and Organizations (DO) Committee, reacting to the "winds of change" sweeping through the Democratic party, recommended that the 1972 convention approve a rule for the 1976 convention whereby each state delegation would be required to select one man, one woman, one delegate under the age of twenty-five, and one member of a minority ethnic group to serve on each convention committee. But the 1972 GOP convention failed to approve this recommendation. Faced with a choice of improving their capacity for better decision-making by reducing convention committee size or increasing the representation of each of the 50 sovereign states and their various constituent elements, both parties have usually opted for large committees.

More Equitable Representation

One priority reform, most political scientists agree, is the need to make conventions (and all other party organs) more representative. The principle of "one Republican (or Democrat), one vote" should be the basis of allocating delegate votes. Throughout the years apportionment systems used in both parties have generally benefited one-party and small states. Thus, despite the number of attempts, starting after the 1912 GOP convention, to reduce the overrepresentation of Southern Republicans in the GOP National Convention, the results fell far short of equality, even as late as 1948, as Table 20 shows.

TABLE 20
MALAPPORTIONMENT AT 1948 REPUBLICAN
NATIONAL CONVENTION

State	Republican Voters per Delegate
New York	29,290
Pennsylvania	19,021
Ohio	27,277
Kansas	24,884
South Carolina	894
Georgia	5,478
Alabama	2,923
Mississippi	630
Louisiana	5,589

Source: "Toward a More Responsible Two-Party System," *American Political Science Review*, Vol. 44 (September 1950), Supplement, p. 29.

Representation at Democratic national conventions before the Supreme Court's ruling of "one-man, one-vote" in the 1964 congressional reapportionment case (*Wesberry v. Sanders*) was grossly distorted in favor of small and heavily rural states.[15] Table 21 shows the gross inequities in representation that existed at the 1948 Democratic convention.

TABLE 21
MALAPPORTIONMENT AT 1948 DEMOCRATIC
NATIONAL CONVENTION

State	Democratic Voters per Delegate
Maine	11,191
Vermont	7,443
Connecticut	21,164
New York	28,960
Pennsylvania	26,955
Illinois	33,245
Wyoming	8,725
Nevada	3,120
Texas	15,014
South Carolina	1,721
Louisiana	5,680

Source: "Toward a More Responsible Two-Party System," *American Political Science Review*, Vol. 44 (September 1950), Supplement, p. 28.

The explanation for this gross imbalance was, of course, caused by an apportionment system based, not on the number of Republican or Democratic voters in the various states, but on statewide population and the consequent apportionment of presidential electors. Theoretically, at least, the delegates represented simple population—Democrats, Republicans, independents, and even the non-voters. Because many malapportioned rural congressional districts might have only one-eighth of the population of an urban district before the Supreme Court's 1964 reapportionment decision, they enjoyed eight times the representation of an urban congressional district at a national convention.

In the South, prior to passage of the Voting Rights Act of 1965, nearly total disenfranchisement of blacks by coercion, literacy tests, and voter registration barriers resulted in heavy overrepresentation of delegates at both the Democratic and Republican conventions. The reason: since the national convention delegate allocations were based upon total population, not voters, the blacks were counted for purposes of allocating the total number of congressional districts to a state—and, thus, the number of convention delegates—though blacks throughout the South had virtually no voice in party decision-making until the late 1960's.

As late as the 1960 convention, Mississippi had one delegate for about 6,300 Democratic voters in the 1956 election and one delegate for every 4,000 Republican voters. In contrast, a competitive state like New York had one delegate for 24,000 Democrats and one for 45,000 Republicans voting in 1956. As for small state overrepresentation, Wyoming had one Democratic delegate at the 1968 Democratic National Convention for every 4,036 Democratic voters in the 1964 election, whereas New York, a large two-party competitive state, had one Democratic delegate allocated for every 24,312 Democratic votes cast in 1964. Convention voting representation should be apportioned more equitably to reflect party voter sentiment in the heavily populated competitive areas of states, not the one-party enclaves or small states. To achieve this kind of representation, the apportionment of delegates should be based on the party vote in each state in the last three presidential elections, not the last census report.

In recent years the most serious effort to revise delegation apportionment was undertaken by the Democratic O'Hara Commission on Rules, established at the same time as the McGovern-Fraser Reform Commission in 1969. Recognizing that any plan based exclusively on the "one Democrat, one vote" principle was not saleable to a Democratic National Committee still consisting of two members from each of the fifty states, O'Hara's panel arrived at its proposed 1972 delegation figures by giving equal weight to population as reflected in the 1970 census and the average Democratic vote for President in the last three Presidential elections—1960, 1964, and 1968. The Democratic National Committee modified slightly the O'Hara formula and other proposals for apportionment on a strict population basis or on a straight Democratic vote by adopting an apportionment formula calculated on the basis of the Presidential vote as 47 percent and Electoral College vote, 53 percent of the formula.

Tension over representation at Republican national conventions has erupted periodically. In 1972, a coalition of conservative Midwestern and Southern states plus several large states—California, Illinois, and Texas—beat back a liberal GOP attempt to substitute a plan giving greater representation to the more populous industrial states. Most party professionals recognized that the old apportionment plan kept party machinery in the hands of the conservative wing. The 1972 GOP Rules Committee fight marked the reemergence of the liberal-conservative cleavage that erupted at the 1964 GOP convention, especially between the Northern, big electoral vote states, on one side, and the small states and the new bailiwicks of GOP conservatism in the "Sun Belt" states, on the other. The conservatives' delegate plan rewarded mostly a heavy Presidential turnout—a proposal especially favored by Southern Republicans who had carried the presidential ticket in their states, even though most congressional and state elective offices remained almost completely in Democratic hands. The plan ratified was also more generous to the small states. Republicans from Massachusetts, Pennsylvania, and New Jersey—along with the Ripon Society, the liberal Republican organization—challenged the Miami compromise plan after the 1972 general election in the courts, but lost.[16] To many veteran newsmen and party leaders the convention-approved apportionment formula closely resembled the 1972 apportionment plan that had been declared unconstitutional by a federal district judge as a violation of the "one-man, one-vote" rule in April 1972. GOP delegates from the large urban states that frequently go Democratic in the presidential race wanted a bonus system that gave a comparable reward for electing Republican congressional and state officeholders, even if the state were carried by a Democratic presidential candidate. Under the 1972 GOP plan adopted, the eight most populous states that cast 52 percent of the 1968 vote for Mr. Nixon received only 37 percent of the delegates at the 1972 convention.

If the liberal, big-state delegate plan had been adopted, the New York delegation would have been increased from 88 delegates to 168 and the California delegation enlarged from 96 to 164. The small and medium-sized states of the South and West would have received only small gains or none at all. No wonder the delegates from the big, industrial states who traditionally favor more liberal Republican presidential candidates were downcast after their substitute apportionment plan was rejected. In any case, the newly approved delegate apportionment plan increased the size of the 1976 GOP convention to approximately 2,200 delegates. Instead of maintaining a convention of manageable size (1,348 delegates in 1972), the Republicans started moving in the direction of the Democrats in converting their conventions into mass rallies. As one big state party leader put it, "More delegates mean more people involved in party activity, thereby attracting young voters and blacks and other minorities to the party cause."

Regular Mid-Term Conventions

Mid-term national conventions were first recommended by the American Political Science Association's Committee on Political Parties in 1950. Dominated by advocates of "responsible parties," the Committee majority insisted that unless some meeting of the entire party was held more frequently than every four years, policy would come to be dominated by the legislative leaders on Capitol Hill who have not always been representative of the party's total national constituency. To strengthen the parties and make them more accountable to the electorate, the Committee recommended that the national conventions meet at least biennially , *"with easy provision for special meetings."*[17] In the words of another biennial convention advocate, "A mid-term convention would allow the other elements of the party to bring their strength to bear, while also providing a means of revitalizing the national organization."[18] Within the out-of-power party a mid-term convention, it has been argued, would give the party a special opportunity to publicize itself and its leadership. For these reasons, as well as those delineated below, it is recommended that both major parties hold mid-term conventions early during the off-year election campaign, that is, 1986, 1990, and so on.

As originally proposed by the political scientist task force, the mid-term convention would be held along the lines of a regular convention at which an incumbent President is to be renominated. The President would be received at the convention as the head of his party, responsible in conjunction with congressional leaders, in directing the off-year campaign for control of Congress. Indeed, the mid-term convention would serve to dramatize the party's campaign to increase its congressional representation, which typically falls off for the in-power party in the off-year election. The mid-term convention would also adopt an updated platform. For the party-out-of-power—the mid-term convention, as originally conceived, would be even more important because it could serve as an important stepping-stone for recapturing the White House. Though the question of party leadership might be in doubt (because the defeated presidential candidate from the last election is not often viewed as the real titular leader of the party), the mid-term convention would serve as a vitally important campaign rally kick-off for the off-year elections as well as pointing the party toward the next presidential election.[19]

Platform issues would be a major item on the mid-term agenda. The mid-term document would help dramatize the differences between the parties and give the American people a fresh opportunity to reassess the out-of-power party's goals, as contrasted with those of the incumbent party. More than two decades ago, the authors of a major study on national conventions concluded, "a mid-term out-party convention could do much to refurbish the party image, put into perspective the relationships between the leaders of the presidential and congressional wings of the party, and tighten up the party organization for the mid-term battle."[20] In actual operation, however, the three Democratic mid-term conventions held thus far have not lived up to the expectations of their original sponsors, as we shall explain in a moment.

Twenty-two years after the Committee on Political Parties proposed that parties hold mid-term conventions, the Democrats decided at their 1972 national convention in Miami Beach to convene their first "mid-term conference" or "mini-convention" in 1974 to approve a new party charter. Originally, a party charter draft was to be presented to the 1972 Democratic convention in Miami Beach for ratification. However, intense opposition from Capitol Hill, trade union leaders, and their allies persuaded the McGovern leadership, in a last-minute goodwill gesture toward party unity, to withdraw the charter from the convention agenda.[21] Subsequently, Democratic National Chairman Jean Westwood appointed former North Carolina Governor Terry Sanford to head a special 165-member Charter Commission to redraft a new party document for consideration at the 1974 mid-term convention.

The original charter drafted in 1972 by party reformers, led by Congressman Donald M. Fraser of Minnesota, co-chairperson of the McGovern-Fraser Reform Commission, had proposed a total restructuring of the party and its national committee along the lines of European parties. The charter draft called for a mid-term National Policy Conference of approximately 3,900 delegates which should "consider and determine party policy and program" independent of the party's elected officials in Congress. The new national committee would be expanded from 110 members to 334, with vastly broadened authority. Between the national committee's infrequent sessions a new National Executive Committee would be established to be responsible for policy and programs. On top of this structure would be the party's national chairman, elected for four years, in mid-term of the Presidency, by all 3,900 delegates to the Policy Conference. As envisaged by the reformers, the party's national chairman would—at least on paper—enjoy prestige equal to that of the party's national presidential candidate. Furthermore, only dues-paying party "members" would be allowed to participate in the selection of members for the National Policy Conference or other party-related activities.[22] But the Sanford Charter Commission draft was a pale carbon copy of Fraser's bold charter draft. Gone were the proposals for party memberships "by periodic personal enrollment," national and regional policy conferences, and a strengthened national committee. (Unlike the Democrats, the GOP has never seriously entertained the idea of holding any mid-term conventions.)

The popular term, "mini-convention," is not entirely accurate, for over 2,038 delegates and 435 alternates attended the 1974 Democratic mid-term convention in Kansas City—more delegates than attended national conventions of either the Democratic or Republican party prior to 1960.[23] The second Democratic mini-convention, held in Memphis in December 1978, was almost as large—1,633 delegates. But the Democratic National Committee scaled down considerably the number of delegates attending the third Democratic mid-term gathering, held in Philadelphia in June 1982. Only 921 delegates—mostly party professionals and elected officials—participated in the Democratic parley in the Quaker City.

How successful have these mid-term conventions been in serving the interests of the Democratic party? In the vivid prose of the *Washington Post*, "The Democratic party's mid-term convention in Kansas City seemed less like a modern political convention than like one of the great church councils of the fourth century" given over to "heresies, doctrinal quarrels, seemingly endless disputes over the meaning of small words, and laborious effort to codify the rules for its communicants."[24] But the record was more impressive than the *Post* editorial implied.

Significantly, the Democratic mini-convention approved its first party Charter. Drafted by the Sanford Commission, the Charter represented the first time in the 145-year history of the Democratic party that it has set forth its basic organization and rules in a formal constitution. This basic working document included sections governing delegate selection processes to national conventions (including proportional representation), stipulated closed primaries, banned the unit rule, established a judicial council to review state delegate selection plans and challenges to these plans, and laid down affirmative action guidelines. The Charter reaffirmed the preeminent status of the national convention as the party's governing body, with an expanded national committee (350 members) exercising power between conventions.[25]

Mini-convention delegates (with the exception of organized labor and its allies) left Kansas City satisfied that they had patched over the deep party rifts left over from the disastrous 1972 McGovern presidential campaign. As columnist David S. Broder put it, "the party proved capable of successfully brokering its most critical internal conflicts in an assemblage of almost 2,000 people representative of the diversity of its constituencies."[26] The party faithful seemed reasonably confident, too, that Democrats could look forward to the 1976 presidential election with a sense of unity and hope for victory. After eight years in exile the Democrats did in fact regain the White House in 1976.

While the first Democratic mini-convention was generally adjudged a success, National Democratic Chairperson Robert Strauss was not an ardent promoter of the mid-term parley; indeed, he regarded it as an expensive nuisance. Strauss shared the concern of Congressional Democrats that they might have to run on a campaign platform hammered out by a non-elected party council. Also, Strauss and the Democratic leaders jointly feared that the 1974 mid-term convention might be a repeat performance of the far-left controlled 1972 Democratic convention, which led to the McGovern debacle in November. Though the 1972 Democratic National Convention resolution stipulated that the party shall, prior to April 1974, issue a call for a conference on "Democratic Party Organization and Policy" to be held in 1974, it did not set a specific date. To avoid any replica of 1972, Strauss therefore chose to schedule the 1974 mid-term conference *after*, not before, the 1974 mid-term congressional elections. Furthermore, Strauss persuaded the Democratic National Committee (DNC) to draw up an agenda that specified that no votes would be taken on anything but the newly drafted Democratic Charter. Requests from California, Texas, and Pennsylvania delegations to open up the convention to votes on such major issues as tax reform, economic policy, and national health insurance were turned down by the Committee on Amendments and the Rules—the DNC-appointed control committee.[27] Instead,

Chairman Strauss and company turned the mid-term convention into a campaign rally, not an issues conference.

High Democratic officials, especially Strauss, had another reason to deplore mid-term conventions: the high price tag. The 1974 Kansas City mid-term convention cost the Democratic party an estimated $685,000—money that could have been diverted in September and October to help win additional congressional seats or to retire the party's long-standing $4 million debt left over from the ill-fated 1968 Presidential election campaign.[28] These scarce funds could also have been used, officials pointed out, to gear up the Democratic National Committee's staff for the 1976 presidential race. Because midterm conventions, unlike the quadrennial national conventions, do not attract the high-level national television coverage, high party officials have had far less enthusiasm for the midterm parley than they have for the quadrennial extravaganzas, which may attract as many as 90 million off-and-on viewers.

Unfortunately for the Democrats, the party did not succeed in maintaining control of the White House after the second mid-term conference. They lost the Presidency, as we know, in the 1980 Reagan landslide. The first telltale signs of impending trouble surfaced at the 1978 Memphis mid-term conclave.[29] Before the second Democratic mid-term conference opened, President Carter and his aides were fearful that it might turn out to be a major embarrassment because Carter's budget-cutting policies and his partial abandonment of Democratic social welfare goals had caused general uneasiness among Democratic liberals. As a result of this apprehension, President Carter and his staff mounted a major floor effort by virtually his entire senior White House staff and Cabinet to avoid a repudiation of his policies by delegates, many of them supporters of Senator Edward Kennedy (D.-Mass.). By careful management of the convention rules and agenda the Carter White House averted any major blowups. To protect the incumbent President from political embarrassment, the Democratic National Committee's Executive Committee voted 13 to 7 on a key decision before the convention opened that all resolutions would have to be approved by a majority of all 1,633 elected delegates—and not just a majority of those present and voting. This action made the odds very heavy against there being 817 votes for any of the four mildly dissenting resolutions against the Carter administration that were to be brought up at the Memphis conclave. To deal with any emergencies at the mini-convention, the Carter strategists established an intricate communications system, similar to the one used by the Carter team in New York City during the 1976 Democratic nominating convention. Though some Carter aides worried that a "dump Carter" movement in favor of Senator Ted Kennedy might arise at the mid-term parley, none developed. But Senator Kennedy did steal the spotlight away from President Carter with a rousing speech on national health insurance and a demand for a full-employment policy. President Carter's address to the convention, in contrast, received only tepid applause.

On the basis of three mid-term conventions held thus far, two conclusions stand out: first, elected officeholders—the President, Senators, and U.S. Representatives—still remain largely immune from or above party policy as formulated by a non-elected party council; and second, Michels' "iron law of oligarchy" is still the order of the day. Early in the twentieth century, Robert Michels, the Swiss sociologist, concluded that in any large organization two castes develop—the oligarchic elite who govern and the masses who are governed.[30] James Madison, one of the Founding Fathers, long ago commented on the same phenomenon in the fifty-eighth *Federalist*, remarking "that in all legislative assemblies the greater the number composing them may be, the fewer will be the men who will in fact direct their proceedings."[31] At all three midterm conventions—Kansas City, Memphis, and Philadelphia—those in power controlled the agenda and all major political decisions and blocked all moves by rank-and-file members that threatened their power base.

Tentatively, it might be concluded that mid-term conferences are better suited when the party is out of power, when the delegates and potential contenders can train their heavy artillery on the opposition party in the White House. While it's still a little early to make a definitive judgment on this point, many party activists feel that it's easier to mount a campaign offensive against an incumbent Administration at these midterm conclaves than to hunker down in defensive fortifications to protect the White House incumbent.

Most presidential contenders in the out-of-power party have discovered that the party's mid-term conference can serve as an excellent launching pad for mounting their presidential drives. Indeed, one veteran political reporter at the 1974 Kansas City mini-convention presciently noted, "One of the big winners in Kansas City was clearly Governor Jimmy Carter of Georgia, whose candidacy had been taken seriously by few politicians before he arrived here. In appearances before more than a dozen state caucuses he performed impressively, especially with such liberal states as Colorado, Wisconsin, and New York, which would not normally be considered fertile turf for a Southerner."[32] Early apprehension that a mid-term convention would exacerbate presidential candidate rivalries and turn the conclave into a party battleground two years before the next national convention was not borne out by experience in Kansas City. Although a flock of presidential candidates—Carter, Jackson, Bentsen, Harris, Wallace, and Udall—held open houses at the midterm convention to promote their announced or soon-to-be-announced candidacies, no serious evidence of hostility or ill-will toward one another surfaced at the parley. Indeed, the abundance of presidential contenders, all vying for the support of the delegates and the attention of the national media, reminded some observers more of a round-robin national basketball tournament than a political elimination contest.

More recently, the 1982 Philadelphia midterm convention also, in the words of one reporter, "turned out to be a beauty pageant of potential presidential candidates."[33] Speeches by six unannounced Democratic presidential hopefuls, led by the defeated 1980 aspirant Senator Edward Kennedy and former Vice President Walter F. Mondale, highlighted the three-day parley. Conference planners, however, who hoped to attract heavy television network coverage of the Philadelphia conference were sadly disappointed. The unexpected resignation of Secretary of State Alexander Haig on the opening day of the party festivities pushed the conference off the evening network television news programs. Then, the closing day of the midterm conference saw the Columbia space shuttle launching preempt heavy network coverage of the final session of the parley.

Unlike the 1978 Memphis conference which was punctuated by frequent criticism of their own incumbent President Jimmy Carter, the 1982 three-day national conference resembled a Democratic love feast. The high-spirited delegates, or the remnants of the original 897 remaining through the final speeches, accepted without debate or dissent a long list of party policy positions. Some party leaders viewed these policy statements as a form of midterm party platform of a type never before devised or used in American politics. This party document was expected to be used to help the party in the 1982 congressional elections.

While the midterm convention offers presidential contenders of the out-of-power party the opportunity to "showcase" their candidacies and a field day for assailing the Republican White House incumbent, the "party-in-the-government" wing of the party—the congressmen and U.S. senators who are responsible for legislating under the separation of powers system—are not warm admirers of mid-term conventions. The remarks of the late Senator Thomas Dodd (D.-Conn.) who spoke out in 1960 against the idea of making a party platform binding on the party's elected officials may be extreme, but they personified the views of many Capitol Hill veterans toward party platforms, and they are just as applicable to midterm conventions. He declared the "concept that a convention platform is binding on the elected representative in the Congress is absolutely inimical to our system of government." Continuing his argument, Dodd asserted that it would be "'the worst betrayal of trust' for a President and Congress. . . to subordinate the four-year deliberative process between the White House and Congress to the four-day drafting process of non-elected members of a party platform committee."[34]

Midterm convention critics on Capitol Hill expressed pleasure with the recent action of the Democratic National Committee to reassert the role of party leaders at the 1982 midterm conference. To achieve greater party official participation, the Democratic National Committee (DNC) in June 1981 voted to shrink the size of the 1982 midterm conference by almost half and allocate most of the seats to elected and party officials.[35] Under the revised DNC plan, the 1982 midterm conclave consisted of about 900 delegates—369 of them the Democratic National Committee members, an equal number to be chosen by state party committees, and 100 to be named by the Democratic National Chairman with the approval of the party executive committee. All Democratic governors, 24 House members, and eight senators were invited. In overturning a resolution passed by the 1980 Democratic National Convention that called for two-thirds of the midterm convention delegates to be chosen by grass-roots Democrats, the DNC action reflected a major shift in attitudes and procedures away from the open, participatory politics of the 1970's. One frustrated party reformer declared beforehand that the newly "downsized" midterm convention will be "no more than an enlarged meeting of the Democratic National Committee."[36] Another critic declared "It's like getting elected to Boy's State."[37] By reducing the size of the 1982 conference and restructuring the framework to limit most of the 900 delegates to party professionals and elected officials (unlike the popularly elected delegates who dominated the 1978 mini-convention in Memphis), the Democratic National Committee also persuaded congressional leaders that the pre-election conference would not be a crippling embarrassment. "Democratic members of Congress," as one former party official observed, "don't want an irresponsible set of resolutions that could be used against them in November."[38]

Nor are incumbent Presidents likely to be ardent supporters of midterm conventions, though in this era of "open politics" presidents would probably be reluctant to state this view publicly. The threat of potential embarrassment to an incumbent President in the form of anti-Administration resolutions or even open challenges to his renomination are ever-present, whether they surface or not. Mid-term conventions are, of course, risky business for presidential incumbents, since they invite in-party criticism of the president in full public view. But as Thomas E. Cronin has observed:

. . . an incumbent president who comes to listen and learn as he meets for a few days with several thousand party regulars and activists is a president who avoids that great temptation for presidents—to become isolated. Further, he gets a chance to see and hear the intensity of concern over contemporary issues. He must hear also about whether or not he is handling the job of president in an appropriate manner. There is much to be said for this mid-term party audit—an audit of the president as well as of party policy positions.[39]

In the years ahead this tension between the party-in-the-government on one side and party activists on the other, over the desirability and viability of mid-term conventions can be expected to persist. Critics have likened national mid-term conventions, which have no responsibility for picking presidential candidates, to playing tennis without a net. Another veteran party-watcher has commented, "If there is a weakness in the mid-term conference, it is the magnifying of minor differences, a preoccupation with verbal distinctions to fill the gap left by the absence of a party convention's usual and all-consuming concern—the nomination of a President."[40]

Still, the experience of three Democratic mid-term conventions held thus far shows that, although they have not lived up to their full potential, they are more than "half-time pep rallies." Mid-term conventions will continue to afford a valuable opportunity to a major party, especially when it is the out-of-power party, to revitalize its national organization. The national convention—the supreme governing body of the national party—meets only four days out of every 1,460 days. Regular mid-term conventions offer the parties a variety of opportunities: to dramatize and contrast issue differences with the opposition party; assess the incumbent party's presidential stewardship at the half-way mark; update the party platform; "showcase" future presidential contenders; strengthen the party for the upcoming congressional elections; and perform the valuable role of educating the American public about the importance of issue and party choice. To expect all of this to happen in the near future is, indeed, a big order. Twenty-four years elapsed, however, before the mid-term convention proposal, first suggested in 1950, became a reality. In light of recent Supreme Court decisions upholding the paramount right of national committees to govern the selection process for picking delegates to national conventions, an enhanced role for mid-term conventions in our political system, even within the Republican party, may not be as utopian as it sounds in this era of drastic social change.

Will there be future midterm conventions? While speculation about future political history is always hazardous, the future of the Democratic midterm convention may well hinge on the party's performance in the next presidential election. The midterm conference may survive into 1986 and beyond if the Democrats are still out of the White House and need a rallying mechanism for focusing attention on the performance of the Republican occupant. But if a Democrat wins the presidency in 1984, memories of President Carter's unhappy experience with the Memphis conference may lead party chieftains to scrap it. Republicans, it might be added, still remain cool to the idea of a midterm conference.

Proposed "Dual Delegate" System

As a result of the Democratic delegate selection "reforms" since 1968, convention delegates have been bound in a way not generally understood by the general public. The delegates have, in effect, become vassals to the presidential candidate and his campaign organization. Delegates, for example, have not only been pledged to vote for a certain candidate (for at least one ballot), but the presidential contender has also been given the prerogative to select the persons who serve as delegates in his behalf. Moreover, the candidate has enjoyed the right to unseat a disloyal delegate who attempts to stray from the fold. Within the GOP presidential candidates have almost the same control over selection and approval of delegates. Indeed, the actual selection of delegates is done by the candidate, his managers, or his designated state party leader. Termed the "new bossism," one recent bipartisan presidential nominating panel meeting at Duke University has asserted:

The delegates are left without any responsibility or authority to speak for the interests of anyone but the candidate. They are handpicked by the candidates to go to the convention and cast their automatic votes the exact way the candidates dictate. In short, the delegates have been reduced to little more than pawns of the candidates. . . .[41]

To defeat the old bosses, the task force reports, "the parties have put into effect rules elevating 'candidate bosses' to new heights of autocratic power."[42]

Most recently, the Democratic convention's 1980 binding delegate rule, originally adopted at the behest of President Jimmy Carter's supporters on the Winograd Commission and the Democratic National Committee, transformed convention delegates essentially into instructed agents or messengers from the primary or caucus-convention states. But as party veterans readily understood, the binding delegate rule injected rigidity into national conventions and reduced the possibility of compromise on candidates and party platforms. Indeed, without a substantial number of uncommitted delegates, the national convention lacks a basic ingredient to facilitate convention "brokering" negotiations if a deadlock should develop. In recent years the spread of binding primaries has threatened to make uncommitted delegates almost an endangered species in the Democratic party— that is, until the Hunt Commission in early 1982 persuaded the Democratic National Committee to mandate that 14 percent of all delegates to the 1984 Democratic convention should be set aside for "uncommitted" elected officials selected by members of Congress and state Democratic committees. Democratic party professionals on the Hunt Commission, after an unfortunate experience with President Jimmy Carter's inept political leadership and his subsequent loss at the polls in 1980, concluded that the national convention should include a sizeable bloc of uncommitted elected officeholders and party professionals. Popularly termed "super delegates," these officials will provide the convention decision-making process with a special group of party veterans familiar with the strengths and weaknesses of the various presidential contenders to help balance off popularly elected delegates who are often less concerned about how a successful presidential candidate can work with Congress and provide strong executive leadership. To a limited degree, this proposed reform will force a presidential contender to seek the support of the same party leaders he will later have to rely on if he gains the Presidency.

Though the binding primaries have also made it harder for Republicans to remain uncommitted, GOP delegates still have more latitude in some states than their Democratic counterparts. Blind primaries (primaries in which delegates are permitted to run uncommitted) are still used, for example, by the Republicans in big states like Illinois, New York, and Pennsylvania. But puzzled Republican voters in the 1980 presidential primaries who wanted to vote for delegates supporting Reagan, Bush, or Anderson and could not figure out how to vote for their favorite candidate have objected to the blind primary ballot. Consequently, Republican voters in some of these states can be expected in the future to insist on the same right Democrats have to decide how the delegates they support will vote at the convention. Illinois Republicans, reacting to voter displeasure, decided to abandon their blind primary soon after the 1980 election.[43] Should this abandonment of uncommitted delegates spread to the other big states, one team of party experts from CBS News recently commented, "It will matter just as little at Republican conventions as it did at the last Democratic convention just who or what the delegates may be. On the main job they are sent there to do, it will only matter which candidate's collar they wear."[44]

To provide greater input from party professionals and elected officeholders in the presidential nominating process, it is recommended that one of several proposals recently advanced to reserve approximately one-third of the national convention delegate seats for these officials be adopted by both major parties.[45] For convenience sake, this plan will be termed the "dual-delegate" system. The Democratic National Committee made one small step in this direction prior to the 1976 Democratic convention. The Mikulski Commission—the second Democratic party reform task force—recommended that the 25 percent at-large portion of a state's delegation be reserved, if necessary, to provide for adequate representation of women, blacks, and young people as well as for the inclusion of party and public officials. But the 1976 "set-aside" for public and party officials was largely negated by the requirement that they be committed to candidates in the same proportion as other delegates. Important public and party officials were mostly unwilling to serve on this basis. Consequently, most of the delegate spots went to minor public and party officials, and they had no visible influence at the convention.[46] After the 1976 convention the third Democratic reform task force— the Winograd Commission—essentially retained the Mikulski Commission's requirement but added a rule that ten percent of the national delegate seats in each state be reserved for party and elected officials.[47]

Under the proposed dual-delegate plan presidential contenders could seek as many pledged delegates as at present in presidential primaries and state conventions— but only from among the 67 percent of the total convention delegate allocation given to each state, whether it used the primary or caucus-convention system. (Delegate allocations to the states have always been handled by the party's national committee.) If any presidential contender could, by prodigious work in the primaries and caucus-convention states, put together a pre-convention majority, there would be scarcely a doubt about his or her appeal and electability; indeed, his right to the nomination would be virtually unassailable.

In most election years the more likely scenario, however, would find some candidate arriving at the convention with a plurality (not a majority) lead over his intra-party rivals. At this point the nominally unpledged bloc of 33 percent of the delegates, including a sizeable bloc of U.S. Representatives and Senators, would then become a major factor in the ultimate convention choice. These uncommitted delegates would hold the balance of power. If the front-running candidate had close to a majority of delegates, the uncommitted bloc would most likely give their stamp of approval promptly to the primary winner. However, if the candidate field were bunched fairly closely, or if two or three candidates were clearly ahead of the pack, the uncommitted bloc could become the convention decision-makers. As in yesteryear, they could be free to shift their support to the candidate that, in their judgment, most closely matched the party prescription for a winning presidential nominee and, if elected, a successful chief executive. Once again, party leaders and legislators would become a major voice in the choice of the nominee, even if two-thirds of the convention delegates were chosen by the rank-and-file voters in the primary states.

While it's difficult to speculate on how this dual-delegate system would operate in real life, one of its most attractive features would appear to be the flexibility it would inject into the nominating process. First of all, part of the delegate selection would once again become a *party* function, rather than a *candidate* function.[48] The bloc of uncommitted delegates could exercise their own judgment in helping to pick the best-qualified candidate for the nomination and to develop a party platform capable of building a winning electoral coalition. This proposal will help the convention once again to become a nominating institution instead of a ceremonial ratification assembly. The dual-delegate system should help check the "new candidate bossism" that has emerged from the election of a large number of pledged delegates originally recruited by the presidential candidate's campaign organization. No longer will the candidate organizations be able to dictate to all of their delegates on how they shall vote on every convention issue. Reducing the number of iron-clad pledged delegates should help prevent conventions from turning into warring candidate camps, such as occurred between the Ford and Reagan forces at the 1976 GOP convention and between the Carter and Kennedy partisans at the 1980 Democratic conclave. Even more important, conventions could once again operate basically as deliberative bodies rather than ratifying assemblies. Uncommitted delegates might be less prone to join bandwagon movements until they had had one final opportunity at the national convention to look over the field. With a larger percentage of veteran federal and state officeholders serving as convention delegates, it is more likely that a nominee would be selected who knows more about being president than just how to win primaries. Furthermore, the presidential nominating process would be more closely tied to the governing process and the political alliances forged during convention negotiations would solidify future working relationships, if the nominee went on to the White House.

Under the dual-delegate system the powerful role of the national media in building up or ignoring candidates would be diluted. The uncommitted delegates, made up of party officials and elected officeholders vested with the heavy responsibility of picking a nominee who has demonstrated or exhibited a willingness to work with congressional leaders of his party, would probably be less susceptible to media influence than rank-and-file voters. (Recent survey data, unlike the early 1940 studies, show that these voters obtain most of their information on presidential candidates from the mass media, not party officials or elective officeholders.)

Best of all, the convention could perform its traditional function of facilitating compromise and fostering consensus. Under the proposed dual-delegate system neither the primary front-runner nor his party competitors nor the public could confidently predict the outcome of the convention midway or earlier in the primary season, such as had happened in 1976 and 1980 in the out-of-power party. No longer would voters in the late-season primaries, especially in the West, feel that the verdict on the nominee had already been made by the primary voters in the early Eastern primary states and, therefore, no point would be served by going to the polls.

The dual-delegate system would not only help counterbalance the disproportionate influence of early primary victories but also the special advantage that federally imposed spending ceilings for all candidates who accept federal subsidies give to the early winners—all magnified by network television. Most party experts believe that the television networks and the national press exert their greatest influence upon the presidential nominating process before the formal selection process begins or in the first month of the primary season. According to these observers, the media have largely displaced the party in winnowing out the presidential candidates who prove to be poor organizers, poor vote-getters, and weak fund-raisers.

Under the present system the media, in effect, "decide" rather early in the race which candidates move into what John Anderson calls the "charmed circle of viable contenders." The dual-delegate plan would help neutralize the powerful impact of the media upon early round candidate performance and give the slow starters a better shot at the nomination. While it is highly unlikely that all 33 percent of the uncommitted delegates would vote as a single bloc, these uncommitted members could concentrate on assessing and pinpointing candidates who possess the ability not only to get elected, but also demonstrate, on the basis of long elective office experience, the talent to govern effectively by working closely with Congress, if elected. Under this proposed dual-delegate system, it seems doubtful that former one-term Georgia Governor Jimmy Carter, a candidate with no experience in foreign affairs or any national administrative or legislative experience, would have attracted the support of this uncommitted bloc in the Democratic party. Nor is it certain that former California Governor Ronald Reagan, a twice-rejected candidate for the nomination who lacked experience in foreign affairs or dealing with Congress, would have been the first choice of these uncommitted GOP delegates.

With the dual-delegate system in operation well-qualified candidates who failed to do well in the early primaries, for example, Senator Edmund Muskie (D.-Maine) in 1972, Senator Henry Jackson (D.-Wash.) in 1976, and Senator Howard Baker (R.-Tenn.) in 1980, might have been encouraged to stay in the race to the finish because the large bloc of uncommitted delegates would be such an attractive prize that few aspirants could resist seeking it—even if it proved ultimately to be out of reach. Under the proposed plan former President Ford, too, might have also decided in 1980 to toss his hat into the ring again. Ford, it will be recalled, could not make up his mind in late February and early March 1980 about seeking another White House term until Ronald Reagan had captured the New Hampshire and several Southern primaries—and then Ford concluded that it was too late to halt the Reagan bandwagon. Unfortunately, the present system with its disproportionate influence of New Hampshire and the other early primaries discourages would-be candidates or first-round losers, no matter how well qualified they may be, to make a full-scale run for the presidency. If these candidates knew that one-third of the entire conventions' delegates remained officially uncommitted, they might be inclined to enter earlier and to remain in the race until decision time at the convention.

Recent reforms in the presidential selection process, it seems clear, have separated nominating politics from electing politics. As Austin Ranney commented recently in a panel discussion, "The process of building the coalition needed to win the nomination is now completely separated from the process of building the quite different coalition needed to govern effectively."[49] To win the presidential nomination in this plebiscitarian era a candidate must be able to appeal to party rank-and-filers who, of course, do not hold responsible government positions or commitments to special interest groups. Skills required to be an effective president require that he be able to negotiate with congressional leaders and committee chairpersons; moreover, he must know how to deal with regulatory agencies and a variety of business and trade union leaders.[50] Equally important, he must be able to surround himself with first-rate advisers. Under the present system, national and state elected officeholders play virtually no role in selecting the party's presidential nominee. But who is better qualified in assessing the strengths and weaknesses of presidential aspirants—especially the ability to make good appointments and sound decisions and to win the cooperation of Congress—than fellow national-state politicians? The average primary voter watching a presidential contender on the television screen is not likely to possess this type of information. Thus, the dual-delegate plan would reinject a form of "peer review" into the nominating system that has been missing so glaringly in the current reform era.[51]

Elected officeholders, especially on the national level, could once again help serve as a screening device or filter between the political party and the mass electorate in weeding out unqualified, but sometimes superficially attractive, presidential contenders. To provide the maximum level of "peer review," Jeane J. Kirkpatrick (most recently the U.S. Ambassador to the United Nations) has proposed that Congress by national legislation provide that the national nominating conventions of each party shall consist entirely of its public officials and party leaders—its congressmen, senators, governors, state party chairs and co-chairs, mayors of major cities, and possibly members of the national committees. Under Kirkpatrick's "closed" nominating system presidential primaries would be banned.[52] While it might be pointed out, as Kirkpatrick and others have noted, that a number of countries universally recognized as democratic, for example, Great Britain, West Germany, and Sweden, all have closed nominating systems, it seems highly doubtful in this era of participatory democracy in America that the Kirkpatrick proposal will be given serious consideration.

In view of the recent (1981) Supreme Court decision in the Wisconsin "open" primary case upholding the national party's paramount authority to regulate the national convention delegate selection process, there is no legal reason why a national party cannot begin openly to encourage states to abandon primaries and even, if necessary, place a ceiling on the percentage of delegates chosen by this means.[53]

Shortly after the Democratic loss of the White House in 1980, Senator Alan Cranston (D.-Calif.), Assistant Minority Leader, proposed another type of "mixed" nominating system for selecting national convention delegates to increase the party's voice in the process. Under the Cranston plan the fifty states and the

District of Columbia would be divided into three groups of 17 each, with each group having approximately the same number of convention delegates. The Canal Zone, Guam, Puerto Rico, the Virgin Islands, and Democrats Abroad would also be worked into the formula in an equitable way.

In the Cranston plan one group of 17 states would have binding primaries, like California's. The second group of states would select delegates through various grass-roots precinct or neighborhood meeting systems. The third group of states would select delegates using the official party structure. For this third group, several variations could be used—some delegates elected by central committees and others chosen by party conventions or caucuses. Under the Cranston plan only delegates from the first group—those with binding primaries—would be legally bound. The remaining two-thirds of the delegates would be free to make up their own minds—or to change their minds—after they arrive at the national convention.[54] Since at least one-third of the delegates would have come through the party-directed selection process, the party's role at the convention would be substantially restored.

The Cranston plan also provides that each of these groups of states would rotate their delegate selection process from one election to the next. Thus, for example, states using the primary system would, four years later, use the grass roots meeting system and then, four years after that, the party structure process. Senator Cranston argues that with this system of balanced delegate selection, national conventions would have a far greater potential for selecting the best available candidate for President and for uniting the party and all its constituencies behind the nominee.

Since the authority of the party's national committee to control the nominating procedures for President, even if the national party rules conflict with state laws, has now been upheld by the highest court in the land, the Cranston plan could be implemented—though it is unlikely to happen. The Cranston plan, while attractive on paper, does violence to so many in-state traditions that its chances of passage are nil. The idea of a rotation system, by which each state would use a different system in each of three successive presidential election years, seems especially unlikely to sell. Undoubtedly, the howls of protest from states, such as Iowa and New Hampshire, which would see their first-round caucus and presidential primary threatened, coupled with complaints from other states using their traditional methods of selecting delegates, would pose mountainous obstacles to the implementation of the Cranston plan. But the Cranston plan does open the dialogue on convention reform. Clearly, it is incumbent upon national committees, congressional and state legislative leaders, and party professionals who study various reform proposals to grope and search until they find a more viable solution to the enormously complex presidential nominating system.

The Road Ahead

National conventions have survived two waves of reform in the twentieth century—the drive to obtain popular control of political parties in the Progressive era before World War I and the post-1968 Democratic party reforms aimed at creating greater intraparty democracy and the streamlining of convention processes. But recent national conventions, especially in the wake of the rapid proliferation of presidential primaries, have seen their deliberative function eroded by the steady influx of mandated delegates whose basic fidelity is to a specific presidential candidate, not the welfare and future of the party.

Paul David and his associates, in their definitive work on national conventions two decades ago, concluded that at the 1952 conventions only 14 percent of the Democratic delegates and 11 percent of the Republican delegates were "firmly bound" to a leading candidate (Eisenhower or Taft). Approximately 15 percent of the Democratic and 11 percent of the Republican delegates were committed to nonleading candidates.[55] Almost twenty years later, James W. Ceaser estimated that 62 percent of the Democratic delegates and 56 percent of the Republican delegates to the 1976 conventions were elected "with national candidate orientation."[56] In 1980, over 90 percent of the Republican delegates, it has been calculated, were committed either to Ronald Reagan or George Bush, and within the Democratic party over 99 percent of the delegates were committed to either President Carter or Senator Edward M. Kennedy.[57] In the words of national columnist David S. Broder, "...delegates in the reformed convention are no longer representatives. In this system they are not chosen for their judgment, experience, or wisdom. They are picked by the candidates as being the most loyal or subservient to discipline among those available from the appropriate demographic groups. A convention with such delegates is not—and cannot be—a political body, let alone a reflective assembly."[58]

Unless this accelerated trend toward total delegate commitment to a presidential candidate is reversed (the Democratic delegate selection rules for 1984 seem to have halted—or at least slowed down—this trend), national conventions may become little more than ceremonial bodies devoted to ratifying the popular choice of the presidential primary race. Indeed, the atrophy of the national convention's deliberative function would be virtually complete and the quadrennial conclave would be transformed into a second Electoral College. If this happened, the convention's duties would be confined merely to giving a formal stamp of approval to the party nominee, chosen, in effect, during the spring primary season. One veteran political scientist has lamented that the Democratic party reforms have made "the convention members not decision-makers but recorders of decision made in other forums."[59]

Will national conventions become obsolescent as decision-making agencies and be transformed into mere ratification assemblies for decisions that have effectively been made elsewhere? Before the obituary is written for the national convention, one should review the possible future impact that the U.S. Supreme Court's recent decision on the dispute between the Democratic National Committee and the State of Wisconsin over the Dairyland State's "open" primary law will have on future national conventions.

The justices, according to one strong advocate of party responsibility, "have signaled to the Democrats that the way is open for them to begin the repair of their own distorted nominating process by curbing the number of delegates chosen in primaries. States may hold primaries according to their own laws, the court said, but the party is obliged to seat delegates only in the manner and number its own rules prescribe."[60]

The far-reaching impact of the Court's decision should, at the very least, strengthen the hand of national party officials who want to cut down drastically on the growing number of presidential primaries and discourage states from jockeying on the timing of early round primaries. According to the Wisconsin open primary case, states can hold primaries as they please. But the national parties now hold the trump card to render them meaningless by refusing to seat the delegates without fear of state or national court challenges.

By its rulings that state and federal courts may not interfere with the process by which political parties choose their presidential candidates, the U.S. Supreme Court has opened the door, especially for the reform-minded Democratic party, to reverse the steady trend toward greater rank-and-file voter participation in the selection of national convention delegates. Parties can now undertake needed reforms, such as requiring that one-third (or a similar fraction or percentage) of all national convention delegate seats in each state be reserved for party leaders, national committee members, and elected officeholders. As indicated earlier, the Democratic National Committee has already taken steps in this direction by reserving 14 percent of the delegate seats to the 1984 Democratic convention for party and elected public officials who would serve as officially "uncommitted" delegates. With clearly established authority now to manage all phases of the presidential nominating process, the national committees can shorten the primary season—or at least shorten the time frame in which national convention delegates are selected. The Democratic National Committee has already decreed that the opening round Iowa precinct caucuses cannot be held until February 27, 1984—five weeks later than in 1980. New Hampshire's first-in-the-nation presidential primary has been pushed back one week to March 6th. This action should help, in a small way, to reduce the scramble of some states, for example, New Hampshire and Massachusetts, to move their presidential primary election dates ever earlier. Under the national committee's reinforced lines of authority, they can now decree that the delegate selection process not begin in January or February without fear of triggering a series of lawsuits from disgruntled states.

These newly established "ground rules" for the 1984 Democratic presidential nominating race were drafted by the party's latest reform panel, the Commission on Presidential Nominations, chosen to gather testimony and make recommendations about improving the party's national convention delegate selection rules. Chaired by Governor James B. Hunt, Jr., of North Carolina, the 69-member task force was appointed by Democratic National Chairman Charles T. Manatt in early July 1981—the fourth Democratic panel chosen since 1969 to reform the rules for nominating a Presidential candidate. (The Republicans also have a 10-member commission, due to report sometime in late 1982, charged with looking into many of the same issues.) The Hunt Commission completed its deliberations in mid-January 1982, and the Democratic National Committee accepted nearly all of its recommendations at its March 1982 meeting, thus putting into effect the delegate selection rules for the 1984 Democratic conclave. The Republicans, unlike the Democrats, already adopted their delegate selection rules for 1984 at the 1980 Detroit GOP National Convention. (Within the Republican party only the GOP national convention has the authority to change the delegate selection rules.) During the Hunt Commission's deliberations, the general feeling among insiders on the commission was that if elected Democrats participated in greater numbers at the 1984 Democratic convention, they would make a more intense effort both to elect the party nominee and to help him govern if elected. Significantly, the Hunt Commission's first public hearing was held in September 1981 in Des Moines, Iowa—capital of the state that holds the first presidential precinct caucuses in mid-winter each quadrennium.[61]

More recently, the AFL-CIO and the Democratic party state chairmen have formally endorsed setting aside 30 percent of the 1984 Democratic convention delegates for elected and party officials. This would mean approximately 1,000 out of the 3,300 delegates (if the Democrats have the same size convention as in 1980) would be party professionals. Also, the House of Representatives Democratic Caucus, through its chairman, Representative Gillis Long of Louisiana, advised the Hunt Commission that House Democrats would participate en masse only if they were allowed to come as uncommitted delegates.[62] Understandably, the Congressmen, all running for reelection in the fall of the presidential election year, did not wish to jeopardize their electoral chances by identifying themselves, in advance, with one contender and against others. If the House members were allowed to come uncommitted, then obviously the governors, mayors, and party officers who would fill the remaining 1,000 reserved delegate seats would demand the same privilege for themselves. The AFL-CIO and the Democratic state chairmen have agreed to allow all Congressional solons to attend as uncommitted delegates.[63] With 1,000 uncommitted delegates on hand, it seems doubtful that any contender could lock up the nomination by sweeping the primaries. In 1980, about 75 percent of the Democratic delegates were committed, directly or indirectly, by the primaries; the remaining 25 percent, mostly committed, came out of the caucuses and conventions. Thus, if 1,000 seats—30 percent—were held by uncommitted delegates, a presidential contender would have to win about nine out of every ten primary delegates to clinch the nomination without any of these uncommitted delegates—a rather tall order. In any event, there appears to be a counterreaction to the Democratic party reform excesses setting in. Members of the Democratic Hunt Commission, among others, appear to be swinging back to the traditional party regular view that elected officials and party officers know more about the various presidential aspirants, their qualifications, and shortcomings than primary election voters.

What does the future hold for national conventions? Unless drastic structural changes are made—which is unlikely—future conventions will probably continue to perform the same valuable functions, in much the same manner as they have since the advent of the age of television. Looking ahead, it seems reasonable to predict that, provided the further spread of presidential primaries is halted, the basic task of national conventions will continue to be to identify and select nominees acceptable to most elements of the party. No other party agency is even a remotely satisfactory substitute for arriving at a reasonable consensus on the party nominee.

Despite several proposals to revamp the vice presidential selection process, national conventions can be expected to continue performing this role, even though it usually means endorsing *pro forma* the presidential nominee's hand-picked choice of running-mate. From time to time, the vice presidential nomination still serves as a valuable consolation prize for a losing faction within the party. Also, by selecting a nationally respected number-two man on the ticket, the convention can help assure the American public that the White House would be in good hands in the event the President-elect were incapacitated or should die in office.

The legitimating function of national nominating conventions has not been weakened with the passage of time. Indeed, next to the selection process itself, the legitimating function is probably the most important function performed by the national conclaves, since it signifies that the party stands behind the nominee and accepts him or her as its legitimate standard-bearer. Since the national convention is the supreme governing body in each of the major parties—and the U.S. Supreme Court by its actions in refusing to substitute the Court's judgment for the Democratic National Convention Credentials Committee in the 1972 credentials challenge litigation over the California delegation has reaffirmed this view—it seems beyond dispute that the legitimating role of national conventions will continue unimpeded.

In the years ahead the national convention will, it seems safe to predict, also continue to perform its mass rally function. With television audiences frequently approaching 90 million viewers both major parties can be expected to continue "showcasing" or advertising their presidential and vice presidential candidates before the American public cost-free. For many of these convention viewers national conclaves offer the first opportunity to assess and "size up" the candidates and their programs. In this sense the national conventions have fulfilled and will continue to perform a valuable educational function that is sometimes overlooked by the critics. Even so, the danger that the decision-making processes of a convention will be subordinated to the demands of the party managers and convention director to put on a mass media extravaganza will continue to be ever present. Free network television time, which can reach, theoretically at least, almost the entire American electorate (approximately 150 million potential voters), poses an almost irresistible temptation to convention managers to concentrate on the mass rally aspect of conventions at the expense of platform-writing, rules changes, and even bargaining over the vice presidential nomination.

Platform-building is unlikely to be discontinued at national conventions in the foreseeable future. Widespread discussion and negotiation undertaken before final convention endorsement of the party document affords a golden opportunity to the various party constituencies and special interest groups to be heard and "paid attention to." The platform continues to be a valuable campaign document, and, as indicated earlier, it belongs to the party, not the presidential candidate. Platforms will continue to serve as a type of road map indicating to party faithful and the burgeoning number of political independents—approximately one-third of the electorate—what course of action the presidential nominee and the party would like to take, if successful, in November.

Unlike the reform-oriented Progressive era dominated by liberal Republicans, the impetus for reform of the presidential nominating process in recent years has come—and probably will continue to come—mostly from the Democratic party. While the Republican convention has done some tinkering with its delegate selection rules, notably improving affirmative action guidelines, the prevailing attitude of the Republican National Committee and its recent national chairmen has been mostly adherence to the maxim, "If it works, why fix it?" And an outside observer assessing the overall results of Republican presidential nominations for the past three decades would probably not quarrel with the prevailing Republican view that we should not tamper unnecessarily with our presidential recruitment procedures. After all, the Republicans have controlled the White House for 20 years out of the past 32 years, or five out of the last eight presidential terms, without any major overhaul of their presidential selection machinery.[64]

Charles Longley, a leading authority on national party organizations, has offered several reasons why the Republicans have not moved very far along the road to reform. First of all, he points to "political" barriers which include the existing formulas favoring small states in both the national convention and the Republican National Committee, plus the view of many GOP National Committee members that the national party is merely an association of state parties. Secondly, Longley has identified several "structural" barriers consisting of a four-stage gauntlet which reform has to run, starting with the Republican National Committee's Rules Committee, the full GOP National Committee, the Rules Committee of the national convention, and finally, the full convention. Three of these stages Longley has described as "structurally biased to advantage those areas traditionally wary of tinkering with the rules of the game."[65] On the GOP convention rules, credentials, and platform committees, for example, all states have equal voting power—"just like the U.S. Senate." Since a gag rule at Republican conventions requires that a measure must have 25 percent minority support on a committee to be reported onto the floor, reform proposals seldom see the light of day. The ten largest states combined, with a majority of the U.S. population and just under a majority of the Electoral College vote, cannot muster even 20 percent of the vote of a GOP convention committee, while the thirteen most sparsely populated states of the Plains and the Rocky Mountains, with a combined population of about three-quarters that of New York state, seldom have trouble marshalling decisive voting strength at GOP conventions.[66]

Final Defense of the National Nominating Convention

In the opening chapter, the national nominating convention received a warm endorsement because of its manifold advantages: it provides a diversity of representation among all constituencies within the party; it possesses a remarkable degree of flexibility to reconcile factional cleavages; it produces a binding nomination acceptable to virtually all elements within the party; and it generally selects nominees who possess a strong likelihood of winning wide voter support. Still, many critics of the national convention remain unpersuaded that the United States should continue to use these quadrennial conclaves to pick our presidential nominees. Throughout this study, however, the case has been made repeatedly that no alternative system fulfills the leadership selection function of this vast country better than the national convention. Indeed, national conventions come closer to maintaining a proper balance between popular participation and party leadership needs than does any other nominating system.

Before resting the case for the national convention, it should be pointed out that the overall record of these quadrennial conclaves is well above average in selecting outstanding leaders—Lincoln, Theodore Roosevelt, Wilson, Franklin D. Roosevelt, and John F. Kennedy. Attention should also be called to some of the highly qualified nominees who, though nominated, failed to reach the White House—Stephen Douglas, Samuel Tilden, Charles Evans Hughes, Alfred E. Smith, Wendell Willkie, Thomas E. Dewey, Adlai E. Stevenson, and Hubert H. Humphrey. (The critics argue, of course, that outstanding nominees were selected despite the system, rather than because of the national convention.) To be sure, the national convention has occasionally come up with some inept, uninspiring, or corrupt nominees who became President—James Buchanan, Ulysses S. Grant, Warren G. Harding, and Richard M. Nixon. But the critics should be reminded that the convention record, on the whole, has been far above the average. In other words, judge the convention system by the overall quality of the product—the number of outstanding Presidents that it has produced—not the mediocrities it has chosen from time to time. No leadership selection system is perfect, but no other system around the world has worked as well in recruiting outstanding leaders during times of national crisis. As James M. Burns has evaluated the national convention: "It has had many triumphs and few failures."[67] Another thoughtful commentator has also observed, ". . . in the eighteen presidential elections between 1900 and 1968, only ten nominations went to candidates who are even arguably second-rate. Twenty-six major party nominations went to evidently first-rate people. For the smoke-filled room, mediocrity was the *exception*; for the primary-dominated system, it has been the *rule*.[68] In the words of another commentator, "The cigar smokers have a better record in summoning first-class men."[69]

Although national parties operating through the national conventions have not always been able to bind all elements of the party into a cohesive team, nevertheless, as the late V.O. Key, Jr., observed, "The total performance of the national

convention as an instrumentality for weaving together the diverse and geographically scattered elements in each party into a national whole constitutes an impressive political achievement."[70] In other words, the national convention choice has
usually been, though not always, a candidate who represents a negotiated party
consensus in most of the 50 states of the Union, instead of merely a wing or
faction of the party. In assessing the "brokerage" function (trading and negotiating) of the national convention, Burns and Peltason remind us, "Those who look
aghast at convention horse trades and hijinks often forget that compromise is the
very essence of democratic politics."[71] Moreover, as one veteran observer, commenting on the convention's brokering function, has noted:

No other agency, surely, is an even remotely satisfactory substitute for decision-making
in a situation in which no one man has been able to demonstrate sufficient popular support
or political acumen to have earned immediate "nomination by ratification."[72]

The "openness" of the national nominating convention system allows a wide
variety of influence to shape the delegates' choice for the party standard-bearer.
Over a span of time that now extends well beyond a year before the general
election, presidential aspirants may compete openly (though they may not have
formally announced their candidacies) for the highest office in the land. In this
"pre-nominating" phase of the race, the public can evaluate the performances of
the aspirants on nationwide televised news panels, such as "Meet the Press" and
"Face the Nation," and also the evening network news programs.

Next, in three dozen presidential primary states the rank-and-file voters can
personally assess the candidates, while the entire nation watches under a variety of election conditions and shifting sets of competitors for a five-month period
from early January to June. After the voters in the presidential primary states
have spoken, a majority of national convention delegates (at least in the Republican party) are still free to make up their own minds on the "best" candidate for
the party to run for President. Also, during the pre-convention period the delegates will have had the opportunity to evaluate the results of national public
opinion poll "trial heats." These polls match the major intra-party contenders
against one another. A second type of pre-convention poll will match the leading
candidates in the out-party against an incumbent President or other prospective
contenders of the in-party, especially if the President has hinted of early retirement. While some voters may still dismiss polls as unreliable and unscientific,
national convention delegates—and the three TV networks—maintain a hawk-
like vigilance in charting the popularity ratings of the various party contenders.
That both parties since World War II have usually nominated the candidate at the
top of the public opinion polls at convention time suggests that the poll results do
influence the delegates.[73]

Whatever the merits or shortcomings of the convention system, it does provide considerable operational flexibility. As Polsby and Wildavsky have noted:
"The convention is sufficiently open to excite great national interest, but it is not

led into perpetual stalemate by pseudo-bargaining in public."[74] In reviewing the overall performance of the national conventions, it will be found that most convention nominees have been experienced, tested leaders committed to the values of a representative system. Over and above this, the convention system has made a valuable contribution to political stability by nominating party moderates (with a few exceptions), thus assuring the electorate that American party politics at the national level are conducted in the middle latitudes of political debate.[75]

In the final analysis, the defenders of the national convention system declare that it should be judged in terms of an alternative system. What other nomination system provides a more satisfactory means to resolve factional differences, competing ambitions, and regional loyalties in selecting a Presidential candidate? Polsby and Wildavsky, for the sake of argument, have posed the question of alternatives—if the convention system were eliminated:

Let us suppose that the smoke-filled room were abolished and with it all behind-the-scenes negotiations. All parleys would then be held in public, before the delegates and millions of television viewers. As a result, the participants would spend their time scoring points against each other to impress the folks back home. Bargaining would not be taking place since the participants would not really be communicating with one another. No compromises would be possible; leaders would be accused by their followers of selling out to the other side. Once a stalemate existed, it would be practically impossible to break, and the party would probably disintegrate into warring factions.[76]

James M. Burns has also defended the smoke-filled room sessions at the national conventions by pointing out:

The smoke-filled room is essential to the convention for it serves as the mechanism that allows party leaders to shift their choices toward a compromise candidate. Without such mechanism there would be eternal deadlock.[77]

In any assessment of the national convention and its integral role in the American party system, it should be kept in mind that we are dealing with a decentralized structure. The national party in the United States, if we may use the term, is composed of 50 autonomous state parties, further fragmented into local party units. Therefore, any convocation of these autonomous units for the purpose of choosing a national political leader is clearly more like a United Nations conference of independent sovereign states than a session of a parliamentary body. The national conventions give cohesion and purpose to the major parties. Indeed, as the late V.O. Key, Jr., observed some years ago, "The national convention represents the solution by American parties of the problem of uniting scattered points of political leadership in support of candidates for the Presidency and Vice Presidency.[78] In the national conventions we have found a compensatory mechanism that provides a modicum of unity within a centrifugal party system.

Upon closer examination, it is evident that many of the criticisms of the national nominating convention are directed at the entire decentralized American party and governmental system. This type of criticism is fair only if we make the assumption that the national conventions should become the ruling bodies in American parties, with authority to bind state and local parties to decisions made at the national level. This assumption also requires that the party conventions should represent exclusively the party voters, instead of electoral units and the general population. These suggested alterations would be appropriate for a highly centralized, "responsible" party system that reflects a mandate for the voters and can enforce party discipline upon recalcitrant party legislators or functionaries. But the model of a centrally directed party system is not germane to a discussion of a decentralized system.[79] Finally, it should not be overlooked that the national convention is the one truly nationalizing political institution in an otherwise highly decentralized and fragmented party system. Though it reemerges, like a mythical Brigadoon,[80] every four years, the national convention brings together hundreds of popularly elected and party-selected delegates from the far corners of the country and the U.S. territories to meet under one huge roof to select nominees for the highest office in the land. The national convention system provides an avenue of advancement to the Presidency, independent of Congress, that offers a degree of openness not found in the leadership selection process of other Western democracies. As the late V.O. Key, Jr., commented some years ago:

[The national convention] does not limit access to the Presidency to those who climb the ladder within the narrow confines of the inner circles of the representative body; nor does it restrict competition to those who gain the deference of their fellows within any narrowly defined group of party notables. The convention operates flexibly with a range of freedom that enables it to elevate to leadership men it judges to be suited to the needs of the time rather than merely to promote those who have worked their way up the bureaucratic ladder of party status.[81]

Over the past century the national convention has profoundly influenced the evolution of the modern Presidency, enhancing the strength and grandeur of this office. Had the congressional caucus by some quirk of fate survived as the method for nominating presidential candidates, the odds are high that the Presidency would have faint resemblance to the powerful institutional Chief Executive that has emerged in the twentieth century.

Though the critics continue to find fault with the national convention system, one would be hard-pressed—repeating the point made throughout our study—to construct another type of presidential nominating machinery that fits so well a vast, sprawling structure of 50 states and several territories, each of whose party structure and activities remain completely independent of one another and, except for the national delegate selection process, completely autonomous from the national party headquarters. To uncover and win over majority support every four years for a presidential ticket among the numerous competing, selfish forces within the decentralized, confederate structure of American parties is no small accomplishment.

More than two decades ago, a team of Brookings Institution scholars in a major study of national conventions concluded that "the continuing contributions made by the conventions to the survival and stability of the American political order are unique, indispensable, and granted our form of Constitution, probably irreplaceable."[82] This judgment still stands, as we approach the two hundredth anniversary of the founding of our federal Republic.

Notes

1. Anthony King, "How Not to Elect Presidential Candidates," in Austin Ranney, ed., *The American Elections of 1980* (Washington, D.C.: American Enterprise Institute, 1981), p. 323.

2. Malcolm Jewell, "Presidential Selection," *Society* (July/August 1980), p. 48, as quoted by James W. Ceaser, *Reforming the Reforms* (Cambridge, Mass.: Ballinger Publishing Company, 1982), p. 95.

3. *Washington Post*, August 13, 1980.

4. Haynes Johnson, *Washington Post*, August 13, 1980.

5. Senator Alan Cranston, Address to California Democratic Convention, Sacramento, California, January 17, 1981. Copy of speech furnished to author by Senator Cranston.

6. For further discussion of the question of deliberation versus participation in candidate selection, see Wilson Carey McWilliams, "The Meaning of the Election," in Gerald Pomper, ed., *The Election of 1980* (Chatham, N.J.: Chatham House Publishers, Inc., 1981), pp. 171-75.

7. James W. Ceaser, *Presidential Selection: Theory and Development* (Princeton, N.J.: Princeton University Press, 1979), p. 344.

8. Kathy Sawyer, *Washington Post*, August 15, 1980.

9. "Toward a More Responsible Two-Party System," *American Political Science Review*, Vol. 44 (September 1950), Supplement, p. 38.

10. Ibid.

11. *New York Times*, September 21, 1969.

12. Gerald Pomper, *Nominating the President* (Evanston, Ill.: Northwestern University Press, 1963), p. 256.

13. According to the 1972 Democratic convention rules, each state, the District of Columbia, Canal Zone, Guam, Puerto Rico, and Virgin Islands could select a number of alternates equivalent to the sum of (a) one alternate for each of the first 20 convention votes; (b) one alternate for each two convention votes in excess of 20 but less than 100 convention votes; and (c) one alternate for each three convention votes in excess of 100 convention votes. *Nomination and Election of the President and Vice President of the United States, Including Manner of Selecting Delegates to National Political Conventions*, compiled under direction of Francis R. Valeo, Secretary of the Senate (Washington, D.C.: U.S. Government Printing Office, 1972), pp. 66-68.

14. Paul T. David, statement before the Commission on rules, Democratic National Committee, cited by Judith H. Parris, *The Convention Problem* (Washington, D.C.: The Brookings Institution, 1972), pp. 79-80.

15. In the Wesberry case the Georgia congressional district in which the city of Atlanta

was located had a 1960 population of 823,000, as compared with the average of 394,000 for all ten Georgia districts. The U.S. Supreme Court held that such a disparity in the population of congressional districts was contrary to the constitutional requirement that representatives in Congress be chosen "by the people of the several states." *Wesberry v. Sanders* 370 U.S. 1 (1964).

16. See Chapter 3, pp. 55-56 for a detailed discussion of this controversy.

17. "Toward a More Responsible Two-Party System," *American Political Science Review*, Vol. 44 (September 1950), Supplement, p. 38.

18. Gerald Pomper, *Nominating the President*, p. 255.

19. Some years ago, a leading spokesperson of the responsible parties school, James MacGregor Burns, declared: "The greatest need of the American Presidency is a potent and competitive Shadow Presidency." Patterned along the lines of the Leader of the Opposition and Shadow Cabinet in the British party system, the Shadow President would be the leader of the out-of-power party. This opposition leader would be chosen by a biennial or annual mid-term convention or party conference. There are a number of reasons why this has not occurred, and Burns quickly put his finger on the chief reason: "The failure of the opposition to take this primitive step is not due to any innate difficulty but mainly to divergent constituencies and institutional jealousies of the Congressional party, which wants to dominate the opposition role even though it fills the role so feebly." In addition to a Shadow President, Burns would have ideally liked to have seen an "annual convention, a dependable system for collecting adequate funds, a large national party staff with regional and state units under it, an effective propaganda apparatus, and talented, articulate and highly visible leadership." James MacGregor Burns, *Presidential Government* (Boston: Houghton Mifflin Company, 1966), pp. 343-344.

20. Paul T. David, Ralph M. Goldman, and Richard C. Bain, *The Politics of National Party Conventions* (Washington, D.C.: The Brookings Institution, 1960), p. 497.

21. *New York Times*, July 13, 1972.

22. A copy of the original draft charter will be found in *Call to Order*, A Narrative Report by the Commission on Rules of the Democratic National Committee (O'Hara Commission Report) (Washington, D.C.: Democratic National Committee, 1972), appendix D, pp. 133-43.

23. The attendees at the Kansas City mini-convention consisted of 343 Governors, Senators, Congressmen, and other elected officials and 1,700 grass-roots representatives who were elected in primaries and conventions earlier in the year.

24. December 9, 1974.

25. See *Charter of the Democratic Party of the United States* (Washington, D.C.: Democratic National Committee, 1974). A copy of the charter is also available in the *New York Times*, December 10, 1974, and *Congressional Quarterly Weekly Report*, Vol. 32 (December 17, 1974), pp. 3334-36. The Democratic Charter has also been summarized in William J. Crotty, *Political Reform and the American Experiment* (New York: Thomas Y. Crowell, 1977), pp. 252-55.

26. David S. Broder, *Washington Post*, December 11, 1974.

27. Ronnie Dugger, "Fast Shuffle at Kansas City," *The Progressive*, Vol. 39 (February 1975), p. 23.

28. The price tag of the 1978 midterm conference was approximately the same—$650,000. The 1982 Philadelphia meeting, numbering less than half the delegates of previous miniconventions, cost the party about $300,000. "Jimmy's Party in Memphis," *Time*, Vol. 112 (December 18, 1978), p. 22; *New York Times*, June 28, 1982.

29. A CBS poll of 800 delegates—almost half of the delegates—conducted during the Memphis mid-term conference showed that 40 percent of the respondents preferred someone other than Carter for President in 1980. *Washington Post*, December 11, 1978.

30. Robert Michels, *Political Parties: A Sociological Study of the Oligarchical Tendencies of Modern Democracy*, trans. by Eden and Cedar Paul (New York: Free Press, 1949).

31. As quoted in Paul T. David, Ralph M. Goldman, and Richard C. Bain, *The Politics of National Party Conventions*, p. 215.

32. R.W. Apple, Jr., *New York Times*, December 9, 1974.

33. Warren Weaver, Jr., *New York Times*, June 27, 1982.

34. Paul T. David, et al., eds., *The Presidential Election and Transition, 1960-61* (Washington, D.C.: The Brookings Institution, 1961), p. 56.

35. David Broder, *Washington Post*, June 6, 1981.

36. *New York Times*, June 27, 1982.

37. "Democrats Meet to Pump Life into Tired Idea," *Congressional Quarterly Weekly Report*, Vol. 40 (June 19, 1982), p. 1468.

38. Ibid.

39. Thomas E. Cronin, "The Presidency and the Parties," in Gerald M. Pomper, ed., *Party Renewal in America* (New York: Praeger, 1981), p. 189.

40. Robert Bendiner, *New York Times*, December 10, 1974.

41. *A Statement of Purpose for Political Parties*, The Forum on Presidential Nominations (Durham, N.C.: Duke University Institute of Policy Science and Public Affairs, 1981), p. 7.

42. Ibid.

43. John S. Jackson, III, Southern Illinois University, is the source of this information. Letter to author dated November 10, 1981.

44. Warren J. Mitofsky and Martin Plissner, "The Making of the Delegates, 1968-1980," *Public Opinion* (October-December, 1980), p. 43.

45. Everett Carll Ladd was among the first to suggest that all Democratic governors, U.S. Senators, and Congressmen be made voting delegates to the national conventions. See Everett Carll Ladd, "A Better Way to Pick Our Presidents," *Fortune*, Vol. 101 (May 5, 1980), pp. 132-42.

46. This author is indebted to Professor Paul T. David for making this observation.

47. *Openness, Participation, and Party Building: Reforms for a Stronger Democratic Party*. Report of the Commission on Presidential Nomination and Party Structure (Washington, D.C.: Democratic National Committee, January 1978), pp. 100-101.

48. *A Statement of Purpose for Political Parties*, p. 10.

49. Jeane J. Kirkpatrick, et al., *The Presidential Nominating Process: Can It Be Improved?* (Washington, D.C.: American Enterprise Institute, 1980), p. 14.

50. Columnist David S. Broder has noted, for example, that at the 1976 Democratic convention that nominated Jimmy Carter for President, only 15 percent of the Democratic senators were delegates. "It was hardly surprising, then, that a Democratic Congress blithely ignored many of the recommendations of that Democratic president." *Washington Post*, November 11, 1981.

51. The term "peer review" has been borrowed from Anthony King, "How Not to Select Presidential Candidates," p. 325. Under the reformed 1984 Democratic delegate selection rules the sizeable bloc of uncommitted party and elected officeholder "super

delegates"—550 of an estimated 3,850 delegates—will help restore an element of "peer" review to the presidential nominating process that has been missing since 1968.

52. Jeane J. Kirkpatrick, et al., *The Presidential Nominating Process: Can It Be Improved*? p. 14.

53. For further discussion on the Wisconsin open primary decision, see chapter 3.

54. Senator Alan Cranston, Democrat Whip, United States Senate, Address to California Democratic Convention, Sacramento, California, January 17, 1981. Copy of speech furnished by Senator Cranston to author.

55. Paul T. David, Ralph M. Goldman, and Richard C. Bain, *The Politics of National Party Conventions*, p. 253.

56. James W. Ceaser, *Presidential Selection: Theory and Development* (Princeton, N.J.: Princeton University Press, 1979), p. 237.

57. *Congressional Quarterly Weekly Report*, Vol. 38 (August 9, 1980), pp. 2268-76.

58. *Washington Post*, August 13, 1980.

59. Gerald Pomper, "The Nominating Contests," in Gerald Pomper, ed., *The Election of 1980*, p. 32.

60. David S. Broder, *Washington Post*, March 1, 1981. The case, *Democratic Party of the United States of America et al. v. Bronson C. LaFollette et al.* 101 S.Ct. 1010, was decided on February 25, 1981. LaFollette, Attorney General of Wisconsin, is the grandson of Robert M. "Fighting Bob" LaFollette—founder of Wisconsin's direct and presidential primaries.

61. *New York Times*, September 24, 1981.

62. David S. Broder, *Washington Post*, November 11, 1981.

63. Ibid.

64. The 1980 GOP Convention did, however, approve a Rules Committee recommendation that a special panel be formed to study proposed revisions of the allocation system and a streamlining of the presidential nomination process. "GOP Convention Rules Adopted without Dispute," *Congressional Quarterly Weekly Report*, Vol. 38 (July 19, 1980), p. 2012.

65. Charles Longley, "Party Reform and the Republican Party," paper delivered at American Political Science Association meeting, New York, 1978. See also John F. Bibby, "Party Renewal in the National Republican Party," in Gerald M. Pomper, ed., *Party Renewal in America* (New York: Praeger, 1981), pp. 102-15.

66. Josiah Lee Auspitz, "A 'Republican' View of Both Parties," *The Public Interest*, Vol. 68 (Spring 1982), pp. 105-6.

67. James MacGregor Burns, "The Case for the Smoke-Filled Room," *New York Times Magazine* (June 15, 1952), p. 26.

68. Wilson Carey McWilliams, "The Meaning of the Election," in Gerald Pomper, ed., *The Election of 1980*, p. 171. McWilliams "second-rater" list includes: Coolidge, Cox, Davis, Goldwater, Harding, Landon, McKinley, Nixon, and Parker, Ibid., p. 187, footnote 4.

69. Nick Thimmesch, *Washington Post*, September 6, 1979.

70. V.O. Key, Jr., *Politics, Parties and Pressure Groups*, 5th ed. (New York: Thomas Y. Crowell Company, 1964), p. 433.

71. James MacGregor Burns and Jack Peltason, *Government by the People*, 4th ed. (Englewood Cliffs, N.J.: Prentice-Hall, Inc., 1960), p. 364.

72. Karl O'Lessker, "The National Nominating Conventions," in Cornelius P. Cotter,

Practical Politics in the United States (Boston: Allyn & Bacon, Inc., 1969), pp. 274-75.

73. See James R. Beniger, "Polls and Primaries," in James W. Davis, *Presidential Primaries: Road to the White House*, 2nd ed. (Westport, Connecticut: Greenwood Press, 1980), pp. 111-133.

74. Nelson W. Polsby and Aaron Wildavsky, *Presidential Elections*, 2nd ed. (New York: Charles Scribner's Sons, 1968), p. 242.

75. Herbert McClosky, "Are Political Conventions Undemocratic?" *New York Times Magazine* (August 4, 1968), p. 10.

76. Nelson W. Polsby and Aaron Wildavsky, *Presidential Elections*, 2nd ed., pp. 232-33.

77. James MacGregor Burns, "The Case for the Smoke-Filled Room," p. 25.

78. V.O. Key, Jr., *Politics, Parties and Pressure Groups*, 5th ed., pp. 269-70.

79. This analysis parallels the general assessment of conventions made by Austin Ranney and Willmoore Kendall, *Democracy and the American Party System* (New York: Harcourt, Brace and World, 1956), p. 317.

80. The metaphor is David Broder's.

81. V. O. Key, Jr., *Politics, Parties and Pressure Groups*, 5th ed., p. 433.

82. Paul T. David., Ralph M. Goldman and Richard C. Bain, *The Politics of National Party Conventions*, p. 494.

Appendix:
Delegate Apportionment for Democratic and Republican Conventions, by State, 1980 and 1984 _____

State	Democratic Party		Republican Party	
	1980	*1984*	*1980*	*1984*
Alabama	45	62	27	38
Alaska	11	14	19	18
Arizona	29	39	28	32
Arkansas	33	42	19	29
California	306	345	168	174
Colorado	40	51	31	34
Connecticut	54	60	35	34
Delaware	14	18	12	18
District of Columbia	19	19	14	14
Florida	100	143	51	82
Georgia	63	82	36	37
Hawaii	19	27	14	14
Idaho	17	22	21	21
Illinois	179	194	102	92
Indiana	80	88	54	50
Iowa	50	58	37	36
Kansas	37	44	32	32
Kentucky	50	63	27	37
Louisiana	51	68	30	41
Maine	22	27	21	20
Maryland	59	74	30	31
Massachusetts	111	116	42	52
Michigan	141	155	82	77
Minnesota	75	86	34	31
Mississippi	32	43	22	30
Missouri	77	86	37	46
Montana	19	25	20	20

State	Democratic Party		Republican Party	
	1980	*1984*	*1980*	*1984*
Nebraska	24	30	25	24
Nevada	12	20	17	20
New Hampshire	19	22	22	21
New Jersey	113	122	66	63
New Mexico	20	28	22	24
New York	282	285	123	136
North Carolina	69	88	40	53
North Dakota	14	18	17	18
Ohio	161	175	77	89
Oklahoma	42	58	34	35
Oregon	39	50	29	31
Pennsylvania	185	195	83	96
Rhode Island	23	27	13	13
South Carolina	37	48	25	35
South Dakota	19	19	22	18
Tennessee	55	76	32	45
Texas	152	200	80	109
Utah	20	27	21	25
Vermont	12	17	19	18
Virginia	64	78	51	49
Washington	58	70	37	43
West Virginia	35	44	18	19
Wisconsin	75	89	34	46
Wyoming	11	15	19	17
Democrats Abroad	4	5	—	—
Guam	4	7	4	4
Latin American Democrats (Canal Zone)	4	5	—	—
Puerto Rico	41	53	14	14
Virgin Islands	4	6	4	4
TOTAL	3,331	3,923	1,994	2,209

Source: Democratic and Republican National Committees.

Note: The 1984 Republican delegate allocations are still tentative as of January 20, 1983, but state allocations will not differ significantly.

Bibliography ⎯⎯⎯⎯⎯⎯⎯⎯⎯⎯⎯⎯⎯⎯⎯

Books

Aldrich, John H. *Before the Convention* (Chicago, Illinois: University of Chicago Press, 1980).

Alexander, Herbert E. *Financing the 1976 Election* (Washington, D.C.: Congressional Quarterly Press, 1979).

Asher, Herbert. *Presidential Elections and American Politics: Voters, Candidates, and Campaigns Since 1952*, rev. ed. (Homewood, Illinois: Dorsey Press, 1980).

Bain, Richard C., and Parris, Judith H. *Convention Decisions and Voting Records*, 2nd ed. (Washington, D.C.: The Brookings Institution, 1973).

Barber, James D., ed. *Choosing the President* (Englewood Cliffs, New Jersey: Prentice-Hall, 1974).

⎯⎯⎯, ed. *Race for the Presidency* (Englewood Cliffs, New Jersey: Prentice-Hall, 1978).

Bickel, Alexander M. *The New Age of Political Reform: The Electoral College, the Convention and the Party* (New York: Harper & Row, 1968).

Bishop, J.B. *Presidential Nomination and Elections: A History of American Conventions* (New York: Scribner, 1916).

Blumler, Jay G., and McQuail, Denis. *Television in Politics* (Chicago: University of Chicago Press, 1969).

Bone, Hugh A. *Party Committees and National Politics* (Seattle, Washington: University of Washington Press, 1958).

Bryan, William J. *A Tale of Two Conventions* (New York: Funk & Wagnalls, 1912).

Campbell, Angus; Converse, Philip; Miller, Warren; and Stokes, Donald. *The American Voter* (New York: John Wiley and Sons, 1960).

Ceaser, James W. *Presidential Selection: Theory and Development* (Princeton, New Jersey: Princeton University Press, 1979).

⎯⎯⎯. *Reforming the Reforms* (Cambridge, Massachusetts: Ballinger Publishing Company, 1982).

Chase, James S. *Emergence of the Presidential Nominating Conventions, 1789-1832* (Urbana, Illinois: University of Illinois Press, 1973).

Chester, Lewis; Hodgson, Godfrey; and Page, Bruce. *An American Melodrama: The Presidential Campaign of 1968* (New York: Viking Press, 1969).

Cotter, Cornelius P., ed. *Practical Politics in the United States* (Boston: Allyn & Bacon, Inc., 1969).

Cotter, Cornelius P., and Hennessy, Bernard C. *Politics without Power: The National Party Committees* (New York: Atherton Press, 1964).

Courtney, John C. *The Selection of National Party Leaders in Canada* (Hamden, Connecticut: The Shoe String Press, Inc., 1973).

Crotty, William J. *Political Reform and the American Experiment* (New York: Thomas Y. Crowell, 1977).

————, ed. *The Party Symbol* (San Francisco: W.F. Freeman, 1980).

————, ed. *Paths to Political Reform* (Lexington, Massachusetts: D.C. Heath and Company, 1980).

Crouse, Timothy. *The Boys on the Bus* (New York: Ballantine, 1973).

Dallinger, Frederick W. *Nominations for Elective Office in the United States* (Cambridge, Massachusetts: Harvard University Press, 1897).

David, Paul T., et al., eds., *The Presidential Election and Transition, 1960-61* (Washington, D.C.: The Brookings Institution, 1961).

David, Paul T., and Ceaser, James W. *Proportional Representation in Presidential Nominating Politics* (Charlottesville, Virginia: The University of Virginia Press, 1980).

David, Paul T.; Goldman, Ralph M.; and Bain, Richard C. *The Politics of National Party Conventions* (Washington, D.C.: The Brookings Institution, 1960).

David, Paul T.; Moos, Malcolm; and Goldman, Ralph M., eds., *Presidential Nominating Politics in 1952*, 5 vols. (Baltimore: The Johns Hopkins University Press, 1954).

Davis, James W. *National Conventions: Nominations under the Big Top* (Woodbury, New York: Barron's, 1972).

————. *Presidential Primaries: Road to the White House*, 2nd ed. (Westport, Connecticut: Greenwood Press, 1980).

Eaton, Herbert. *Presidential Timber: A History of Nominating Conventions* (New York: Free Press of Glencoe, 1964).

Farley, James A. *Behind the Ballots* (New York: Harcourt, Brace and World, Inc., 1938).

Fishel, Jeff, ed. *Parties and Elections in an Anti-Party Age* (Bloomington, Indiana: University of Indiana Press, 1978).

Foley, John; Britton, Dennis A.; and Everett, Eugene B., Jr. *Nominating a President: The Process and the Press* (New York: Praeger, 1980).

Germond, Jack W., and Witcover, Jules. *Blue Smoke and Mirrors: How Reagan Won and Why Carter Lost the Election of 1980* (New York: The Viking Press, 1981).

Goldman, Ralph M. *Search for Consensus: The Story of the Democratic Party* (Philadelphia: Temple University Press, 1979).

Goldstein, Joel K. *The Modern American Vice Presidency: The Transformation of a Political Institution* (Princeton, New Jersey: Princeton University Press, 1982).

Graber, Doris A. *Mass Media and American Politics* (Washington, D. C.: Congressional Quarterly, Inc., 1980).

Hadley, Arthur T. *The Invisible Primary* (Englewood Cliffs, New Jersey: Prentice-Hall, 1976).

Harwood, Richard, ed. *The Pursuit of the Presidency, 1980* (New York: Berkley Books, 1980).

Herring, Pendleton. *The Politics of Democracy* (New York: W. W. Norton, Inc., 1940).

Hyman, Sidney. *The American President* (New York: Harper & Brothers, 1954).

Johnson, Donald B. *National Party Platforms*, 2 vols. (Urbana: University of Illinois Press, 1978).

Johnson, Walter. *How We Drafted Adlai Stevenson: Story of the Democratic Presidential Convention of 1952* (New York: Knopf, 1955).

Keech, William R., and Matthews, Donald R. *The Party's Choice* (Washington, D.C.: The Brookings Institution, 1976).

Key, V.O., Jr., *Politics, Parties, and Pressure Groups*, 5th ed. (New York: Thomas Y. Crowell Company, 1964).

————. *Southern Politics* (New York: Alfred A. Knopf, 1949).

Kirkpatrick, Jeane J. *The New Presidential Elite: Men and Women in National Politics* (New York: Russell Sage Foundation and the Twentieth Century Fund, 1976).

Kraus, Sidney, and Davis, Dennis. *The Effects of Mass Communication on Political Behavior* (University Park, Pennsylvania: Pennsylvania State University Press, 1976).

Lang, Kurt, and Lang, Gladys E. *Politics and Television* (Chicago: Quadrangle Books, 1968).

Lengle, James I., and Shafer, Byron E., eds. *Presidential Politics* (New York: St. Martin's Press, 1980).

Lurie, Leonard. *The King Makers* (New York: Coward, McCann and Geoghegan, 1971).

MacNeil, Robert. *The People Machine* (New York: Harper & Row, 1968).

Marshall, Thomas R. *Presidential Nominations in a Reform Age* (New York: Praeger, 1981).

Martin, Ralph G. *Ballots and Bandwagons* (Chicago: Rand McNally, 1964).

Matthews, Donald R., ed. *Perspectives on Presidential Selection* (Washington, D.C.: The Brookings Institution, 1973).

May, Ernest R., and Fraser, Janet, eds. *Campaign '72: The Managers Speak* (Cambridge, Massachusetts: Harvard University Press, 1973).

McGinniss, Joe. *The Selling of the President* (New York: Trident Press, 1969).

McKee, Thomas H. *The National Conventions and Platforms of All Political Parties, 1789-1905: Convention, Popular and Electoral Vote* (New York: AMS Press, 1971).

McNitt, Virgil B., ed. *A Tale of Two Conventions: An Account of the Republican and Democratic Conventions of June 1912* (New York: Arno Press, 1974).

Mendelsohn, Harold, and Crespi, Irving. *Polls, Television and New Politics* (Scranton, Pennsylvania: Chandler, 1970).

Mendelsohn, Harold, and O'Keefe, Garrett. *The People Choose a President* (New York: Praeger, 1976).

Moore, Jonathan, and Fraser, Janet, eds. *Campaign for President* (Cambridge, Massachusetts: Ballinger Publishing Company, 1977).

Moos, Malcolm C., and Hess, Stephen. *Hats in the Ring* (New York: Random House, 1960).

Morgan, H. Wayne. *From Hayes to McKinley: National Party Politics, 1877-1896* (Syracuse, New York: Syracuse University Press, 1969).

Mowry, George E. *Theodore Roosevelt and the Progressive Movement* (Madison: University of Wisconsin Press, 1947).

Murray, Robert K. *The 103rd Ballot: Democrats and the Disaster in Madison Square Garden* (New York: Harper and Row, 1976).

National Party Conventions, 1831-1976 (Washington, D.C.: Congressional Quarterly, Inc., 1979).

Nie, Norman H.; Verba, Sidney; and Petrocik, John R. *The Changing American Voter* (Cambridge, Massachusetts: Harvard University Press, 1976).

Nimmo, Dan, and Savage, Robert L. *Candidates and Their Images* (Pacific Palisades, California: Goodyear, 1976).

Novak, Michael. *Choosing Our King: Powerful Symbols in Presidential Politics* (New York: Macmillan, 1974).

O'Lessker, Karl. *The National Nominating Conventions* (New York: Robert A. Taft Institute of Government, 1968).

Ostrogorski, M. I. *Democracy and the Organization of Political Parties*, 2 vols. (New York: The Macmillan Company, 1902).

Overacker, Louise. *The Presidential Primary* (New York: The Macmillan Company, 1926).

Parris, Judith H. *The Convention Problem* (Washington, D.C.: The Brookings Institution, 1972).

Patterson, Thomas E. *The Mass Media Election* (New York: Praeger, 1980).

————, and McClure, Robert D. *The Unseeing Eye: The Myth of Television Power in National Politics* (New York: Putnam, 1976).

Perry, James M. *Us and Them: How the Press Covered the 1972 Election* (New York: Clarkson N. Potter, Inc., 1973).

Polsby, Nelson W., and Wildavsky, Aaron. *Presidential Elections*, 5th ed. (New York: Charles Scribner's Sons, 1980).

Pomper, Gerald. *Nominating the President* (Evanston, Illinois: Northwestern University Press, 1963).

————, ed. *The Election of 1980* (Chatham, New Jersey: Chatham House Publishers, Inc., 1981).

Pomper, Gerald with Lederman, Susan S. *Elections in America*, 2nd ed. (New York and London: Longman, Inc., 1980).

Ranney, Austin. *Curing the Mischiefs of Faction* (Berkeley, California: University of California Press, 1975).

————, ed. *The American Elections of 1980* (Washington, D.C.: American Enterprise Institute, 1981).

————, and Kendall, Willmoore. *Democracy and the American Party System* (New York: Harcourt, Brace and World, Inc., 1956).

Reeves, Richard. *Convention* (New York: Harcourt Brace Jovanovich, 1977).

Roseboom, Eugene H. *A History of Presidential Elections* (New York: The Macmillan Company, 1957).

Rubin, Richard. *Press, Party and President* (New York: W.W. Norton, 1980).

Saloma, John S. III, and Sontag, Frederick H. *Parties* (New York: Alfred A. Knopf, 1972).

Sanford, Terry. *A Danger of Democracy* (Boulder, Colorado: Westview Press, 1981).

Sorauf, Frank O. *Party Politics in America*, 4th ed. (Boston: Little, Brown and Company, 1980).

Stoddard, H.L. *Presidential Sweepstakes: The Story of Political Conventions and Campaigns* (New York: Putnam, 1948).

Sullivan, Denis, et al. *Explorations in Convention Decision Making: The Democratic Party in the 1970's* (San Francisco: W.H. Freeman, 1976).

Sullivan, Denis G.; Pressman, Jeffrey L.; Page, Benjamin I.; and Lyons, John J. *The Politics of Representation* (New York: St. Martin's Press, 1974).

Tillett, Paul, ed. *Inside Politics: The National Conventions, 1960* (Dobbs Ferry, New York: Oceana Publications, Inc., 1962).

Thompson, Hunter S. *Fear and Loathing: On the Campaign Trail '72* (New York: Fawcett Popular Library, 1973).

Watson, Richard A., *The Presidential Contest* (New York: John Wiley & Sons, 1980).

Wayne, Stephen J. *The Road to the White House* (New York: St. Martin's Press, 1980).

White, Theodore H. *The Making of the President* (New York: Atheneum, 1961, 1965, 1969, and 1973).

———. *America in Search of Itself: The Making of the President, 1956-1980* (New York: Harper & Row Publishers, 1982).

Witcover, Jules. *Marathon: The Pursuit of the Presidency, 1972-1976* (New York: The Viking Press, 1977).

Wykoff, Gene. *The Image Candidates* (New York: Macmillan, 1968).

Articles

Arterton, F. Christopher. "Strategies and Tactics of Candidate Organizations," *Political Science Quarterly*, Vol. 92 (Winter 1977-1978), pp. 663-71.

Auspitz, Josiah Lee. "A 'Republican' View of Both Parties," *The Public Interest*, Vol. 68 (Spring 1982), pp. 105-6.

Bendiner, Robert. "The Presidential Primaries Are Haphazard, Unfair, and Wildly Illogical," *New York Times*, February 17, 1972.

Beniger, James R. "Winning the Presidential Nomination: National Polls and State Primary Elections, 1936-1972," *Public Opinion Quarterly*, Vol. 40 (Spring 1976), pp. 22-38.

Burns, James M. "The Case for the Smoke-Filled Room," *New York Times Magazine* (June 15, 1952), pp. 9, 24-26.

Carleton, William G. "The Collapse of the Caucus," *Current History*, Vol. 25 (September 1953), pp. 144-50.

———. "The Revolution in the Presidential Nominating Convention," *Political Science Quarterly*, Vol. 72 (June 1957), pp. 224-40.

Center, Judith A. "1972 Democratic Convention Reforms and Party Democracy," *Political Science Quarterly*, Vol. 89 (1974), pp. 325-50.

Collat, Donald S.; Kelley, Stanley, Jr.; and Rogowski, Ronald. "The End Game in Presidential Nominations," *American Political Science Review*, Vol. 75 (June 1981), pp. 426-35.

Costain, Anne N. "An Analysis of Voting in American National Nominating Conventions, 1940-1976," *American Politics Quarterly*, Vol. 6 (January 1978), pp. 95-120.

David, Paul T. "Party Platforms as National Plans," *Public Administration Review*, Vol. 31 (May/June 1971), pp. 303-15.

Dugger, Ronnie. "Fast Shuffle at Kansas City," *The Progressive*, Vol. 39 (February 1975), pp. 22-25.

Eisenhower, Dwight D. "Our National Conventions Are a Disgrace," *Reader's Digest*, Vol. 89 (July 1966), pp. 76-80.

Epstein, Leon D. "Political Science and Presidential Nomination," *Political Science Quarterly*, Vol. 93 (Summer 1978), pp. 177-95.

Hickey, Neil. "It's a $40 Million Circus," *TV Guide*, July 13, 1980.

Hyman, Sidney. "Nine Tests for the Presidential Hopeful," *New York Times Magazine* (January 4, 1959), pp. 11, 47-50.

"Inside the Jerry Ford Drama," *Time*, Vol. 116 (July 28, 1980), pp. 16-19.

Jackson, John S. III; Brown, Barbara Leavitt; and Bositis, David. "Herbert McClosky and Friends Revisited: 1980 Democratic and Republican Party Elites Compared to Mass Public," *American Politics Quarterly*, Vol. 10 (April 1982), pp. 158-80.

Jackson, John S., III; Brown, Jesse C.; and Brown, Barbara. "Recruitment, Representation, and Political Values: The 1976 Democratic National Convention Delegates," *American Politics Quarterly*, Vol. 6 (April 1978), pp. 187-211.

Janosik, Edward. "The American National Nominating Convention," *Parliamentary Affairs*, Vol. 17 (Summer 1964), pp. 321-39.

Johnson, Loch K., and Hahn, Harlan. "Delegate Turnover at National Party Conventions, 1944-1968," in *Perspectives on Presidential Selection*, Donald R. Matthews, ed. (Washington, D.C.: 1973), pp. 143-55.

Kirkpatrick, Jeane J. "Representation in the American National Conventions: The Case of 1972," *British Journal of Political Science*, Vol. 5 (July 1975), pp. 313-22.

Knebel, Fletcher. "One Vote for the Convention System," *New York Times Magazine* (August 23, 1964), pp. 21, 89-91.

Ladd, Everett Carll. "A Better Way to Pick Our Presidents," *Fortune*, Vol. 101 (May 5, 1980), pp. 132-42.

———. "Reform Is Wrecking the U.S. Party System," *Fortune*, Vol. 96 (November 1977), pp. 177-88.

Marshall, Thomas R. "Caucuses and Primaries: Measuring Reform in the Presidential Nomination Process," *American Politics Quarterly*, Vol. 7 (April 1979), pp. 155-174.

McClosky, Herbert. "Are Political Conventions Undemocratic?" *New York Times Magazine* (August 4, 1968), pp. 10-11, 62-68.

McClosky, Herbert; Hoffman, Paul J; and O'Hara, Rosemary. "Issue Conflict and Consensus among Party Leaders and Followers," *American Political Science Review*, Vol. 54 (1960), pp. 406-27.

McGinniss, Joe. "The Resale of the President," *New York Times Magazine* (September 3, 1972), pp. 8, 17-23.

McGrath, Wilma E., and Soule, John W. "Rocking the Cradle or Rocking the Boat: Women at the 1972 Democratic National Convention," *Social Science Quarterly*, Vol. 55 (June 1974), pp. 141-50.

McGregor, Eugene B., Jr. "Rationality and Uncertainty at National Nominating Conventions," *Journal of Politics*, Vol. 35 (May 1973), pp. 459-78.

Mitofsky, Warren J., and Plissner, Martin. "The Making of the Delegates, 1968-1980," *Public Opinion*, Vol. 3 (October-November 1980), pp. 37-43.

Munger, Frank, and Blackhurst, James. "Factionalism in the National Conventions, 1940-1964: An Analysis of Ideological Consistency in State Delegation Voting," *Journal of Politics*, Vol. 27 (May 1965), pp. 375-93.

O'Neil, Paul. "Conventions: Nominations by Rain Dance," *Life*, Vol. 65 (July 5, 1968), pp. 19-28.

Paletz, David L., and Elson, Martha. "Television Coverage of Presidential Conventions: Now You See It, Now You Don't," *Political Science Quarterly*, Vol. 91 (Spring 1976), pp. 109-31.

Pomper, Gerald. "Factionalism in the 1968 National Conventions: An Extension of Research Findings," *Journal of Politics*, Vol. 33 (August 1971), pp. 326-830.

————. "If Elected I Promise: American Party Platforms," *Midwest Journal of Political Science*, Vol. 11 (August 1967), pp. 318-52.

Pressman, Jeffrey L., and Sullivan, Denis G. "Convention Reform and Conventional Wisdom: An Empirical Assessment of Democratic Party Reforms," *Political Science Quarterly*, Vol. 89 (Fall 1974), pp. 539-62.

Reiter, Howard. "Party Factionalism: National Conventions in the New Era," *American Politics Quarterly*, Vol. 8 (July 1980), pp. 303-18.

Reston, James. "The Convention System: A Five-Count Indictment," *New York Times Magazine* (July 11, 1948), pp. 7, 36-37.

Roback, Thomas. "Amateurs and Professionals: Delegates to the 1972 Republican National Convention," *Journal of Politics*, Vol. 37 (1975), pp. 436-68.

Robinson, Michael. "Television and American Politics, 1956-1976," *The Public Interest*, No. 48 (Summer 1977), pp. 3-39.

Soule, John W., and Clarke, James W. "Amateurs and Professionals: A Study of Delegates to the 1968 Democratic National Convention," *American Political Science Review*, Vol. 64 (September 1970), pp. 888-98.

Soule, John W. and McGrath, Wilma. "A Comparative Study of Presidential Nominating Conventions: The Democrats 1968 and 1972," *American Journal of Political Science*,Vol. 19 (August 1975), pp. 501-18.

Sullivan, Denis G. "Party Unity: Appearance and Reality," *Political Science Quarterly*, Vol. 92 (Winter 1977-1978), pp. 635-45.

"Toward a More Responsible Two-Party System," *American Political Science Review*, Vol. 44 (September 1950), Supplement, pp. 1-99.

Vance, Cyrus R. "Reforming the Electoral Reforms," *New York Times Magazine* (February 22, 1981), pp. 16, 62-69.

Walker, Jack. "Reforming the Reforms," *Wilson Quarterly*, Vol. 5 (Autumn 1981), pp. 88-101.

Waltzer, Herbert. "In the Magic Lantern: Television Coverage of the 1964 National Conventions," *Public Opinion Quarterly*, Vol. 30 (Spring 1966), pp. 33-53.

Weinberg, Martha Wagner. "Writing the Republican Platform," *Political Science Quarterly*, Vol. 92 (Winter 1977-1978), pp. 655-62.

Wicker, Tom. "Why the System Has Failed," *New York Review of Books* (August 14, 1980), pp. 11-15.

Wildavsky, Aaron B. "On the Superiority of National Conventions," *Review of Politics*, Vol. 24 (July 1962), pp. 307-19.

Documents

Call to Order. A Narrative Report by the Commission on Rules (O'Hara Commission) (Washington, D.C.: Democratic National Committee, 1972).

Mandate for Reform. A Report of the Commission on Party Structure and Delegate Selection to the Democratic National Committee (McGovern Commission) (Washington, D.C.: Democratic National Committee, April 1970).

Nomination and Election of the President and Vice President of the United States, Including Manner of Selecting Delegates to National Political Conventions. Compiled under direction, Secretary of the Senate (Washington, D.C.: U.S. Government Printing Office, 1968, 1972, 1976, and 1980).

Openness, Participation, and Party Building: Reforms for a Stronger Democratic Primary. Report of the Commission on Presidential Nomination and Party Structure (Winograd Commission) (Washington, D.C: Democratic National Committee, 1978).

Report of the Commission on Presidential Nomination (Hunt Commission), Washington, D.C.: Democratic National Committee, 1982.

Monographs

Choosing Presidential Candidates: How Good Is the New Way? (Washington, D.C.: American Enterprise Institute, 1980).

Kirkpatrick, Jeane J. *Dismantling the Parties: Reflections on Party Reform and Party Decomposition* (Washington, D.C.: American Enterprise Institute, 1978).

————, et al. *The Presidential Nominating Process: Can It Be Improved?* (Washington, D.C.: American Enterprise Institute, 1980).

The Presidential Nominating System: A Primer (Cambridge, Mass.: Institute of Politics, John F. Kennedy School of Government, Harvard University, 1979).

Ranney, Austin. *The Federalization of Presidential Primaries* (Washington, D.C.: American Enterprise Institute, 1978).

————. *Participation in American Presidential Nominations* (Washington, D.C.: American Enterprise Institute, 1977).

A Statement of Purpose for Political Parties, The Forum on Presidential Nominations (Durham, North Carolina: Duke University, 1981), pp. 1-14.

Index

About the Author

JAMES W. DAVIS is Dean of the College of Arts and Sciences at Western Washington University in Bellingham. His previous books include *Presidential Primaries: Road to the White House* (2nd edition, Greenwood Press, 1980) and *National Conventions: Nominations Under the Big Top*.

208045